Psalms Old and New

Psalms Old and New

Exegesis, Intertextuality, and Hermeneutics

Ben Witherington, III

Fortress Press
Minneapolis

PSALMS OLD AND NEW
Exegesis, Intertextuality, and Hermeneutics

Cover design: Joe Reinke

Print ISBN: 978-1-5064-2057-8
eBook ISBN: 978-1-5064-2058-5

The paper used in this publication meets the minimum requirements of American
National Standard for Information Sciences — Permanence of Paper for Printed
Library Materials, ANSI Z329.48-1984.

Manufactured in the U.S.A.

This book was produced using Pressbooks.com, and PDF rendering was done by
PrinceXML.

"The Psalter is the prayer book of Jesus Christ in the truest sense of the word. He prayed the Psalter and now it has become his prayer for all time.... We understand how the Psalter can be prayer to God and yet God's own Word, precisely because here we encounter the praying Christ ... because those who pray the psalms are joining in with the prayer of Jesus Christ, their prayer reaches the ears of God. Christ has become their intercessor."

—Dietrich Bonhoeffer[1]

"The human heart is like a ship on a stormy sea driven about by winds blowing from all four corners of heaven.... The Book of Psalms is full of heartfelt utterances made during storms of this kind. Where can one find nobler words to express joy than in the Psalms of praise or gratitude? In them you can see into the hearts of saints as if you were looking at a lovely pleasure-garden, or were gazing into heaven. How fair and charming and delightful the flowers you will find there."

—Martin Luther, *Preface to the Psalms*

"The Psalms have a unique place in the Bible because most of the Scripture speaks to us while the Psalms speak for us."

—Athanasius

"Poets exist so that the dead may vote."

— Elie Wiesel[2]

1. Bonhoeffer, *Psalms: The Prayer Book of the Bible,* (Minneapolis: Augsburg Fortress, 1974), see pp. 13–21.
2. W. Brueggemann, *The Spirituality of the Psalms,* (Minneapolis: Fortress Press, 2001), xiv.

"Even though the meaning of the words [of psalmody] be unknown to you, teach your mouth to utter them meanwhile. For the tongue is made holy by the words when they are uttered with a ready and eager mind. . . . No one in such chanting [with a ready and eager mind] will be blamed if he be weakened by old age, or young, or have a rough voice, or is altogether ignorant of rhythm. What is here sought for is a sober soul, an alert mind, a contrite heart, sound reason, and a clear conscience. If having these you have entered into God's sacred choir, you may stand beside David himself. There is no need of zithers, nor of taut strings, nor of a plectrum, nor skill, nor any instruments. But if you will, you can make yourself into a zither, mortifying the limbs of the flesh, and forming full harmony between body and soul. For when the flesh does not lust against the spirit, but yields to its commands, and perseveres along the path that is noble and admirable, you thus produce a spiritual melody."*

—St. John Chrysostom, PG 58, 158, *Commentary on Psalm 41*

"The material is universal, for while the particular books of the Canon of Scripture contain special materials, this book has the general material of theology as a whole. . . . [For] the work of God is fourfold, namely that of creation . . . governance . . . reparation [i.e., salvation] . . . glorification. . . . There is a complete treatment of all these things in [the Psalms]. . . . And this will be the reason the Psalter is read more often in the Church, because it contains the whole of Scripture."*

—Thomas Aquinas, *Commentary on the Psalms*, Introduction

Contents

Abbreviations

ABRL	Anchor Bible Reference Library
Ant.	Josephus *Jewish Antiquities*
b. Ber.	Babylonian Talmud Berakot
BCOTWP	Baker Commentary on the Old Testament Wisdom and Psalms
Bib	*Biblica*
b. Meg.	Babylonian Talmud Megillah
b. Šabb	Babylonian Talmud Šabbat
b. Sanh	Babylonian Talmud Sanhedrin
b. Sop	Babylonian Talmud Sopherim
BTCB	Brazos Theological Commentary on the Bible
BZAW	Beihefte zur Zeitschrift für die alttestamentliche Wissenschaft
CBET	Contributions to Biblical Exegesis and Theology
CBQ	*Catholic Biblical Quarterly*
CBQMS	Catholic Biblical Quarterly Monograph Series
CBSC	Cambridge Bible for Schools and Colleges
CC	Continental Commentaries
ConBOT	Coniectania Biblica Old Testament Series
CRINT	Compendia Rerum Iudaicarum ad Novum Testamentum
Dial.	Justin Martyr *Dialogue with Trypho*
EBS	Encountering Biblical Studies
Ep. Marcel.	Athanasius *Letter to Marcellinus on the Interpretation of the Psalms*

Exod. Rab.	Rabbah Exodus
FAT	Forschungen zum Alten Testament
f(f).	following
frag.	fragment
Gen. Rab.	Rabbah Genesis
HB	Hebrew Bible
Int	*Interpretation*
ITQ	*Irish Theological Quarterly*
JBL	*Journal of Biblical Literature*
JSOTSup	Journal for the Study of the Old Testament Supplement Series
Leg.	Philo *Legum allegoriae*
LXX	Septuagint
Midr.	Midrash
MS(S)	manuscript(s)
MT	Masoretic Text
NA28	*Novum Testamentum Graece*, Nestle-Aland, 28th ed.
NIB	*New Interpreter's Bible*. Edited by Leander E. Keck. 12 vols. Nashville: Abingdon, 1994–2004.
NCBC	New Cambridge Bible Commentary
NovTSup	Supplements to Novum Testamentum
NTS	*New Testament Studies*
NTSI	New Testament and the Scriptures of Israel
Num. Rab.	Rabbah Numbers
OG	Old Greek
OTL	Old Testament Library
par(r).	parallel(s)
Pesiq. Rab.	Pesiqta Rabbati
PG	Patrologia Graeca. Edited by Jacques-Paul Migne. 162 vols. Paris, 1857–1886.
pl.	plural
Proof	*Prooftexts: A Journal of Jewish Literary History*

SBLMS	Society of Biblical Literature Monograph Series
SCS	Septuagint and Cognate Studies
SJLA	Studies in Judaism in Late Antiquity
SJOT	*Scandinavian Journal of the Old Testament*
SNTSMS	Society for New Testament Studies Monograph Series
SPhilo	*Studia Philonica*
STDJ	Studies on the Texts of the Desert of Judah
Tg. Isa.	Targum Isaiah
TOTC	Tyndale Old Testament Commentaries
TTE	*The Theological Educator*
TynBul	*Tyndale Bulletin*
WTJ	*Westminster Theological Journal*

Fore-words

In the first volume in this series, which seeks to read the Old Testament (OT) both forward (in its original contexts) and backwards (in light of the Christ event and of the use of the OT by the earliest Christians), we studied Isaiah at some length.[1] We are focusing in these studies on the portions of the OT most often quoted, alluded to, or echoed in the NT, and trying to understand why these particular texts were so important to the earliest Christians, especially as they proceeded to articulate their understanding of Christ, his person and work, and of his *ekklēsia,* Jew and gentiles united in Christ.

On the one hand, since all the earliest followers of Jesus were Jews, it is easy to understand why the OT was overwhelmingly the sacred source for their reflection on Christ, but why did their reflections often go beyond (and in different creative directions), what the original authors seem to have focused on? On the other hand, why *only* these texts? Why, for example, is there almost no mention of Job or any use of the rich material in the book of Job in the New Testament (NT), when the NT texts are so full of reflection on suffering, especially the suffering of Christ and his followers? Why is there so frequent a turning not only to Isaiah but to the Psalms, again and again and again? This in turn leads to the question, What exactly do the Psalms and Isaiah have in common that they were the "go to" texts for the earliest Christians as they tried to understand and articulate the Christ event and its impact?

In the first volume in this series I made the following suggestions: (1) the Psalter and Isaiah (especially Second and Third Isaiah) share in

---

1. Ben Witherington III, *Isaiah Old and New: Exegesis, Intertextuality, and Hermeneutics* (Minneapolis: Fortress, 2017).

common the fact that they are poetry, exalted sacred poetry, and (2) as poetry their language partakes of all the characteristics of poetry: rhythm, rhyme, assonance, alliteration, and the creative use of metaphor, images, and the like. The language of analogy is to the fore, again and again and again, and not just any kinds of analogies but analogies, particularly in the Psalms, that draw on some of the most common human experiences—trials, tribulations, suffering, rescue—as experiences in both the present and the future. While historical context is all-important in understanding a good deal of Isaiah, more generic human context and experience are critical in understanding many of the Psalms. Yes, there are Psalms linked to specific experiences, such as those of David when he was confronted by Nathan about Bathsheba. But most of the Psalms are not like that, and most of the uses of the Psalms in the NT, especially to articulate the Christ event, draw on the broader sort of psalm material.

To be clear, Isaiah is prophecy in poetic form, whereas the Psalms are songs in poetic form. The Psalms, by genre, are not inherently prophecy, by which I mean, they are not oracular speech from God's lips to the prophet's ears; nor are they visionary speech, though occasionally there is a quoted oracle included in a song. This is not to say that the songs could not be interpreted prophetically, and indeed the Psalms were, because in fact the earliest Christians saw *all of the OT* as prophetic of the Christ event in the broad sense of the term *prophetic*. That is, it all foreshadowed, even if it did not all foretell, the coming of the Messiah, and in their view, like John the Baptist, it prepared the way for his coming in one way or another.

In fact, the Psalter is rather unique in the OT in its being a revelation of the human heart poured out to God in sung prayer. The Psalter is not just any kind of songbook, it is a sacred songbook of praise, thanksgiving, lament, celebration, and pilgrimage in which God is addressed again and again. St. Athanasius was on the right path in suggesting that while prophecy reveals the character of God as he speaks to us, the Psalms reveal the true character of humankind and of the human heart as we speak to God.

This explains one of the conundrums that has puzzled expositors of the Psalms over many ages, namely, why do we have things like the imprecatory psalms urging God to smash the heads of the Edomite babies on the rocks (Psalm 137)? The answer is, *the Psalms are a true revelation of the human heart always, but the human heart is not always in accord with the character, nature, and plan of God. Yes, the Psalter does at times reveal God's character and will as mirrored in the human heart, but it always reflects with transparency and clarity the intricacies of the human heart.*[2] We must never forget this fact as we work through the Psalms and their use in the NT. If we use it and the insights already mentioned above in this study, we will be on the right path to understanding.

Furthermore, the Psalms are indeed songs, and as songs they speak to and from the affective side of human nature, showing forth the whole gamut of human emotions. Music reaches and speaks for the parts of human nature that are not merely cognitive. Studying the lyrics to songs as if they were literal theological treatises is a mistake, and yet many commentators on the Psalms over the ages have fallen into this trap.[3] This is not because there are no profound thoughts to be found in the Psalms. It is because too often we ignore the very genre or character of the Psalms, which are so full of dramatic hyperbole. Nothing is more discouraging and deadening than watching someone attempt a literal reading of figurative language. But that of course was not the intent of the psalmist in the first place, and fortunately the earliest Christians knew this. They do not ponder "how exactly" the hills might skip like rams when theophany happens, or whether literally "God's nose burned" as the Hebrew suggests when he "waxed wroth." The Psalms were read and spoken and sung, and must be approached with full sensitivity to the kind of literature they are: lyric poetry. So let us see if we can still hear the music, though we don't know the tunes anymore. Let us see if we can still be caught up in love and wonder and praise, as were the original psalmists, and find out why these very texts transfixed and transfigured the earliest Christians.[4]

2. This is precisely why Calvin, in the first paragraph of his Preface to his *Commentary on the Psalms,* says, "I have been accustomed to call this book, I think not inappropriately, 'An Anatomy of all the Parts of the Soul' for there is not an emotion of which any one can be conscious that is not here represented as in a mirror. Or rather, the Holy Spirit has here drawn to the life all the griefs, sorrows, fears, doubts, hopes, cares, perplexities, in short, all the distracting emotions with which the minds of men are wont to be agitated. The other parts of Scripture contain the commandments that God enjoined his servants to announce to us. But here the prophets themselves, seeing they are exhibited to us as speaking to God, and laying open all their inmost thoughts and affections, call, or rather draw, each of us to the examination of himself in particulars in order that none of the many infirmities to which we are subject, and of the many vices with which we abound, may remain concealed. It is certainly a rare and singular advantage, when all lurking places are discovered, and the heart is brought into the light, purged from that most baneful infection, hypocrisy." John Calvin, *Commentary on the Psalms,* vol. 1, https://www.ccel.org/ccel/calvin/calcom08.vi.html.
3. Notice the warning of even so conservative a commentator as Tremper Longman III, *Psalms: An Introduction and Commentary,* TOTC (Downers Grove, IL: InterVarsity Press, 2014), 9: "It is crucial to note that the book of Psalms is not a theological textbook, but rather the libretto of the most vibrant worship imaginable."
4. In fact the followers of Jesus seem to have been some of the first to speak of a "Book of Psalms" as a distinct entity; see Luke 20:42 and Acts 1:20.

A final word of caution is in order before we begin, since most of my readers are Christians. Walter Brueggemann has rightly warned about certain tendencies on the part of Christians to gloss over or ignore the darkness in the Psalms, and other parts of the Bible. He stresses:

> Much Christian piety and spirituality is romantic and unreal in its positiveness. As children of the Enlightenment, we have censored and selected around the voice of darkness and disorientation, seeking to go from strength to strength, from victory to victory. But such a way not only ignores the Psalms; it is a lie in terms of our experience. Brevard S. Childs is no doubt right in seeing that the Psalms as a canonical book is finally an act of hope. But the hope is rooted precisely in the midst of loss and darkness, where God is surprisingly present. The Jewish reality of exile, the Christian confession of crucifixion and cross, the honest recognition that there is untamed darkness in our life that must be embraced—all of that is fundamental to the gift of new life.[5]

Brueggemann is warning us that our rather gnostic and all too postmodern approach to the Psalms as Christians is in danger of glossing over the most prevalent theme in the Psalms, namely, *lament,* which comes out of crisis. But if we do that we will not understand, for example, why Jesus said, "My God, my God why have you forsaken me," quoting the beginning of Psalm 22, and not any of the rest of it. Too much of Christian piety today ignores the old warning of William Penn, written when he was suffering in the Tower of London in 1682: "No pain, no palm; no thorns, no throne; no gall, no glory; no cross, no crown."[6]

A detailed study of the Psalms, old and new, can help us not only by correcting for our blind spots, but by reminding us that life, including devout Christian life, involves both tragedy and triumph, and the Psalms again and again tell us that we must go through, not around the darkness, in order to reach the dawn. In the end, even Psalm 23, so beloved by Christians, would not be able to help us much had the psalmist never walked through the valley of deep darkness before he dwelt in the house of the Lord forever.

No one knew better that the Psalms were honest about both the darkness and light of life than an English soldier who was incarcerated during World War II in a Nazi concentration camp. This soldier had been praying fervently, with the help of the Psalms, for direction and

---

5. Walter Brueggemann, *Spirituality of the Psalms*, Facets (Minneapolis: Fortress, 2002), xii.
6. William Penn, *No Cross, No Crown* (London, 1682).

help from God. He had prayed that God would show him how he might get beyond his current situation so that he might serve him fulltime in some sort of ministry. He had been reading one of the "rescue" psalms, in this case Psalm 91, and asked God to show him what to do to get out of prison. In prayer, he says, he heard God tell him, "you live under the protection of the Most High" (Ps 91:1). He felt led to use that phrase to extricate himself from the horrors of the death camp.

One day he walked up to the guard at the inner gate and was asked where he was going. He replied: "I am under the protection of the Most High." Unbeknownst to most of the prisoners, Hitler was regularly called by the title "the Most High," so when the guard heard the prisoner say this, he stood to attention and let the man pass. The man arrived at the outer gate to the prison and followed the same routine, saying, "I am under the protection of the Most High," and again the guards came to attention and let the man pass. For a long time he wandered through the countryside of Germany until he finally made his way back to England. The recitation of Psalm 91 had set him free.[7]

My hope is that those who read this book will arrive at new or renewed appreciation for the power and beauty of the Psalms, and perhaps, by studying and ruminating on the Psalms, even something liberating will happen.

Eastertide 2017

7. This is a story that Corrie Ten Boom often told in her speaking tours. I was fortunate enough to hear her in North Carolina in the 1960s and in New England in the 1970s when she was on one of her last tours. As for Psalm 91, see ch. 6, below.

1

Tuning Up

An Introduction to the Psalter

We now have before us one of the choicest parts of the Old Testament, wherein there is so much of Christ and his Gospel, as well as of God and his Law, that it has been called the summary of both Testaments . . . this book brings us into the sanctuary, draws us off from converse with men, with the philosophers or disputers of this world, and directs us into communion with God.
—John Wesley[1]

For poetry too is a little incarnation, giving body to what had been before invisible and inaudible.
—C. S. Lewis[2]

It is an interesting fact that while the study of prophecy, for instance of the book of Isaiah, has involved all sorts of scholarly debates and disagreements about the nature of prophecy (e.g., debates about the character of the oracles, whether they are in any sense predictive of

---

1. John Wesley, *Psalms: Explanatory Notes and Commentary* (Middletown, DE: Hargreaves, 2016), 6. This is a reprint taken from Wesley's *Explanatory Notes on the Old Testament*, which in turn was his presentation based on a close reading of Matthew Henry and Matthew Poole's notes on the OT, without Henry's Calvinistic orientation.
2. C. S. Lewis, *Reflections on the Psalms* (London: Bles, 1958), 5. I would add that poetry adds beauty to truth.

the future or not, whether pseudonymous prophecy should really be considered prophecy or just "history" masked as prophecy), when it comes to the study of the Psalter, there has in fact been a rather clear consensus of most scholars as to what kind or genre of material the Psalms are. Ever since the landmark studies of Hermann Gunkel, who analyzed the psalms according to literary type or genre, and then Sigmund Mowinckel, who tied the types of psalms to their various uses in worship, scholars have been in agreement that we are dealing with the poetic lyrics to songs. This is Hebrew poetry that was used in Israelite worship, and particularly in worship in the temple in Jerusalem as well as elsewhere.[3] In short, we are dealing with a form of literature, some would say wisdom literature, that is different in kind and function from prophecy, even though it shares a poetic character with prophecy such as we find in most of Isaiah. It is thus important that we set up our discussion of particular texts with a general orientation to the kind of material we will be examining.[4]

The Recital: Reviewing the Sheet Music

The Greek term ψαλμός refers to a striking of instrumental strings, and in fact the Latin term *psalter* refers to the stringed instrument itself in the first instance. The Hebrew term, however, that is translated by that Greek word in the LXX, namely מִזְמוֹר (*mizmôr*), means praises, specifically melodic sung praises. The traditional title for the book in Hebrew was *sepher tehellim*, book of praises. Both terms make quite clear that we are not simply dealing with ordinary prayers; rather we are dealing with music, which in various cases involves sung prayers. But we ignore the musical side of the equation at our peril.[5] That we are dealing with music should be evident from the musical directions and cues we find from time to time as parts of the prescripts to various psalms.

---

3. See, e.g., Hermann Gunkel, *The Psalms: A Form-Critical Introduction*, Facets 19 (Philadelphia: Fortress, 1967); Sigmund Mowinckel, *The Psalms in Israel's Worship*, 2 vols. (Nashville: Abingdon, 1962).
4. Let me be clear that I'm not suggesting that interest in the Psalms has waned in the scholarly world of the twenty-first century, to the contrary, there is plenty of ferment and fervor in the study of the Psalms recently, and some important new things have come to light; see, e.g., Philip S. Johnson and David Firth, eds., *Interpreting the Psalms: Issues and Approaches* (Downers Grove, IL: InterVarsity Press, 2005).
5. Note that only a few of the psalms have the Hebrew word prayer, *tephilla*, in the prescript or title: Psalms 17, 86, 90, 102, 142, though clearly more than just these psalms can be characterized as prayers of some sort. Just as importantly, fourteen psalms contain the word *sîr*, or song, with an additional fifteen being called a song of ascents (e.g., Psalm 120). One psalm, Psalm 45, is called a wedding song.

Some 116 of the 150 psalms in the book contain some sort of pre-script and various of them are directions given to the choir director or musician in charge of performing the psalm. For example, Psalm 67 says "to the leader, with stringed instruments," or Psalm 69 says "to the leader, according to the lilies" (which presumably is a particular tune). Some of the psalms are of course connected with a famous figure, usually a king, such as David or Solomon (Psalms 72, 127), but since the Hebrew construction "*le Dawid*" can mean "for David," "by David," or "about David," we cannot always be sure which of these are being attributed to David as the composer of the psalm, though it is probable that several of them were originally composed by him (e.g., Psalm 23, Psalms 51–53?).[6]

Probably, Longman is right in suggesting that "there are sufficient reasons to believe that the [final] editors did intend . . . to attribute authorship."[7] Certainly, the historical titles indicate that the early editors took the phrase that way. There are thirteen psalms, all connected to David, that have a historical title (Psalms 3, 7, 18, 34, 51, 52, 54, 56, 57, 59, 60, 63, and 142). The title of Psalm 18 is particularly noteworthy, since it speaks explicitly of David's "writing activity."[8] This is not quite correct, because what that prescript actually says is that David sang the words of this song to the Lord when he was delivered from his enemies.

There is indeed a considerable body of evidence that David was a musician (cf. 1 Sam 16:15–23; 2 Sam 1:17–27; 23:1–7; 1 Chr 6:31; 15:16; 16:7–36; 25:1; 2 Chr 29:30; Ezra 3:10; Neh 12:24–27; Psalm 18; 2 Samuel 22; Amos 6:5). What this suggests is that David is the one who started the tradition of writing sacred songs, and some of his original ones were kept and included in the book of Psalms, and presumably others added to this Davidic tradition later. (For example, some of the psalms that have David's name in the prescript also speak of temple worship, which happened after his time.)

Bernhard W. Anderson is worth quoting at this juncture:

> Even on critical grounds . . . the association of David with the Psalter is substantially valid. There was an ancient tradition to which the prophet Amos appealed in the eight century B.C. (Amos 6.5) that David was skillful

---

6. While the ending of Psalm 51, which speaks of the rebuilding of the walls of Jerusalem, suggests a time later than the time of David, we must remember that the original songs, by David or others, were adopted and adapted, edited and reframed, in various ways when they were put into a collection for later use in the worship life of Israel. It is not necessary then to conclude that the core of Psalm 51 is not by David and about his experience.

7. Longman, *Psalms*, 25.

8. Ibid.

with the lyre. It was this skill which brought him into the court of Saul, according to a well-known story (1 Samuel 16.14-23). Moreover, David gave great impetus to Israel's worship by bringing the ark of the covenant to Jerusalem (2 Samuel 6) and by laying plans for the building of the temple (2 Samuel 7). Further, there must be some truth in the view expressed in the relatively late Chronicler's history that David sponsored the composition of psalms and was active in organizing the music and liturgy of Israel's worship (1 Chronicles 13-29). In light of all this it may be assumed that embedded in the Psalter are poems or poetic fragments actually composed by David or by those in his court.[9]

But clearly, there are many other contributors to this hymnbook, noting the psalms associated with Jeduthun (Psalms 39, 62, 77), Moses (Psalm 90), the sons of Korah (Psalms 42–49, 84, 85, 87, 88), Asaph (Psalms 50, 73–83), Heman the Ezrahite (Psalm 88), and Ethan the Ezrahite (Psalm 89). These latter three names are the names of musicians, and they are listed first among the musicians in 1 Chronicles 15:17 who presented sacred music when the ark of the covenant was brought up to Jerusalem. According to 1 Chronicles 6:31–47, these three were in charge of music first at the tabernacle and then at the temple once Solomon built it (1 Chr 6:31–47).

First Chronicles 16:7 also implies that Asaph was in charge of temple music, and the one who accepted a psalm of David for use in worship. Asaph would later be remembered in Hezekiah's day as more than a musician (as a seer; see 2 Chr 29:30), and in fact some of his psalms include divine oracles (Psalms 50, 75, 81–82). Note as well that his descendants were apparently involved in Second Temple worship (Ezra 2:41; 3:10; Neh 11:22; 12:46). Possibly that family became the keepers and passers-on of the psalms from the preexilic period to the postexilic period. It may have been a family tradition.[10]

It is important to bear in mind that the Psalms, unlike various other parts of the OT, served four functions at once: (1) as material for singing in the temple and elsewhere; (2) as Scripture to be read in the temple and later in the synagogue (and memorized); (3) as prayers that could be recited privately or in corporate worship; and (4) as a source for teaching and preaching. Neither

---

9. Bernhard W. Anderson and Steven Bishop, *Out of the Depths: The Psalms Speak for Us Today*, 3rd ed. (Louisville: Westminster John Knox, 2000),16.

10. In *Isaiah Old and New*, Appendix D, I suggested that a possible solution to the issue of the three Isaiahs could be found in the text of Isaiah itself (see Isaiah 6–8), which seems to suggest that Isaiah had descendants who may have carried on the Isaianic prophetic tradition in the exile and beyond. Perhaps this is how the psalm tradition was passed on as well, through the hands of a particular family, that of Asaph. We should not underestimate how very important family connections and ancestral traditions passed on in families were to early Israelite culture.

the Pentateuch nor the Prophets could serve as many different purposes as the Psalms did.[11] Furthermore, none of the material in the NT seems to have been as multifunctional as the Psalms either, with the possible exception of the christological hymns such as we find in Philippians 2:5–11.[12] In their current forms, however, all these psalms, whatever their origins, have been adopted and adapted for worship. Furthermore, there is evidence of their having been edited into several collections, and then finally into one large compilation of these collections.

The final form of the canonical book of Psalms involves five books:

1. Book 1: Psalms 1–41;
2. Book 2: Psalms 42–72;
3. Book 3: Psalms 73–89;
4. Book 4: Psalms 90–106; and
5. Book 5: Psalms 107–150.

It is not clear whether the material was divided into five books based on the precedent of the Pentateuch, but it is possible. That there is overlap in these collections (cf. Psalms 14 and 53, though with different Hebrew terms for God in each) has made clear to scholars that originally there were several separate collections that got combined at some late stage, probably in the postexilic period, into one large hymnbook. In this regard, the process that produced the Psalms is much like the process that has produced denominational hymnbooks in the modern era as well.

Of the collections within the Psalms, scholars have identified the following:

1. Davidic psalms: Psalms 3–41; 51–72; 138–45;
2. Korahite psalms: Psalms 42–49; 84–85; 87–88;

---

11. There are some exceptions to this rule, namely when we find songs or psalms sprinkled in narrative or prophetic texts that are otherwise not lyrics to songs. Consider, e.g., the Song of the Sea in Exod 15:1–18, based on the Song of Miriam in Exod 15:20–21; the Song of Moses in Deut 32:1–43; the Song of Deborah (Judg 5:1–31); the Song of Hannah (1 Sam 2:1–10), which proves a major resource for some of the material in Luke 1–2; the song of thanksgiving of David in 2 Sam 22:2–51; the sung prayer of Habakkuk in Hab 3:2–19; or songs of lament in Jer 15:15–18; 17:14–18; 18:19–23; or Sir 39:14b–35. Sometimes the prayer of Jonah in Jonah 2:2–9 is also listed, but not all prayers are songs, and not all songs are prayers; so one has to be careful from a form-critical point of view. E.g., while Sir 51:1–12 is a prayer of thanksgiving (cf. Tobit 13), is it also a song? By contrast, Sirach 39:14b–35 actually refers to singing, so this one seems to be more than a spoken prayer.
12. But they are not prayers properly speaking, so even they are less multipurposed than the Psalms.

3. Elohistic psalms (i.e., psalms in which God is called Elohim): Psalms 42–83;
4. Asaph (a choir director and/or major composer of songs) collection: Psalms 73–83; and
5. the Songs of Ascents, or Pilgrimage Psalms for traveling to Jerusalem: Psalms 120–134.

The conclusion of Walter Brueggemann and W. H. Bellinger about all this is worth quoting: "It is fair to say that the Davidic collections form the core of the book of Psalms, and these psalms are primarily the prayers of individuals. The psalms of the Korahites and of Asaph add community prayers and begin the move toward more psalms of praise, a move that continues in books IV–V (probably the later books added to the collection)."[13] Anderson rightly points out that the notice at the end of Psalm 72—"the prayers of David, the son of Jesse, are ended"—probably means that at some early stage this was the original end of a particular collection of psalms. It is interesting that this notice was left in the collection when more materials from a Davidic collection were added after this notice (e.g., Psalms 108–10 and 138–45).[14] The evidence of compilations of songs in various stages is rather clear. This process may have been brought to some sort of closure well before the Herodian temple was built, because otherwise it is hard to account for the overall similarity of content and order between the MT and the LXX, save of course for Psalm 151 in the LXX.[15]

Occasionally, but not usually, there are specific notes in the prescript, tagging a song to a particular historical situation or circumstance (e.g., Psalm 57, which refers to this being a Davidic "*miktam*," which possibly means a golden poem, when David fled from Saul in the cave). Most of these songs are less context-specific and more generic in character, which is one reason they have been able to be used in so many different eras. They have a more universal human character to them, like much of wisdom literature in general.

When it comes to types of psalms, the most common form of song is the lament, or as we might call it, "a blues song." The following can be called individual laments: Psalms 3–7, 9–11, 13, 16–17, 22, 25–28, 31,

---

13. Walter Brueggemann and W. H. Bellinger, *Psalms*, NCBC (Cambridge: Cambridge University Press, 2014), 3.
14. Anderson, *Out of the Depths*, 11.
15. Enumeration is a different matter. Psalms 9–10 and Psalms 114–15 appear as two psalms in the Hebrew Bible but only one in the Greek Bible. On when the Psalter was substantially a closed collection see R. T. Beckwith, "The Early History of the Psalter," *TynBul* 46 (1995): 1–27.

35–36, 38–40, 42–43, 51–52, 54–57, 59, 61–64, 69–71, 77, 86, 88, 94, 102, 109, 120, 130, 140–43. In addition, there are a goodly number of corporate or group laments: Psalms 12, 14, 44, 53, 58, 60, 74, 79–80, 83, 85, 90, 106, 108, 123, 126, and 137. Interestingly, this focus on laments distinguishes the Hebrew Psalter from some later Christian hymnbooks, which focus mainly on songs of praise and thanksgiving. The Hebrew Psalter not only has no problems with individuals or groups complaining and crying out to God, *it in fact emphasizes and stresses these sorts of songs more than the other types* (cf. the whole book of Lamentations, especially Lamentations 5 to Psalm 137).

There are both individual and corporate thanksgiving songs in the Psalter as well: (1) individual (Psalms 30, 34, 41, 66, 92, 111, 116, 118, 138), and (2) corporate (Psalms 67, 75, 107, 124, 129, 136). Scholars distinguish these sorts of songs from what seem to be more formal general hymns (Psalms 29, 33, 68, 100, 103, 105, 113–15, 134–35, 139), and it should be noted that the whole Psalter closes with a series of such hymns (Psalms 145–50 with the exception perhaps of Psalm 138). Psalms 146–50 seem to be spinning out some of the main themes and motifs of Psalm 145 rather like a musical coda.

Other categorizations of the remaining psalms seem to be not so much based on form critical considerations as on content, so for example we have a series of so-called royal psalms, psalms having to do with the king (Psalms 2, 18, 20–21, 45, 72, 89, 101, 110, 132, and 144). These quite naturally lent themselves to being applied to later kings including the messiah, as is especially evident from what the earliest Christians did with a hymn like Psalm 110. There are in addition a series of wisdom and creation songs: (1) wisdom (Psalms 1, 37, 49, 73, 78, 89, 101, 119, 127–28, 132), and (2) creation-themed psalms (Psalms 8, 19, 65, 104, 148). There are a series of psalms about Zion (Psalms 46, 48, 76, 84, 87, 122). Finally, there are hymns which focus on the theme of trusting God, though I would say these could also be included under the heading of general hymns or praise songs of a sort (Psalms 23, 91, 121, 125, 131).

In general, we can say that some of these are preexilic, a few are exilic (Psalm 137), and some are postexilic in origin. The book of Psalms obviously had a very long gestation period, not concluded before the postexilic period. The fact that songs from a long history of Israel's relationship with her God were carried forward in the worship life of God's people tells us that song in a largely oral culture was an important vehicle of preserving community memory and of creating continuity between the past and the present, and even the future. But again, in all generations these songs reflect the human heart in paraphrase, the soul in pilgrimage, to borrow phrases from George Herbert's famous poem about prayer. As such, they are true revelations about the character and concerns on the hearts of the devout, and *not usually* direct revelations of God's heart, will, or plan. There is evidence that even though a particular historical incident may have prompted the writing of a psalm, upon editing, the song was made more generic in character so it would be appropriate to describe a range of human experiences. Thus, for example, Longman points to Psalm 51, which simply speaks of cleansing from sin, not cleansing from the specific sin of adultery, though that was the presenting issue in David's case.[16] *What this suggests is that from the time these psalms were part of a sacred collection the editors already had in mind framing things in a more generic or universal way to be relevant to as wide an audience as possible.*

Precisely because we have lost the original tunes and sounds of these songs in Hebrew,[17] they have tended to be treated by Christians as either: (1) prayers without music, or (2) have been adopted and adapted as Christian hymns used to address God in some manner, or (3) have become part of special readings to the congregation from the Psalter (sometimes responsive readings), or (4) special choir numbers performed for the congregation. To examine the NT use of the Psalms is to see how this material was *first used* by the earliest Christians, often for christological purposes and ends. But to some extent they were following earlier precedents, even messianic precedents, as we can see, for example, from the way the Psalms come up for discussion in the Qumran literature. In fact, it appears that the messianic and eschatological reading of a psalm like Psalm 2 began already in the postexilic period when there was no Davidic king, but the text was assumed to still be relevant to the hopes and dreams of God's people.[18]

Is there some sort of ordering principle in the book of Psalms, as well as clues to its composition? In regard to the former issue there is some-

---

16. Longman, *Psalms*, 32.
17. Though we appear to have names of some of the tunes: Psalm 9 "the death of the son," Psalm 22 "the does of the morning," Psalms 45, 69 "lilies," Psalm 56 "a dove on distant oaks," Psalms 57, 58, 59, 75 all share the title "do not destroy," Psalm 60 has "the lily of the covenant" as does Psalm 80 except lilies is plural in that title. The references to stringed instruments are not infrequent, and rule out the notion that the early Israelite worship was strictly a capella; see Psalms 4, 6, 54, 55, 61, 67, and 76. We are not sure what the word *selah* means but it occurs seventy times in the Psalms, and also in the poem in Habakkuk 3. It *seems* to indicate that the singer or listener is to pause and allow reflection, but we cannot be sure. That it only occurs in poems suggests it is some kind of technical term.
18. See Longman, *Psalms*, 35, 59–64.

thing to be said for the view that the overall flow of the hymnbook is moving from laments to praises, with the former predominating at the outset of the book and hymns of praise predominating in book 5 of the Psalter. Each book ends with a doxology indicating that all of the songs were intended for use in worship. There may also be something to the suggestion that because Psalm 1 is a torah song, and because the book was divided into five parts that perhaps the Psalms are to be seen as David's torah, on the pattern of the Pentateuch being seen as Moses's torah.[19] Those scholars are probably right as well to suggest that the use of the sacred names in particular patterns tells us something of the earlier stages of collections. For example, in book 1 we find YHWH 272 times, but Elohim only 15, whereas book 2 has just the opposite pattern with Elohim 207 times but YHWH 74 times. Book 3 has fewer uses of the sacred names, in this case YHWH 13 times and Elohim 36 times. Books 4 and 5 use YHWH some 339 times but Elohim only 7 times. As already mentioned, what is particularly telling is finding the same psalm in two different books, one with YHWH and the other one with Elohim used as the sacred name (cf. Psalms 14 and 53).

But even in early Israelite worship it was not just about singing and praying to God; it was also about God speaking to his people, so it is no surprise that we have psalms where God speaks to his people (Psalms 50, 81), and other psalms which are not oracles as a whole, but they contain oracles (Psalms 75, 92, 110). But it is not just God as ruler who speaks to his people, sometimes the human king does as well or is the subject of a song (Psalm 20). These are called royal psalms, and with good reason.

What may we reasonably expect from these songs? They depict God and humankind in relationship through imagery, personification, parallel construction, and a host of other poetic devices. These songs should be evaluated like one would evaluate impressionistic paintings, say Monet's various paintings of Rouen cathedral. The work of art *is referential*, but it is not *literally descriptive*. As Roland Murphy says, we have to approach this literature with "a certain sensitivity to poetry, a yielding to the imagery."[20] It works by analogy and seeks to leave an impression, make an emotional impact. Its method is indirection and its message is big picture, often generic and universal. Not surprisingly,

---

19. See C. L. Seow, "An Exquisitely Poetic Introduction to the Psalter," *JBL* 132 (2013): 275–93.
20. Roland E. Murphy, *The Psalms, Job*, Proceedings (Philadelphia: Fortress, 1977), 12–13. Karl Rahner even reportedly said that in general one needs a "poetic ear" to properly hear the word of God in the words of human beings (quoted by Murphy, ibid.).

in the NT it provides a religious vocabulary and religious imagery that can be applied in various ways, and used to describe the experience of Christ and various early Christians; and it has a decided ethical edge as Gordon Wenham has rightly stressed.[21] It is intended to affect not just one's thinking but one's behavior, not just one's thoughts but one's affections and actions.

We should not think however that the Psalms were only a part of public worship; it is clear that in early Judaism they were also a part of private piety. For example, as Steve Moyise and Maarten J. J. Menken point out:

> in 4 Maccabees, a book that was probably written sometime between 19 and 54 CE [we find that] a large part of it concerns the story of the martyrdom of a mother and her seven sons under the Syrian king Antiochus IV Epiphanes, who took a series of vehement anti-Jewish measures in the period between 167 and 164 BCE. When the mother reminds her sons of their deceased father, one of the many things she says about him is: "He used to sing to you the psalmist David who says 'many are the afflictions of the righteous'" (4 Macc 18:15; quoting Ps 34:20). A clause from a psalm ascribed to David is immediately applied to the situation of a family suffering persecution under Antiochus Epiphanes.[22]

The Psalms by the Numbers

When it comes to numbers and the Psalms, things can get confusing. The Hebrew text and the Jewish Greek Text of the Psalms have different chapter numbers (and sometimes different verse numbers too), and the English translations normally follow the numbering that comes with the Hebrew text. For example, Psalm 100 in the Hebrew text is Psalm 99 in the LXX. We will be following the normal numbering found in your English translations to prevent confusion, *even when we are talking about the LXX text.* But there are other sorts of numbers to consider as well at this juncture.

It will do well here at the outset to also lay out where the Psalms are mainly used in the NT, and where they are not. For a start, there are a whole series of books in the NT that neither quote nor *clearly* allude to the Psalms (though there are *often* echoes) and some of these are quite surprising: Philippians, 1 and 2 Thessalonians, the Pastoral Epis-

---

21. Gordon J. Wenham, *Psalms as Torah: Reading Biblical Song Ethically* (Grand Rapids: Baker Academic, 2012).

22. Steve Moyise and Maarten J. J. Menken, eds., *The Psalms in the New Testament*, NTSI (London: T&T Clark, 2004), 1.

tles, Philemon, James, 2 Peter, the Johannine Epistles, and Jude.[23] Some of this can be accounted for by the fact that the quoting from or alluding to the OT *in general* is almost entirely absent in various of these documents. One could theorize that perhaps the converts in Thessalonike, for example, were so overwhelmingly from a pagan background that Paul refrained from using a sacred text with which they would be totally unfamiliar. But this hardly explains the almost total absence of Psalm material in the Pastoral Epistles or James or Jude, for example. A better explanation will be required as we work through the data. What the above data do reveal is that some thirteen of the twenty-seven books of the NT do not really provide much material for discussion of citations or clear allusions in this particular study, whereas the Gospels, Acts, some Pauline letters, and Revelation do provide a lot of source material of all sorts. Nevertheless, this study seeks to go beyond where even some detailed studies of citations of and allusions to the Psalms go, to show how pervasive the influence of the language, thought world, and subject matter of the Psalms is on the NT in general. In each major exegetical chapter that follows, we will conclude with a section called the lexicon of faith, a study of minor allusions and echoes and use of Psalter language that is usually overlooked or neglected in the study of the impact of the Psalms on NT literature. Here is a starter kit for those beginning to look at the obvious visible and direct impact of the Psalms on the NT.

Psalms Quotes/Allusions in the New Testament[24]

Matt 4:6 // Luke 4:10–11	Ps 91:11–12 (90:11–12 LXX)
Matt 13:35	Ps 78:2 (77:2 LXX)
Matt 21:9 // Luke 13:35 and 19:38 // John 12:13	Ps 118:26 (117:26 LXX)
Matt 21:16	Ps 8:2
Matt 21:42 // Mark 12:10–11 // Luke 20:17 // Acts 4:11 // 1 Pet 27	Ps 118:22–23 (117:22–23 LXX)
Matt 22:44 // Mark 12:36 // Luke 20:42–43 // Acts 2:34–35 // Heb 1:13	Ps 110:1 (109:1 LXX)
Matt 27:35 // John 19:24	Ps 22:18 (21:18 LXX)

23. See ibid., 2.
24. Cf. the similar list compiled in 1999 by Joel Kalvesmaki, http://www.kalvesmaki.com/LXX/NTChart.htm. I have reviewed his list, added to it, and made some modifications.

Luke 23:46	Ps 82:6 (81:6 LXX)
John 2:17 // Rom 15:3	Ps 69:9 (68:9 LXX)
John 10:34	Ps 82:6 (81:6 LXX)
John 13:18	Ps 41:9 (40:9 LXX)
John 15:25	Ps 69:4 (68:4 LXX)
John 19:36	Ps 34:20 (33:20 LXX)
Acts 1:20	Ps 69:25 (68:25 LXX) and Ps 109:8 (108:8 LXX)
Acts 2:25–28 and Acts 13:35	Ps 16:8–11 (15:8–11 LXX)
Acts 4:25	Ps 2:1–2 (2:1–2 LXX)
Acts 13:22	Ps 89:20 (88:20 LXX)
Acts 13:33 // Heb 1:5 // Heb 5:5	Ps 2:7
Rom 2:6	Ps 62:12 (61:12 LXX)
Rom 3:4	Ps 51:4 (50:4 LXX)
Rom 3:10–18	Ps 14:1–3 (13:1–3 LXX) Ps 53:1–3 // Ps 5:9 // Ps 140:3 // Ps 10:7 (cf. Ps 5:10 // 139:4 // 9:28 // 59:7–8 // 35:2 LXX)
Rom 4:7–8	Ps 32:1–2 (31:1–2 LXX)
Rom 8:36	Ps 44:22 (43:22 LXX)
Rom 10:18	Ps 19:4 (18:4 LXX)
Rom 11:9	Ps 69:22–23 (68:22–23 LXX)
Rom 15:9	Ps 18:49 (17:49 LXX)
Rom 15:11	Ps 117:1 (116:1 LXX)
1 Cor 3:20	Ps 94:11 (93: 11 LXX)
1 Cor 10:26	Ps 8:4–6 (Ps 8:4–6 LXX)
1 Cor 15:27 // Heb 2:6–8	Ps 8:4–6 (Ps 8:4–6 LXX)
2 Cor 4:13	Ps 116:10 (115:10 LXX)
2 Cor 9:9	Ps 112:9 (and 111:9 LXX)
Eph 4:8	Ps 68:18 (67:18 LXX)
Eph 4:26	Ps 4:4 (4:4 LXX)
Heb 1:5	Ps 2:7 (2:7 LXX)

Heb 1:7	Ps 104:4 (103:4 LXX)
Heb 1:8, 9	Ps 45:6–7 (44:6–7 LXX)
Heb 1:10–12	Ps 102: 25–27 (101:25–27 LXX)
Heb 2:12	Ps 22:22 (21:22 LXX)
Heb 3:7–11 // 3:15 // 4:3–7	Ps 95:7–11 (94: 7–11 LXX)
Heb 5:6 // 5:10 // 7:17 // 7:21	Ps 110:4 (109:4 LXX)
Heb 10:5–9	Ps 40:6–8 (39:6–8 LXX)
Heb 13:6	Ps 27:1 // 118:6 (26:1 // 117:6 LXX)
1 Pet 3:10–12	Ps 34:12–16 (33:12–16 LXX)
1 Pet 5:7	Ps 55:22 (54:22 LXX)
Rev 2:7	Ps 2:9

This list can be compared to the older one compiled by A. F. Kirkpatrick in 1902[25]:

Psalm 2:1, 2	Acts 4:25, 26
2:7	Acts 13:33; Heb 1:5; 5:5
2:8, 9	Rev 2:26, 27; 12:5; 19:15
4:4	Eph 4:26
5:9	Rom 3:13
6:3a	John 12:27
6:8	Matt 7:23; Luke 13:27
8:2	Matt 21:16
8:4–6	Heb 2:6–8
8:6	1 Cor 15:27; Eph 1:22
10:7	Rom 3:14
14:1c, 2b, 3	Rom 3:10–12
16:8.–11	Acts 2:25–28
16:10b	Acts 13:35

25. A. F. Kirkpatrick, *The Book of Psalms*, CBSC (Cambridge: Cambridge University Press, 1902).

13

Psalm 18:2b	Heb 2:13
18:49	Rom 15:9
19:4	Rom 10:18
22:1	Matt 27:46; Mark 15:34
22:7	Matt 27:39; Mark 15:29; Luke 23:35
22:8	Matt 27:43
22:18	John 19:24; cf. Matt 27:35; Mark 15:24; Luke 23:34
22:22	Heb 2:12
24:1	1 Cor 10:26 [28]
31:5a	Luke 23:46
32:1, 2	Rom 4:7, 8
34:8	1 Pet 2:3
34:12–16	1 Pet 3:10–12
34:20	John 19:36
35:19b	John 15:25
36:1b	Rom 3:18
37:11a	Matt 5:5
38:11	Luke 23:49
40:6–8	Heb 10:5–7
41:9	John 13:18
41:13	Luke 1:68
42:5	Matt 26:38; Mark 14:34
44:22	Rom 8:36
45:6, 7	Heb 1:8, 9
48:2	Matt 5:35
51:4	Rom 3:4
53:1–3	Rom 3:10–12
55:22	1 Pet 5:7
62:12	Matt 16:27; Rom 2:6

Psalm 68:18	Eph 4:8
69:4	John 15:25
69:9a	John 2:17
69:9b	Rom 15:3
69:21	Matt 27:34, 48; Mark 15:36; Luke 23:36; John 19:28, 29
69:22, 23	Rom 11:9, 10
69:25	Acts 1:20
72:18	Luke 1:68
78:2	Matt 13:35
78:24	John 6:31
82:6	John 10:34
86:9	Rev 15:4
88:8	Luke 23:49
89:10	Luke 1:51
89:20	Acts 13:22
90:4	2 Pet 3:8
91:11, 12	Matt 4:6; Luke 4:10, 11
91:13	Luke 10:19
94:11	1 Cor 3:20
94:14	Rom 11:1, 2
95:7–11	Heb 3:7–11, 15, 18; 4:1, 3, 5, 7
97:7	Heb 1:6
98:3	Luke 1:54
102:25–27	Heb 1:10–12
103:17	Luke 1:50
104:4	Heb 1:7
105:8, 9	Luke 1:72, 73
106:10	Luke 1:71
106:45	Luke 1:72

Psalm 106:48	Luke 1:68
107:9	Luke 1:53
109:8	Acts 1:20
109:25	Matt 27:39
110:1	Matt 22:44; Mark 12:36; Luke 20:42, 43; Acts 2:34, 35; Heb 1:13; cf. Matt 26:64; Mark 14:62; 16:19; Luke 22:69; 1 Cor 15:25; Eph 1:20; Col 3:1; Heb 1:3; 8:1; 10:12, 13; 12:2; 1 Pet 3:22
110:4	Heb 5:6; 6:20; 7:17, 21
111:9a	Luke 1:68
111:9c	Luke 1:49
112:9	2 Cor 9:9
116:10	2 Cor 4:13
117:1	Rom15:11
118:6	Heb 13:6
118:22, 23	Matt 21:42; Mark 12:10, 11; Luke 20:17; Acts 4:11; 1 Pet 2:4, 7
118:25, 26	Matt 21:9; 23:39; Mark 11:9; Luke 13:35; 19:38; John 12:13
132:5	Acts 7:46
132:11	Acts 2:30
132:17	Luke 1:69
135:14a	Heb 10:30
140:3b	Rom 3:13
143:2b	Rom 3:20
146:6	Acts 4:24; 14:15[26]

Felix Just has provided a somewhat more comprehensive list of all citations or allusions to the OT in the NT, as follows:[27]

---

26. Anderson, et al. *Out of the Depths*, 225–28 lists some eighty-nine, but they are limiting themselves to specific quotes or clear allusions.

27. Felix Just. Found at http://catholic-resources.org/Bible/Quotations-NT-OT.htm.

NT Passage	OT Source	NT Passage	OT Source
Matt 1:3b–6a	Ruth 4:18–22	Matt 11:23a	Isa 14:13, 15
Matt 1:23a	Isa 7:14	Matt 12:7	Hos 6:6
Matt 1:23b	Isa 8:8, 10	Matt 12:18–21	Isa 42:1–4
Matt 2:6	Mic 5:2	Matt 12:40	Jonah 1:17
Matt 2:15	Hos 11:1	Matt 13:14–15	Isa 6:9–10
Matt 2:18	Jer 31:1–15	Matt 13:35	Ps 78:2–3
Matt 2:23	Isa 11:1	Matt 15:4a	Exod 20:12
Matt 3:3	Isa 40:3	Matt 15:4a	Deut 5:16
Matt 4:4	Deut 8:3	Matt 15:4b	Exod 21:17
Matt 4:6	Ps 91:11–12	Matt 15:8–9	Isa 29:13
Matt 4:7	Deut 6:16	Matt 18:16	Deut 19:15
Matt 4:10	Deut 6:13	Matt 19:4	Gen 1:27
Matt 4:15–16	Isa 9:1–2	Matt 19:4	Gen 5:2
Matt 5:21	Exod 20:13	Matt 19:5	Gen 2:24
Matt 5:21	Deut 5:17	Matt 19:7	Deut 24:1
Matt 5:27	Exod 20:14	Matt 19:18–19a	Exod 20:12–16
Matt 5:27	Deut 5:18	Matt 19:18–19a	Deut 5:16–20
Matt 5:31	Deut 24:1	Matt 19:19b	Lev 19:18
Matt 5:33	Lev 19:12	Matt 21:5	Zech 9:9
Matt 5:33	Num 30:2	Matt 21:9	Ps 118:25–26
Matt 5:38	Exod 21:24	Matt 21:13	Isa 56:7
Matt 5:38	Lev 24:20	Matt 21:16b	Ps 8:2–3
Matt 5:28	Deut 19:21	Matt 21:42	Ps 118:21–23
Matt 5:43	Lev 19:18	Matt 22:24	Deut 25:5
Matt 8:17	Isa 53:4	Matt 22:32a	Exod 3:6, 15
Matt 9:13a	Hos 6:6	Matt 22:37	Deut 6:5
Matt 10:35–36	Mic 7:6	Matt 22:39	Lev 19:8
Matt 11:10	Mal 3:1	Matt 22:44	Ps 110:1

NT Passage	OT Source	NT Passage	OT Source
Matt 23:39	Ps 118:26	Mark 12:29–30	Deut 6:4–6
Matt 24:15	Dan 9:27b; 11:31; 12:11	Mark 12:31	Lev 19:18
Matt 24:29	Isa 13:10	Mark 12:32a	Deut 6:4
Matt 24:30	Dan 7:13	Mark 12:32b	Deut 4:35
Matt 26:31	Zech 13:7	Mark 12:32b	Isa 45:21
Matt 26:64a	Ps 110:1	Mark 12:33a	Deut 6:5
Matt 26:65b	Dan 7:13	Mark 12:33b	Lev 19:18
Matt 27:9–10	Zech 11:12–13	Mark 12:36	Ps 110:1
Matt 27:46	Ps 22:1	Mark 13:26	Dan 7:13
		Mark 14:37	Zech 13:7
Mark 1:2	Mal 3:1	Mark 14:62a	Ps 110:1
Mark 1:3	Isa 40:3	Mark 14:62b	Dan 7:13
Mark 4:12	Isa 6:9–10	Mark 15:34	Ps 22:1
Mark 7:6–7	Isa 29:13		
Mark 7:10a	Exod 20:12	Luke 2:23	Exod 13:2, 12, 15
Mark 7:10a	Deut 5:16	Luke 2:24	Lev 12:8
Mark 7:10b	Exod 21:17	Luke 3:4–6	Isa 40:3–5
Mark 10:4	Deut 24:1, 3	Luke 4:4	Deut 8:3
Mark 10:6	Gen 1:27	Luke 4:8	Deut 6:13
Mark 10:5	Gen 5:2	Luke 4:10–11	Ps 91:11–12
Mark 10:7–8	Gen 2:24	Luke 4:12	Deut 6:16
Mark 10:19	Exod 20:12–16	Luke 4:18–19	Isa 61:1–2
Mark 10:19	Deut 5:16–20	Luke 4:18	Isa 58:6
Mark 11:9–10	Ps 118:25–26	Luke 7:27	Mal 3:1
Mark 11:17	Isa 56:7	Luke 8:10	Isa 6:9
Mark 12:10–11	Ps 118:22–23	Luke 10:27a	Deut 6:5
Mark 12:19	Deut 25:5	Luke 10:27b	Lev 19:18
Mark 12:26	Exod 3:6, 15	Luke 13:25	Ps 118:26

NT Passage	OT Source	NT Passage	OT Source
Luke 18:20	Exod 20:12–16	John 19:36	Num 9:12
Luke 18:20	Deut 5:16–20	John 19:37	Zech 12:10
Luke 19:38	Ps 118:26		
Luke 19:46	Isa 56:7	Acts 1:20a	Ps 69:25
Luke 20:17	Ps 118:22	Acts 1:20b	Ps 109:8
Luke 20:28	Deut 25:5	Acts 2:17–21	Joel 2:28–32
Luke 20:37	Exod 3:6	Acts 2:25–28	Ps 16:8–11
Luke 20:42–43	Ps 110:1	Acts 2:30	Ps 132:11
Luke 21:27	Dan 7:13	Acts 2:31	Ps 16:10
Luke 22:37	Isa 53:12	Acts 2:34–25	Ps 110:1
Luke 22:69	Ps 110:1	Acts 3:13	Exod 3:6, 15
Luke 23:30	Hos 10:8	Acts 3:22	Deut 18:15–16
Luke 23:46	Ps 31:5	Acts 3:23a	Deut 18:19
		Acts 3:23b	Lev 23:29
John 1:23	Isa 40:3	Acts 3:25	Gen 22:18
John 2:17	Ps 69:9	Acts 3:25	Gen 26:4
John 6:31	Ps 78:24	Acts 4:11	Ps 118:22
John 6:45	Isa 54:13	Acts 4:25–26	Ps 2:1–2
John 10:34	Ps 82:6	Acts 7:3	Gen 12:1
John 12:13	Ps 118:25–26	Acts 7:5	Gen 17:8
John 12:15	Zech 9:9	Acts 7:6–7	Gen 15:13–14
John 12:38	Isa 53:1	Acts 7:7	Exod 3:12
John 12:40	Isa 6:10	Acts 7:18	Exod 1:8
John 13:18	Ps 41:9	Acts 7:27–28	Exod 2:14
John 15:25	Ps 35:19	Acts 7:30	Exod 3:2
John 15:25	Ps 69:4	Acts 7:32	Exod 3:6
John 19:24	Ps 22:18	Acts 7:33	Exod 3:5
John 19:36	Exod 12:46	Acts 7:34	Exod 3:7–8, 10

NT Passage	OT Source	NT Passage	OT Source
Acts 7:35	Exod 2:14	Rom 4:3	Gen 15:6
Acts 7:37	Deut 18:15	Rom 4:7–8	Ps 32:1–2
Acts 7:40	Exod 32:1	Rom 4:9	Gen 15:6
Acts 7:40	Exod 32:23	Rom 4:17	Gen 17:5
Acts 7:42–43	Amos 5:25–27	Rom 4:18a	Gen 17:5
Acts 7:49–50	Isa 66:1–2	Rom 4:18b	Gen 15:5
Acts 8:32–33	Isa 53:7–8	Rom 4:22	Gen 15:6
Acts 13:22a	Ps 89:20	Rom 7:7	Exod 20:17
Acts 13:22b	1 Sam 13:14	Rom 7:7	Deut 5:21
Acts 13:33	Ps 2:7	Rom 8:36	Ps 44:22
Acts 13:34	Isa 55:3	Rom 9:7	Gen 21:12
Acts 13:35	Ps 16:10	Rom 9:9	Gen 18:10,14
Acts 13:41	Hab 1:5	Rom 9:12	Gen 25:23
Acts 13:47	Isa 49:6	Rom 9:13	Mal 1:2–3
Acts 15:16–17	Amos 9:11–12	Rom 9:15	Exod 33:19
Acts 23:5	Exod 22:28	Rom 9:17	Exod 9:16
Acts 28:26–27	Isa 6:9–10	Rom 9:25	Hos 2:23
		Rom 9:26	Hos 1:10
Rom 1:17	Hab 2:4	Rom 9:27–28	Isa 10:22-23
Rom 2:24	Isa 52:5	Rom 9:29	Isa 1:9
Rom 3:4	Ps 51:4	Rom 9:33	Isa 8:14
Rom 3:10–12	Ps 14:1–3	Rom 10:5	lev 18:5
Rom 3:10–12	Ps 53:1–3	Rom 10:6	Deut 9:4
Rom 3:13a	Ps 5:9	Rom 10:6–8	Deut 30:12–14
Rom 3:13b	Ps 140:3	Rom 10:11	Isa 28:16
Rom 3:14	Ps 10:7	Rom 10:13	Joel 2:32
Rom 3:15–17	Isa 59:7–8	Rom 10:15	Isa 52:7
Rom 3:18	Ps 36:1	Rom 10:16	Isa 53:1

NT Passage	OT Source	NT Passage	OT Source
Rom 10:18	Ps 19:4	1 Cor 1:31	Jer 9:24
Rom 10:19	Deut 32:21	1 Cor 2:9	Isa 64:4
Rom 10:20	Isa 65:1	1 Cor 2:16	Isa 40:13
Rom 10:21	Isa 65:2	1 Cor 3:19	Job 5:13
Rom 11:3	1 Kgs 19:10, 14	1 Cor 3:20	Ps 94:11
Rom 11:4	1 Kgs 19:18	1 Cor 5:13	Deut 17:7
Rom 11:8	Isa 29:10	1 Cor 6:16	Gen 2:24
Rom 11:8	Deut 29:4	1 Cor 9:9	Deut 25:4
Rom 11:9–10	Ps 69:22–23	1 Cor 10:7	Exod 32:6
Rom 11:26–27a	Isa 59:20–21	1 Cor 10:26	Ps 24:1
Rom 11:27b	Isa 27:9	1 Cor 14:21	Isa 28:11–12
Rom 11:34	Isa 40:13	1 Cor 15:27	Ps 8:6
Rom 11:35	Job 41:11	1 Cor 15:32	Isa 22:13
Rom 12:19	Deut 32:35	1 Cor 15:45	Gen 2:7
Rom 12:20	Prov 25:21–22	1 Cor 15:54	Isa 25:8
Rom 13:9a	Exod 20:13–15, 17	1 Cor 15:55	Hos 13:14
Rom 13:9a	Deut 5:17–19, 21		
Rom 13:9b	Lev 19:18	2 Cor 4:13	Ps 116:10
Rom 14:11a	Isa 49:18	2 Cor 6:2	Isa 49:8
Rom 14:11b	Isa 45:23	2 Cor 6:16	Lev 26:12
Rom 15:3	Ps 69:9	2 Cor 6:16	Ezek 37:27
Rom 15:9	Ps 18:49	2 Cor 6:17a	Isa 52:11
Rom 15:10	Deut 32:43	2 Cor 6:17b	Ezek 20:34
Rom 15:11	Ps 117:1	2 Cor 6:18	2 Sam 7:8, 14
Rom 15:12	Isa 11:10	2 Cor 8:15	Exod 16:18
Rom 15:21	Isa 52:15	2 Cor 9:9	Ps 112:9
		2 Cor 10:17	Jer 9:24
1 Cor 1:19	Isa 29:14	2 Cor 13:1	Deut 19:15

NT Passage	OT Source	NT Passage	OT Source
Gal 3:6	Gen 15:6	Heb 1:8–9	Ps 45:6–7
Gal 3:8	Gen 12:3	Heb 1:10–12	Ps 102:25–27
Gal 3:10	Deut 27:26	Heb 1:13	Ps 110:1
Gal 3:11	Hab 2:4	Heb 2:6–8	Ps 8:4–6
Gal 3:12	Lev 18:5	Heb 2:12	Ps 22:22
Gal 3:13	Deut 27:26	Heb 2:13a	Isa 8:17
Gal 3:16	Gem 12:7	Heb 2:13b	Isa 8:18
Gal 4:27	Isa 54:1	Heb 3:7–11	Ps 95:7–11
Gal 4:30	Gen 21:10	Heb 3:15	Ps 95:7–8
Gal 5:14	Lev 19:18	Heb 4:3, 5	Ps 95:11
		Heb 4:4	Gen 2:2
Eph 4:8	Ps 68:18	Heb 5:5	Ps 2:7
Eph 4:25	Zech 8:16	Heb 5:6	Ps 110:4
Eph 4:26	Ps 4:4	Heb 6:13–14	Gen 22:16–17
Eph 5:31	Gen 2:24	Heb 7:1–2	Gen 14:17–20
Eph 6:2–3	Exod 20:12	Heb 7:17, 21	Ps 110:4
Eph 6:2–3	Deunt 5:16	Heb 8:5	Exod 25:40
		Heb 8:8–12	Jer 31:31–34
Phil 2:10–11	Isa 45:23b	Heb 9:20	Exod 24:8
		Heb 10:5–7	Ps 40:6–8
1 Tim 5:18	Deut 25:4	Heb 10:16–17	Jer 31:33–34
		Heb 10:28	Deut 17:6; 19:15
2 Tim 2:19	Num 16:5	Heb 10:30	Deut 32:35–36
		Heb 10:37–28	Hab 2:3–4
Heb 1:5a	Ps 2:7	Heb 11:5	Gen 5:24
Heb 1:5b	2 sam 7:14	Heb 11:18	Gen 47:31
Heb 1:6	Deut 32:43	Heb 11:21	Gen 47:31
Heb 1:7	Ps 104:4	Heb 12:5–6	Prov 3:11–12

NT Passage	OT Source		NT Passage	OT Source
Heb 12:20	Exod 19:12–13		1 Pet 2:6	Isa 28:16
Heb 12:21	Deut 9:19		1 Pet 2:7	Ps 118:22
Heb 12:26	Hag 2:6		1 Pet 2:8	Isa 8:14
Heb 13:5	Deut 31:6, 8		1 Pet 2:9a	Isa 43:20
Heb 13:6	Ps 118:6		1 Pet 2:9b	Exod 19:6
			1 Pet 2:9c	Isa 43:21
Jas 2:8	Leb 19:18		1 Pet 2:22	Isa 53:9
Jas 2:11	Exod 20:13, 14		1 Pet 3:10–12	Ps 34:12–16
Jas 2:11	Deut 5:17, 18		1 Pet 3:14	Isa 8:12
Jas 2:23	Gen 15:6		1 Pet 4:18	Prov 11:31
Jas 4:6	Prov 3:34		1 Pet 5:5	Prov 3:34
1 Pet 1:16	Lev 19:2		1 Pet 2:22	Prov 26:11
1 Pet 1:24–25	Isa 40:6–8			

What we learn from all such lists is that no matter how one counts it, while there are numerous quotes and allusions to the Psalms in the NT, the number pales in comparison to the number of direct quotes or allusions from Isaiah. Counting quotations, including multiple uses of the same verse from the Psalms in different NT texts, and allusions and echoes, I can only get to about 200 or so such distinct references, which is barely a third of the number of references compared to the use of Isaiah in the NT.[28] This, however, only deals with quotations and clear allusions; it does not tell a very significant part of the story.

On the surface of things, the Psalms seem very important in the Gospels to the telling of the story of Jesus, and in the synopses of the early preaching about Jesus in Acts. The Psalms comes up for especially important use in the Gospel of John, as we shall see. Romans and Hebrews, among the epistles also call on the Psalms for citation and allusion rather frequently. This contrasts with the entire lack of such use in other epistles, and the bare direct mention of a few Psalm texts in Revelation. *But again, there are many echoes and uses of language from*

---

28. However the index in NA28, 783–88, gives some nine columns to perceived references to the Psalms, but only eight to Isaiah! See Appendix A below for their complete list. What this shows, is that there are trace elements of the Psalms in the forms of echoes, key phrases, ideas in many places where there is no citation or clear and direct allusion to the Psalms.

the Psalms in Revelation and some of these other NT books that do not directly cite or allude to the Psalms. We should heed the hints in texts like Ephesians 5:19 that the Psalms were regularly sung by early Christians. This led to residual influence of the language of the Psalms in all kinds of early Christian literature.

On the surface, it would appear from the NT itself that the Psalms were more often used for preaching and teaching—especially on matters christological—than for strictly liturgical purposes, although we have some clear evidence that Christians sang the Psalms when in distress (Acts 16:25).[29] These sorts of initial impressions will need to be confirmed or disconfirmed in the course of the study that follows. These are some of the questions we will need to be asking along the way:

- Is the Psalm text being "exegeted" in the NT text?

- Is the Psalm text being used simply for its imagery or religious language?

- Is the Psalm text being used homiletically to make a point the original author was not making and if so is it being used in a way that goes beyond the original meaning but not against it (e.g., in the royal psalms)?

As we shall see, *how the Psalter is used in the NT, not how often it is directly cited or clearly alluded to* is perhaps the most crucial issue.[30]

---

29. Anderson, *Out of the Depths*, 22 is prepared to say "Early Christians were not interested in the literary quality of the psalms but in their theological—or rather, their Christological—meaning." There are about 970 references in the index to different Psalms texts in the helpful *Commentary on the New Testament Use of the Old Testament*, G. K. Beale and D. A. Carson, eds. (Grand Rapids: Baker Academic, 2007), but of course one has to analyze these closely because many of them are just suggesting parallel texts in the Psalms to the ones they are actually discussing, often *not* indicating that these particular references involve a citation, an allusion, or an echo of the Psalm text in some NT text. There are references to every Psalm in this index except Psalms 64, 126, and 150 (following the Hebrew/ English numbering system). Interestingly, there are almost no references to the Psalms of Ascent (Psalms 120–34), or in general any of the psalms in the last thirty in the Psalter. Perhaps this reflects the fact that early Christianity was not a temple-centered religion, and apart from some of the Jewish Christians like Paul, few were making pilgrimages to Jerusalem to participate in worship there. Note as well that many of the references in this commentary index involve a list of texts where a particular Greek or Hebrew word is used in a particular way in some verse in a psalm, not a reference to that verse as a whole being cited or alluded to.
30. As with the previous study on Isaiah, because I have written published commentaries on all the NT books, I will let the interested reader turn to them for the more detailed exegesis of the NT texts in this study, in so far as the discussion goes beyond the use of the OT in the NT. Here we must concentrate on presenting a basic exegesis of some important psalms and on the NT use of the Psalms and matters germane to the discussion of intertexuality.

2

The Psalter in Early Judaism

And now David being freed of wars and dangers, and enjoying for the future a profound peace, composed songs and hymns to God of various meters; some he made in trimeters, and some in pentameters.
—Josephus, *Ant.* 7.305[1]

The Psalter is the book of all saints, and everyone, whatever his situation may be, finds psalms and words in it that fit his situation and apply to his case so exactly that it seems they were put in this way only for his sake.
—Martin Luther[2]

---

1. Interestingly enough, in all his voluminous works, Josephus never once quotes the Psalms. And here, he is either referring to some Greek version of the Psalms, or he is assuming that the Psalms were composed not according to synthetic, accumulative, and antithetical parallelism such as we find in Hebrew poetry, but according to Greek poetry! Ralph Brucker, "Observations on the *Wirkungsgeschichte* of the Septuagint Psalms in Ancient Judaism and Early Christianity," in *Septuagint Research: Issues and Challengers in the Study of the Greek Jewish Scriptures*, ed. Wolfgang Kraus and R. Glenn Wooden, SCS 53 (Atlanta: Society of Biblical Literature, 2006), 360 stresses: "Josephus obviously feels a certain lack about the Greek Psalms, as they don't follow the standards of Greek religious poetry. In fact, the translator of the Psalms did not try to create pieces of Greek metrical poetry but preferred a translation into rhythmical prose. Now Josephus, in order to meet the expectations of his Greco-Roman readers, claims that the missing meters are actually there but in the Hebrew original (which of course none of his original readers could check)." Josephus (cf. *Ant.* 2.346 and 4.303) even tries to suggest that the songs of Moses in Exodus 15 and Deuteronomy 32 follow the "heroic" meter of Homer!
2. Martin Luther in *Reading the Psalms with Luther: The Psalter for Individual and Family Devotions*, ed. Bruce A. Cameron (St. Louis: Concordia, 2007), 9.

In his classic introductory study on the Psalms, Bernard Anderson tells the tale of Natan Sharansky, a Jewish dissident in Soviet Russia who was imprisoned for nine long years by the KGB, years which often involved his going on hunger strikes. Of those nine years, one was spent in a "punishment" cell, barely six feet square, where he was incessantly questioned and where his only positive companion was a copy of the Psalter, which his wife Avital had given him. Sharansky was not a particularly religious man, but he began reading and even memorizing the Psalms. "To his astonishment he found a striking affinity between his experience of bondage and the distresses articulated by many of the psalmists. Their prayers of lament became his own and their hope of deliverance became a gleam of light in his cell."

After nine grueling years of interrogation without his resistance being broken, Sharansky was finally transported to the airport in Moscow to be flown to East Germany and freedom. The authorities had confiscated his Psalm book once again, and refused to give it back to him. They wanted a photo opportunity at the airport showing how merciful they were. When the cameras were rolling, Sharansky once again said "Where's my Psalm book?" and was told he had been given all that was permitted. Sharansky dropped to the snow in front of the plane and said, "I won't move until you give me back my Psalm book." When his demand was not met, he lay down in the snow and started shouting, "Give me back my Psalm book!" at which point the authorities did so, and the cameramen pointed their cameras toward the sky. Having been given back his Psalm book, he quietly boarded the plane. Sharansky had made a promise to himself that his first act of freedom would be to read Psalm 30: "I extol you O Lord/ for you have lifted me up and not let my enemies rejoice over me/ O Lord my God,/ I cried out to you/and you healed me./ O Lord, you brought me up from Sheol/ preserved me from going down into the pit."[3] Sharansky's experience with the Psalms clearly has many centuries of precedent in the faith life of many Jews, including the Jews who lived just before and during the time of Jesus. They found their own experiences, their own lives, exegeted by the Psalms.

The very earliest Christians were all Jews who grew up in the Jewish environments of Galilee and Judaea. As such their exposure to the Psalter, and to the way the Psalter was being used, was much the same as other early Jews from all we can tell. It follows from this that we

---

3. Anderson, *Out of the Depths*, 1–2; the quotation is from p. 1.

would do well to examine how the Psalter was used in early Judaism before doing our "before and after" examination of the Psalter in its original context and in the NT. This should hopefully provide us with some clues about the connection between the Psalter in its original context, and in its use by the earliest Christians.

The Psalms at Qumran

We will begin with the Qumran community because there is considerable evidence from that source that the Psalms were very important to those devout Jews. In fact, the Qumran Psalms scrolls represent the largest number of manuscripts of any single biblical book. There are some thirty-seven such scrolls, three from Cave 1, an impressive twenty-seven from Cave 4, four from Cave 11, and one each from Caves 5, 6, and 8. But that is not all. The aforementioned scrolls are simply copies of Psalms, but there are in addition seven other manuscripts with significant citations from the Psalms. To give some perspective on this, about two hundred of the nine hundred Qumran scrolls are biblical in character, citing some or much from the OT. The Psalms scrolls make up some 20 percent of these biblical scrolls. Unfortunately, nineteen of these scrolls contain just tiny fragments of a Psalm.[4] Most importantly, *the Psalms represent the largest number of manuscripts for any biblical book.* Qumran was a community that devoted a great deal of attention to the Psalms in various ways. Perhaps the most important thing to focus on is *how* the Psalms seem to have been used at Qumran.[5]

First of all, there were collections of copied psalms, but there is no scroll that contains all the psalms from Qumran, which is no surprise because such a scroll would have been too huge to be really useful. Even taken altogether, only 126 of the canonical Psalms show up in some form. Perhaps the most important of the scrolls with multiple psalms is 11QPsa, which contains some 49 Psalms, which takes up some five meters of scroll. Compare this to the great Isaiah scroll (1QIsaa), which is only seven meters long *in toto*. Even the famous Temple Scroll (11QTa) is just eight meters long.[6] Most of these manuscripts contain psalms from only Psalms 1–89, but there are some that have psalms beginning with Psalm 90, and 1QPsa has fragments from both some

---

4. There are in addition a few Psalm scrolls from two other nearby locations, one from Naḥal Ḥever, and two from Masada.
5. See Dwight D. Swanson, "Qumran and the Psalms," in *Interpreting the Psalms: Issues and Approaches*, ed. Philip S. Johnson and David Firth (Downers Grove, IL: InterVarsity Press, 2005), 247–61.
6. On all this see Peter Flint, *The Dead Sea Scrolls and the Book of Psalms*, STDJ 17 (Leiden: Brill, 1997), 48.

of the later psalms from the Psalms 1–89 collection and some fragments from Psalms 92–119. It is not viable to conclude that the Qumran Psalter ended with Psalm 119 (though as we will see that was a very important Psalm at Qumran), for the six fragments we have of 1QPsb have portions of Psalms 126–28. Frankly, so many of these manuscripts are so fragmentary, that it is just too speculative to theorize about whether the Qumran community had a complete Psalter as we find it in the LXX or the later MT, or whether the Psalter was not yet a complete or closed collection. What we do know is the Psalter was very important to that community.

Perhaps the most interesting insight to be derived from a close study of the Psalms at Qumran comes from manuscripts that cite, and in some cases comment on the Psalms. There are seven such scrolls from Qumran; three are pesharim where the Psalms are being contemporized or applied in a way that is directly relevant for that community, and there is also 4QFlorilegium, 4QTanhumim, 4Q Catena A, and most famously 11QMelchizedek. The pesharim provide us with examples of a sort of exposition that otherwise we find only for the prophetic works at Qumran. It seems clear that the commentary was seen as an inspired running commentary on the biblical text of relevance for a community who believed they lived in the eschatological age, and were beginning to experience "the end of days." This probably indicates that there were Qumranites who saw the Psalms as having a prophetic character like Isaiah or Hosea, or Zechariah, which have similar sorts of treatment in that community's manuscripts. In particular, we find the Qumranites applying Psalms 37, 68, and 118 to their own community and its experiences, as we also find in the NT. In the NT, such texts were applied especially to Christ's passion, whereas at Qumran the discussion was more about the suffering of the community, but both communities did look forward to the coming of messianic figures, and they saw the Psalms as helping them understand the eschatological situation.[7]

A word of caution however is necessary about such comparisons. There were some major differences between the nascent Jesus movement and the Qumran movement, if we may call it that, and one of the differences comes directly to light when we consider one psalm in particular: the great torah psalm, Psalm 119. This psalm was the subject of much study and interest at Qumran, as is shown by the fact that

7. See Swanson, "Qumran and the Psalms," 260–61.

4QPsg and 4QPsh are manuscripts that contain Psalm119 *alone* (and this is possibly the case with 5QPs as well). Those manuscripts were stand-alone manuscripts, not part of a Psalter collection.

Contrast this with the fact that Psalm 119, not to mention Psalm 1 is just barely visible in the NT, either as a quote, an allusion, an echo, or as a source for religious imagery and language.[8] In other words, unlike at Qumran, there is little use of the two famous torah psalms in the NT, whereas they were an important source for the faith life of the Qumranites. The teaching of Jesus, in parables, aphorisms, and riddles took the form of wisdom literature, not a new torah, and so on the one hand it is not surprising that his followers often used the Psalms to flesh out their religious thoughts as did the Qumranites (for the Psalms were clearly neither law, nor like classical prophecy), but on the other hand the followers of Jesus stood out from various of their contemporaries *including the Qumranites* in not being torah-centric in their theological reflections on messiah and the Christ event.[9]

It is equally telling that while the Qumran community drew on some form of the Hebrew text of the Psalter, the earliest Christians seem overwhelmingly to have relied on the LXX or some other form of the Old Greek translation of the Psalter. There is more: the Qumranites seem mainly to have copied and used psalms in stichometric form, which is to say in poetic form. We can debate however how much the Greek Psalter is in poetic or prosaic form, perhaps it is best to say it is a sort of poetic prose.

On the whole, it appears that the earliest Christians used the Psalter because of various of its key ideas, not in the main because of its genre or literary form. There is evidence they knew it was poetry, but their concern was more with content than form when they used the Psalter. *It may be suggested that since Hebrew poetry is easier to memorize than straight prose, one of the reasons why the poetic form of a psalm like Psalm 119 was preserved in the copying at Qumran is because the scribes were partly concerned with memorizing not just mining the psalms.*[10]

Of course it may also be asked: What was the function of the Greek translation of the Psalter in the first place? Was it just used to convey

---

8. See, rightly, G. J. Brooke, "The Psalms in Early Jewish Literature in the Light of the Dead Sea Scrolls," in Moyise, *Psalms in the New Testament,* 7–8.

9. On the character of Jesus's teachings, see Ben Witherington III, *Jesus the Sage: The Pilgrimage of Wisdom* (Minneapolis: Fortress, 2001).

10. As Brooke points out in "Psalms in Early Jewish Literature," 8, the aforementioned Psalm 119 manuscripts involve not only a stichometric layout, but also the use of a large *lamed* in the margin to indicate where one stanza ended and another begin. It is worth comparing 4QDeutq, which contains the Song of Moses, and which is also laid out in stichometric form.

the content of the Psalms (sometimes in a paraphrase) to Greek-speaking Jews?[11] But there is also evidence from Qumran (see frag. 3 of 4QPsn) that psalms could be excerpted and combined into a sort of catena on the basis of similar ideas or catchword connections. The fragment in question has Psalm 135:11–12 directly followed by Psalm 136:23–24, with a link made by having Psalm 135:12a and b have a key phrase found throughout Psalm 136.[12]

Without question the great psalm scroll from Qumran, 11QPsa is of relevance for our discussion of the use of the Psalms in the NT because it bears strong witness to the Davidic messianism of the community and the attempt to make clear that the whole collection should be seen as Davidic in character. Particular attention has to be given not only to Psalm 151, the autobiographical poem in column 28 of the manuscript, but also to "the compositions of David" paragraph which is in prose and reads as follows: "And he [David] wrote psalms: 3,600; and the songs to be sung before the altar over the perpetual offering of every day, for all the days of the year: 364; and for the Sabbath offerings 52 songs; and for the offering for the beginning of the month, and for all the days of the festivals, and for Yom Kippur, 30 songs. And all the songs he composed were 446. And the songs to be sung over the possessed, 4 songs. The total was 4,050. *He composed them all through the spirit of prophecy which had been given to him from before the most High.*" (11QPsa 27:4–13, emphasis added). It was not just the earliest Christians who saw the Psalms as prophetic in character, for this last sentence in the prose interlude makes clear that at least some at Qumran saw David as inspired by the spirit of prophecy when he wrote all his songs.

This view of the Psalms should be compared to what is said, for instance in 1 Peter 1:10–12 about prophecy, a discussion that is followed by a citation of a catena of "stone" texts involving material from both Isaiah and the Psalms. The OT in general was seen as pregnant with messianic prophecy, even in texts that were not oracular or visionary in character, including especially the Psalms. But the autobiographical poem now called Psalm 151 does not just show up at Qumran, it shows up in translated form at the end of the LXX Psalter. What the various psalms collections at Qumran, which differ one from another, *may* suggest is that the Psalter was not a closed book of 150 songs at the beginning of the NT era. If this is true, you would not know

---

11. In other words, I'm asking whether the LXX Psalter might not have served the same sort of purpose as Eugene Peterson's *The Message* does as a version of the NT.
12. Again see Brooke, "Psalms in Early Jewish Literature," 8.

it from the NT, which only quotes or alludes to portions of what came to be called the canonical psalms, found in the MT and the LXX. There is no use of Psalm 151 in the NT.

At this juncture we should also point out that there is evidence in the NT that the writers (and perhaps Jesus himself) distinguished the Psalms from "the Law and the Prophets." I'm referring to Luke 24:44 which should be compared to the reference to the "Law and all the prophets" in Luke 24:27. And yet at the same time, Luke 24:44 makes clear that the Psalms as well are considered prophetic in some sense: "everything written about me in the Law of Moses, the prophets, *and the Psalms* must be fulfilled" (emphasis added). Whether the Psalms are simply seen as foreshadowing the Christ or actually predicting his person and work, either way, the Psalms are seen as something that were being fulfilled in Christ. In this approach to the Psalms there is resonance with what we have already found at Qumran.

One of the questionable aspects of Brooke's otherwise excellent discussion of the Psalms in early Jewish literature is his assumption that the Psalms were, as he calls them "timeless poems" later historicized by associating them with a particular event in David's life or more generally associated with David through the *le Dawid* prescript. He then hypothesizes that

> part of the shift from poetry to history is the way in which the Psalms are viewed as some kind of oracular text which is in unfulfilled. . . . As some superscripts identify the subject matter of many poems with their author David, so the eschatological reader is able to recognize the typological implications of what the Psalm may say in relation to the Davidic messiah. More than most texts, probably because of their associations with David, the Psalms become the scriptural basis for messianic fulfillment, seen in the New Testament in the historicized proof-texting of the Passion narratives, as well as in such works as the Epistle to the Hebrews."[13]

From Generic to Specific, or Vice Versa?

This whole approach begs a lot of questions, and provides answers to complex questions without any significant substantiation. In the first place, the whole OT was seen as prophetic in character by not only the earliest Christians, but by other eschatologically inclined groups like that at Qumran (or e.g., it would appear by John the Baptizer and his movement). It was not some singular association with King David

---

13. Ibid., 15.

of a particular portion of the OT that inclined early Jews to read the OT prophetically, or even to speculate about the messiah. It must be remembered that the Qumranites spoke of both a priestly and a kingly messiah to come. The former at least, was not necessarily envisioned as Davidic in character.

Secondly, as we noted in our previous study, *the go-to source for material to help early Christians understand the Christ event was Isaiah.* The prophecies in Isaiah do not mainly feature the Davidic connections of the coming messiah. The Psalms are *quoted* less than half as much as Isaiah in the NT to discuss such matters, and in fact the Psalms are regularly used to discuss eschatological matters *other than the messiah* in the NT (e.g., they are used to talk about the community of Jesus's followers).

It can just as easily be argued that some particular psalms were later made more generic in character to make them more suitable for universal liturgical use. The *"relecture"* sometimes seems to have required this. And it needs to be noted that various of the prescripts in the Psalms attribute them to musicians other than King David, and we even have one attributed to Moses. This surely had nothing to do with later Davidic messianism or typology. I do not think the "later historicizing by adding prescripts to make the Psalter more messianically Davidic" theory stands up to close scrutiny.

Furthermore, there are almost as many citations from the Pentateuch as from the Psalms in the NT, especially from Deuteronomy. Jesus himself is presented as claiming in John 5:46 that "Moses wrote of me." What we find in the use of the Psalms is not different from what we find in the use of the prophets or the law of Moses. *All of it is seen as prophetic in some way, and in some sense prophetic of the Christ in the NT, as Luke 24 makes evident.*

It may also be doubted that the Psalter is particularly appealed to by the earliest Christians *just because of its associations with David.* The earliest Christians saw Jesus as much more than the Davidic messiah, though they certainly viewed him that way as well. Indeed, we are even told in Mark 12 that Jesus himself viewed the messiah, as not merely the offspring of David, but more importantly as David's Lord (Mark 12:35–37). In short, a more careful and convincing reading of the use of the Psalms in early Judaism and by the earliest Christians is required.

The Psalms in the Apocrypha

Brooke also canvases other early Jewish works to see how the Psalms may have been used, but at best these works (Apocalypse of Abraham, Tobit, Wisdom of Solomon, Testament of Levi) reflect authors whose religious ideas and imagery and vocabulary has been influenced somewhat by the Psalms, but "there is virtually no explicit use of the Psalms in any of these writings."[14] Even more strikingly, Devorah Dimant notes only two explicit quotations of the Psalms in the whole of the Apocrypha, both in the Maccabean literature (Ps 79:2–3 in 1 Macc 7:16–17 and Ps 34:20 in 4 Macc 18:15).[15] When one does seem to find some allusion to the Psalter in this apocryphal body of literature, for example in Testament of Levi 13, what we find is an echo of the praise of the law found in Psalm 1, something that we do not find in the NT, or even more tellingly in Testament of Levi 4.2 where Psalm 2:7's reference to the "son" seems to be taken to refer to the priestly heir of Levi, something never later claimed of Jesus by the earliest Christians.

More promising is a close examination of the Wisdom of Solomon in comparison to the Psalms.[16] The Wisdom of Solomon involves a great deal of poetry, poetry influenced by the style and language and imagery and some of the ideas of the Psalms in their Greek translation. Patrick W. Skehan is prepared to conclude after a detailed analysis of phrases, ideas, and images in Wisdom of Solomon that the author had a knowledge of the complete Psalter as we have it in Greek.[17] Be that as it may, we do not find the sort of citing or quoting or paraphrasing of the Psalms to make messianic or eschatological points in this body of literature as we do in the NT.

The detailed study of David Runia on Philo's use of the Psalms concludes that of the some 1161 quotations from the OT in Philo, only 41 are from texts outside the Pentateuch, and of these only 20 are from the Psalms.[18] They are basically used as a secondary support for the allegorical exegesis Philo wants to do, particularly of the Pentateuch. Runia concludes that "the Book of Psalms is thus at a considerable

---

14. Ibid.
15. Devorah Damant, "Use and Interpretation of Mikra in the Apocrypha and Pseudepigrapha," in *Mikra: Text, Translation, Reading, and Interpretation of the Hebrew Bible in Ancient Judaism and Early Christianity*, ed. Martin J. Mulder, CRINT 2/1 (Philadelphia: Fortress, 1988), 385, 390–91.
16. See Patrick W. Skehan, *Studies in Israelite Poetry and Wisdom*, CBQMS 1 (Washington, DC: Catholic Biblical Association of America, 1971).
17. Ibid., 149.
18. David Runia, "Philo's Reading of the Psalms," *SPhilo* 13 (2001), 102–21.

remove from the use of the Psalter both in the Qumran and in the Early Christian writings," and that includes in Hebrews.[19]

While the cupboard is not bare, what we learn from such surveys is that really, only the Qumran literature provides us with some substantive parallels to the NT when it comes to the use of the Psalms. This is in part because like the earliest Christians, the Qumranites were eschatological and to some extent messianic in their orientation, and also like the earliest Christians they were at odds with the Jerusalem temple hierarchy, and the perceived corruption of praxis in the Herodian temple. Overall, the conclusion of Brooke is right when he says "the individual concerns of the authors of the New Testament books control much of their use of the Psalms, and their writing in Greek often restricts their base material to the Psalms as known in the LXX."[20] But then, as Ulrich Dahmen makes clear, the same could be said for the reception and use of the Psalms at Qumran, in regard to their own urgencies dictating how the Psalms were used.[21]

The Psalms in Early Christian Noncanonical Literature

Finally, it is interesting to compare the considerable use of the Psalms for various purposes, especially theological ones, in the NT, and what we discover in the noncanonical early Christian literature from at the end or soon after the NT era. For example, 1 Clement contains a significant portion of quotations and use of the Psalms: (1) 1 Clement 18 has Psalm 50:3–19; (2) 1 Clement 22 has Psalm 33:12–18; (3) 1 Clement 35:7–12 has Psalm 49:16–23. Among the Apologists, Justin's *Dialogue with Trypho* is replete with Psalm quotations, in fact he seems to have been the earliest example of a Christian to quote whole Psalms (e.g., Psalm 23 at *Dial.* 36.3–4; Psalm 44 at *Dial.* 38.3 and cf. 63.4; Psalm 49 at *Dial.* 22.7; Psalm 81 at *Dial.* 124.2; Psalm 95 at *Dial.* 73–74; Psalm 98 at *Dial.* 37.2; Psalm 109 at *Dial.* 32.6, and these are just some of the examples).[22] Clearly, the Psalms continued to be important in early Chris-

19. Ibid., 119.
20. Brooke, "Psalms in Early Jewish Literature," 24.
21. Ulrich Damen, *Psalmen-und Psalter-Rezeption im Frühjudentum: Rekonstruktion, Textbestand, Struktur und Pragmatik der Psalmenrolle 11QPs³ aus Qumran*, STDJ 49 (Leiden: Brill, 2003). His study is especially helpful with trying to figure out what is going on with 11QPSa. What it shows is the creative handling, and in some cases rearranging of materials from especially the last two books of the Psalter (see, e.g., the chart on p. 312). But then, the NT writers also handled the Psalms in creative and rhetorical ways too, see Appendix B below.
22. For the full list see Brucker, "Observations," 367.

tianity at and after the end of the NT era. Now however, having laid some of the groundwork for the main focus of our study, it is time to turn to the exposition of the Psalms old and new, in earnest.[23]

---

23. For the discussion of recent trends in scholarly study of the Psalms see now David M. Howard, "The Psalms in Current Study," in Johnson, *Interpreting the Psalms*, 23–40.

3

———

Psalter Book 1 (Psalms 1–41)

The Agony and Ecstasy

The Psalms are among the oldest poems in the world, and they still rank with any poetry in any culture, ancient or modern, from anywhere in the world. They are full of power and passion, horrendous misery and unrestrained jubilation, tender sensitivity and powerful hope.
—N. T. Wright[1]

According to Benedict's scheme, the community reads through . . . the entire book of Psalms every week. The monks are therefore exposed . . . to all the despairing, doubtful, bitter, vindictive, jingoistic, nationalistic, and seemingly racist passages in the Psalter. It is not that every sentiment expressed by a psalmist is admirable, but that in praying the Psalms, we confront ourselves as we really are. The Psalms are a reality check to keep prayer from becoming sentimental, superficial, or detached from the real world.
—Richard H. Schmidt[2]

As with our earlier book on Isaiah, we will always begin by presenting a translation of both the MT (the Masoretic Text) and the LXX (the Septuagint text) so the reader may notice the differences comparing

---

1. N. T. Wright, *The Case for the Psalms: Why They Are Essential* (New York: HarperOne, 2013), 2.
2. Richard H. Schmidt, *God Seekers: Twenty Centuries of Christian Spiritualities* (Grand Rapids: Eerdmans, 2008), 73–74.

and contrasting the two.[3] In general, it is clear that the earliest Christians, some due to language limitations and others due to the need to express their thoughts in the lingua franca of the age, almost always used some preexisting Greek text of the Psalms when they quoted, paraphrased, or excerpted material. In part this may be put down to the fact that the early Christian movement was overwhelmingly an evangelistic venture meant to spread the news about Jesus of Nazareth to all and sundry. In this respect especially we may contrast this Jewish movement with the one that had a base camp at Qumran, and spent time pondering mainly the Hebrew text of the Psalms and other OT texts. We need to keep these things in mind as this study progresses.

Our modus operandi here will be the same as in our *Isaiah Old and New* volume: we will present the two translations first then comment on the meaning of the psalm in its original context and then on how the psalm is used in the NT. One note more before we start: *the earliest Christians seem more apt to use the language and imagery of the Psalms to describe and explain the Christ event, rather than doing some sort of exegesis of a psalm at length or in context. They used key phrases, little excerpts, to present the story of Jesus for the most part, rather than doing extended commentary.* I would call this a homiletical and didactic use of the Psalms rather than an exegesis of the Psalms per se. As such they should not be faulted for bad exegesis, when that was not what they were trying to do in the first place. However, we will also occasionally see the Psalms expounded at more length, often christologically.

---

3. As mentioned in Witherington, *Isaiah Old and New*, 22–25, in our discussion of the LXX, we realize that there seem to have been several Old Greek texts that are thought to have been in play by the NT era, including efforts to revise the original LXX back toward a more literal translation of the Hebrew. This matter is complex; see now J. Ross Wagner, *Reading the Sealed Book: Old Greek Isaiah and the Problem of Septuagint Hermeneutics*, FAT 88 (Waco, TX: Baylor; Tübingen: Mohr Siebeck, 2013). For the sake of clarity we have simply provided the translation of the LXX and will comment as needed on the possibilities of NT writers following some *other* old Greek text on a case-by-case basis. Florian Wilk, in his meticulous analysis of the use of the Greek OT of Isaiah in Paul's letters concludes: "Paul's quotations from Isaiah show a certain, though not consistent, tendency towards the Alexandrian text type, and they testify to an ongoing process of scribal work on the Septuagint that was intended to align it with the Hebrew text." ("Letters of Paul as Witnesses to and for the Septuagint Text," in Kraus, *Septuagint Research*, 268). What is important to note about this is that the LXX is not being jettisoned, but simply revised where necessary. It is not necessary to call this evidence of a *different* Old Greek translation, any more than one would call the latest edition of the NIV a completely different translation than the original NIV. See however R. Timothy McLay, *The Use of the Septuagint in New Testament Research*, (Grand Rapids: Eerdmans, 2003) for appropriate warnings about the complexity of this matter, not least because of the freedom and variety of ways the NT writers use the OT. McLay is, however, wrong about several key matters; see Appendix B below.

A Regal Start: Psalm 2[4]

MT Psalm 2	LXX Psalm 2
1 Why do the nations conspire and the peoples plot in vain? 2 The kings of the earth rise up and the rulers band together against the Lord and against his anointed, saying,	1 Why did nations grow insolent, and peoples contemplate vain things? 2 The kings of the earth stood side by side, and the rulers gathered together, against the Lord and against his anointed,
	Interlude on strings
3 "Let us break their chains and throw off their shackles." 4 The One enthroned in heaven laughs; the Lord scoffs at them.	3 "Let us burst their bonds asunder and cast their yoke from us." 4 He who resides in the heavens will laugh at them, and the Lord will mock them.
5 He rebukes them in his anger and terrifies them in his wrath, saying,	5 Then he will speak to them in his wrath, and in his anger he will trouble them.
6 "I have installed my king on Zion, my holy mountain." 7 I will proclaim the Lord's decree: He said to me, "You are my son; today I have become your father. 8 Ask me, and I will make the nations your inheritance, the ends of the earth your possession. 9 You will break them with a rod of iron; you will dash them to pieces like pottery."	6 "But I was established king by him, on Zion, his holy mountain; 7 by proclaiming the Lord's ordinance: The Lord said to me, 'My son you are; today I have begotten you. 8 Ask of me, and I will give you nations as your heritage, and as your possession the ends of the earth. 9 You shall shepherd them with an iron rod; like a potter's vessel you will shatter them.'"
10 Therefore, you kings, be wise; be warned, you rulers of the earth.	10 And now, O kings, be sensible; be instructed, all you who judge the earth.
11 Serve the Lord with fear and celebrate his rule with trembling. 12 Kiss his son, or he will be angry and your way will lead to your destruction, for his wrath can flare up in a moment. Blessed are all who take refuge in him.	11 Be subject to the Lord with fear, and rejoice in him with trembling. 12 Seize upon instruction, lest the Lord be angry, and you will perish from the righteous way, when his anger quickly blazes out. Happy are all who trust in him

Psalm 2 has been traditionally called a royal psalm, a song about the

4. All Scripture quotations from the translation of the MT of the Psalms, unless otherwise indicated are from the NIV; all LXX translations are from NETS.

king. Interestingly it is one of the psalms in the first book of the Psalter that does not have a prescript telling us it is for, about, or by David. It is possible that this was the first psalm in some collection of the Psalter, because one variant reading of Acts 13:33 quotes from this psalm and calls it "the first psalm" (but see below). Were Psalms 1 and 2 originally seen as two parts of one psalm? This seems unlikely for Psalm 1 makes a nice preamble for the whole collection and is a wisdom and torah psalm, unlike Psalm 2.[5] It has been thought to be better, by some scholars, to see Psalm 1 as a preamble to the Psalter, with Psalm 2 to be taken as the proper first psalm, as the variant reading in Acts 13:33 found only in manuscript D seems to suggest.

Another way to view this would be to suggest that while Psalm 1 and 2 have independent origins originally, they were placed here as a two-part preamble to the whole Psalter, noting some similar themes in the two psalms (e.g., Psalm 1 begins with a wisdom theme about blessing, and Psalm 2 ends with a word to the wise for the nations, a word about how they can be blessed).[6] This is possible but would not explain what Acts 13:33 suggests. In any case, the Psalm divides neatly into four subsections: (1) vv. 1–3 describe the nations' plans; (2) vv. 4–6 Yahweh's response to such plans; (3) vv.7–9 the king's own response, and finally (4) vv.10–12 the word to the wise for the nations. The poem thus has an ABB'A' sort of structure.[7]

As a royal psalm it is a song about the installation of the king, a coronation ode of sorts. Perhaps the major difference between the MT and the LXX in this psalm can be seen in v. 6 where in the Hebrew we have direct speech by Yahweh, whereas in the LXX it is a comment by the king himself. We also must note the change from "kiss the son, lest he be angry" to "seize upon the instruction, lest the Lord be angry" which, as I. Howard Marshall says, makes it easier to see the whole last stanza as part the instructions from the king to the nations.[8]

The logic of the narrative in the poem seems to be as follows: in vv. 1–3 we hear of the revolt of the foreign nations against Yahweh and his king. This is followed by the reaction of Yahweh to such a revolt in vv. 4–6. God's answer to the problem is the investiture or anointing of

---

5. Here I agree with Hans-Joachim Krauss, *Psalms 1-59: A Commentary*, CC (Minneapolis: Augsburg, 1988), 114 in arguing against the notion that Psalms 1-2 were originally a single psalm.
6. See the discussion in John Goldingay, *Psalms: Volume 1; 1-41*, BOTCWP (Grand Rapids: Baker Academic, 2006), 94–95.
7. See ibid., 96.
8. I. Howard Marshall, "Acts", in *Commentary on the New Testament Use of the Old Testament*, ed. G. K. Beale and D. A. Carson (Grand Rapids: Baker Academic, 2007) 552.

the king and giving him power and authority to rule, with a promised future coming judgment on the nations by Yahweh's anointed one (vv. 7–9). This in turn is followed by a warning or ultimatum to the nations that they had better behave, lest Yahweh get angry and the wrath of God fall upon them. They would do well to serve Yahweh as his king does. The close connection between Yahweh and his king needs to be stressed; those who oppose the king will find themselves at odds with Yahweh as well.[9]

While attempts have been made to see this Psalm as part of a coronation *liturgy*, this seems unlikely because the speaker here is either God or the king himself, and the king seems to be the basic narrator of the whole poem. It is possible that this song was sung at the investiture of a king (say, David or Solomon) but we cannot be sure. What is more certain is that interregnums, or the change in reign from one king to another, were often times when vassal states, under the thumb of the previous king, would try to revolt in order to gain their independence.

In some ways this poem, if it is not just an example of rhetorical hyperbole, better suits the reign of Solomon because we know that not only were enemies like the Philistines defeated, but that he expanded the territory of the Holy Land in various directions, irritating various foreign powers. Even so, the language is still extravagant, *but it is precisely the extravagance of the language that made it more easy to use in an eschatological and messianic way (see Psalms of Solomon 17:26).* The psalmist expresses extreme surprise that the foreign rulers would be so foolish as to revolt against the one true God and his king. The tenor of the discussion is, "How foolish! They should have known better than to plot and plan pointless revolts."

But the king knows something these foreign rulers do not even imagine: that there is a singular God who rules over the whole earth, not a bunch of national or tribal deities with limited power and domain. Notice as well that Yahweh is viewed as a God who is not merely well informed as to what is going on in the world, but who is

---

9. While Ellen T. Charry, *Psalms 1-50: Sighs and Songs of Israel*, BTCB (Grand Rapids: Brazos, 2015), 5–9 is probably right that this text in its original context was not intended to refer to some future messianic figure, nor to "salvation" from sin in the later Christian sense, nevertheless, the use of this psalm at Qumran and elsewhere in early Judaism in a messianic way showed that the multivalency of poetry allowed for such a reading of this psalm, especially after the demise of the Davidic line courtesy of the Babylonians. As Goldingay suggests, there was prophetic potential in this poetic language, and some of the statements in the psalm could only be pure hyperbole if applied to David or Solomon, or the rest of the known Davidic monarchy; and yes, as Charry suggests, the poem seems to sanction violence against enemies, as does the later use of the psalm messianically in Revelation, but there only the Lord is allowed to take vengeance.

paying active attention to the machinations of humans, and "will have them in derision." He laughs at their puny plans and foolish plots. This God may dwell in heaven, but he is hands-on in his involvement on earth, and especially on behalf of his king and his people. Indeed, he has his own special holy mountain on earth, Mt. Zion, as v. 6 indicates.

It is important to speak for a moment about what has been called the anthropomorphisms in a text like this, namely the predication of human emotions, like mirth or wrath, to God. Some have seen this as merely an attempt to indicate that God is just as much a *personal* being as humans are, without actually suggesting that God has feelings, or that his feelings wax and wane, or change according to circumstances. Some church fathers, for example Chrysostom, grounded deeply in Greek philosophy, and in particular in the notion that a deity must be impassable (i.e., not given to "irrational" feelings) objected to the idea of God having feelings. Commenting on Psalm 6, Chrysostom reassures his audience that of course God does not really feel anger or wrath, for God is without passions (*Psalms 1:95-96*). Goldingay rightly responds "If so, it was risky of God to speak so consistently in the Psalms and elsewhere about having such passions (e.g., Isa 10:6; Jer 49:37; Ezek 7:14; Zeph 3:8)."[10] I quite agree.

When the Bible talks about God being unchanging, it is referring to the reliable character of God, not his impassability, or his immutability for that matter. From a Christian point of view, it should be obvious from the incarnation that God can incorporate change into the divine being, without an alteration of character, and from the OT it should be clear that God is a being of deep, though *not irrational* feelings. We should speak of the pathos of God as Abraham Joshua Heschel taught us to do so long ago in his study of the prophets.[11] When one reads the Psalms, or a text like Hosea 11 it simply becomes impossible to doubt that the biblical writers were convinced God was a being of deep feelings, not the least of which is love.

Verse 5 is important for it tells us that God, in his own good time, will intervene, will step in and do something about this revolting development. The Hebrew word "then" (אָז 'āz) here likely refers to some future propitious moment. Here, as in Isaiah 7 the coming of the king produces a negative reaction by foreign powers, not least because it is a judgment not only on their politics but also on their theology.

These foreign powers do not realize that this Davidic king has been

---

10. Goldingay, *Psalms: Volume 1*, 9n12.
11. Abraham Joshua Heschel, *The Prophets* (New York: HarperPerennial, 2001).

anointed and appointed by the God of the universe, and God is angry with these powers. The announcement of this king's investiture is frightening to the powers that are already established in the region. God's king has been established on a particular hill, Zion, and at a particular time, for the biblical God is one who works his will in human history. In due course, all the world will know who is the true God who has established the true king. Philippians 2:5-11 is similar in its conclusion that a day will come when everyone will know the truth about Jesus being Lord "and every knee will bow." As we shall see, Psalm 22 ends with a similar proclamation about the future. Verse 6 tells us where the psalmist stands on these matters. The "I" here is emphatic, "But as for me, *I* have set."[12]

At the enthronement of the king, the words of investiture are "you are my son, I myself have begotten you today." These are words spoken by God to the king himself, not presumably to the general public who might have been present at the coronation. While the idea was common in the ancient Near East that a king was the "son" of some deity (cf. Ps 89:26, 27; 2 Sam 7:13, 14; 1 Chr 28:6), Psalm 2 is not referring to an actual begetting, but rather to a change of role and status by the empowerment and authorization of the deity. While it is possible that the investiture is viewed as a process of adoption, this is not clear, and texts like Genesis 30:3 and 50:23 do not provide clear analogies, as they are nonroyal in character.

It is natural to associate this psalm with 2 Samuel 7, which is the other place in the OT that the Davidic king is called God's son. There are differences however. The subject in 2 Samuel 7:8-17 is about what Yahweh will do with David's *heir*, Solomon, not with David. It is Solomon who will build God's house, and Solomon whose throne God will establish ʿad ʿôlām, and it is Solomon to whom God says he will be like a father and Solomon will be like a son. Furthermore this passage does not record an investiture ritual nor is it a poem. It can also be noted that this passage in 2 Samuel 7 says nothing about begetting or even adopting. It talks about how God will relate to Solomon and vice versa.[13]

What is promised to the king in vv. 8-9 is breathtaking, nothing less than world dominion, not just one kingdom among many, and the

---

12. See Derek Kidner, *Psalms 1-72: An Introduction and Commentary on Books I and II of the Psalms*, TOTC (Downers Grove, IL: InterVarsity Press, 1973), 51.
13. Neither text refers to a ritual of covenanting complete with sacrifice and the like. They are talking about an ongoing relationship God already has with the Davidic king and his heir.

power to judge the other nations, and even smash them to pieces like a clay jar if they do not submit. Again, we see this theme echoed in Philippians 2:5-11 where we are told that a time will come when every knee will bow.

In vv. 10-12 it is the human king himself who warns the nations to act wisely, which in this case means to fear the real God, Yahweh, even to serve him, and treat him as the true king.[14] The ancient ritual of kissing the boot or feet of the ruler as a sign of subservience is referred to here, only the king in question is Yahweh himself and so this is a dramatic metaphor for submission to the will of the biblical God. If they do submit to Yahweh, they will live a blessed existence. "At the centre of history is no longer the struggle of the great world powers for existence, but God, whose relationship with the earthly powers will determine their destiny."[15]

This of course raises the whole issue not merely of divine wrath, but of divine violence. The threat of such genuine divine judgment is seen as real here, and note that the end of the psalm does *not* suggest that the king will be the implementer of final judgment; rather it is Yahweh whose anger may blaze. The theme "vengeance is mine, says the Lord" is not less present in the NT than in the OT, if anything it is just as present, for instance in a book like Revelation or a text like 2 Thessalonians 2, not least because the NT is much more definitive and clear about the afterlife and last judgment than the OT is.[16] "God's patience is not placidity, any more than his fierce anger is loss of control, his laughter cruelty or his pity sentimentality. When his moment comes for judgment, in any given case, it will be by definition beyond appeasing or postponing."[17]

It is not hard at all to see why this psalm seems to have been very important for early Christians. James L. Mays puts it this way: Psalm 2 "is the only text in the Old Testament that speaks of God's king, messiah, and son in one place, the titles so important for the presentation of Jesus in the Gospels."[18] While in its present context in the Psalter it served as something of an introduction to the other royal psalms

---

14. Kidner, *Psalms 1-72*, 52 is right to stress that we must not press the literary categories too hard; a royal poem about authorization can have wisdom elements, as this one does, "the Bible never drives a wedge between authority and truth, or between wisdom and obedience."
15. Artur Weiser, *The Psalms: A Commentary*, OTL (Philadelphia: Westminster, 1962), 111.
16. For some helpful reflections on divine violence see Goldingay, *Psalms: Volume 1*, 104-6.
17. Kidner, *Psalms 1-72*, 53.
18. James L. Mays, *Psalms*, Interpretation (Louisville: John Knox, 1994), 44.

(Psalms 18, 20, 21, 45, 72, 89, 110, 144), in the hands of the earliest Christians it became a rich resource for talking about Jesus.

But the Davidic monarchy, as is well known, came to an abrupt halt in about 587 BCE. It never achieved the sort of world dominion that seems to be promised in this psalm. The very poetic hyperbole of the text if applied even to the reigns of David or Solomon or Hezekiah or Josiah, lent itself quite naturally to thoughts about a future ideal king, a messianic figure, and this of course is what happened at Qumran; and is also the case in early Christian appropriation of this text, but with a difference. The Qumran community seems to have still looked to the future for the royal figure to appear, whereas the Christians applied this and other psalms to a historical figure that the earliest among them had known *personally*, Jesus of Nazareth. What was seen as a promise and prophecy in OT times and thereafter by early Jews, was seen as a reality already being fulfilled and to be fulfilled by Jesus, the once and future king.

What happened in ancient Near Easter coronation rituals? Among a variety of things, one thing that regularly happened was the pouring of consecrated oil from above, from a sacred horn, on the head of the god's anointed one. It symbolized the imbuing of the person with power and authority, and the direct address "you are my son" to the royal figure was meant as a confirmation of the same thing.

There is no better place to begin our discussion of the use of the Psalms in the NT, and this psalm in particular, than with the primitive form of the story of Jesus's baptism by John found in Mark 1:10–11. As I have pointed out at length elsewhere, the baptismal scene is presented as a case of Jesus receiving a vision from heaven with both an auditory and a visual component meant for him in particular. The vision does not happen before or during the baptism but rather as he is coming up out of the water, and the language of the heavens "rent asunder," the Spirit descending like a dove, and the divine voice all should be compared to the description of an apocalyptic vision we have, for instance, in Revelation 1:10–15 or in Revelation 4.[19] This then was originally a private revelation to Jesus, which he must have shared with his disciples later.[20]

For our purposes, what is critical is that the voice from heaven

---

19. See the discussion in Ben Witherington III, *Jesus the Seer and the Progress of Prophecy* (Minneapolis: Fortress, 2014), 246–92, and more specifically on this particular Markan text, Ben Witherington III, *The Gospel of Mark: A Socio-rhetorical Commentary* (Grand Rapids: Eerdmans, 2001), 74–77.
20. Notice how in Matt 3:13–17 it becomes a public declaration, "This is my son"; surely a later reframing of the story; contrast Luke 3:22.

involves a conglomerate scripture citation partly from Psalm 2:7 ("you are my son") and partly from Isaiah 42:1,[21] and perhaps Genesis 22:2. The psalm text should be seen as primary, not least because there are no royal associations in the use of the son language in Genesis, whereas the title "Son" or "Son of God" is a crucial title in the Gospels used to indicate Jesus's messianic character and identity. There is furthermore the issue that Jesus doesn't assume the role of messiah, anointed one of God, until after the baptism, just as the king didn't assume office until after his coronation and anointing. But Jesus had no symbolic anointing with oil, he was literally anointed with the Holy Spirit according to Mark. It is of a piece with the apocalyptic character of the Markan scene that Jesus does not hear the voice from heaven until the Spirit has descended upon him (cf. similarly John in Revelation 1, "I was in the Spirit, on the Lord's Day . . . and I heard . . . and I saw").

Not to be missed is the fact that in Psalms of Solomon 17 we have something of a running commentary on Psalm 2, with the messiah being the figure to whom the nations are subjugated. Of equal importance is 4Q174 1, I, 10–19 where Psalm 2:1 is related to the "end of days" when the reign of the Davidic messiah will be established. In both these texts, Psalm 2 is read as a prophecy of eschatological days involving the messiah, and something similar is going on in Mark 1,[22] except in Mark 1 the future is now, or at least already and not yet. [23] As Rikki Watts points out, the use of Psalm 2 here at the outset of Mark's Gospel sets up and prepares for the use of Psalm 118 in 11:9–10 and 12:10–11, Psalm 110 in Mark 12:36 and 14:62, and Psalm 22 in Mark 15:24, 34,[24] not to mention the voice from heaven at the transfiguration in Mark 9:7 where we have a modified form of Psalm 2:7 directed to the inner circle of the disciples.[25]

Acts 4:25–26 provides us with a *relecture* of Psalm 2:1–2, only in this case those who are furiously raging are not the foreign rulers, but the Jewish one (Herod Antipas) and the gentile one (Pilate), raging against the notion of Jesus as the Jewish messiah and against his disciples who are proclaiming him as such. The context here is important, namely a gathering of followers of Jesus after the release of Peter and John, and

21. It is the Targum on Isa 42:1 that uses the phrase "beloved."
22. See also the discussion in Peter Doble, "The Psalms in Luke-Acts," in Moyise, *Psalms in the New Testament*, 101–4.
23. See the discussion in Rikki Watts, "Mark" in Beale, *Commentary on the New Testament*, 122–28.
24. Ibid., 128.
25. See also Watt's much fuller discussion in "The Psalms in Mark's Gospel," in Moyise, *Psalms in the New Testament*, 25–45.

the psalm text is quoted in the context of a corporate prayer, not a preached message. Verse 25 is especially important as it says "it is you who said by the Holy Spirit through our ancestor David, your servant" indicating that the psalm is: (1) a word of God, (2) spoken by King David, who was (3) God's servant before Jesus was, and (4) spoken about the situation Jesus and his followers found themselves in when Jesus was opposed and then killed by the authorities and his followers likewise found themselves called on the carpet for continuing to claim after his death that Jesus was the messiah.

Notice the pointing up of the quotation in v. 27 making clear that the person in question in the psalm text is Jesus, God's anointed servant. The text of the psalm here is clearly the LXX, but at that juncture the LXX follows the MT quite closely (see the translations above). There are, in addition, textual difficulties in these verses in Acts 4.[26] Luke is using this psalm not only to make clear that Jesus was foreseen by David, but that the difficulties the earliest Christians were facing with the authorities were also foreshadowed in Psalm 2. Of course the implication is that David was hinting that this psalm was not about himself but rather a later king! It is also important to note that Peter is portrayed as praying this psalm, and so acting in continuity with one of the main ways the Psalms were used in the worship life of Israelites from the time of David onward. Furthermore, Peter in v. 28 makes clear that there was no reason for the Christians to be dismayed by what happened to Jesus or by what had just happened to Peter and John, because in both cases it had been part of God's plan all along.

In Acts 13:33, which we have already referred to, Psalm 2 is called the "first" psalm in the variant text in D and in some church fathers that seem to have followed the reading of D. Nevertheless, the NT textual committee is quite clear that the reading which should be preferred is "in the second Psalm," which is attested to by many early and good manuscripts such as p74, ℵ, A, B, C, and numerous others, and this reading seems likely to be original.[27] It is unfortunate that there is some tex-

---

26. See Ben Witherington III, *The Acts of the Apostles: A Socio-rhetorical Commentary* (Grand Rapids: Eerdmans, 1998), 201–3. As I mentioned there, this is surely Luke's use of the LXX as it may be doubted that Peter, who according to Papias spoke in Aramaic, would pray in Greek using the LXX in the midst of a group of Aramaic-speaking Jewish Christians. On the textual problems here see Bruce M. Metzger, *Textual Commentary on the New Testament: A Companion Volume to the United Bible Societies' Greek New Testament,* 2nd ed., 4th revision (Stuttgart: Deutsche Bibelgesellschaft, 1998), 279–81. On the other hand, Peter well might speak in Greek if he had a mixed audience at Pentecost some of whom only knew Greek.

27. See the discussion in Metzger, *Textual Commentary*, 363–65. There is some possibility that in fact p45 has the earliest reading where we simply have "in the Psalms."

tual uncertainty here, as this is the only place in the whole NT where the precise location of a NT citation is given.

The text referred to in Acts 13:33b is Psalm 2:7, again. There is room for considerable debate as to whether Psalm 2:7 is used by Paul here, in the first lengthy synagogue sermon attributed to him in Acts, to refer to: (1) the raising up of Jesus in general (and so to the virginal conception), which would make good sense of the begetting reference in the quotation, and then the reference to Jesus's resurrection from the dead comes in 13:34 and is supported by the reference to Psalm 16:10. This makes good logical sense of the passage, and also in terms of the theology of Luke-Acts, because clearly in Luke 3:22, as in Mark 1, the language of Psalm 2:7 is used of an event prior to the death and resurrection of Jesus. (2) it is possible that Acts 13:33 uses Psalm 2:7 to refer to the resurrection of Jesus, which could be supported by the fact that, according to many scholars, some early Christian traditions associate Jesus's resurrection with his becoming Son (see Rom 1:3-4; Heb 1:3-6).

There is a problem with this conclusion however, because what Romans 1:3-4 does not say is that Jesus *became* Son of God at the resurrection, but rather that he assumed the role of Son of God *in power* at the resurrection, and elsewhere Paul is clear enough that he views Jesus as God's Son before the resurrection. Furthermore, in Hebrews 1:3-6 the author tells us that God created all worlds through his Son (v. 2b) and that God spoke to us through his Son (v. 2a) and that God brought his firstborn (Son) into the world (v. 6). It must be doubted then that Heb 1:5 should be taken as a reference to Jesus's resurrection, where again Psalm 2:7 shows up once more![28] As Marshall says, "begetting is not an obvious metaphor for the resurrection."[29] In any case, Paul is depicted in Acts 13 as using Psalm 2:7 messianically to indicate that God had planned for Jesus to be Israel's messiah all along. What we have seen so far is both the christological use of the Psalms, but also the use of the Psalms to explain events not only in the life of Jesus, but also events in the lives of the earliest Christians, such as Peter and John.[30]

In Hebrews 5:5-6 we have a double quotation from the Psalms first from Psalm 2:7 and then from Psalm 110:4. The use of Psalm 2:7 in both Hebrews 1:5 and in Hebrews 5:5 should be studied together, for, as Guthrie has pointed out, this same text is used to introduce two major sections of the homily we call Hebrews, two sections which make two

28. See. George H. Guthrie, "Hebrews," in Beale, *Commentary on the New Testament*, 927
29. Marshall, "Acts," 585.
30. On the whole sermon in Acts 13 see Doble, "Psalms in Luke-Acts," 105-11.

different christological points: (1) that the Son is greater than all the angels because of his unique relationship to the Father (in Hebrews 1); and (2) that the Son is greater than all the ordinary priests as he is a priest forever.[31]

This christological use of Psalm 2:7 is not a surprise since, as Guthrie points out, this same text had been used messianically for various centuries before and after the NT was written (cf. 1Q28a II, 11–12; 4Q174 1 I, 10–II,5; Psalms of Solomon 17:14–20 Testament of Levi 4.2; b. Sukkah 52a).[32] It seems clear as well that the author of Hebrews is simply using the LXX translation since it is unlikely he would have independently come up with the same translation of the Hebrew as we find in the LXX.[33] It may be the case that Psalm 2:7 in Hebrews 5:5 primarily plays a structural role since the focus at that juncture is on finding a smooth way to introduce Psalm 110:4 into the discussion, and so to introduce the major unique christological theme of the book: the heavenly high priesthood of the son. We will say much more on the latter text later in this study.

Psalm 2:8–9 comes up for repeated use in Revelation 2:26–27; 12:5; and 19:15, and in different and fascinating ways. On the one hand, the use of Psalm 2:8–9 in Revelation 2:26–27 involves Christ rather than Yahweh speaking the psalm text and promising to the potential martyrs that if they remain faithful to him to the end he will give *them* authority over the nations just as his father has given him. In Revelation 12:5 by contrast we hear about the birth of Christ who is destined to rule the nations with an iron rod, and in Revelation 19:15 we see him doing so, having returned from heaven at the eschaton to bring final judgment to the earth.

As Steve Moyise points out, interpretation of the use of Psalm 2:8–9 in these passages hinges in part on what we take the key verb ποιμαίνω to mean in these passages. Does it have a different sense or the same sense in all these texts?[34] On the one hand, the verb can mean "to shepherd" in a positive sense, but the OT background and also the accompanying portions of the quoted text (John seems to be following the LXX in Revelation 2 where we have the fuller citation) do not suggest such a meaning; how does one shepherd by breaking pots? The context of Revelation 12 speaks about satan, and the context does not encour-

---

31. Guthrie, "Hebrews," 925–29, 960.
32. Ibid., 926.
33. Ibid., 927.
34. Steve Moyise, "The Psalms in the Book of Revelation," in Moyise, *Psalms in the New Testament*, 233–34.

age the translation shepherding, especially with the mention of the rod of iron. Finally, in Revelation 19:15 the context is full of death and destruction and the striking down of the nations, and the rider on the white horse is using the rod of his mouth to accomplish this. Again, this is hardly a positive context.

Moyise suggests that the breaking pots metaphor refers to smashing the resistance of the opposition, rather than smashing them, and this might be correct but it doesn't fit very well with the use in Revelation 19:15 where "ruling" involves judging, including punitive judgment at the eschaton. What is important to note is that in all three texts the action is seen as transpiring not "now" or in "heaven," but at "the end of days" when Christ returns and reigns with his martyrs before and during the millennium (see Revelation 20). This eschatological use of the psalm is similar to what one finds in 1Q174 (see above). Like in so much of Jewish apocalyptic literature, the point is to comfort the afflicted, the persecuted and prosecuted, and even the executed, reassuring them that in the end God will make sure justice is done on their behalf (cf. Rev 6:9–11). Here again, a combination of christological and eschatological use is made of the psalm in question.

An Ode on Creation: Psalm 8

Psalm 8 is the first praise song in the Psalter, and it is unlike any of the others not only in its structure, but because unlike any other song or hymn in the OT (with the exception of Exod 15:1–18) it is entirely addressed directly to God.[35] Both Psalm 8 and Exodus 15 share in common that they are songs of an individual addressing God, and in the case of Exodus 15 a famous individual, Moses, as might also be the case with Psalm 8 if it is truly "of David."[36] Sirach 17 could be said to be a further exposition on the same subject, influenced by the theology and character of Psalm 8. This psalm, following as it does the introductory psalms (Psalms 1–2) and the first set of lament psalms (Psalms 3–7) is perhaps put here because the last verse of Psalm 7 says that the speaker vows to sing Yahweh's praise, and Psalm 8 fulfills that promise.[37]

35. See May, *Psalms*, 65.
36. Krauss, *Psalms 1–59*, 179.
37. See Brueggemann and Bellinger, *Psalms*, 58.

MT Psalm 8	LXX Psalm 8
For the director of music. According to *gittith*. A psalm of David. 1 Lord, our Lord, how majestic is your name in all the earth! You have set your glory in the heavens. 2 Through the praise of children and infants you have established a stronghold against your enemies, to silence the foe and the avenger. 3 When I consider your heavens, the work of your fingers, the moon and the stars, which you have set in place, 4 what is man that you are mindful of him, and the son of man that you care for him? 5 You have made him a little lower than the angels and crowned him with glory and honor. 6 You made him rulers over the works of your hands; you put everything under their feet: 7 all flocks and herds, and the animals of the wild, 8 the birds in the sky, and the fish in the sea, all that swim the paths of the seas. 9 Lord, our Lord, how majestic is your name in all the earth!	1 Regarding completion. Over the wine vats. A Psalm. Pertaining to David. 2 O Lord, our Lord, how admirable is your name in all the earth, because your magnificence was raised beyond the heavens. 3 Out of mouths of infants and nurslings you furnished praise for yourself, for the sake of your enemies, to put down enemy and avenger, 4 because I will observe the heavens, works of your fingers—moon and stars—things you alone founded. 5 What is man that you are mindful of him or son of man that you attend to him? 6 You diminished him a little in comparison with angels; with glory and honor you crowned him. 7 And you set him over the works of your hands; you subjected all under his feet, 8 sheep and cattle, all together and further the beasts of the plain, 9 the birds of the air and the fish of the sea —the things that pass through paths of seas. 10 O Lord, our Lord, how admirable is your name in all the earth!

One of the major motifs in the Psalms is praising God for his work as creator. Psalm 8 is the perfect example of this sort of psalm, manifesting the normal structure of invocation (v. 1 expanded by a who clause in v. lc), motive for praise in vv. 3ff., and refrain in v. 9. There is little reason to doubt this psalm was sung in Israelite worship services. The psalm could be said to be a meditation on a particular text from the Pentateuch, Genesis 1:26–28.[38]

Two of the great imponderables are addressed in this sublime hymn: Who God is and what the role of humanity on earth is in light of who

38. See Mays, *Psalms*, 67.

God is. This hymn has clear echoes of Genesis 1: the discussion of creation, the mention of humankind in the image of God, and the task of dominion given to humans by God. If one considers this in light of the ancient Near Eastern background then it is appropriate to remember that in some of those cultures the king was particularly said to be in the image of some god and that deity's plenipotentiary on earth. For example, on a stele of Amenhotep II the Pharaoh is praised as "the beloved physical son of Ra, the lord, the image of Horus on the throne of his father, great in power."[39]

Here, in a sense, the whole race is said to be God's king on earth—called to rule over the rest of creation.[40] This whole line of thinking makes it easier to understand why, for example, the writer of Hebrews was able to see Christ as the one this hymn was primarily talking about. In any case, the *image* theology suggests humans have been uniquely made for personal relationship with God, and as persons like unto God they are able to share some of his majesty, both by being an image-bearer and by fulfilling the task of having dominion over the earth. The Hebrew terms used for humans in v. 4 are אֱנוֹשׁ (*'enôš*) *and* בֶּן־אָדָם (*ben-'ādām*), which by itself provides an echo of Genesis 1. The first of these terms is often associated with the frailty of humankind.[41]

The tone of this psalm is set from the opening invocation: it expresses awe, wonder, and joy. The central theme of the psalm could be said to be the majesty and magnificence of God as it is revealed in nature and human nature and human roles. Verse 2 is the most difficult to make sense of. How could the stammering praises of children and infants in arms be a bulwark against God's enemies, if that's what the Hebrew text means (cf. 2 Macc 7:27)? Possibly the praise of children drowns out the cacophony of the nonbelievers? Is true praise what really puts to shame and defeats God's foes?[42] The "free confession of love and trust is a devastating answer to the accuser and his arsenal of doubts and slanders."[43]

In Wisdom of Solomon 10:21 wisdom is said to "untie the tongue of the little one." Or does true praise and piety bring God's intervention on behalf of his people? Is praise God's weapon of war or at least the

---

39. Quoted by Kraus, *Psalms 1–59*, 184. See also the study by Catherine McDowell, *The "Image of God" in the Garden of Eden: The Creation of Humankind in Genesis 2:5–3:24 in Light of the mīs pî pīt pî and wpt-r Rituals of Mesopotamia and Ancient Egypt*, Siphrut 15 (Winona Lake, IN: Eisenbrauns, 2015).
40. Ibid.
41. Brueggemann and Bellinger, *Psalms*, 59.
42. See the discussion in Kraus, *Psalms 1–59*, 181–82.
43. Kidner, *Psalms 1–72*, 66–67.

last line of defense for his people? This whole line of thinking reminds one of the famous story of when Mother Theresa was crossing from Jordan into Israel, and an Israeli guard at the border asked her if she had any weapons, to which she immediately replied, "Yes. I have my prayer books."[44] In any case, as we shall see, this verse is applied by Jesus to the hosannas of the children as he enters Jerusalem, and their praise confounds Jesus's enemies. It is possible as well, as Samuel Terrien suggests, that Paul has these verses in mind when he says in 1 Corinthians 1:27 that God has chosen the weak things of this world to confound the things which are mighty.[45]

At v. 3 the psalmist begins to reflect on creation, which because of its vastness and beauty causes a sense of human insignificance. Notice that only at v. 3 do we hear the individual voice speaking, "when I consider . . ." the rest of the song is a group expression. The psalmist is pondering the significance of his personal insignificance, so to speak, in the face of so vast a creation.[46] What kind of God could it be that could make all of this? In view of the size and scope of the universe, what are tiny human beings that God should pay any attention to them? The Hebrew here could be rendered "remember and visit." What kind of God remembers and visits human beings? And yet God *is* mindful of his human creatures, not only caring for them but in fact exalting them to a place of honor.[47] We are told that they are made but a little less (or lower) than 'elōhîm. Now 'elōhîm might mean angels (this is how both the Greek OT and Heb 2:6-8 take it, cf. 1 Sam 28:13; Ps 82:1-7) or it might mean God or even gods (plural). It is probably not the latter, since our psalmist recognizes only one God, but like other writers of the OT he does recognize the existence of lesser supernatural beings.

We are told that humankind is bequeathed both glory and the functions of God (though on a lesser scale), that is, to rule over all of creation.[48] Notice that it is God who is the actor in all these actions ("you

44. The source of the Mother Teresa quote is http://www.iskandar.com/waleed911/mothertheresa.html, and her visit to Gaza is confirmed at http://al-bushra.org/memories-of-mother-teresa-s-visit-to-jordan-resurrected/.

45. Samuel L. Terrien, *The Psalms: Strophic Structure and Theological Commentary* (Grand Rapids: Eerdmans, 2003), 129.

46. See the telling reflections of Patrick D. Miller in his essay on "What Is a Human Being?" in his collected essays entitled *The Way of the Lord: Essays in Old Testament Theology* (Grand Rapids: Eerdmans, 2004), 226-36; the apt phrase "the significance of our insignificance" is from James Mays, quoted by Miller, ibid., 230.

47. As Kidner, *Psalms 1-72*, 67 points out, the term "mindful" when predicated of God doesn't just mean remembering or bearing in mind, but always implies God's movement toward and taking action in regard to the person or group that has come to mind.

48. Noticing how Job 7:17 draws on Ps 8:4, with Job lamenting that his suffering amounts to a loss of

made . . . you put"). We are not talking about human accomplishment or what humans deserve, but rather the plan and gift of God. We were meant and made to be rulers over all the works of God's hands.

As Anderson reminds us, this stress on human dominion over creation was a revolutionary doctrine. Other ancient Near Eastern cultures saw the gods as part of nature, and all humans as slaves of the gods (cf. *enuma eliš*) under the sway of the stars (hence the need for astrology).[49] But it is not by recognizing nature as humankind's mother, but rather God as its father, that human beings come to understand why they are here. Only by God's special revelation through his word do humans learn of their true place and task in life. But the psalmist suggests that everyone can know the existence of an almighty God simply by observing and reflecting on the creation (cf. Rom 1:20). Humans are to be God's governor or representative on earth. "The import of these verses is to impress upon the psalm's singers that within the vast scope of divine wisdom, which created and controls the cosmos, God deigns to treat humanity with incredible dignity and respect."[50] Indeed, amazingly enough God has made creation, or at least the human sphere of creation, our galaxy, our sun, our planet, our environment, so that it will support human life. In that sense, God made creation for us, an astounding fact, but perhaps a little less dumbfounding when one takes into account that the sons of Adam are created in God's image, uniquely so.[51]

Interestingly, this hymn does not remind us that we have taken the great power and privilege granted us by God and often used it to exalt ourselves and serve our own ends. While that is a prevalent theme elsewhere in the Psalter, the focus here is not on how "dominion has become domination; rule has become ruin; subordination in the divine purpose has become subjection to human sinfulness."[52] By contrast, this hymn reminds us of the positive character of being God's image bearer, but at the same time insists "we can say 'human being' only after we have learned to say 'God.'"[53] It can be debated whether the psalmist is reflecting on humankind in its prefallen state still crowned with glory and honor, or whether the author has no theology of human

glory. Could Paul's "we have all sinned and lack the glory of God" (Rom 3:23) reflect Ps 8:4 by way of Job's lament?

49. Anderson, *Out of the Depths*, 134–37.
50. Charry, *Psalms 1–50*, 43.
51. See Miller, "What Is a Human Being?," 230–31.
52. Mays, *Psalms*, 70.
53. Goldingay, *Psalms Volume 1*, 161.

fallenness, but surely Thorsten Moritz is right that the links with the Genesis 1 material suggests the former rather than the latter.[54] Notice how the reflections on humans are framed by the insistence at the beginning and end of the psalm that the person with the most excellent name and nature throughout the earth is the biblical God who created it all. "Human dignity enjoys its full stature within the grandeur of divine majesty."[55]

The NT develops the theme of this psalm quite a bit further than the original author by applying this task of having dominion especially to Christ, the one unfallen human who will not abuse creation and who can rule it justly (cf. 1 Cor 15:27; Eph 1:22; Heb 2:6–8).[56] Paul suggests that ultimately, when Christ returns, he will reveal the sort of dominion humans were meant to have over creation, for he will order all things under himself (1 Corinthians 15). He is viewed by Paul as the last Adam, the one who fulfills properly and finally the task given to the first Adam. When he accomplishes this, then humanity will have dominion, and there will be a new heaven and a new earth. Then again will the closing words of this hymn ring out, "O Lord, our ruler, how magnificent is your name in all the earth."

If we look closely at the NT use of Psalm 8, various things come to light. Matthew 21:16 has a quotation of some form of Psalm 8:2, in particular the quotation is considerably closer to the LXX, "out of the mouths of infants and nurslings you furnish praise for yourself" whereas the Hebrew text reads, "through the praises of children and infants you have established a stronghold against your enemies."[57] Notice that the Hebrew reverses the order of the praising, with the older child first, and notice that in both Matthew 21 and the LXX we have reference to how the mouths of the children have prepared or furnished praise for God. What prompts the citation of the psalm in Matthew 21 is children shouting hosanna to the son of David on the way into Jerusalem with Jesus and his disciples and even in the temple (cf. Matt 21:9, 15), but of course the psalm is about children praising

---

54. Thorsten Moritz, "The Psalms in Ephesians and Colossians," in Moyise, *Psalms in the New Testament*, 184–87. It may be suggested further, that for the author of Hebrews, who assumes a theology of human fallenness, which Christ has not participated in (see Heb 4:16), Psalm 8 must have been seen as a discussion of unfallen humanity or else it would not have been applied to Jesus.

55. Charry, *Psalms 1–50*, 41.

56. See Brevard Childs, "Psalm 8 in the Context of the Christian Canon," *Int* 23 (1969): 20–31 for a survey.

57. This is clearly the most difficult verse in this psalm, hence the various translations of it. Part of the issue is whether we should render the Hebrew term עֹז as "strength' or as "praise." See Charry, *Psalms 1–50*, 42. The LXX renders it "praise."

Yahweh himself, yet another example of transferring to Jesus what in the OT was applied to God. As Blomberg points out, this portion of the story of the temple cleansing is unique to Matthew, including the quotation of the psalm.[58]

First Corinthians 15:22 (cf. Eph 1:22) seems to involve a partial quotation of Psalm 8:6b, but Paul is applying the words to the risen Jesus, not to humankind in general. This however comports with his presentation in that very chapter of Christ as the representative human being, the last or eschatological Adam.

The most full and important use of Psalm 8 in the NT comes at Hebrews 2:5–9 with a citation of the Greek text of Psalm 8:5–7 in some form. Famously, the author of Hebrew has not merely "he made them a little lower than the angels" but rather "you have made them *for a little while* lower than the angels" something that neither the MT nor the LXX in themselves *necessarily* suggest. However, there is no change in the Greek expression βραχύ from the LXX. The word can mean either "for a little while" or simply "a little," and our author chooses to use the adverb as part of a diachronic construction such that the "crowned with glory and honor" transpires at a different point in time than "for a little while lower than the angels." Subjection comes before exaltation in this reading of the psalm, but the clauses in the psalm are in the reverse order, with the crowning mentioned before the being a little lower. The author is however preparing for his suggestion that Jesus is the one who has already fulfilled the promise of this psalm, and that by the incarnation he was "for a little while" lower than the angels, but is not so any more, being the exalted Son of God at the right hand of the Father.

There is something going on here because already in Hebrews 1 the author goes out of his way to make clear that Christ: (1) is no mere angel, rather he is God's Son, and (2) that he is in no way inferior to the angels, even though during his human life he was for a while quite literally lower than the angels in heaven. One has to wonder if the author also picked Psalm 8 to make his point because it is the only psalm that refers to "the son of man," and Christ is called that repeatedly in the Gospel tradition. In any case, Harold Attridge is right that the Psalm text uses the singular, not the plural, though man and son of man are collective nouns in the psalm. If one translates this humankind or uses

---

58. This may suggest that the form of the quotation comes from Matthew whose audience will be listening in Greek, and are perhaps familiar with the LXX. Blomberg, "Matthew", *Commentary on the NT Use of the OT*, 68–70.

the plural "them" one obscures the fact that the singular noun made it easy for a christological application of the psalm to Christ.[59]

Besides the difference noted above, the author of Hebrews follows the LXX closely in his citation of Psalm 8 except that according to some manuscripts of Hebrews (p46, B, D2) he omits the clause "you have set him over the works of your hands."[60] The author of Hebrews is clear that humankind has not yet seen or experienced all of creation subject to them, but they have seen Jesus to whom God subjected all things and who reigns from heaven in the present. It should not be missed that the author of Hebrews is not just talking about the submitting of this present world to Christ, but also the submitting of the world to come to him. This becomes especially clear in Hebrews 2:5 where we have the negative statement that God has not submitted the coming world to angels. Here is the first place in the book of Hebrews that the author offers something of a midrashic commentary on the OT text, applying it to Christ.[61] This is quite different than what we find in 1QS III, 17–18 and 1QS XI, 20 where Psalm 8 seems to be used to emphasize the insignificance of human beings in comparison to the magnificent God (cf. 3 Enoch 5:10 and Gen. Rab. 8:6). Fourth Ezra 6:53–54 is of relevance to our discussion because there we have the same notion that humans do not possess the world as their inheritance nor have dominion over it. Our author simply says yes we do, but "in Christ."[62]

A Deliverance Ode: Psalm 18

Psalm 18 is in a sense the sequel to Psalm 2, for in the earlier psalm God sets up and anoints the king for service and promises him dominion, and here we are told that God has delivered on his promise in a time of crisis or need.[63] This is a song of praise for God's deliverance, and it is one of the longest in the Psalter, only Psalms 78 and 119 are longer.[64] Its basic structure involves: (1) introductory praise in vv. 1–3; (2) a report of difficulties in the past in vv. 4–5; (3) a direct appeal to God in v. 6; (4) a report of the answer provided by God in vv. 16–19; and (5) lengthy praises of God as a result of the deliverance in vv. 31–42. There are several vivid descriptions along the way to punctuate the psalm's mes-

---

59. Harold W. Attridge, "The Psalms in Hebrews," in Moyise, *Psalms in the New Testament*, 204.
60. See ibid., 203.
61. See the discussion in Guthrie, "Hebrews," 944.
62. See the helpful discussion by ibid., 945–46.
63. Mays, *Psalms*, 90.
64. Goldingay, *Psalms: Volume 1*, 251.

sage: (1) a theophany description in vv. 7–15; (2) a description of the righteous king in vv. 20–24; (3) a description of the perfection of God in vv. 25–30.[65]

One of the more unique features of this particular psalm is the way it changes voicing, for example, it begins with the speaker speaking in the second-person singular, addressing God directly, then it shifts to the third-person singular speaking about God to the psalmist's own audience, then to the first-person singular to speak about the psalmist's own experience with God, and back and forth between these voicings.[66] The psalm is also found in 2 Samuel 22 with some minor variants.

MT Psalm 18	LXX Psalm 17
For the director of music. Of David the servant of the Lord. He sang to the Lord the words of this song when the Lord delivered him from the hand of all his enemies and from the hand of Saul. He said: 1 I love you, Lord, my strength. 2 The Lord is my rock, my fortress and my deliverer; my God is my rock, in whom I take refuge, my shield and the horn of my salvation, my stronghold. 3 I called to the Lord, who is worthy of praise, and I have been saved from my enemies. 4 The cords of death entangled me; the torrents of destruction overwhelmed me. 5 The cords of the grave coiled around me; the snares of death confronted me. 6 In my distress I called to the Lord; I cried to my God for help. From his temple he heard my voice; my cry came before him, into his ears.	1 Regarding completion. Pertaining to David the servant of the Lord, what he said to the Lord, the words of this ode in the day in which the Lord rescued him from the hand of all his enemies and from the hand of Saoul. 2 and he said: I will love you, O Lord, my strength. 3 The Lord is my firmness and my refuge and my rescuer; my God is my helper, and I will hope in him, my protector and horn of my deliverance, my supporter. 4 When I praise, I will call upon the Lord, and from my enemies I shall be saved. 5 Pangs of death encompassed me, and wadis of lawlessness alarmed me; 6 pangs of Hades encircled me; snares of death outran me. 7 And when I was being afflicted, I called upon the Lord, and to my God I cried. From his holy shrine he heard my voice, and my cry before him will enter into his ears.

---

65. Mays, *Psalms*, 90–91.
66. Charry, *Psalms 1–50*, 84.

7 The earth trembled and quaked,
and the foundations of the mountains
shook;
they trembled because he was angry.

8 Smoke rose from his nostrils;
consuming fire came from his mouth,
burning coals blazed out of it.
9 He parted the heavens and came down;
dark clouds were under his feet.
10 He mounted the cherubim and flew;
he soared on the wings of the wind.

11 He made darkness his covering, his
canopy around him—
the dark rain clouds of the sky.
12 Out of the brightness of his presence
clouds advanced,
with hailstones and bolts of lightning.
13 The Lord thundered from heaven;
the voice of the Most High resounded.
14 He shot his arrows and scattered the
enemy,
with great bolts of lightning he routed
them.
15 The valleys of the sea were exposed
and the foundations of the earth laid bare
at your rebuke, Lord,
at the blast of breath from your nostrils.

16 He reached down from on high and
took hold of me;
he drew me out of deep waters.

17 He rescued me from my powerful
enemy,
from my foes, who were too strong for
me.
18 They confronted me in the day of my
disaster,
but the Lord was my support.
19 He brought me out into a spacious
place;
he rescued me because he delighted in
me.
20 The Lord has dealt with me according
to my righteousness;
according to the cleanness of my hands
he has rewarded me.
21 For I have kept the ways of the Lord;
I am not guilty of turning from my God.

8 And the earth shook and was atremble,
and the foundations of the mountains
were disturbed
and shook, because God was angry with
them.
9 Smoke went up in his wrath,
and fire flamed from before him;
coals were ignited by him.
10 And he sloped heaven and came down,
and thick darkness was under his feet.
11 And he mounted upon cheroubin and
flew;
he flew upon the wings of winds.
12 And he made darkness his hideaway;
around him was his tent,
dark water in clouds of air.
13 From the brightness before him the
clouds passed,
hail and coals of fire.
14 And the Lord thundered from heaven,
and the Most High gave forth his voice.
15 And he sent out arrows and scattered
them;
and lightnings he multiplied and con-
founded them.
16 And the springs of the waters
appeared,
and the foundations of the world were
uncovered
at your rebuke, O Lord,
at the blast of the breath of your wrath.
17 He sent out from on high, and he took
me;
he took me to himself out of many
waters.
18 He will rescue me from my powerful
enemies
and from those that hate me,
because they were too stout for me.
19 They outran me in the day of my ill-
treatment,
and the Lord became my buttress.
20 And he brought me out into spaciousness;
he will rescue me, because he wanted me.
21 And the Lord will reward me according to my righteousness,
and according to the cleanness of my
hands he will give back to me,
22 because I kept the ways of the Lord
and did not impiously depart from my
God,

22 All his laws are before me;
I have not turned away from his decrees.

23 I have been blameless before him
and have kept myself from sin.

24 The Lord has rewarded me according
  to my righteousness,
according to the cleanness of my hands
  in his sight.
25 To the faithful you show yourself
  faithful,
to the blameless you show yourself
  blameless,
26 to the pure you show yourself pure,
but to the devious you show yourself
  shrewd.
27 You save the humble
but bring low those whose eyes are
  haughty.
28 You, Lord, keep my lamp burning;
my God turns my darkness into light.

29 With your help I can advance against a
  troop;
with my God I can scale a wall.
30 As for God, his way is perfect:
The Lord's word is flawless;
he shields all who take refuge in him.
31 For who is God besides the Lord?
And who is the Rock except our God?
32 It is God who arms me with strength
and keeps my way secure.
33 He makes my feet like the feet of a
  deer;
he causes me to stand on the heights.
34 He trains my hands for battle;
my arms can bend a bow of bronze.
35 You make your saving help my shield,
and your right hand sustains me;
your help has made me great.

36 You provide a broad path for my feet,
so that my ankles do not give way.

37 I pursued my enemies and overtook
  them;
I did not turn back till they were
  destroyed.

23 because all his judgments were before
  me
and his statutes I did not put away from
  me.
24 And I shall be blameless with him,
and I shall keep myself from my lawlessness.
25 And the Lord will reward me according to my righteousness
and according to the cleanness of my
  hands before his eyes.
26 With the devout you will be deemed
  devout,
and with the innocent man you will be
  innocent,
27 and with the select you will be select,
and with the crooked you will pervert,

28 because it is you who will save a humble people,
and the eyes of haughty you will humble,
29 because it is you who will light my
  lamp, O Lord—
O my God, you will light my darkness—
30 because in you I shall be rescued from
  a pirate's nest,
and in my God I will scale a wall.
31 My God—blameless is his way,
the sayings of the Lord, tried by fire;
he is a protector of all who hope in him,
32 because, who is god except the Lord?
  And who is god besides our God?—
33 God who girded me with power,
and he made my way blameless,
34 refitting my feet like a deer's
and setting me on the heights,

35 training my hands for battle,
and my arms you made a bronze bow.
36 And you gave me protection for my
  deliverance,
and your right hand supported me,
and your instruction set me straight
  completely.
37 You made spacious my strides under
  me,
and my footsteps did not weaken.
38 I will pursue my enemies and overtake
  them,
and I will not turn away until they fail.

38 I crushed them so that they could not rise; they fell beneath my feet. 39 You armed me with strength for battle; you humbled my adversaries before me.	39 I will much afflict them, and they will not be able to stand; they shall fall under my feet. 40 And you girded me with power for battle; you shackled under me those who rise up against me under me.
40 You made my enemies turn their backs in flight, and I destroyed my foes. 41 They cried for help, but there was no one to save them— to the Lord, but he did not answer. 42 I beat them as fine as windblown dust; I trampled them like mud in the streets.	41 And as for my enemies—you gave me their back, and those who hated me you destroyed. 42 They cried out, and there was no one to save, to the Lord, and he did not listen to them. 43 And I will pulverize them like dust before the wind; like the mire of streets I will grind them down.
43 You have delivered me from the attacks of the people; you have made me the head of nations. People I did not know now serve me,	44 You will rescue me from disputes with people; you will appoint me as head of nations; a people whom I did not know was subject to me.
44 foreigners cower before me; as soon as they hear of me, they obey me. 45 They all lose heart; they come trembling from their strongholds. 46 The Lord lives! Praise be to my Rock! Exalted be God my Savior!	45 At the ear's hearing, it obeyed me. Sons of strangers lied to me. 46 Sons of strangers grew old and limped from their paths. 47 The Lord lives! And blessed be my God, and let the God of my deliverance be exalted,
47 He is the God who avenges me, who subdues nations under me, 48 who saves me from my enemies. You exalted me above my foes; from a violent man you rescued me.	48 the God who gives me vengeance and subdues peoples under me, 49 my rescuer from my irascible enemies; from those who rise up against me you will lift me up; you will rescue me from an unjust man.
49 Therefore I will praise you, Lord, among the nations; I will sing the praises of your name. 50 He gives his king great victories; he shows unfailing love to his anointed, to David and to his descendants forever.	50 Therefore I will acknowledge you among nations, O Lord, and make music to your name, 51 magnifying the acts of deliverance of his king and doing mercy to his anointed, to David and his offspring forever.

As particularly the second half of this psalm makes clear, this is a royal psalm, a psalm about the king, and the prescript links it particularly to David's rescue from the pursuit of Saul.[67] So it is not, ostensibly, about

---

67. Kidner, *Psalms 1–72*, 90 notes the small clues that this psalm in some form likely goes back to the period of David, because it mentions combat on foot, whereas later kings took to chariots to wage war (1 Kgs 22:34; 2 Kgs 9:21).

61

the rescue of just anyone, but more particularly about the rescue of the king. Of course, when David eluded Saul, it was Saul who was actually the king, but this song is about King David and even in the end of the psalm about the Davidic line.[68]

The continual use of "my" in this psalm speaks of a personal relationship and a personal rescue of the psalmist by God. God is said to be "my strength" and "my rock," a characterization that is the most frequent epithet used of God in the psalms, and elsewhere in Hebrew poetry. The image of the rock suggests both something that is permanent and strong, on the one hand, and a place where one could hide, a refuge, on the other;[69] and of course David did hide in a cave at one juncture while running from Saul (cf. 1 Sam 23:25–28). But the psalm is cast in very generic terms. Mays stresses: "the psalm moves at a mythopoeic theological level; it unfolds a narrative plot and prospect that could interpret many historical occasions."[70] This is correct, and one can debate whether this means the psalm was originally more specifically about David and after his time was made more generic in character, or the reverse process. It is hard not to see the very first verse as the singular expression of a particular person. The word אֶרְחָמְךָ (’erḥāmkā) is an Aramaic cognate of the Hebrew verb "to have mercy" but in this particular verbal form with the suffix indicating its object it means "I am deeply devoted to you," or as R. Alter has it "I am impassioned of You."[71]

A careful reading of vv. 4–19 makes clear that the author sees salvation not as a purely subjective personal experience, though it certainly has personal effects, but as a cosmic sort of drama where God comes down in a theophany cloud, like at Mt. Sinai, and in this case deals with the king's adversaries.[72] While human adversaries are in view, the

---

68. On the variety of names applied to Yahweh in the psalm as a key to a tenth century date for its composition, see Goldingay, *Psalms: Volume 1*, 252, who cites David Noel Freedman's study of these names/titles; on the interrelationship between the version of this song in 2 Samuel 22 and the version here in Psalm 18 (likely two recensions of the same original) see Frank Moore Cross and David Noel Freedman, "A Royal Song of Thanksgiving," *JBL* 72 (1953): 15–34. There are Aramaisms in vv. 1 and 25 according to Goldingay which are not found in the 2 Samuel 22 version, but does that make it likely to be the earlier or later form? I would say later.

69. Longman, *Psalms*, 112 is right to note that the psalmist is not talking about a rock one can hold in one's hand, but rather one large enough to hide in as 1 Sam 23:14–29 says David did. This becomes especially clear when the next term used to describe this refuge really means something like mountain fortress (v. 2b).

70. Mays, *Psalms*, 91.

71. See Charry, *Psalms 1–50*, 85 and Robert Alter, *The Book of Psalms: A Translation with Commentary* (New York: Norton, 2007), 52.

72. For God as a divine warrior, see Tremper Longman and Daniel G. Reid, *God is a Warrior* (Grand Rapids: Zondervan: 1995).

ultimate enemy here is death and Sheol (cf. Ps 116:3), depicted as like a large body of chaotic waters, which accordingly leads to the image of salvation being a rescue from drowning. God heard the cry of the psalmist, came down from heaven and snatched the king from the jaws of death and Sheol, snatched him out of the chaos waters.

If rock, as a part of and the foundation of the land, is the perpetual image of stability in the psalms and elsewhere, water is the image of instability, chaos in the Hebrew lexicon. This sort of thought pattern can be seen in Genesis 1 where land is formed out of the chaos waters, and it recurs throughout the Bible, so, for instance, famously John's image of the perfecting of the new creation after the second coming involves not merely the sea giving up its dead (Rev 20:13a) and death and Hades, the land of the dead, also giving up their dead (Rev 20:13b), but finally, once and for all, we have the proclamation "the first earth had passed away *and there was no more sea*" (Rev 21:1, emphasis added). John envisions new heavens and a new earth, but not a new sea, for in the final state of affairs no chaos, instability, or death can remain.

When God comes down, the imagery of thunder and lightning and hail are used, as well as the imagery of earthquakes, and even volcanoes can be used. If the intervention is prompted in part by the anger of God over his chosen one or ones being under attack, then we also have images of smoke and fire to depict the anger. When God descends in the theophany cloud, the earth and all that is in it reacts and is affected. We are told at v. 10 that God rides his throne chariot down from heaven "riding on the cherubim" (cf. Ps 104:3-4; Isa 19:1; Ezekiel 1). All hell breaks loose from heaven as God descends in his anger and rescues his king. Verse 15 seems to be an echo of the Red Sea crossing, with the laying bare of the ground at the bottom of the sea by the breath of God's nostrils. But what should we make of this description?

Goldingay argues that Judges 4-5 is instructive. The poetic account is paralleled by a prosaic one that depicts God working through human processes to produce victory over the foe. It was not a torrent that swept Sisera away, it was a tent peg driven through his head! It is true as well that Psalm 18 says that God enabled the king to conquer his foes. This suggests that we should surely not press the imagery in this psalm when it comes to the mode of divine intervention. The dramatic and metaphorical imagery can be seen as a vivid way of saying Yahweh will move heaven and earth to help his king.[73]

Verses 20-30 are interesting because they involve the king or psalmist giving testimony that he's been good! In fact the psalmist is prepared to say something we certainly do not hear in the Pauline epistles, "the Lord rewarded me according to my righteousness, according to the cleanness of my hands, he recompensed me, for I have kept the Lord's ways, and have not wickedly departed from Him. . . . I was blameless before him and kept myself from guilt." Now this description might be compared, for instance, to Paul's saying that in regard to a righteousness defined by the Mosaic law, he was blameless in his pre-Christian days (Phil 3:6), but Christians were more apt to suggest that this, if not mere braggadocio, was most apt if a description of God's final king, the messiah, Jesus. It is particularly this portion of the psalm that has led some scholars to suggest it is probably written *for* David, during his lifetime, perhaps at or near the end of his reign.[74] Would David really have said this of himself, glossing over his major sins?

There is in any case an inherent rhetorical metaphorical hyperbole not only in the description of God and his intervention but also in the description of the psalmist's protestation of his righteousness. At the mundane level what is probably meant is that the king was a law keeper, and loyal and obedient to Yahweh. He was not a rebel against God, or someone who regularly violated God's will. He exemplifies the kind of right living attributed to the blessed person in Psalm 1.[75] "The claim is not a cross assertion of self-righteousness by the King but a confession that he has been true to the righteousness in which the divine choice to be king had set him. . . . He had fulfilled the vocation given to the King to embody the law of the divine King."[76] Since this song is placed at the end of David's career, perhaps we are meant to think that this is how in the end the psalmist thinks one should evaluate David's life, not on the basis of his sin of passion, lusting after Bathsheba, which led to a further sin against her husband Uriah the Hittite. Charry even suggests that perhaps we should see this as God having mercy on David and counting him as "in right standing" for the sake of the nation, in order to show his own "perfection" and trustworthiness, because having jettisoned Saul, there were reasons to have doubts about Yahweh's constancy.[77]

As for God, God is not merely righteous, he is "perfect!" The Hebrew

---

73. See Goldingay, *Psalms: Volume 1*, 260.
74. See Goldingay's discussion in ibid., 254–56 of the five or so possible views of the authorship of this psalm.
75. Charry, *Psalms 1-50*, 87.
76. Mays, *Psalms*, 93.
77. Charry, *Psalms 1-50*, 88.

word תָּמִים (*tāmîm*) is a critical one in the Psalter, and deserves our close attention. It has various nuances to it, and can be translated "whole," "complete," or "blameless" (see vv. 23, 25 where it is applied to the king himself). The term refers to God being a person of total integrity and honesty; his word is his bond, and his deeds reflect his words and character. His conduct is reliable, consistent, coherent, and dependable because that is also his character.[78] What you hear and see is what you get. The appropriate human response is "obedience and trust [which are] not thought of as separate but thought of as a single feature of human conduct in relation to God. Obedience is trust and trust is obedience."[79] This is so because human conduct should reflect human character in a positive sense, so that for God's people, just as for God, there is consistency in thought, word, deed, and character.

Verses 31–50 come across as something of a victory ode. God is the savior, and as a result the king is the victor as well, including a victor in battle. It is God who has enabled the king to accomplish much and as a result the king lavishes great praise on God. It is God who girded the king with strength (vv. 32, 39). It is interesting that this psalm is atypical in the OT in portraying the king as the one who triumphs over his foes, as the actor who defeats the enemies, instead of God, who has simply equipped the king to do so. Contrast this with Exodus 15 where it is Yahweh who has gone into battle and done-in the enemy; and importantly, even when there was no king in Israel, the psalm was still seen as valid and valuable as a promise or even a prophecy of the future ideal king who would one day come, hence the jubilant note at the end, "to David and his descendants forever" (v. 50). Verse 35 is important because it strikes the balance, avoiding attributing everything to David's prowess or alternately all to God with no enabling of David. Weiser puts the matter this way: "the final sentence of v. 35, stating that the king owes his rise to greatness to the 'condescension' of God, a statement which is unique even in the language of the Old Testament, clearly removes the danger that the King might transgress the bounds of humility."[80]

In an interesting and unusual occurrence, a slightly altered version of this same psalm occurs in 2 Samuel 22, at the conclusion of David's

---

78. See Kidner, *Psalms 1-72*, 95.

79. Mays, *Psalms*, 93.

80. Weiser, *Psalms*, 195. The use of עֲנְוַתְךָ (*'anwatkā*) of Yahweh, translated merely as "help" in the NRSV is rather daring. God is not merely a God who helps from afar, he comes down to earth and helps in person. The translation as "condescend" comports nicely with the vivid imagery of the theophany in this psalm.

career, as perhaps an exegesis of all the battles and escapes of David the warrior king. This suggests once more that the psalm in some form goes back to David, or perhaps the chronicler of his life.[81] That placement of this psalm makes clear that songs did not just belong in the Psalter, they belonged in and helped interpret narrative contexts as well. "Theologically the expansion from a specific to a general context teaches that the virtuous pattern of life of the righteous works at both the personal and international level. God commends a single standard of living no matter the setting."[82]

Here in the Psalter we are told what tune this song should be sung to, "the servant of the Lord," the same as in Psalm 36. This suggests that the poem was adapted for liturgical use after the fact. It originally was part of the summing up of David's career in a narrative context. "The duplication of the text assures David's place as the poet laureate of ancient Israel."[83] A final note is in order before we consider the NT use of this material: the climax of this psalm is the exclamation in v. 46, "the Lord lives!" When Yahweh is called a living God, the qualifying term did not mean that he was alive as opposed to dead, but that he was active as opposed to passive, or ineffective, or even indifferent.[84]

This song of theophany is important to the study of the NT if for no other reason than how it contrasts with the means by which the evangelists depict God coming down in the person of Jesus. Divine condescension can take several forms it would appear. According to the Gospels, while an angel spoke to Mary and the Spirit overshadowed her, there was no dramatic theophany, no parting of the clouds, no *Sturm und Drang*. In gospel time, God did not come as the mighty warrior, but as the prince of peace, not riding on his throne chariot, but wrapped in bands of cloth and laid in an animal trough and then later riding on a donkey in Jerusalem. What a contrast.

When you set Psalm 18 side by side with Luke 1 you can hardly believe you are talking about the same subject, namely God coming to rescue his people. Yet clearly both Psalm 18 and Luke 1 are about God coming down to rescue his people, the main difference is that in Psalm

---

81. So Weiser, *Psalms*, 186. He says that nothing in the psalm itself could not have been said during the close of David's reign. Longman, *Psalms*, 110 notes that vv. 43–44 are things only a king could say.

82. Charry, *Psalms 1-50*, 85. This insight supports the thesis that the direction of editing of these psalms went from more specific to more generic as time went on. In other words, the prescripts on the whole are more likely to tell us about the original context from which the psalm came, not the later contextualizing of a generic song.

83. Ibid., 83.

84. Mays, *Psalms*, 90.

18, it is the king who is being rescued, whereas in Luke 1 it is the king who is doing the rescuing. At the level of ideas there is a close affinity between the two texts; God is hands-on with his people to save and deliver them, although theophany is one thing and incarnation takes things a step further. At the level of means of accomplishing this end, the difference is stark, even allowing for the metaphorical character of the psalm; the psalm depicts God as a warrior and one who enables devout warriors to win their battles, whereas Jesus comes as the Prince of Peace and nonviolence.

If we turn to quotations, allusions and echoes, and not just analogous ideas, Paul in Romans 15:9 seems to have read Psalm 18 with Jesus speaking in the first person in v. 49: "Therefore I will praise you among the gentiles, I will sing the praises of your name."[85] The odd thing here is that the first clause is closer to the MT, whereas the second clause which speaks of singing the praises of God's name is closer to the LXX and the following quotation from Psalm 117:1 is from the LXX. Some commentators have found Romans 15:9a odd because Jesus during his ministry did not praise or proclaim God among the gentiles, but this is forgetting Romans 15:18 where Paul tells the audience that Christ was working through him, and through the apostolic ministry in general, to bring about the obedience of the gentiles.[86]

But in the original text it is David speaking, and what he is saying is that he has had military triumphs over the gentiles in his area and that is how he has imprinted the divine name on them, showing who the living and real God is. It is decidedly not after proclaiming the good news to the gentiles like Paul has been doing, as Richard Hays rightly points out.[87] This contrast in the use of the psalm compared to its original contextual significance is much like the contrast in theophanies we pointed out above.

In his helpful examination of the catena of quotes in Romans 15, Wagner points out that it is the last verse of the psalm, which speaks of not just David but also "his seed forever" which "helped to hold Psalm 18 open to interpretation in terms of later historical monarchs and, after the fall of the house of David, in terms of an eschatological

---

85. See Longman, *Psalms*, 117.
86. See rightly J. Ross Wagner, *Heralds of the Good News: Isaiah and Paul in Concert in the Letter to the Romans*, NovTSup 101 (Leiden: Brill, 2002), 310.
87. Richard B. Hays, *Echoes of Scripture in the Letters of Paul* (New Haven: Yale University Press, 1989), 72; but see also Sylvia C. Keesmaat, "The Psalms in Romans and Galatians," in Moyise, *Psalms in the New Testament*, 156. Also see Mark A. Seifrid, "Romans" in Beale, *Commentary on the New Testament Use*, 688–89.

king. That Paul has read this psalm as the words of Christ is therefore not terribly surprising."[88] In fact, Wagner suggests that Paul may have read Psalm 18 as generally applicable to Christ, indeed as his testimony to his own experiences of being rescued from death and Sheol, or in vv. 44–45a being saved from the arguments of the people, and being established as a leader of a people whom he did not know, a people who became obedient to him.[89] This may be so. Certainly, royal psalms lent themselves to later messianic reflections. As. Wilk has pointed out, it does not appear that Paul is simply using a preexisting catena of texts, because Romans 15 reflects wider verbal links to and knowledge of other verses from Psalm 18.[90]

One of the more interesting passages in this long psalm is the segment at vv. 20–27. Our focus here will be on vv. 20 and vv. 25–27.

> 20 The Lord has dealt with me according to my righteousness;
> according to the cleanness of my hands he has rewarded me.
> 25 To the faithful you show yourself faithful,
> to the blameless you show yourself blameless,
> 26 to the pure you show yourself pure,
> but to the devious you show yourself shrewd.
> 27 You save the humble
> but bring low those whose eyes are haughty.

If one reads carefully through James 4:6–8 one can see the similarities immediately.

> 6 That is why Scripture says:
> "God opposes the proud
> but shows favor to the humble."
> 7 Submit yourselves, then, to God. Resist the devil, and he will flee from you. 8 Come near to God and he will come near to you. Wash your hands, you sinners, and purify your hearts, you double-minded.

It is odd that some translations have *only* suggested that Proverbs 3:34 is being quoted in James 4:6, which is true, when in fact Psalm 18:20–27 is closer to the whole context of this passage in James. You have the concept of clean hands in both texts. There is also the concept of reciprocity. God is faithful to the faithful is just another way of saying that if you draw near to God he will draw near to you, and you hear about

88. Wagner, *Heralds*, 312.
89. Ibid., 313.
90. Wilk, "Letters of Paul as Witnesses," 262–63.

God helping the humble and opposing the proud. True, Proverbs 3:34 in the LXX reads "The Lord resists the arrogant, but he gives grace to the humble" so properly speaking this is being cited here, but in the context of this passage in James there are also various echoes or allusions to Psalm 18. This is not surprising since both texts are drawing on fundamental wisdom themes, as is Proverbs of course. Of a very different ilk is our next psalm to consider, Psalm 22.

The Cry of Desolation: Psalm 22

In terms of understanding the passion of Jesus, there are few psalms of more importance than Psalm 22, which according to both Mark and Matthew Jesus quoted the first line of, in either Hebrew or Aramaic, probably the latter. Jesus himself then seems to have provided the impetus for the use of some of the rest of this psalm to describe and explain the crucifixion of Jesus and its surrounding circumstances (cf. e.g., Ps 22:7 mockery and shaking of heads; Ps 22:18 division of garments).[91] In fact, the Matthean crucifixion narrative seems to be deliberately cast in light of Psalm 22, showing how the end of Jesus's life fulfilled this psalm. It is a mistake however to not compare this individual lament to the many other laments in the Psalter, and as Brueggemann and Bellinger themselves lament "for many [Christians] it is the only lament known or used at all."[92]

MT Psalm 22	LXX Psalm 21
For the director of music. To the tune of "The Doe of the Morning." A psalm of David. 1 My God, my God, why have you forsaken me? Why are you so far from saving me, so far from my cries of anguish? 2 My God, I cry out by day, but you do not answer, by night, but I find no rest. 3 Yet you are enthroned as the Holy One; you are the one Israel praises. 4 In you our ancestors put their trust; they trusted and you delivered them.	1 Regarding completion. Over the support at dawn. A Psalm. Pertaining to David. 2 God, my God, attend to me; why did you forsake me? Far away from my deliverance are the words of my transgressions. 3 O my God, I will cry by day, and you will not listen, and by night, and it becomes no folly for me. 4 But you, the commendation of Israel, reside in a holy place. 5 In you our fathers hoped; they hoped, and you rescued them.

91. On this see Weiser, *Psalms*, 226.
92. Brueggemann and Bellinger, *Psalms*, 113.

5 To you they cried out and were saved;
in you they trusted and were not put to
shame.
6 But I am a worm and not a man,
scorned by everyone, despised by the
people.

7 All who see me mock me;
they hurl insults, shaking their heads.

8 "He trusts in the Lord," they say,
"let the Lord rescue him.
Let him deliver him,
since he delights in him."
9 Yet you brought me out of the womb;
you made me trust in you, even at my
mother's breast.
10 From birth I was cast on you;
from my mother's womb you have been
my God.
11 Do not be far from me,
for trouble is near
and there is no one to help.
12 Many bulls surround me;
strong bulls of Bashan encircle me.
13 Roaring lions that tear their prey
open their mouths wide against me.
14 I am poured out like water,
and all my bones are out of joint.
My heart has turned to wax;
it has melted within me.
15 My mouth is dried up like a potsherd,
and my tongue sticks to the roof of my
mouth;
you lay me in the dust of death.

16 Dogs surround me,
a pack of villains encircles me;
they pierce my hands and my feet.
17 All my bones are on display;
people stare and gloat over me.
18 They divide my clothes among them
and cast lots for my garment.

19 But you, Lord, do not be far from me.
You are my strength; come quickly to
help me.
20 Deliver me from the sword,
my precious life from the power of the
dogs.
21 Rescue me from the mouth of the
lions;
save me from the horns of the wild oxen.

6 To you they cried and were saved;
in you they hoped and were not put to
shame.
7 But as for me, I am a worm and not
human,
a reproach of mankind and despised by
people.
8 All who saw me mocked at me;
they talked with the lips; they moved the
head:
9 "He hoped in the Lord; let him rescue
him;
let him save him, because he wanted
him,"
10 because it was you who drew me from
the belly,
my hope from my mother's breasts.
11 On you I was cast from the womb;
from my mother's stomach you have
been my God.
12 Do not keep away from me,
because affliction is near,
because there is no one to help.
13 Many bull calves encircled me;
fat bulls surrounded me;
14 they opened their mouth at me,
like a lion that ravens and roars.
15 Like water I was poured out,
and all my bones were scattered;
my heart became like wax
melting within my belly;
16 my strength was dried up like a potsherd,
and my tongue is stuck to my throat,
and to death's dust you brought me
down,
17 because many dogs encircled me,
a gathering of evildoers surrounded me.
They gouged my hands and feet;
18 I counted all my bones,
but they took note and observed me;
19 they divided my clothes among themselves,
and for my clothing they cast lots.
20 But you, O Lord, do not put my help
far away!
Attend to my support!
21 Rescue my soul from the sword,
and from a dog's claw my only life!

22 Save me from a lion's mouth,
and my lowliness from the horns of uni-
corns!

22 I will declare your name to my people; in the assembly I will praise you.	23 I will tell of your name to my kindred; in the midst of an assembly I will sing a hymn to you:
23 You who fear the Lord, praise him! All you descendants of Jacob, honor him! Revere him, all you descendants of Israel!	24 You who fear the Lord, praise him! All you offspring of Jacob together glorify him; let all the offspring of Israel fear him,
24 For he has not despised or scorned the suffering of the afflicted one; he has not hidden his face from him but has listened to his cry for help.	25 because he did not despise or scorn the petition of the poor, nor did he turn away his face from me, and when I cried to him, he listened to me.
25 From you comes the theme of my praise in the great assembly; before those who fear you I will fulfill my vows.	26 From you comes my commendation in a great assembly; my vows I will pay before those who fear him.
26 The poor will eat and be satisfied; those who seek the Lord will praise him— may your hearts live forever!	27 The needy shall eat and be satisfied, and those who seek him shall praise the Lord; their hearts shall live forever and ever!
27 All the ends of the earth will remember and turn to the Lord, and all the families of the nations will bow down before him,	28 All the ends of the earth shall remember and turn to the Lord, and all the paternal families of the nations shall do obeisance before him
28 for dominion belongs to the Lord and he rules over the nations.	29 because kingship is the Lord's, and it is he who is master over the nations.
29 All the rich of the earth will feast and worship; all who go down to the dust will kneel before him— those who cannot keep themselves alive.	30 All the fat ones of the earth ate and did obeisance; all who descend into the earth shall fall down before him. And my soul lives for him,
30 Posterity will serve him; future generations will be told about the Lord.	31 and my offspring will serve him; the coming generation will be announced to the Lord,
31 They will proclaim his righteousness, declaring to a people yet unborn: He has done it!	32 and they shall announce his righteousness to a people to be born, because the Lord acted.

In terms of its form, this psalm is an individual psalm of lament, and it follows the pattern of many of them in moving from the report of the distress, to affirming of trust, to further lamenting, to a petitionary prayer for help, to a promise to publicly praise God if delivered from whatever the crisis was. Because this is often the pattern of these songs, some scholars have suggested that Jesus cited this psalm because even though he was suffering he knew how the psalm ended. This attempt to take the edge off of Jesus's anguish, or sense of God-forsakenness, is probably not justified, any more than it would be justified to think that the original psalmist was not deadly serious about his distress, just because the psalm seems to have "a possible happy ending." This psalm possibly stands out from some laments however because of a dramatic statement of reversal in v. 21b, "you have answered me!" (MT). However, עֲנִיתָנִי ('anîtānî) could be translated as a vocative plea, "please do answer me." So let us consider the psalm in its original context and in terms of its original content first. If we envision this originally applied to David, then the second question at the beginning must exegete the first one as Kidner suggests. By this I mean, that the cry of desolation in fact means "why are you so far from helping me" in David's case.[93] For Jesus, the meaning of the cry seems to have been much more profound—and troubling.

This is one of many psalms that laments unjust suffering of a pious or righteous Israelite (cf. also Psalms 14, 41, 42, 43, 69, etc.). The theme of the vindication of the righteous sufferer was rather common in early Judaism (cf. Wis 2:12–24; 5:1–8; 2 Baruch 15:7–8; 48:49–50). It is however odd that the Qumran literature nowhere directly cites the righteous sufferer psalms, though some of the ideas and imagery do show up in places like 4Q88. More importantly, there is no evidence as of yet that Psalm 22 was seen as messianic in character prior to the time of Jesus. While it was fine to talk about Israel suffering unjustly, the avoidance of predicating this of the messiah is notable even when discussing a text like Isaiah 52–53 (see Tg. Isa. 52:13—53:12).

These laments come from people who have an ongoing relationship with the biblical God, but some crisis has arisen that makes them think they have been abandoned by God, despite his promises of faithfulness and protection.[94] Though the complainer says he has been forsaken, he still addresses God as "my God." The psalmist has not entirely given up hope or abandoned his faith in Yahweh, but he believes he has himself been abandoned by the one he has trusted.[95] The psalmist here appeals to God's track record; in the past when called upon, Yahweh has come to the rescue, and the assumption is that by reciting this fact, God could be motivated to take action again and rescue the psalmist.

The psalm begins with the psalmist, perhaps David, in deep distress. The cry "my God, my God" indicates that the psalmist has not forsaken

93. Kidner, *Psalms 1–72*, 106.
94. See Brueggeman and Bellinger, *Psalms*, 114–15.
95. In Mark's Gospel this becomes more pointed because the only place in Mark where Jesus calls God simply "God" and not Abba or some other term of endearment or of close relationship, is on the cross. Even in the garden of Gethsemane, Jesus addresses God as Abba, Father.

Yahweh, but it appears to him that he has been forsaken by Yahweh, hence the urgency of the cry. What is especially striking about this is that the psalmist does not first ask why these things are happening to him, but instead asks why God has seemingly abandoned him in his hour of need. His complaint is not so much "why have you allowed this to happen," but rather "Where are you when I need you so badly?" The biblical God is deeply concerned and compassionate and will come to the rescue. As Weiser says, we should not see these words as an attempt to berate God for not doing his job, but as a cry of desperation.[96]

Nonetheless, the psalmist is clearly terrified by his God-forsaken-ness, especially because he is beset by a fierce and powerful foe. Verse 1b reads literally "far from help [or helping me] are the words of my roaring." Even his most vehement shouting seems useless, stressing how far away God seems, not even hearing the psalmist's strongest cries. As Peter Craigie notes, even though the psalmist had been taught to trust God (the verb for trust occurs three times in vv. 4–5) and was crying to him both day and night, nonetheless his experience seems to give the lie to his theology.[97] How very often does our experience cause us to doubt, reject, or reshape our theological assumptions? Then at v. 3, the psalmist begins to think of the character of God: he is holy and enthroned on the praises of Israel. Maybe it is because God is so holy that he seems so distant. He is literally set apart from the human scene, as the word קָדוֹשׁ (qādôš) suggests. The psalmist seems to be remembering the worship service when Israel would sing praises. They would lift God up and exalt him in song. Perhaps he is envisioning the ark on which God was enthroned above the cherubim (the creatures who were thought to lift him up). Some have seen here the incense, a symbol of prayer and praise, rising up to God during worship.

At v. 4 the psalmist looks back over the history of God's people. He remembers that there was precedent for God rescuing his people when they were in dire straits, but then the psalmist seems to think, "but they were worthy of such help, and I am not; I am but a worm." The psalmist is probably envisioning the Exodus here, for he uses the verb נִמְלָטוּ (nimlāṭû) which means "to slip through" (cf. v. 6 to Judg 3:26). God helped them to slip through the hands of Pharaoh and escape Egypt. They were not put to shame or disappointed. Yet the psalmist is overcome by his sense of unworthiness. A worm is something trampled under human feet, not treated decently as a person should be. Some-

---

96. Weiser, *Psalms*, 220–21.
97. Peter C. Craigie and Marvin E. Tate, *Psalms 1-50*, 2nd ed., WBC 19 (Dallas: Word, 2004), 197–98.

times when people are abused in this fashion they begin to wonder whether perhaps they deserve such treatment.

After all, wonders the psalmist, why does everyone despise me? It is bad enough to be suffering, but to suffer while being taunted by one's people and seemingly abandoned by one's God is intolerable. Verse 7 speaks of derision. Verse 7b reading literally "they separate with the lip," in other words, they sneer at him and shake their heads (cf. Matt 27:39; Mark 15:29). What is especially galling is that the crowd taunts him in regard to his faith: "He rolled his burden to the Lord, so let the Lord deliver him." The psalmist had petitioned God openly and now awaited the response, for it is clear the crowd would not help him. Notice that his detractors seem to assume that God operates at our convenience and when we need him to do so, not on the basis of his will and plan.[98]

Verse 8 must be seen as the words of the enemy, but at v. 9 we return to the psalmist's reflections. He says to himself, "Why would God stop caring now?" After all, God drew him forth from the womb and placed him at his mother's breast. Indeed, God had cared not only for the forefathers but also for the psalmist himself, so there was good reason to expect it to happen again. Yet God seems so distant that the psalmist implores, "Do not be distant!"

Beginning in v. 12 the adversaries are described as bulls of Bashan (cf. Amos 4:1, "cows of Bashan," and Deut 32:14). The fertile pastureland east of the Jordan was well known for its strong breeds of cattle. At v. 13 we have a different metaphor: the foes are like hungry lions ready to rend one in pieces and roar, or possibly we should read "ready to rage and roar." These sorts of images were often used of savage leaders in antiquity, for instance of the Assyrian conquerors (cf. the beasts in Daniel 7).[99] At v. 17 we hear of dogs surrounding the psalmist, standing around waiting for a carcass to dismember.

The self-description in v. 14 is very moving. The word translated "potsherd" often denotes pieces of broken earthenware, but here the subject seems to be the palate or mouth. The author feels totally washed out, like a bag of disjointed bones. Indeed, his foes are already casting lots for his clothes, as though he were already dead. The psalmist is emaciated, and his tongue clings to the roof of his mouth. Verse I5b indicates that God ultimately put the psalmist in the dust of death.

---

98. Kidner, Psalms 1-72, 106.
99. Mays, Psalms, 110. That imagery was also used of demons, but that does not seem relevant here.

The most difficult verse in the entire psalm is 16c. How are we to render כָּאֲרִי (*kāʾarî*)? Its obvious sense is "like a lion," but how does that relate to hands and feet? John Calvin points out that if we do render it literally, then we must supply the verb from the previous clause, "encompassed" or "beset."[100] The LXX at this point has "they pierced my hands and feet." It is important to note that the NT cites this verse and mentions the nailing of Jesus's hands and feet only *after* the resurrection (cf. John 20:25–28). Now if the original psalm text had read "they pierced my hands and feet," then it is surprising that no evangelist cites this verse in their Passion narrative. Thus I suggest that we take it in its most natural sense and translate, "like a lion they beset me, hands and feet," that is, all around or completely. The image could be of hands and feet being gnawed or mauled. Since the lion metaphor had already been used, it is natural to see a development of it here. Verse 21b can be seen as transitional, not least because after it we simply have praise for God and his mighty works. The verb can be taken as past tense, "he answered me," or possibly as imperative, "do thou answer me."[101]

Beginning at v. 23 is an address to the whole congregation, and v. 25 in all likelihood means that the psalmist would not have sung this part had he not had a change of fortune. Thus this whole psalm cannot be applied to Jesus as it is, for Jesus died, but the psalmist did not. Verse 28 is interesting. Here the psalmist gives a more universal perspective on things. The Lord is seen as one who rules over all nations and to whom, one day, all the ends of the earth and all nations will turn and bow down. The nations are seen as converted by the all-encompassing rule of God. Then at v. 29 we hear, "lo those who sleep in the earth must worship him, before him all must bow who went down into the dust." Here clearly we have the consummation of human history, and this seems to allude to life beyond death, if not resurrection of the body per se.[102] It appears to refer to conscious life beyond the grave, though in what form is unclear. The point is that no one gets beyond God's rule, not even the dead. We can see a clear progression here: (1) in v. 28 all present nations must worship; (2) in v. 29 all past human beings will do

100. Found at: http://biblehub.com/commentaries/calvin/psalms/22.htm.
101. See Alter, *Book of Psalms*, 75n22. Cf. the discussion in Charry, *Psalms 1–50*, 109n3. The Hebrew translation at www.mechon-mamre.org, which comes from Jerusalem and is intended for Jews and gentiles alike has "do thou answer me." Kraus, *Psalms 1–59*, 293–98 is quite clear that we should take v. 21b as an interjection "you have heard me" which explains the change in tone and content of the psalm thereafter. What begins as lament ends as thanksgiving.
102. Mays, *Psalms*, 113.

so; and (3) in v. 30 all future persons will do so. When one dies, one's descendants will then serve God and tell their descendants to do so, so the reign of God will be passed down from generation to generation.[103]

Thus this magnificent psalm is full of rich ideas including the afterlife, the problem of evil, and rescue by God in times of trouble. There was one God-forsaken person to whom this psalm was especially appropriately applied. Christ endured our God-forsakenness, taking it upon himself, so that we would not have to bear it any longer. Notice how this psalm ends, as Philippians 2 does, with every knee bowing and every tongue confessing the true God.

The NT use of this psalm, in various ways, is noteworthy, as it is a text that is not only quoted, but influences the way the passion narrative is told, to mention but two things. Brueggemann and Bellinger are surely right that Christians should avoid the temptation to "tone down the raw aloneness of verse 1, a raw aloneness essential to any serious 'theology of the cross.'"[104] This is exactly right. What should have been asked is, Is Christ depicted as experiencing our God forsakenness, our alienation from God on the cross, on our behalf?[105] But it is not just in the passion narrative that Psalm 22 comes up for use in the NT, as we shall now see. While Matthew 27:46 // Mark 15:34 should be the starting point for any discussion of the Christian use of this psalm, and one can readily expand the discussion to the use of other verses of this psalm in those same narratives as part of the narrative rather than as a quote, there is more to be considered.

For example, Psalm 22:3 speaks of crying to God both day and night, and Jesus in his commentary on his own parable of the persistent widow asks this rhetorical question in Luke 18:7, "and will not God grant justice to his chosen ones who cry to him day and night?" One wonders if this fact was not in his mind when he recited Psalm 22:1 from the cross. Like the psalmist, Paul in Philippians 1:20 expresses his hope that he will not be put to shame, just as his ancestors were not put to shame (Ps 22:5). Or Jesus says in Mark 9:12 that the son of man will be treated with contempt, a telling portrait of what that looks like can be found in Psalm 22:6–7. Psalm 22:8 speaks in the voice of the suffer's adversaries suggesting that the sufferer must commit his cause to God

---

103. See the discussion of "the dead" in Charry, *Psalms 1–50*, 114. She is right that usually in the psalms we are told that the dead do not praise God (e.g., Pss 6:5; 88:10; 115:17), but it is possible that this is an exilic or postexilic psalm when there was a growing theology of a positive afterlife.

104. Brueggemann and Bellinger, *Psalms*, 120.

105. See the powerful discussion in Jürgen Moltmann's classic study *The Crucified God: The Cross of Christ as the Foundation and Criticism of Christian Theology* (New York: Harper & Row, 1974).

"let him deliver him, let him rescue the one in whom he delights." This may be echoed in Luke 23:35 where we hear, "and the people stood by watching but the leaders scoffed at him saying 'he saved others let him save himself if he is the Messiah of God, his chosen one'" or the fuller version of the same scoffing in Matthew 27:43.

All four gospels mention the dividing of Jesus clothes by the soldiers (Matt 27:35; Mark 15:24; Luke 23:34; John 19:24) and there is no controversy about the text of Psalm 22:18 which speaks of this very thing in neat Hebraic parallelism. that is, speaking of the same thing in two different ways (the clothes are divided by means of the casting of lots to see who gets what). Paul exclaims in 2 Timothy 4:17 that he was rescued from the lion's mouth, and no sooner do we hear at Psalm 22:21 the cry, "rescue me from the lion's mouth" than we have only a few words later, "you have answered me!" In Hebrews 2:12 we are told Jesus himself is the speaker of Psalm 22:22, "I will tell of your name to my brothers and sisters. In the midst of the congregation I will praise you." The exhortation to the saints in Revelation 19:5 echoes the same exhortation to the same sort of audience in Psalm 22:23. Or one could compare the statement in Psalm 22:24 to the statement about Jesus's prayer response and how God heard him in Hebrews 5:7. Granted, once again some of this is just using the language of the psalms to talk about analogous matters, but in some of these cases the psalm is quoted or alluded to very clearly with the implication that it is being fulfilled in the life of Jesus and/or his followers. Some of this we must discuss further now.

First of all, we have to come to grips with the fact that in the passion narrative, especially in Matthew, but also in the other narratives, there is an interaction of historical event, historical account, and reflection on the OT texts, especially the psalms in these narratives. It is not merely a process of the psalms providing commentary on the narrative, but the language of the psalms being used in the composition of the narrative.[106] Psalm 22:1 in the LXX adds the phrase "you received me" or perhaps "attend to me."

> Mark includes only the portion of the text found in the MT, transliterates the Aramaic paraphrase, but follows the LXX version for the Greek translation of Jesus' words, except for the slight alteration in the expression for "why." Matthew mostly follows Mark but changes the spelling of "my

106. Ben Witherington III, *Matthew*, SHBC (Macon, GA: Smyth & Helwys, 2006), 512–13.

God" in transliteration and changes the Greek nominative used for direct address to the actual vocative.[107]

While the psalms, including Psalm 22, foreshadow what will happen to Jesus in several ways, it is well to remember that the psalmist himself experienced reversal short of death, not after death, so not all of the psalm is applicable to the story of Jesus, and consequently not all of it is used. Psalm 22 is not an allegory of the death of Jesus out of due season, it is the story of a righteous sufferer in his own age, who foreshadows some of the things that will happen to the quintessential righteous sufferer, Jesus. Jesus above all could be said to fulfill that role since he was not a sinner, and did indeed suffer entirely unjustly, from a human point of view.

Turning now to Hebrews 2:12, in Hebrews 2:10–18 the author is seeking to show Jesus's solidarity with believers in various ways. The quotation from Psalm 22:22 is part of this endeavor. In Hebrews 2:12–13, Psalm 22:22 is juxtaposed with Isaiah 8:17b–18. The author of Hebrews did not have to choose between the MT and the LXX (if he knew Hebrew) because his Greek Jewish Scripture directly corresponds to the MT at this point. The psalm text is used to reinforce the point of Hebrews 2:11 that Christ is not ashamed to call believers his brothers and sisters. These verses were probably picked by the author of Hebrews because they speak of the universal aspect of the proclamation about God the deliverer and how at some juncture all flesh will recognize this God.

It would be hard not to see a prophetic cast to this psalm in light of the gospel story, and also the later proclamation of the good news to gentiles.[108] Attridge is right that the most interesting part "is the use of the Psalms to give voice to Jesus. Ironically, the one who delivers the final word of God to the world speaks in Hebrews only in the words of Scripture, and principally in the words of the Psalms."[109] The Christians who had never met Jesus nor heard his voice, those of the second and third generations, nonetheless are being told that Jesus was speaking to them through a text like Psalm 22:22.

It has often been noted that Paul found himself in the text of Isaiah, or at least he found his calling and mission described there.[110] But one can also make a case for Paul seeing his life as at least analogous to the

107. Craig Blomberg, "Matthew" in Beale, *Commentary on the New Testament Use*, 99.
108. See Guthrie, "Hebrews," 949.
109. Attridge, "Psalms in Hebrews," 212.
110. On which see the relevant passages in Witherington, *Isaiah Old and New*.

righteous sufferer in the Psalms as well. So, for example, when we hear in Psalm 22:21 about being rescued from the lion's mouth, and we find exactly the same language being used of Paul in 2 Timothy 4:17 (where the lion may well be a cipher for the emperor, or perhaps death in the arena), the writer seems to see his life as like that of the sufferer in the Psalms. Philip H. Towner, in a detailed discussion, in fact argues that Paul adopted and adapted Psalm 22 as an "interpretive compass" to explain to himself and Timothy his own situation of abandonment (4:16), suffering, trial, vindication, and proclamation to both believers and the gentile world. He puts it this way:

> Paul's discourse [in 2 Timothy 4] moves from the historical level to the theological level by making various connections with Ps. 21 LXX. The purpose is to interpret his final episode of suffering for the gospel in terms of the tradition of Jesus' passion. By incorporating the psalmist's vision for the Gentiles, this interpretive application of the suffering figure of the psalm to his apostolic ministry actually takes Paul to a place that Jesus would go only through the apostolic mission—to the Gentiles. This is in keeping with the place at which the Pauline story begins and ends and the distinctive role that he plays in relation to God's promise to save the nations. Paul's suffering, the abandonment he experienced, and his impending death all fit the Jesus mold. Yet his experience in no way supercedes that of Jesus; rather it is the complementary outworking of one who has taken to himself the cruciform character and behavior of the Lord.[111]

In a very interesting exposition, Goldingay reflects on what it would mean to see this whole psalm on Jesus's lips. For instance, "in remembering vss. 9–10, Jesus would be recollecting his experience of being the child of Mary. When choosing the mother of the Lord, God had sought out a young woman who was willing to be totally available to God. . . . The psalm would testify to God's making him dependent on her and meeting his needs through her as he grew."[112] But suppose we take this one step further. Suppose Jesus's citing of this psalm on the cross indicates that he *had* thought through and carefully reflected on his life and ministry on the basis of this psalm. He certainly wouldn't have been the first Jew to see himself and his own experiences in the words of a psalm. Suppose in addition Jesus had right in front of him his mother at the foot of the cross as John 19 indicates and he began

---

111. Philip H. Towner, "1–2 Timothy and Titus," in Beale, *Commentary on the New Testament*, 912–13.
112. Goldingay, *Psalms: Volume 1*, 342.

to recite this psalm. Then surely vv. 9–10 would have the resonance for Jesus himself that Goldingay is speaking of. This psalm can of course be seen as the voice of every devout person who suffers unjustly, including Paul, but there is no one that better fits the description than Jesus himself. The many uses of this psalm in the NT suggest that many of the writers of the NT truly believed it was relevant to their situation and concerns, especially their christological concerns.

Tasting the Lord, Breaking No Bones: Psalm 34

Psalm 34 is an alphabet acrostic poem, with basically two line couplets for each letter of the twenty-two letter Hebrew alphabet.[113] Naturally enough, this fact is basically lost in most translations. This psalm begins with an "irregular" prescript which reads quite literally "David's" and then describes the occasion in his life which is thought to prompt this poem.[114] The thing about alphabet acrostics is that they usually try to cover a subject, as we would say, from A to Z, for instance like the more famous example on the torah, Psalm 119 (or cf. Psalm 25). Basically the psalm is about reverencing Yahweh in the midst of a fearful situation as the key to deliverance from danger.[115]

The similarity to the advice we find in Proverbs ("the reverence of God is the beginning of wisdom" and cf. Prov 1:7, 8, 29; 3:1–2; 4:1) has led some to see this as a wisdom psalm.[116] The header refers to the episode in 1 Samuel 21:13 where David deliberately acted abnormally, or in a crazy manner, disguising his good sense. It urges others to use good sense in a crisis or abnormal situation. This is more of a teach-

---

113. As Mays, *Psalms*, 151 notes: "In both [Psalm 25 and Psalm 34] the letter *waw* is omitted and a final line beyond the alphabetic sequence is added to make twenty-two lines."

114. There seems to be some confusion in the text at this point because the header seems to allude to the story in 1 Sam 21:13 which involves a king named Achish, not Abimelech who is a figure in the Pentateuch (Genesis 20 and 26) from Gerar, and probably a Philistine king. But could this be a reference to the son of the famous priest Abiathar who is also called Abimelech (1 Chr 18:16) and did live in the time of David? Probably not, since the reference to David acting like a madman seems to be referring to his rolling around in the dirt and drooling into his beard to save his skin. The name Abimelech in any case means "my father's the king" and seems to refer to several different people in the OT (e.g., the one in Genesis 20 doesn't seem likely to be the same one referred to in Genesis 26). According to Jewish tradition, however, Achish is called Abimelech in honor of the king of Gerar because "Achish, though a heathen, was pious, for which reason he is called Abimelech in the Psalms after the king of Gerar who was also noted for his piety" (Louis Ginzberg, Bible Times and Characters from the Joshua to Esther, vol. 4 of The Legends of the Jews, trans. Henrietta Szold and Paul Radin [Baltimore: Johns Hopkins University Press, 1998], 89), cited by James Nogalski in "Reading David in the Psalter: A Study in Liturgical Hermeneutics," HBT 23 (2001): 173.

115. Goldingay, *Psalms: Volume 1*, 478.

116. Weiser, *Psalms*, 296–97 is right to note that the advice given in this psalm is like the maxims in wisdom literature in that it involves the recasting of personal experiences into generally or usually valid claims.

ing song than a thanksgiving song, and ostensibly provides a testimony to encourage the faithful. The setting or *Sitz im Leben* for the psalm is surely the worship service where one will both praise God and hear wise teaching and words of reassurance and exhortation. Bruggemann and Bellinger suggest that the worshiper went to the temple to pray, and there received a word of encouragement from the priest leading the worship.[117] Notice again how the generic descriptions of the problems and the solutions make the psalm suitable for many applications and many situations. Let us consider the two translations.

MT Psalm 34	LXX Psalm 33
Of David. When he pretended to be insane before Abimelek, who drove him away, and he left. 1 I will extol the Lord at all times; his praise will always be on my lips.	1 Pertaining to David. When he changed his face before Abimelech, and he let him go, and he went away. 2 I will bless the Lord at every opportunity; continually shall his praise be in my mouth.
2 I will glory in the Lord; let the afflicted hear and rejoice.	3 In the Lord my soul shall be commended; let the meek hear and be glad.
3 Glorify the Lord with me; let us exalt his name together. 4 I sought the Lord, and he answered me; he delivered me from all my fears.	4 O magnify the Lord with me, and let us exalt his name together. 5 I sought the Lord, and he hearkened to me, and from all my sojournings he rescued me.
5 Those who look to him are radiant; their faces are never covered with shame.	6 Come to him, and be enlightened, and your faces shall never be put to shame.
6 This poor man called, and the Lord heard him; he saved him out of all his troubles. 7 The angel of the Lord encamps around those who fear him, and he delivers them. 8 Taste and see that the Lord is good; blessed is the one who takes refuge in him. 9 Fear the Lord, you his holy people, for those who fear him lack nothing.	7 This poor one cried, and the Lord listened to him, and from all his afflictions he saved him. 8 An angel of the Lord will encamp around those who fear him and will rescue them. 9 O taste, and see that the Lord is kind; happy the man who hopes in him. 10 O fear the Lord, you his holy ones, because those who fear him have no want.
10 The lions may grow weak and hungry, but those who seek the Lord lack no good thing.	11 The rich became poor and hungry, but those who seek the Lord shall not suffer decrease in any good thing.

117. Brueggemann and Bellinger, *Psalms*, 169.

	Interlude on strings
11 Come, my children, listen to me; I will teach you the fear of the Lord. 12 Whoever of you loves life and desires to see many good days, 13 keep your tongue from evil and your lips from telling lies. 14 Turn from evil and do good; seek peace and pursue it. 15 The eyes of the Lord are on the righteous, and his ears are attentive to their cry; 16 but the face of the Lord is against those who do evil, to blot out their name from the earth. 17 The righteous cry out, and the Lord hears them; he delivers them from all their troubles. 18 The Lord is close to the brokenhearted and saves those who are crushed in spirit. 19 The righteous person may have many troubles, but the Lord delivers him from them all; 20 he protects all his bones, not one of them will be broken. 21 Evil will slay the wicked; the foes of the righteous will be condemned. 22 The Lord will rescue his servants; no one who takes refuge in him will be condemned.	12 Come, O children; hear me; the fear of the Lord I will teach you. 13 What person is he who wants life, coveting to see good days? 14 Stop your tongue from evil and your lips from speaking deceit. 15 Turn away from evil, and do good; seek peace, and pursue it. 16 The Lord's eyes are on the righteous, and his ears are toward their petition. 17 But the Lord's face is against evildoers, to destroy the remembrance of them from earth. 18 The righteous cried, and the Lord listened to them, and from all their afflictions he rescued them. 19 The Lord is near to the brokenhearted, and the humble in spirit he will save. 20 Many are the afflictions of the righteous, and from them all he will rescue them. 21 The Lord will guard all their bones; not one of them will be crushed. 22 The sinners' death is wretched, and those who hate the righteous shall go wrong. 23 The Lord will redeem his slaves' souls, and none of those who hope in him will go wrong.

The psalmist first declares that he will worship and praise Yahweh at all times. The reason for this is not long in coming; he sought help in his vulnerable state from Yahweh and God answered him, delivered him. This is of course a very common theme in the Psalter, especially in the laments, but here the psalmist is instructing others to follow his example, and to expect the same results.

Notice the parallel construction in line 1, where "continually" matches "at all times," and "praise" parallels "will worship." Exuberant worship in which the human spirit exults itself in God is what the psalmist has in mind. But the mentioning of all this has a didactic purpose: so the weak will listen to this testimony and join in the rejoicing. At v. 3 there is more than an implied exhortation, there is an invitation to join with the psalmist in singing Yahweh's praises, exalting his name, by which is meant his nature and actions.

Verses 4-6 tell us the psalmist prayed, and God responded, and not just in an ephemeral way, but rather he rescued the psalmist from the source of all his fears. The Hebrew term מְגוּרוֹתַי (megûrôtay), if we compare other occurrences (Prov 10:24; Isa 66:4) suggests that the psalmist is not just complaining he has been delivered from *feelings* of terror or dread, but the source of the fear. In vv. 5-6 we have both an observation ("if people will look to Yahweh they will shine, their faces will not show shame") and a testimony. The image here is of the shekinah glory of God reflecting off the faces of those who trust him and have been rescued by him. Verse 6 reverts to testimony, the psalmist was in a weak and vulnerable condition and he looked to Yahweh and Yahweh listened and delivered him.

Verses 7-22 seem to go together as a unit, and the changes are rung early on, on the theme of revering Yahweh (vv. 7, 9, 11). Verse 7 likely refers to a frequently mentioned character in the OT, the angel of the Lord (מַלְאַךְ-יְהוָה mal'ak YHWH). Here we are told that this emissary of God surrounds and protects those who fear God (cf. Josh 5:14).[118] The thing about this emissary is that he is mysterious. Is this just another way of talking about God in his imminence? Is this a separate being? Verses 8-9 seem to be parallel lines and in v. 9 we are told it is Yahweh in whom the faithful person shelters.[119] It is true that there was a concept in Hebrew thought that "a man's agent is as himself" and has the same power and authority of the one who sent him. So perhaps "the angel of the Lord" is seen as God's authorized representative, his šaliah. One of the things that the author of Hebrews is later adamant about is that the preexistent Son of God is no mere angel however exalted (see Hebrews 1-2), a memo that some later church fathers seem not to have gotten or understood when they suggested that Jesus = the angel of the Lord in the OT.

Verse 8 is the first clear imperative in the section and is the psalm's most familiar verse, "taste and see that the Lord is good." "'Taste' is used here in the sense of 'find out by experience.'"[120] Quite rightly 1 Peter 2:3 picks up this verse and uses it to talk about the fact that experiencing God deeply, and trusting him completely, leads to the discovery of just how good God is.[121] The repeated call to "fear the Lord"

---

118. See the discussion in Alter, *Book of Psalms*, 118.
119. See Kidner, *Psalms 1-72*, 140.
120. Mays, *Psalms*, 153.

needs to be understood in context. "Fear here has to do with being in awe of the divine or revering or respecting God."[122] This sort of relationship with God is at the opposite end of the spectrum from that described in v. 10, namely those who are apostate are like lions who are starved for real meat, but those who seek help from God are well nourished! "There is no lack for those who revere God" (v.9b).

Verse 11 provides a further exhortation to listen and learn what reverence for Yahweh looks like. The speaker refers to his audience as children. The exhortation is needed because people are always trying to take control and run their own lives. The psalmist is like a parent saying, "if you know what's good for you, then you will. . . ." In this case, if you delight in life and desire to live a long one and see lots of blessings and good things, then reverence for Yahweh and trusting him is the key.

In a sense, this is the same sort of advice one finds the sage in Proverbs 1–9 giving to the "children" or learners in that book as well.[123] But enjoying the good involves abstaining from the bad, so v. 13 insists that one must guard his tongue and avoid speaking deceitfully. "Bad behavior generates bad experience."[124] So one must deliberately and intentionally turn away from the bad and do good, and this also involves seeking one's own well-being and vigorously pursuing it. Dishonesty in speech can lead to dishonesty in relationships, and the initial focus here is on speech. But then too, doing good for others is a key to pursuing well-being for one's self. "In contrast to a piety that would counsel passivity when under duress, waiting patiently for God to *do something,* the editor is quite comfortable having David act on his own behalf without drawing the conclusion that self-help in any way detracts from the power of God to rescue. . . . God acts in and through acts of self-preservation."[125]

Verse 15 tells us that Yahweh's eyes are carefully watching, and watching out for the faithful, and his ears are well attuned to their cries for help. When he sees the faithful in distress or danger he responds (see Ps 33:18–19). Verse 16 tells us the opposite is true when it comes to those who do evil—his face is so set against them he would even blot out their sordid memory from the land.

Now of course, this is poetry, and it is in this same Psalter that we

---

121. See Goldingay, *Psalms: Volume 1,* 481.
122. Brueggemann and Bellinger, *Psalms,* 169.
123. Kidner, *Psalms 1–72,* 140.
124. Goldingay, *Psalms: Volume 1,* 483.
125. Charry, *Psalms 1–50,* 181.

hear the question: Why do the wicked prosper and the righteous suffer? We must remember that any one psalm is only expressing a part of the truth about God and reality. But the urgency of these verses is based on the assumption that the main form of "afterlife" is that if one does good, one lives on in the memory of those who have been blessed by one's good influence and good words and good deeds. By contrast, we are being told that the memory of the wicked, like a bad dream, will be erased or forgotten. In other words, no positive afterlife, no positive legacy to posterity.

Verse 18 stresses the compassion of Yahweh: he is near to the broken-hearted and reaches out to deliver those whose spirit is crushed. This is talking about depression and discouragement not some kind of positive spiritual brokenness.[126] Verse 19 is quite candid in admitting that bad things do frequently happen to the faithful, but "Yahweh will rescue them from them all" reassures the psalmist. By contrast, a bad experience can finish off the faithless, and in fact those who oppose the faithful may expect punishment down the road (v. 21). God's protection of the faithful is "in detail"; v. 20 says he guards all the faithful person's bones so that not one is broken (on which see below on the application to Christ). Not only so, but as v. 22 says for those who rely on God, they need not fear facing punishment in the future.

This psalm is quite frank, and sobering, about the fact that the faithful will face many trials and tribulations in life, including from their enemies as well as natural difficulties of health and the like. There will even be times when one is inwardly crushed, despondent, in despair, depressed. But what is also said is that God is on red alert and closely watching over the life of the faithful, and ready to intervene and rescue, and that the psalmist himself is not just theorizing, but has experienced such a rescue by God.[127] "The true happiness of a godly life consists in the nearness of God and in the living experience of his help and not in being spared suffering and affliction."[128]

This psalm doesn't try to answer why bad things happen to God's people, it admits that they do, but it is adamant that this does not negate the reality of God, or the need to continually worship God, or the fact that God intervenes and helps the weak, the terrorized, those in danger and difficulty. The mystery of why life involves both good and bad, even for the faithful, when there is a singular almighty God,

---

126. See Goldingay, *Psalms: Volume 1*, 484.
127. Brueggemann and Bellinger, *Psalms*, 171.
128. Weiser, *Psalms*, 299.

is not explained, it is simply accepted. The psalmist pushes neither the inscrutable divine sovereignty button, nor the "everyone has free will button," he simply admits actions have moral consequences, and if one wants to live a good life with less internal turmoil, true worship and good behavior are a key, while at the same time stressing that Yahweh does intervene and help the faithful.

As Craigie once put it: "The fear of the Lord . . . may mend the broken heart, but it does not prevent the heart from being broken; it may restore the spiritually crushed, but it does not crush the forces that may create oppression. The psalm, if fully grasped, dispels the naiveté of that faith which does not contain within it the strength to stand against the onslaught of evil."[129]

Psalm 34:21 is likely alluded to in John 19:36. That text is clearly closer to Psalm 34:21 than it is to Exodus 12:10, 46 or Numbers 9:12, which thematically also do not really fit, for they are about the eating of the Passover lamb and not breaking its bones, whereas the psalm text is about human bones, and again John's citation is verbally closer to the psalm text.[130] For example, John 19:36 has exactly the same verbal form συντριβήσεται as Psalm 34:20 LXX.[131] In fact, Jewish beliefs about the resurrection may be in play here as well, because, on the basis of Ezekiel 37:1–14 the preservation of Jesus's bones could be seen as a pledge of his resurrection.[132]

It is true to say that the use of the psalm here is an attempt to provide further evidence that Jesus is the messiah, and it was all along part of God's plan that he die on the cross, and the psalm especially promotes the Davidic connection because it is so clearly a Davidic psalm.

129. Craigie and Tate, Psalms 1–50, 282.
130. See, rightly, Marianne Meye Thompson, "'They Bear Witness to Me': The Psalms in the Passion Narrative of the Gospel of John," in The Word Leaps the Gap: Essays on Scripture and Theology in Honor of Richard B. Hays, ed. J. Ross Wagner, C. Kavin Rowe, and A. Katherine Grieb (Grand Rapids: Eerdmans, 2008), 278–79.
131. There is a further problem with thinking the evangelist has in mind those texts from the Pentateuch. If you read them closely they are about what to do with the bones once the Passover has been eaten. But in the Johannine text Jesus dies on the day of preparation for the Passover and for the Sabbath (19:31), not on Passover. See however Andreas J. Köstenberger, "John" in Beale, Commentary on the New Testament Use, 503 for the suggestion that all three texts, the two from the Pentateuch and the one from the Psalms, stand in the background here.
132. See the discussion in Margaret Daly-Denton, "The Psalms in John's Gospel" in Moyise, Psalms in the New Testament, 135–36. It is not clear to me that Jubilees 49:13 helps make the case for associating the Pentateuch texts with Psalm 34 and hence with the righteous sufferer. That text again has to do with not breaking the bones of the Passover lamb. The part of the verse that has muddied the waters reads: "for of the children of Israel no bone shall be crushed," but this follows the instructions about the animal, and is in turn followed by more instructions about the animal. It would surely be better to read that phrase to mean "for by means of the children of Israel no bones of the Passover lamb should be crushed."

Jesus is not like just any righteous sufferer. He is like a specific one, David.[133] Charry has some helpful reflections at this point. She points out that Jesus's suffering did not shame him nor did it morally degrade him. It degraded his tormentors. Suffering in itself is not shameful, indeed it may even be a badge of righteousness in a fallen and wicked world full of abuse and violence. So despite the fact that many ancients saw crucifixion as the most shameful way to die, in the divine calculus and in the case of Jesus, this was not so. "Shame accrues to the perpetrators of violence, not to its victims . . . a victim can be physically injured but not morally harmed." This is in part because while we cannot control all our circumstances to prevent all suffering, "moral dignity is something over which one has control, and Ps. 34 calls us to guard it well. No one can take it away or damage it; only we can do that."[134]

The most extensive OT quotation, of many quotations in 1 Peter is the quoting of Psalm 34:13-17 in 1 Peter 3:10-12. The Greek text of 1 Peter 3:10-12 closely follows the LXX, which in turn is almost a verbatim rendering of the Hebrew, except that in v. 5b the Hebrew word is taken not to be the word for "my fears" but rather the word for "my sojourning" or "place of residence."[135] There are however a few variations from the LXX in the quoted passage in 1 Peter 3. In particular, there is: (1) the omission of the phrase "what person is he," which as Sue Woan suggests is probably necessary for the sake of the flow of the argument using the quoted passage, and the addition of "for" in 1 Peter 3:10 helps the transition back from the quotation to the argument in the letter; (2) the question "which of you desires life?" has been altered to "those who desire life" also in 1 Peter 3:10; (3) the second-person imperatives in the psalm have been altered into third-person; (4) possibly Psalm 34:17b is omitted since the author is addressing Christians, and so he need not include warnings about the fate of the wicked.[136] Peter does not try to follow the alphabet acrostic feature of the original, but his quotation does retain some poetic effects, some assonance and rhythm.

It has been suggested that in fact 1 Peter is something of a meditation on Psalm 34 and the plight and rescue of the righteous sufferer.

---

133. See the discussion in Köstenberger, "John," 503.
134. Charry, *Psalms 1-50*, 185.
135. On this see Lars O. Eriksson, *"Come Children, Listen to Me!" Psalm 34 in the Hebrew Bible and in Early Christian Writings*, ConBOT 32 (Stockholm: Almquist & Wiksell, 1991), 99.
136. See the discussion by Sue Woan, "The Psalms in 1 Peter" in Moyise, *Psalms in the New Testament*, 220.

For example, Woan points to 1 Peter 2:1 "rid yourselves, therefore of all malice and all guile" could be alluding to Psalm 34:14 LXX where the same words are used for malice and guile and there is a thematic continuity as well; this is followed almost immediately by 1 Peter 2:3 where we have a quite clear use of Psalm 34:9 in the form of "if indeed you have tasted that the Lord is good." The Lord, here of course refers to Christ, and this is taken as obvious; it is not argued for. Woan argues that the quote in 1 Peter 3:10–12 both looks back to the allusions just mentioned, summarizing it and introducing what follows. She is able to demonstrate the clear verbal links between 3:10–12 and what comes before and after, for example, the words for evil, righteousness, and doing good found in 3:10–12 recur in 3:13–17. Even phrases like "those who desire life and to see good days" (Psalm 34:10) could be said to prepare for the discussion in 1 Peter 4:7–13, which speaks of the eschatological end of days, and 1 Peter 5:1–6 which focuses on the "good days" coming for the faithful.[137] As it turns out it was not just the tale of the righteous sufferer in Isaiah 53 that led Peter to reflect on that subject.[138]

There are a variety of suggested allusions to Psalm 34 in the NA28 index to the Greek NT, some more convincing than others. For example, is Matthew 5:3 "blessed are the poor in spirit" really alluding to the broken-hearted and crushed in spirit in Psalm 34:18? Or is the bare mention of Joseph being rescued from all his afflictions in Acts 7:10 really an allusion to Psalm 34:19 which speaks in a very general way of the afflictions of the righteous and how the Lord rescues the righteous from them all? But this is a common notion in the Psalms, as elsewhere in the OT. The taming of the tongue is a common theme in wisdom literature, and James gives several examples of this theme (Jas 1:26; 3:3–12) a theme we also find in Psalm 34:13, which also warns to keep one's tongue from evil and one's lips from deceit. The theme is the same, but James is working out a horse bridle and bit metaphor that we don't find in Psalm 34, and there are no close verbal parallels between the two texts.

More plausible is the suggestion that Psalm 34:2–3 provides some of the language for the beginning of the Magnificat in Luke 1:46, "my soul magnifies the Lord, and my spirit rejoices in God my savior." Psalm 34:7 speaks of the angel of the Lord surrounding and delivering the faithful,

137. See ibid., 223–25.
138. For a more extensive list of possible echoes of Psalm 34 in 1 Peter see D. A. Carson, "1 Peter," in Beale, *Commentary on the New Testament Use*, 1037.

and in view of the copious use of the Psalms already in Hebrews 1, it is just possible that the author had this verse in mind when he speaks of angels in Hebrews 1:14 as being spirits in the divine service, sent to serve those who are to inherit salvation. Possible allusions and echoes have to be given very close scrutiny in regard to plausibility, for sometimes when one starts looking for such things, parallelomania takes over. Bearing that caution in mind, we will turn in the final section in this chapter to other possible allusions and echoes in the NT to the Psalms in the first book of the Psalter, and even perhaps a citation or two, that bear the imprint of some portion of the first book of the Psalter.

The Lexicon of Faith: The Broader Use of Psalms 1–41

Through prayer, and singing, through public reading out loud, teaching, and memorization, the language of the Psalms gradually became the language of many early Jews, which they used to express their own thoughts and feelings. Because the Psalms are poetry, and are often more generic and universal in character, they lent themselves quite naturally to expressing common human experiences of the pious Jew of the NT era, including Jesus himself. This kind of use of the Psalms was apparently common and was not so much a kind of exposition of the OT text as an appropriation of the language of the Psalms to describe a similar thought, feeling, or experience of the Jewish speaker. Devout early Jews spoke a kind of "biblese" and the OT, particularly texts like the Psalms or Isaiah, provided the vocabulary, the lexicon for self-expression, or articulation about current events. In this section of this chapter we are going to illustrate this point through the use of various texts that briefly quote or paraphrase or allude to the Psalms found in Psalms 1–41.

Let us start by taking Acts 24:5 which the NA28 critical apparatus suggests echoes in some way Psalm 1:1. In the latter text we have the threefold characterization of a person to avoid: the wicked, the sinner, the scoffer. In Acts 24:5 Paul is characterized as a pestilent fellow, an agitator, a ringleader. This is a sapiential, and rhetorically apt way of stigmatizing a person in both cases, but the terminology differs. Clearly this is not a case of quoting or paraphrasing or even alluding to Psalm 1, but an example perhaps of how the threefold cadence and characterization could have affected the speech material we find in Acts 24:5. Tertullus after all is a rhetor, but one may doubt he is saturated in the language of the Psalms, in which case this diction may reflect Luke's knowledge of the LXX (where the NETS translation renders it "the impious, the sinner, the pestiferous"). Again the characterization of Paul has to do with his actions stirring up, even organizing trouble, whereas the Psalm is about the character of a wicked individual.

Or again NA28 suggests a comparison of Psalm 1:5 to Matthew 13:49, but what these two texts share is simply the idea that the wicked will one day be judged. Jesus is not quoting the psalm, he is simply using an idea also found in the psalm. More promising is the comparison of Psalm 4:4 with Ephesians 4:26; the latter reads "be angry but do not sin; do not let the sun go down on your anger" whereas the former text says, "When you are angry, do not sin; ponder it on your beds, and be silent." Here the Pauline text is closer to the LXX, for the MT has "tremble and do not sin." This I would say does qualify as an allusion to the psalm, and I agree that the better rendering of Ephesians 4:26 is "when you are angry . . ." because Paul is not encouraging anger, he is trying to contain it. But Paul is not simply reciting the psalm, he is providing pastoral advice that goes beyond pondering things on one's bed. He seems to suggest that one should resolve a difference before the day is over. The influence of the psalm is clear, but Paul is neither merely quoting nor expounding the psalm. He is adopting and adapting the language for his own purposes.

Romans 3:13 is in the midst of a catena of citations by Paul, and Psalm 5:9 does indeed lie in the background here. It reads "For there is no truth in their mouths, their hearts are destructive, their throats an open grave," but the LXX is a little different, "Because there is no truth in their mouth, their heart is vain; their throat is an opened grave; with their tongues they would practice deceit." Paul has "their throats are open graves, they use their tongues to deceive" which is clearly closer to the final phrases in the LXX both in the order and the wording of the clauses.

As Romans 3:10 indicates, Paul is citing, and he knows he is, probably from memory. The principle of association between all these conglomerated texts is they all characterize the wicked in similar ways. The assumption is that human beings are just as sinful in Paul's day as in the psalmist's and so the descriptions of the wicked are just as apt in both cases. This is what may be called an ethical appropriation of the language of the Psalter, not a christological or eschatological one.[139] Paul is making clear that all, both Jews and gentiles, are consigned under sin, whereas the psalmist is talking about his own enemies. However, a careful reading of the last half of Psalm 5 makes clear that the psalmist is probably also referring to Jews who have rebelled against God. Paul is using the rhetorical technique of "accumulation," saying the same thing in slightly different ways using different scriptural texts to make crystal clear "there is none righteous, no not one." We might call this "overkill."

In Matthew 7:23 // Luke 13:27 we have a verbally close allusion to Psalm 6:8, "depart from me all you evil doers." In the Synoptic context the saying is eschatological in character and voiced by Jesus, speaking of those who will not be saved. In the psalm, the saying is found on the lips of the psalmist, and is his directive to those who are bothering him and causing him pain in the present. He expresses trust that God will deal with them whereas the Synoptic saying indicates that "on that eschatological day" Jesus will deal with them. One thing we do see quite often in the psalm references in the NT is the transfer of a divine role to Jesus whether in salvation or judgment. The saying in the Synoptic is closer to the MT form of the psalm, for the LXX speaks of workers of lawlessness, not evil-doers.

In Psalm 9:8 we have the statement that Yahweh will judge the world in righteousness, and we may compare the same basic idea in Acts 17:31 and Revelation 19:11, but again the action is predicated of Christ in the Acts text and of the rider on the white horse in Revelation 19, which is to say in both cases it is predicated of Christ (Acts 17 even speaks of the man God has appointed to judge the world in righteousness). Both texts are closer to the LXX of the psalm, because the Hebrew could be rendered "rules the world in righteousness," whereas the LXX speaks of "judging," as do the NT references. Again we have a case of transference of the divine activity from Yahweh to Christ.

In Matthew 16:18 we have a reference to the gates of Hades, the land of the dead, which probably echoes Psalm 9:13b, which speaks of the gates of death. Here we are dealing with the appropriation of a theological idea, rather than a quoting of the psalm in question. Nor is the larger psalm context alluded to in the context of Matthew 16:18 either. The Psalms provided a ready font for both theological and ethical ideas used by early Jews, including Jewish Christians.

Psalm 10:7 provides another item in Paul's catena of quotations in Romans 3:13–14. Paul renders the text "their mouths are full of cursing

---

139. See the fine study by Wenham, *Psalms as Torah*, 139–66 on what the Psalter says about virtues and vices.

and bitterness" which seems mostly closest to the MT "their mouths are filled with cursing and deceit and oppression" rather than the LXX, which has the singular "his mouth."

We find the notion of a forever reign of God in Psalm 10:16, and we may compare this to the famous verse in Revelation 11:15. "the kingdom of the world has become the kingdom of our Lord and of his Messiah, and he will reign forever and ever." Again this is not a citation, and what we have here is addition rather than substitution. In the psalm God being king forever is contrasted with the nations, which will perish from his land. In Revelation the nations, indeed all the world including the Holy Land, are God's and Christ's domain and they will reign over it together.

In Psalm 11:4 we find the notion that God's throne is in heaven, and to this we may compare both Matthew 5:34 and Revelation 4:2. In Matthew 5:34 Jesus says that heaven *is* the throne of God, whereas in Revelation 4:2 John sees a throne in heaven with one seated on it, which is clearly closer to the idea in the psalm. Again the Psalms provide not merely a lexicon, but a font of ideas for the NT writers to use in various ways without feeling the need to quote or directly allude to the psalm in question. In such cases we are not really dealing with metalepsis, the idea that the larger context of the quoted OT text is assumed to be known by the audience, but not mentioned.

Another use of the theological ideas in a psalm can be found if one compares Psalm 11:6, "on the wicked he will reign coals of fire and sulphur," to Revelation 14:10 which says of those who worship the beast that they will be "tormented with fire and sulphur in the presence of the holy angels." The psalmist is referring to a temporal judgment, whereas John may be referring to a final judgment, since he says the torment goes on forever.

Psalm 14:1–7 provides an interesting case study in how similar sounding ideas turn out to be somewhat different when the context is considered. Psalm 14 is a wisdom psalm that uses the stock character of the "fool," in this case the fool who says in his heart there is no God, to contrast such people who have all gone astray, with the righteous and the pious poor for whom God is their refuge. Here the key repeated phrase is "there is no one who does good" (vv. 1 and 3, which is amplified in the latter verse by the phrase "no not one"). To this we may compare Paul's first quote in his catena of references that follows the Scripture citation formula in Romans 3:10, "there is no one who is righteous, not even one, there is no one who has understanding," and by *no one* Paul doesn't just mean all the fools in the world, he means no Jew or gentile, all humans have sinned and gone astray. Even with the differences noted, Paul's citation is closer to the MT than to the LXX of the psalm verses in question. The psalmist thinks there are at least a few righteous and pious ones whom God protects from the majority of those who neither understand nor believe in nor seek God. Not so Paul. Yet it is clear that Psalm 14 provides a rhetorical resource, particularly the telling phrase "there are none . . . no not one," but also the lament about no understanding of God. Has Paul just tailored the psalm to suit his own purposes?[140]

Psalm 16:8–11 comes up for brief mention in a citation by Peter in Acts 2:25–28, and Peter indicates that David is describing the experience of Christ. As Marshall says, the Acts text is following the LXX here, but omitting the last line of the psalm "pleasures at your right hand forever."[141] But who is the "Lord" in this psalm, originally, and in the interpretation of Peter? While the LXX version would allow a rendering that indicates someone is raised from the dead, can the MT also be read that way, or should we see it as simply referring to rescue from premature death? Further, what exactly is Peter trying to prove with this citation? Is he trying to provide a proof text for the resurrection of Jesus, or is he trying to demonstrate that Christ is truly the Jewish messiah of whom David speaks?

Several things can be said: (1) clearly it is assumed by Peter (or Luke) that David is the author of the psalm and is speaking about Jesus. This much is evident from v. 25a; (2) Peter in v. 29 makes quite clear that the psalm is not speaking of David himself and his future, because David died, was buried, and is still buried in Jerusalem when Peter is speaking; (3) in the original Hebrew psalm there is no question but that "Lord" refers to Yahweh throughout Psalm 16, and the psalm is about giving help to the person who sends up the distress signal, the psalmist, who probably refers to his being rescued from premature death; (4) the LXX could at least be rendered "you will not abandon my soul unto Hades" (εἰς ᾅδην), which could be interpreted to refer to either not leaving someone in Hades, or preventing one from going there. While it is true enough that Peter would likely have been quoting the Hebrew text if the audience was just the Aramaic-speaking disciples, *that is not the audience here.* Peter is speaking to a mixed audience, including Greek speakers, and the default citing form for such a mixed audience would

---

140. See the discussion in Wagner, *Heralds*, 287–88, 349–50.
141. Marshall, "Acts," 537.

be Greek; (5) in terms of the original song itself, "my inner being" and "me" are surely parallel in vv. 9–10, but again in the LXX "my inner being" might refer to one person "and your holy one" could possibly be someone else.

So here is how Peter seems to read Psalm 16, the Lord = the messiah, as does "my holy one." David is speaking of his confidence that the Lord will support him in his distress and therefore his heart is glad and he will live in hope (of the resurrection). Furthermore, God will not let his messiah see corruption at all, or leave him in Hades even for a short period of time. The application in Acts 2:31 makes clear Peter thinks the psalm refers to the resurrection of the messiah who did not decay in the grave as, self-evidently, David has done since he is still in his grave in Jerusalem. Once again we see the christological transfer of things previously said of Yahweh now being said of Jesus: he is the Lord in this psalm according to Peter.[142] Paul is said to use one verse of this same psalm to make the same point at Acts 13:35 about Christ avoiding corruption.[143]

The use of Psalm 19 is brief and sprinkled throughout the non-Gospel portions of the NT from Romans to Revelation. While we may find the influence of Psalm 19:1–2 in Romans 1:20 where Paul says that we can know God exists and is powerful by examining the things he has made, his creation, the psalmist is less prosaic and talks of creation pouring forth speech about God's glory and handiwork. There is a connection but only at the conceptual level. Romans 10:18 involves a brief paraphrase of Psalm 19: 4, "yet their voice goes out throughout all the earth, and their words to the end of the world." As Keesmaat has pointed out, Paul's use of the psalm here in Romans 10 is rather different than the bare allusion in Romans 1, for here the message that has gone out and been heard is the message not of God's existence but of the good news about Jesus Christ.[144] Furthermore, while the psalm is talking about a message to all humankind, Paul is talking about a message that Jews have heard, and largely rejected, while many gentiles have accepted it. So ironically the Jews are proving more disobedient to the "message" than the gentiles in Paul's experience. Once again it needs to be said that this quotation, which is part of a catena, involves

---

142. See the helpful discussion by Doble, "Psalms in Luke-Act," 92–97, and also Marshall, "Acts," 536–39.
143. On the detailed exegesis, and Luke's tendency to "Septuagintalize" his source material including his narrative material see Witherington, *Acts of the Apostles*, 142–45.
144. Keesmaat, "Psalms in Romans and Galatians," 153.

a rhetorical use of the psalm, not really an exegesis per se of its meaning.

Perhaps one of the biggest surprises along the way is how seldom the ever-popular Psalm 23 comes up in the NT. In fact, it's opening phrases in vv. 1 and 2b are paraphrased in Revelation 7:17 and applied to Jesus only here in the NT. "for the Lamb at the center of the throne will be their shepherd and he will guide them to springs of the water of life." Apart from this, the psalm comes up for no quotes or paraphrases at all in the NT. Yes, the general idea can be said to be lurking in the background in the discussion of Jesus as the Good Shepherd (whereas Yahweh is the shepherd in Psalm 23) to some degree in John 10, but even there Psalm 23 is not quoted.

A further surprise comes in the case of Psalm 24. Whereas one might at least expect the second half of Psalm 24 to come up for some comment or use in the NT since it is an entrance liturgy involving a king coming to town, especially with the use of the title "king of glory"; in fact this falls into the category of something of a missed opportunity.[145] In 1 Corinthians 10:26 we do have a brief citation or allusion from the first half of the psalm, from the very first verse, "the earth is the Lord's and the fullness thereof," which Paul sees as the basis for the conclusion that one should be able to eat whatever one wants. The LXX follows the MT and Paul follows it exactly.[146] Again, this is not exegesis of the psalm, but the idea in the psalm is taken to be a support or basis for the conclusion Paul wants to draw. H. H. Dake Williams suggests that Paul uses the psalm to extend his argument.[147] There is the added idea that the food should be received with thanksgiving. Second Peter 3:5 draws on the concept found in Psalm 24:2 that God founded the earth on the seas and established it on the rivers, but with a variation suggesting that the earth was formed out of water and by means of water. The connection is at the level of ideas.

In Psalm 27:12 we have "false witnesses have risen up against me, and they are breathing out violence," which may have affected the way

---

145. It is true that 1 Thess 4:16–17 draws on the concept of the return of a king to his city and the greeting committee going out to meet him, but there are not even any clear echoes of Psalm 24 in this Pauline text.

146. Roy E Ciampa and Brian Rosner, "1 Corinthians," in Beale, *Commentary on the New Testament Use*, 730.

147. H. H. Drake Williams III, "The Psalms in 1 and 2 Corinthians," in Moyise, *Psalms in the New Testament*, 167–69. He is right that Paul is at least implicitly indicating that since the earth and its food belong to God, that one needs to obey God's will when it comes to others that one might eat with, indeed obey God in all one's conduct. It is interesting that in later rabbinic literature Ps 24:1 seems to have been used to thank God for the food at meals (b. Ber. 35a; b. Šabb. 119a).

Mark has framed his narrative at Mark 14:56, which reads "for many give testimony against him," but there is no citation or direct allusion here. Matthew 27:59 however brings to bear two of the ideas in that psalm verse, namely both the false testimony and desire to do violence against the person in question. The narrative is not created out of the psalm, but the psalm provides ideas and vocabulary for telling the story of Jesus, in this case the story of his passion. At Psalm 29:3 we find the phrase God of glory, which is used at Acts 7:2 (cf. Eph 1:17, "father of glory"). The psalms provide these speakers or writers with a theological vocabulary. It also provides Jesus with his last saying before he passed away according to Luke. Psalm 31:5 reads "into your hand I commit my spirit, you have redeemed me, O Lord, faithful God." Luke 23:46 has "Father into your hands I commend my spirit." As David W. Pao and Eckhardt J. Schnabel suggest, Jesus's use of this verse intimates that he believes God will protect him in death and his life will continue.[148] Along the same lines is the conclusions of *Dr. Eliyahu (Eli) Lizorkin-Eyzenberg who argues that the Hebrew verb here means something more like "deposit" rather than merely "commit/commend," and that the implication is that he expects to get his spirit back, that is, he doesn't see his death as the end of his story.*[149]

Psalm 32:1–2 reads "Happy are those whose transgression is forgiven, whose sin is covered. Happy are those to whom God imputed no iniquity" and it is cited in Romans 4:7.[150] Paul follows the LXX here very closely, shifting the singulars to plurals as does the LXX with the Hebrew text.[151] There is a good reason for this: to make the universality of sin and the universal possibility of forgiveness clear. It is interesting however, as Seifrid points out, that while the psalm is very concerned with confession of sins (v. 5), Paul makes no mention of it here.[152]

At Psalm 32:5 we hear about confession of sin, and forgiveness of the guilt of sin. At the level of ideas, 1 John 1:9 is possibly drawing on this verse for it reads "if we confess our sins, he who is faithful and just will forgive us our sin and cleanse us of all unrighteousness" according to some reckonings. But since the idea of confession, forgiveness of sin, cleansing of guilt is a very prevalent idea in the OT and in early Jewish thinking this is probably overpressing things.

---

148. David W. Pao and Eckhardt J. Schnabel, "Luke," in Beale, *Commentary on the New Testament Use*, 399.
149. This comes from the emails he sends out to lots of folks on the Israel Study Center mailing list, and was sent in July 2016.
150. See Keesmaat, "Psalms in Romans and Galatians," 148.
151. Seifrid, "Romans," 624.
152. Ibid.

More convincing is the suggestion that James 3:3 is drawing on Psalm 32:9, which speaks of bit and bridle to curb the temper of a horse or mule, but James puts the metaphor to different use. He says the bit and bridle are meant to make a horse obey the rider, and it is used to control the whole body. He is drawing an analogy in order to talk about taming the tongue.

The use of Psalm 33 in the NT provides us with another good example of how much one misses if one just concentrates on quotations or clear allusions of the OT in the NT. One also misses just how widespread the influence of the language and ideas of the psalms are in the NT. Focusing on Psalm 33, we have echoes or language usage from this psalm in Luke, John, 1 Corinthians, 2 Corinthians, 2 Thessalonians, Hebrews, and Revelation. In other words, at least five of the writers of the NT reflect a knowledge of and use of the psalms at the most elementary level, probably even at an unconscious level. The psalms have affected their very vocabulary and the way they frame their discourse or narrative. So, for example, working through the psalm in order, Psalm 33:3, which calls for the singing of a new song, is picked up in Revelation 14:3 where harpists in heaven are playing and singing "a new song" which John overhears. It cannot be an accident that Psalm 33:2 mentions the playing of a harp or stringed instrument, and we find this in Revelation 14:2–3. The psalm has funded the imagination of John in the way he will describe his vision. He is not saying "this is a fulfillment of that," though perhaps he is implying this is one sort of example of that.

The idea of God creating things by speaking a word, or alternately destroying things by "the breath of his mouth" comes up. So, for example, Psalm 33:6 says the heavens were made by God's word (so also v. 9) and the hosts of heaven by the breath of his mouth. John 1:3 indicates that all things came into being through "the Word," which here refers to the preexistent Son of God. Hebrews 11:3 says that the worlds were "prepared" by the word of God. At the other end of the spectrum is 2 Thessalonians 2:8 which tells us that the returning Christ will destroy the lawless one by the breath of his mouth.[153]

The notion that God has a plan or counsel for humankind is a common one in the OT and we find it at Psalm 33:10–11. Luke 7:30 even suggests God has a purpose and plan for the Pharisees and their legal

---

153. First Corinthians 1:19 seems primarily to be a partial quote of Isa 29:10, however it is also close at the level of ideas to Ps 33:10, "the Lord brings the counsel of the nations to nothing, he frustrates the plans of the peoples."

experts, but their behavior toward Jesus was frustrating that purpose or plan. This is the opposite of Psalm 33:10 where it says God frustrates human plans, but Luke 7:30 says humans can frustrate God's plans for their lives. Finally, 2 Corinthians 1:10 speaks of Paul's being rescued from deadly peril, an idea frequent in the crisis psalms, so there is no need to think that this is particularly echoing Psalm 33:19, which speaks of God delivering persons from death.

Psalm 35:9 reads "then my soul shall rejoice in the Lord, exulting in his deliverance," which is partially echoed in the opening line of the Magnificat, "my soul magnifies the Lord, and my spirit rejoices in God my savior" (Luke 1:46–47). While John 15:25 says that the partial quotation is from "the Law" and reads, "it was to fulfill the word that is written in their Law, 'They hated me without a cause,'" this is probably an allusion to Psalm 35:19, "do not let my treacherous enemies rejoice over me, or those who hate me without a cause wink the eye." Law then would be used in the broad sense of all of torah. While John 20:28 has often been seen as an echo of the claims of the Emperor Domitian (*deus et dominus noster*), we do find the phrase "my God and my Lord" in Psalm 35:23 followed by "O Lord, my God" in the following verse.

Psalm 36:1, "there is no fear of God before their eyes," comes up for brief citation in Romans 3:18 as part of the larger catena of quotes by Paul. The metaphor of God being like a giant bird under whose wings all people can take refuge is found in Psalm 36:7 and is applied by Jesus to himself in regard to Jerusalem in Matthew 23:37 // Luke 13:34, "How often have I desired to gather your children together as a hen gathers her brood under her wings, and you were not willing." This is not a citation or really an allusion, it is simply the transferred application of a metaphor used of Yahweh in the psalm, now applied to Jesus.

The concept of seeking God first and getting blessings thereafter as a result comes into play in Psalm 37:3–4, "Trust in the Lord and do good; so you will live in the land, and enjoy security. Take delight in the Lord, and he will give you the desires of your heart." Something similar is being said, without quoting or alluding to these verses directly when Jesus says "seek first the Kingdom of God and its righteousness, and all these things will be given to you as well" (Matt 6:33), with "all these things" being defined as the basic necessities of life: food, clothing, and shelter mentioned in the previous verses in Matthew 6. There are various echoes of the psalms in the Sermon on the Mount, and another one is found in the beatitude in Matthew 5:5 which assures the audience that "blessed are the meek, for they shall inherit the earth." This is a partial quote of Psalm 37:11 "but the meek shall inherit the land, and delight in abundant prosperity." The LXX here simply has "the meek will inherit land/earth" as its reading of the Hebrew. The Hebrew probably has "the holy land" in mind. If so, Jesus's vision was broader.

Psalm 38:11 reads "my friends and companions stand aloof from my affliction, and my neighbors stand far off." Has this influenced Luke's language at Luke 23:49, "but all his acquaintances, including the women who had followed him from Galilee, stood at a distance watching these things." Here there seems to be more of a connection because Psalm 38 is a Davidic psalm about the speaker enduring extreme suffering, which is of course analogous to what was happening to Jesus at this juncture in the Lukan text. The psalm of course is in the first person, the sufferer is speaking, whereas Luke is narrating the passion in his text. What is especially intriguing is that Luke's verbiage is closer to the MT here than to the LXX, which reads, "My friends and my fellows approached opposite me and stood, and my next of kin stood far off." Is Luke simply remembering a scriptural phrase and applying it to an analogous circumstance? This is possible, but it is also possible that Luke had meditated on laments like that found in Psalm 38, and thought it apt language in general to describe the experience and circumstances of Christ and his followers as he hung on the cross.

The index of NA28 suggests a connection between Psalm 39:3, "my heart became hot within me" and Luke 24:32, "did not our hearts burn within us," but if so, it is purely a matter of similar language, not an adoption of the ideas in Psalm 39, where the context is a person becoming angry when he is goaded by the wicked but trying to keep his mouth shut, something at the opposite end of the spectrum from what the "heart-warming" experience is said to entail in Luke 24.

Sometimes it is impressive just to take stock of how many different NT writers draw on the Psalms, either quoting, alluding to, echoing, or using the diction and imagery and ideas of the Psalms in one way or another. Take for example Psalm 40 (39 in the LXX). We find evidence of the influence of this psalm in Revelation, Ephesians, and Hebrews, all by different authors, and all using this psalm in differing ways. For example, in Ephesians 5:2 there is the use of the phrase "offering and sacrifice to God," which may echo Psalm 40:6, which says that God does not desire sacrifice and offering of animals. But if there is a connection, it is surely an ironic one, as in Ephesians 5:2 we hear about the sacrifice, a human sacrifice, that was acceptable to God and part of his plan, the sacrifice of his Son. The use of Psalm 40 is much more clear in Hebrews 10:5–7, which quotes Psalm 40:6–8 and which is then explained christologically in Hebrews 10:8–10. It appears clear that the author of Hebrews is using some form of the LXX text that reads:

> 7 "Sacrifice and offering you did not want,
> but ears you fashioned for me
> [some Greek MSS read "a body you fashioned for me"]
> Whole burnt offering and one for sin you did not request.
> 8 Then I said, "Look, I have come;
> in a scroll of a book it is written of me.
> 9 To do your will, O my God, I desired—
> and your law, within my belly."

The author of Hebrews of course assumes Christ is actually the speaker of this psalm, and he follows the reading which has "a body you fashioned for me" because he will go on to stress that believers are sanctified through the offering by God of Christ's body in sacrifice, once for all. The author of Hebrews also uses this quotation to support his view that Christ abolishes the Mosaic sacrifices, supplanting them with a once-for-all sacrifice in the person of himself. Christ knew the animal sacrifices were not going to effectively deal with the sin problem, and so he comes in person to do God's perfect will. The author assumes as well that Christ himself believed that psalms like Psalm 40 are examples of the fact that "in the scroll of a book it is written of me." Not only does Christ speak in the psalm, the psalm speaks of him.

One of the interesting aspects about Martin Karrer's discussion of Hebrews and the use of the LXX, is that he shows that when our author uses a citation formula, he is less apt to take poetic license and alter the text than when he is simply alluding to the OT text.[154] Our author uses the Psalms more than any other scriptural source in his sermon (the Psalms some fourteen times, and the Pentateuch some thirteen times, with the prophets used far less). Here we see a procedure just the opposite of Philo, who was singularly fixed on expositing the Pentateuch according to his Hellenistic and allegorical methods. Here, "the Law is quoted after Psalms and . . . by so using the Psalms, the author of Hebrews turns upside down the normal assessment of Scripture, according to which the Law would determine exegesis."[155]

This is a clue not to be missed in our study of the use of the OT in the NT. One of the main reasons for the impressive dependence on Isaiah and the Psalms in

---

154. Martin Karrer, "Epistle to the Hebrews and the Septuagint," in Kraus, *Septuagint Research*, 335–53.
155. Ibid., 338.

the creation of various NT books is because they could most easily be read in christological and eschatological ways. To find OT clues about and foreshadowing of Jesus, one needed to start with the Psalms and Isaiah, and bring in other material, including material from the Pentateuch (especially Deuteronomy) for support.

There is probably a further reason as well: various NT writers such as the author of Hebrews and Paul did not think that Christians were under the Mosaic covenant any longer. What would be the point in focusing on the law, when, as the author of Hebrews says, it is obsolete, having been fulfilled and completed by Christ? There was thus an ethical as well as a theological reason for focusing on something other than the law when explaining the Christ event and its significance.

The author of Hebrews is clearly committed to using some form of the Greek OT, for as Karrer points out, we have no hints or relics of Aramaic or Hebrew in his Scripture citations,[156] and furthermore, he reflects some of the peculiarities of the Greek grammar of the LXX (e.g., the unusual negation using εἰ, Heb 3:11 and 4:3, 5 using Ps 94:11 LXX). Hebrews tends to have more extended OT quotations than other NT books, for example, the quotation of Psalm 94:7–11 in Hebrews 3:7–11 is longer than any other quoting of the Psalms in the NT. Furthermore Psalm 110 (in particular vv. 1 and 4) shows up some one dozen times either by citation or allusion.[157] What this suggests to Karrer, probably rightly, is that our author had a scroll of the Psalms in Greek to work from, and was not just citing or alluding to the OT on the basis of his memory.[158] On the other hand, what we find in the catena of scriptural phrases in Hebrews 1, largely from Psalm 2:7, 103:4, and 109:1 (and also Pss 44:7–8 and 101:26–28) may give us pause, for the reading "fire flame" for Psalm 103:4 is not found in the main LXX manuscripts. Notably, this catena also shows up, with some difference in order of the citations of the Psalms in 1 Clement 36 and with some of the same non-LXX readings such as "fire flame."

Obviously, one of the things that most needed to be explained in regard to the story of the passion of Jesus was why it was a member of his inner circle who betrayed him, handing him over to the Jewish authorities. Sometimes in the use of the Psalms in the NT there is an apologetic tone and motive detectible and the use of Psalm 41:9, "even my friend in whom I trusted, who ate of my bread, has lifted the heel

---

156. Ibid., 339.
157. See Attridge, "Psalms in Hebrews," 197.
158. Karrer, "Epistle to the Hebrews," 342.

against me" is the most obvious example. In its original context, the story the poem tells us is of a person who is sick, perhaps even deathly ill, and even his supposed friends are abandoning him, as was the case with Job (see v. 3), but that is not all. This person believes he has also sinned against God and needs spiritual healing (v. 4). Obviously, the whole of this psalm could not be applied to Jesus, and in fact in this case it is not helpful to argue that this psalm is used in the NT in a way that suggests that the readers were supposed to go back and consider the whole psalm. We are not dealing with that kind of intertextuality here; we are dealing with the use of only the particular verse that is seen as apt and as fulfilled in the life of Jesus.[159]

This psalm verse is either alluded to or quoted in Mark 14:18, John 13:18, and Acts 1:16. In Mark there is a mere allusion, not a citation. Jesus says he will be betrayed by one who is then eating with him. By contrast, John 13:18 has a much fuller context and use of the text, which is worth quoting at length, "I am not referring to all of you; I know those I have chosen. But this is to fulfill this passage of Scripture: 'He who shared my bread has lifted his heel against me.'" Here not only is the Scripture quoted fairly literally on the basis of the Hebrew, not the LXX, text, but it is stressed that Judas's action was foreseen and so was a fulfillment of Scripture. In fact Acts 1:16 takes this whole sort of apologetic use of the psalm text one step further by saying, "Brothers, the Scriptures had to be fulfilled, which the Holy Spirit through David foretold concerning Judas, who became a guide for those who arrested Jesus." Notice: (1) Psalm 41 is not quoted here, but (2) the reference to David makes clear Peter is referring to a psalm, and (3) interestingly the foreteller in this case is said to be the Holy Spirit, speaking in the psalm through David. Once again the psalm is seen as prophetic in character, even with its very generic original character. The point of what is going one in John and Acts is to make clear that Jesus's demise was not a tragic accident of human history, rather it was part of God's plan all along, however strange that might seem, but as we are told elsewhere in the Psalms (Ps 76:10), God can even use the wrath of human beings for good, even for his praise.

---

159. There is however evidence that one other verse of this psalm, the last one, "blessed be the Lord, the God of Israel, from everlasting to everlasting. Amen" was influential in the NT. The last phrase of Ps 41:13 in the LXX form is probably influencing the diction of Paul's little doxology in Rom 9:5, and probably also the one in Luke 1:68.

Conclusions

The first and the last books of the Psalter are by far the longest in the collection, with forty-one and forty-three psalms respectively in the two books. The first book places before the reader some thirty-seven psalms out of a total of forty-one with the name of David somewhere in the prescript. The other four (or three if Psalms 1-2 are taken together as two parts of one composition) are simply anonymous. Accordingly, the compilers of this collection must have intended to emphasize the Davidic nature of this first book, whether David is the composer, the inspiration, or the honoree of these psalms that bear his name. Equally clearly, some of these "Davidic" psalms encourage the listener to think not only of David himself, but of the Davidic line of kings, as we have already seen. When the southern monarchy fell "into shadow" in 587 BCE or so, it became only natural that these psalms would be read messianically in early Judaism, and especially by the followers of Jesus who had actually appeared on the scene in the Holy Land and had ridden a donkey into Jerusalem (like earlier Davidic kings), during the lifetime of some of the writers of various NT books. They were eager to search the Scriptures once more, with the impetus of Jesus himself, to see whether what was told and foretold and foreshadowed in the Hebrew Scriptures might help them understand and interpret what had just happened—the Christ event, and its significance, and the meaning of Jesus's words and deeds and life.

Other than Isaiah, no book was more helpful in their quest for understanding and provided more fuel for their evangelistic fires than the Psalms. In part, this is perhaps because of the great familiarity of pious Jews with the Psalms, which as we have mentioned were prayed, taught, sung in worship, meditated on, and memorized in ways and to a degree that other parts of the OT were not. The lexicon of faith and piety for early Jews, the source that provided them with a lion's share of their religious vocabulary and many of their thoughts and ideas, was the Psalms.

It is then no surprise at all, to find the *language* of the Psalms being used over and over again to talk about Jesus, and about the events of his life, and of the events in the subsequent Jesus movement. Their thoughts and prayers and speech were saturated with the language of the Psalms. It was the language of the Psalms that also helped them interpret and express their own experiences, just as Jesus had used it to express his experiences, including on the cross. The Psalms became all the more useful because there were so many laments in the Psalter, so much verbiage about the righteous sufferer, and both Jesus and his first followers quite naturally found those kinds of words readily coming to mind when there was resistance and even persecution for the sharing of the good news about Jesus. *This kind of use of the Psalms is very frequent in the NT, and it does not really involve the actual contextual exegesis or exposition of the Psalter. Similar experiences led to the use of familiar sacred religious language to express one's own perspectives on such experiences.*

Psalm 22 is poetry, and not in the first place a prophecy about Jesus, if by prophecy we mean something that was originally and intentionally written to predict the coming messiah from of old, and then fulfilled in Jesus and in no one else. No, this psalm is about a righteous sufferer who is rescued from death's door, rather than going through death, and celebrates his rescue in the latter portion of the psalm. *Nevertheless,* both Jesus and his followers saw the Psalms, like the rest of the OT, as in the broad sense prophetic, foreshadowing things to come, and they found that particular verses, phrases, passages in psalms like Psalm 22 fit no one better than Jesus and his life. They were not unique in reading various of these psalms in a messianic way. In other words, they were happy to read the Psalms forward, but also were keen to read them backwards in light of more recent events and experiences. Since God's word was seen as a living thing, this seemed perfectly natural and appropriate. It had a meaning for God's people in all generations. The meaning might become clearer with time and later experiences. It might be amplified and expanded upon in light of the Christ event, but the writers were clear enough, it had always had this meaning or at least implication and application, waiting to be understood by God's people, on further review. The review, of necessity, had to happen when it was believed the messiah had shown up, and things didn't entirely go according to some conventional expectations.

In addition to this sort of use of the first book of the Psalter, we also saw a variety of other kinds of usage. For example, psalms which spoke of Yahweh doing this or that were used to talk about Christ doing this or that. He became the good shepherd of Psalm 23. He became the Lord who ruled over the enemies of God's people. Even more daringly, both Paul and the author of Hebrews *place psalms on the lips of Jesus himself as the speaker*, and not just during his ministry, but as the risen and exalted Lord. This "transference" approach was both creative, and must have been shocking to some early Jewish listeners.

Furthermore, we found the ethical use of the Psalms, especially in the Epistles and in places like James (which is a sermon), where key affirmations about the character of God—and what ought to be the character of his followers—are stressed: mercy, faithfulness, constancy, humility, purity, and so much more. The character of God had not changed through the ages, but the cost of discipleship had gone up as a result of Jesus. So the ethical teaching in the OT had to be supplemented, and indeed interpreted through the lens of the teachings of Jesus. It is not an accident that there are some twenty or more echoes and phrases from the Sermon on the Mount found in James, which also spends a lot of time drawing on OT wisdom literature and the Psalms for its homily.[160] It is also not an accident that when Paul turns to ethics in Romans 12–15 he draws on both the OT and the teachings of Jesus when addressing a largely gentile audience that he had mostly not converted.

At times, there were fuller quotations from the Psalms, for instance in 1 Peter 3:10–12, and something like contextual exegesis is done after a fashion, but regularly with a christological or eschatological application. In a few cases, one gets the sense that the NT writer expects at least some in the audience to know where the quoted material came from, and perhaps some of its original context, but most of the use of the Psalms that we have examined thus far is not of that nature. This is why I have stressed that mostly what we find in the use of the Psalms in the NT falls under the heading of a *homiletical* use of the psalms, rather than straight exegesis and application of the Psalms, though the latter is not entirely lacking in the NT.

The writers of the NT are clearly of the persuasion that Jesus is the Christ and he has ushered in the eschatological age when the proclamation of the good news about the messiah must go forth to the world, to Jew and gentile alike. They are all convinced true believers when it comes to this matter. As a result of believing this, there is a stress on the fact that they are living in the era of the fulfillment of the prophecies, the promises, and the proclamations of the OT. They are living in the era when what was foreshadowed or foretold in the OT is coming to pass. What this also meant was they were living in the era when the new covenant foretold by Jeremiah was believed to be in play, and "new occasions taught new duties." The Mosaic covenant was not seen as being renewed, but rather temporary, according to Galatians 3–4 and Hebrews. The new covenant reaffirmed some of the old, but also

---

160. See Witherington, *Letters and Homilies for Jewish Christians: A Socio-rhetorical Commentary on Hebrews, James, and Jude* (Downers Grove, IL: InterVarsity Press, 2007), 416–555.

broke new ground in various ways, especially in ways that made it possible for gentiles to follow Jesus without becoming Jews. All of this kind of thinking affected how the earliest Christians approached the Psalms, again and again.

We noted earlier in this chapter, for example, that it seemed plausible to conclude that the reason the NT writers fastened so firmly and overwhelmingly on the Psalms and Isaiah to help them interpret the Christ event over and over again rather than focusing primarily on texts from the Pentateuch, is precisely because their eschatological GPS suggested that the hour was late, and it was high time to move on to and implement the new covenant, in particular the teachings of Jesus about the new way to live a holy life. The time was at hand, and Christ had fulfilled the Mosaic law as a way of righteousness (Rom 10:4). We pointed to the dramatic contrast between Philo and his fixation on the Pentateuch in his numerous writings, and a writer like the author of Hebrews, or even Paul, for whom the Psalms and the prophets were where the focus needed to be. Philo had not gotten the memo about the eschatological hour, or for that matter the coming of the messiah.

At times, the NT writers could be very creative in their handling of the Psalms, for example, the sort of use of Psalm 8 we find in Hebrews 1–2, where a creation ode about the relationship of humankind in general to God, an ode which reflects on Genesis 1, is used as a commentary on the special son of man, the last Adam and the arc of his career. In the hands of this NT author, the psalm speaks of one who was "for a little while" lower than the angels, but now reigns in glory and honor with God in heaven. The author is not doing hermeneutical gymnastics here, he is exploiting the ambiguity and metaphorical capacity of the poetic language of Psalm 8 to use it in a way that the original psalmist probably never imagined, which brings up a key point.

Not only is the language of poetry often metaphorical, especially when it is more generic and universal, as is the case in Psalm 8; it can also be said to be multivalent, having a surplus of meaning, or at least, in its opaqueness leaving the door open for multiple possible legitimate readings of its meaning. The author of Hebrews boldly walked through that door, using Psalm 8 to comment on things christological, things that angels longed to look into in times gone by, but had to wait for further revelation to break forth with the answers and clarifications about fulfillment.

Taking things one step further, we also noted that the historical

Jesus himself seems to have interpreted not only his death, but also his commissioning and empowerment at his baptism with the help of the Psalms. He heard his Father speaking to him in the language of the Psalms, and he expressed his own experiences with that language. As we shall see when we get to Psalm 110 and other key texts, Jesus indeed had his own convictions about who he was in relationship to David and the Davidic line, and he expressed these convictions by interpreting the Psalms as speaking about him, not merely as the son of David, but as David's Lord. It is no surprise then that the writers of the NT followed his lead in using texts like Psalm 2 or Psalm 22 or Psalm 110 in their christological reflections.

At times, in Revelation, but also elsewhere in the NT, the writers of the NT focused on the final horizon, the end of the end of days. When they did so, they found the poetic language of the Psalter exceedingly helpful in expressing their thoughts, whether about when God's Son would finally put all of the enemies of God's people under his feet, or when justice would finally be done for the oppressed, or when all the nations would worship the God of the Bible, or when the resurrection of the dead and the life everlasting would come to pass, or when the chaos waters would finally be drained from the earth, and evil would be no more. As we turn now to the second book of the Psalter, Psalms 42–72, we will be looking closely to see if these sorts of the uses of the Psalms continue in that book as well.

4

Psalter Book 2 (Psalms 42–72)

True Confessions

There is in the Psalms no quick and easy resignation to suffering. There is always struggle, anxiety, doubt. God's righteousness, which allows the pious to be met by misfortune but the godless to escape free, even God's good and gracious will, is undermined (Ps 44:24). His behavior is too difficult to grasp. But even in the deepest hopelessness God alone remains the one addressed.
—Dietrich Bonhoeffer[1]

"Whenever I read the psalms, I feel like I am eavesdropping on a saint having a personal conversation with God."
—commonly attributed to R. C. Sproul

The second book of the Psalter is shorter (some 30 songs) than the first, and of a different character in various regards. For one thing, it starts out with mostly Korahite psalms. David doesn't show up in the prescript until the famous Psalm 51, but thereafter all the songs up through Psalm 65 have David in the header, with some of them tagging the song to a particular experience in David's life. Psalms 66–68 have headers but mention an anonymous leader, perhaps the lead musician. Psalms 68–70 once again mention David in the header, Psalm 71

---

1. Dietrich Bonhoeffer, *Psalms: The Prayer Book of the Bible* (Minneapolis: Augsburg, 1970), 47.

is anonymous with no header, and Psalm 72 ends this collection with the header "of Solomon," and famously at the end of Psalm 72 we hear "the prayers of David, son of Jesse are ended," but in fact they are not since Psalm 86 is attributed to David, as are Psalms 101 and 103, and then in the final book of the Psalter we have a whole series of Davidic psalms, beginning with Psalms 108–110, then three more at Psalms 122, 124, and 131, and finally Psalms 138–145. What the final line of Psalm 72 attests to is that there were several collections of psalms over many years, and book 2 of the Psalter was probably one of the earlier ones, to which was added other collections, with some Davidic psalms, thereafter.

If one carefully compares the NA28 index of references to the Psalms in the NT[2] to the list of Davidic psalms in the Psalter, a pattern begins to emerge: the Christians tended to gravitate to and use the Davidic psalms when appropriating material from the Psalter to talk about Jesus and his life and work. This is not entirely the case, but it is a significant pattern. Perhaps it was assumed that they were more naturally adapted and adopted and applied to the Christ event, and to the story of his followers and their mission. We will examine several of the more quoted, alluded to, or echoed psalms from book 2 of the Psalter at length in what follows, and then look more broadly at the echoes and allusions and partial quotations found in the rest of book 2 of the Psalter.

The Longing for God: Psalms 42 and 43

In various manuscripts of the Hebrew Psalter, Psalms 42 and 43 are part of one psalm, and it is not hard to see why. A brief comparison of Psalm 42:5 and 11 and Psalm 43:5 will demonstrate that these three verses share the same refrain. In addition, Psalm 42:9 is repeated almost verbatim at Psalm 43:3. In fact only Psalm 43:1–2 and 4 really provides any distinct content in that song from what we find in Psalm 42. For this reason among others, most scholars have rightly concluded that we should treat this material together as one psalm. It needs to be remembered that the later Christian division into chapters and verses in the Bible we owe to the work of Archbishop Stephen Langton of Canterbury, and there is nothing inspired or original about his divisions. But this is not the entire story. Clearly enough, at least by the time the LXX was produced, Psalms 42 and 43 had already been divided up by editors, and a Davidic header had been added to Psalm 43

2. See Appendix A.

to make it distinct from the previous psalm. Perhaps, as Goldingay suggests, what has happened here is that Psalm 43 has been separated from Psalm 42 to facilitate liturgical use—as seems to have happened to Psalms 9-10. The alternative is Psalm 43 was composed to accompany Psalm 42, but in either case, they belong together.[3]

Quite apart from the headers, there are notable differences between books 1 and 2 of the Psalter. For one thing there is marked preference for the term אֱלֹהִים ('elōhîm "God"), in this book as opposed to Yahweh, which predominates in book 1. For this reason scholars have spoken of the second book of the Psalter as the Elohistic Psalter.[4] Some have even suggested that since אֱלֹהִים was the preferred term in the north and Yahweh in the south, perhaps a goodly portion of this book originated there. In any case, some variant of אֱלֹהִים occurs some eighteen times in these sixteen verses of Psalms 42-43, which makes this opening to the second book stand out from the first one.[5]

A theological observation is in order at this point. The Psalms again and again make clear that God's covenant with his people is not a unilateral affair. The psalmists do not think that whatever happens is all part of God's plan, and so ultimately for the best. As Charry stresses "The psalmists have a different understanding of covenant as a bilateral arrangement. According to this view, they do not hesitate to call God to account, so convinced are they of God's responsibilities to Israel. The poet does not fear brutal honesty in that relationship because God and Israel are both responsible for protecting it."[6] Just so.

The relationship between God and the psalmist is not a one-way street, even verbally. As a relationship, it involves both parties freely participating in the relationship, otherwise love given and love received are not possible in the relationship. Love cannot be compelled, coerced, or predetermined. It would cease to be love were it all predetermined, because love requires at least a modicum of freedom to respond or initiate on one's own; and that of course means there is risk in this relationship, a quality so very clear when one reads through the Psalter as a whole, especially the laments, without preconceived theological notions.

Because we are dealing with the beginning of the psalms (Psalms 42-49), which seem to have been composed by the sons of

---

3. John Goldingay, *Psalms: Volume 2; Psalms 42-89*, BOTCWP (Grand Rapids: Baker Academic, 2007), 21.
4. On this subject see Laura Joffe, "The Elohistic Psalter: What, How, and Why?," *SJOT* 15 (2001): 142-66.
5. See Charry, *Psalms 1-50*, 220.
6. Charry, *Psalms 1-50*, 233.

Korah (see also Psalms 84, 87–88), it is well to bear in mind that Korah was a Levite and a leader of the guild or company of songwriters (1 Chr 9:19; 2 Chr 20:19).[7] In Exodus 6:21, Numbers 25:58, and 1 Chronicles 6:7 they are said to be Levites. This psalm may chronicle a crisis in the life of a worship leader. This is understandable if, as some scholars think, the several references to being distant from the temple suggest that the man is in exile, he is over Jordan, he is far from where he used to worship. This may be correct, but on the other hand, Kraus says there is no real indication the person is in exile, rather he seems to be at the sources of the Jordan river,[8] in the mountains in the north, near Mt. Hermon, and unable to get back to Jerusalem.[9] Notice that the solution to the problem is not viewed as a retreat where one can be alone, but rather an advance to the worship place where one can join the congregation, play one's lyre, and sing (43:4–5).

MT Psalms 42–43	LXX Psalms 41–42
For the director of music. A *maskil* of the Sons of Korah. 1 As the deer pants for streams of water, so my soul pants for you, my God. 2 My soul thirsts for God, for the living God. When can I go and meet with God? 3 My tears have been my food day and night, while people say to me all day long, "Where is your God?" 4 These things I remember as I pour out my soul: how I used to go to the house of God under the protection of the Mighty One with shouts of joy and praise among the festive throng.	1 Regarding completion. Regarding understanding. Pertaining to the sons of Kore. 2 Just as the doe longs for the springs of water, so my soul longs for you, O God. 3 My soul thirsted for the living God. When shall I come and appear to the face of God? 4 My tears became my food day and night, while it was said to me day after day, "Where is your God?" 5 These things I remembered, and I poured out my soul upon me, because I shall proceed to a place of a marvelous tent, as far as the house of God, with a sound of rejoicing and acknowledging, a noise of one who is feasting.

7. See Brueggemann and Bellinger, *Psalms*, 204.
8. Kraus, *Psalms 1–59*, 438 and see especially p. 440, where he points out that the "little mount" would be a particular peak in the Hermon range, and the plural "Hermons" definitely refers to the mountain range. Weiser, *Psalms*, 348 thinks we can be quite specific. For some reason the psalmist is in exile in the place which was later called Caesarea Philippi.
9. See Goldingay, *Psalms: Volume 2*, 27, 32.

5 Why, my soul, are you downcast?
Why so disturbed within me?
Put your hope in God,
for I will yet praise him,
my Savior and my God.

6 My soul is downcast within me;
therefore I will remember you
from the land of the Jordan,
the heights of Hermon—from Mount
    Mizar.
7 Deep calls to deep
in the roar of your waterfalls;
all your waves and breakers
have swept over me.
8 By day the Lord directs his love,
at night his song is with me—
a prayer to the God of my life.

9 I say to God my Rock,
"Why have you forgotten me?
Why must I go about mourning,
oppressed by the enemy?"

10 My bones suffer mortal agony
as my foes taunt me,
saying to me all day long,
"Where is your God?"
11 Why, my soul, are you downcast?
Why so disturbed within me?
Put your hope in God,
for I will yet praise him,
my Savior and my God.

[Psalm 43]

Vindicate me, my God,
and plead my cause
against an unfaithful nation.
Rescue me from those who are
deceitful and wicked.

2 You are God my stronghold.
Why have you rejected me?
Why must I go about mourning,
oppressed by the enemy?

6 Why are you deeply grieved, O my soul,
and why are you throwing me into confu-
    sion?
Hope in God, because I shall acknowledge
    him;
my God is deliverance of my face.
7 My soul was troubled at myself;
therefore I shall remember you
from a land of Jordan and Hermoniim,
from a small mountain.

8 Deep calls to deep
at the sound of your cataracts;
all your surges and your billows passed
    over me.
9 By day the Lord will command his
    mercy,
and at night an ode is with me,
a prayer to the God of my life.
10 I will say to God, "My supporter you
    are;
wherefore did you forget me?
Why must I walk about sullenly,
as the enemy oppresses me?"

11 As my oppressors crushed my bones,
they insulted me,
while they say to me day after day,
"Where is your God?"
12 Why are you deeply grieved, O my
    soul,
and why are you throwing me into confu-
    sion?
Hope in God, because I shall acknowledge
    him;
my God is the deliverance of my face

[Psalm 42]

1 A Psalm. Pertaining to David.
Vindicate me, O God, and defend my
    cause
from a nation not devout;
from a person, unjust and deceitful, res-
    cue me!
2 Because you, O God, are my empower-
    ment;
why did you reject me?
And why do I walk about sullenly
as the enemy oppresses me?

3 Send me your light and your faithful care, let them lead me; let them bring me to your holy mountain, to the place where you dwell. 4 Then I will go to the altar of God, to God, my joy and my delight. I will praise you with the lyre, O God, my God. 5 Why, my soul, are you downcast? Why so disturbed within me? Put your hope in God, for I will yet praise him, my Savior and my God.	3 O send out your light and your truth; these led me, and they brought me to your holy mountain and to your coverts. 4 And I will enter to the altar of God, to God who makes glad my youth. I will acknowledge you with a lyre, O God, my God. 5 Why are you deeply grieved, O my soul, and why are you throwing me into confusion? Hope in God, because I shall acknowledge him; deliverance of my face and my God he is.

This song has three stanzas (42:1–5, 42:6–11, 43:1–5), each finishing with the same refrain, where the introspective psalmist encourages himself to hope in God. In fact Charry suggests we translate the refrain "how depressed I am and growling, yet I wait for God and still expect his rescue" (42:5, 11; 43:5).[10] Translators have had difficulty with this refrain, for it is terse, merely twelve words in the Hebrew (contrast twenty-nine in the NRSV). The psalmist is realistic about his frame of mind or state of soul, but has not despaired to the point of giving up on God's help. Still, his adversaries keep mocking him asking, "Where is your God now?"

The first stanza of the song likens the longing for the living God to an animal's deep thirst for water (cf. Ps 63:1). By living water was meant running water, spring water that is fresh and not brackish, thirst-quenching, clean, and clear. In other words, the need for God is basic, fundamental to life—like eating, drinking, sleeping, breathing. It is something the psalmist can't do without, and yet, this psalmist says his soul is parched, his inner spirit dry as a bone. The only water around is his salty tears, and they can quench no thirst. The problem for the psalmist is not just doubting God, but also self-doubt, and those two things often go together.

He remembers how confident he was when he was singing boldly with the congregation in corporate worship.[11] He was on an emotional high. Not only did he participate in vibrant worship, he says "I led the

10. Charry, *Psalms 1–50*, 221.
11. Apparently the reference for the term festive, is to a festival, and hence to a particularly important point in the religious calendar: Passover, Pentecost, or the like. See Longman, *Psalms*, 194. If the psalmist was leading that, then he indeed is a priest of some sort.

114

procession . . . with glad shouts and songs." He asks himself, in view of such exhilarating experiences in worship, why in the world am I now depressed and restless in my spirit? Notice the verb about leading here. This matches with the header, which says "to the leader." Perhaps he is the worship leader. A crisis of faith in the case of a leader is not just a personal matter, it has repercussions for the other faithful. Chaucer once had a parson say:

And this figure he added eek therto,
That if gold ruste, what shal iren do?
For if a preest be foul, on whom we
    truste,
No wonder is a lewed man to ruste;
	And this metaphor he added thereunto:
	That, if gold would rust, what shall iron
	    do?
	For if the priest be foul, in whom we
	    trust,
	No wonder that a layman thinks of lust?[12]

This is a good place to talk a bit about the Hebrew word *nepeš* here called "my *nepeš*" (נַפְשִׁי). This term does not refer to the later Greco-Roman notion of the immortal soul and translating it as "soul" creates confusion for those who have inherited the later Christian reflections on this subject, beginning already with the Greek church fathers. The *nepeš* refers to the inner self, the human spirit, the very being of the person. Thus, sometimes the word can simply mean "being"; so, for example, God breathed into Adam and he became a "living being" (לְנֶפֶשׁ חַיָּה: *lenepeš hayāh* Gen 2:7).

The water imagery continues in the second stanza, only now the psalmist is thinking of the river Jordan, and presumably the springs and waterfalls that come down from Mt. Hermon, the highest mountain in the region, and Mt. Mizar as well.[13] One source of water calls to another drowning out the psalmist. His explorations of nature somehow calm his spirit, perhaps through reflecting on what God may be like who has made this remarkable creation which supplies our basic needs for air, water, and shelter. The result is that at least at night he is able to sing and pray to God. Yet the voices of his adversaries keep nagging at him, causing some doubts. On the one hand he can boldly assert "by day the Lord commands his steadfast love, and at night his song is with me" (v. 8), but when he remembers what those who mock

---

12. Geoffrey Chaucer, *The Canterbury Tales*, "The Prologue to the Parson's Tale," lines 501–4; text and translation from http://www.librarius.com/canttran/genpro/genpro479-530.htm.
13. Goldingay, *Psalms: Volume 2*, 27 notes the plural of Hermon, perhaps suggesting the Hermon mountain range rather than one peak. Also, we do not otherwise know of a Mt. Mizar, so Goldingay suggests the translation "Little Mount."

him keep saying, he wonders and asks God, "Why have you forgotten me?" One thing is clear, the psalmist realizes that it is God alone who makes life possible, and God's presence alone which makes one's spiritual life possible, much less flourishing.[14]

Here something should be said about God's חֶסֶד, (ḥesed), sometimes translated loving kindness or steadfast love, and some have even suggested it means "covenant love," God's love for his chosen people, a love he has promised to give to a specific group of people. Here in this psalm the word seems to mean no more than a reliable and constant compassion, which is characteristic of the biblical God. On the one hand, it is clear enough that this word can be used of persons other than God, for example, Jacob asks Joseph to promise to deal with him with compassion or mercy (Gen 47:29). An even better example is in the exchange between Rahab and the Hebrew spies in Joshua 2:12–14 where Rahab says that since she has dealt with the spies with חֶסֶד, she asks them to swear they will deal with her family with חֶסֶד. Rahab is hardly a covenant member or covenant keeper, and the term cannot mean "covenant love" here, but it does refer to mercy or compassion, and again we have a context where promising or swearing to act kindly is involved. If one looks at the paradigmatic example in Exodus 20:6 (cf. Exod 34:7) we are told that God shows "mercy/compassion to the thousands of those who love me and keep my commandments." Clearly this word is not about some unilateral or purely divine love. It is about a quality that is supposed to characterize a good relationship, and one gets the sense that the term emphasizes what we would call mercy or compassion, or less probably kindness. The formulaic use of the term in say Numbers 14:18, where it is paired with on the one hand God's being slow to anger, and on the other hand with forgiveness of sin, again suggests a reliable, ongoing, constant, merciful love, merciful in both its slowness to anger and its forgiveness of sins. In Deuteronomy 5:10 again we have the formulaic saying, which indicates that God's mercy is responsive and relational, he shows his steadfast compassion to those who love him and keep his commandments. In Judges 8:35 we hear about faithless Israelites who failed to show "mercy" or one might even translate it "loving compassion" to the household of Gideon. We cannot tarry here to deal with the more than sixty examples where this term shows up in the OT, of which some fourteen are found in the Psalter (Pss 18:50, 25:10, 32:10, 33:5, 52:1, 61:7,

---

14. See Brueggemann and Bellinger, *Psalms*, 205.

85:10, 86:5, 86:15, 89:2, 89:14, 101:1. 103:4, 141:5),[15] but Ruth 1:8 deserves close scrutiny. Here Naomi commends Ruth, a Moabitess, for dealing "kindly" with her and her now dead sons, and says "may the Lord deal mercifully [חֶ֫סֶד] with you." Clearly enough, God was under no obligation to do so, as he had no covenant with Ruth. For that matter it would be stretching things to say Ruth had some sort of covenant obligation to Naomi and her lost loved ones. After all, Ruth's marriage was at an end and she certainly had no covenant with Naomi herself. This is why the translation "kindness" or "kindly" or even "mercy" is in order in such a text. In short, while there are contexts where this term refers to a kind of kindness and loyalty that God has promised to give, even then it is not seen as unilateral, but rather reciprocal, and responsive to those who love God, and the term can be used in noncovenantal contexts as well to simply refer to kindness, something unexpected and compassionate, or to mercy. It is the context, not the content of the word that decides such matters, and humans as well as God can and do exhibit this quality.

In the third stanza (43:1–5) the psalmist decides what he must do: ask God for vindication against the ungodly who taunt him. In short, he asks God to be his defense attorney to deal with his detractors and mockers.[16] He chooses trust over doubt, faith over fear.[17] It seems clear that the psalmist is himself a leader of some sort, and he needs his faith to lead the faithful. Charry is partially right in noting: "Faith is not a calculated commitment but is organic to a person's emotions and attachments. Even coherent arguments cannot unseat God from a person's body. God is embedded there."[18] But faith surely does involve one's reason as well as one's emotions, one's thoughts as well as one's experiences. It is a commitment, but of the whole self, and often the heart hangs on even when the mind has doubts, as the dialogue with self in this song shows.

Finally, there is an irony in the double psalm, namely the psalmist keeps complaining about God's absence, but God's name is present

---

15. Not surprisingly, in a context of prayer and songs praising God, it is God's חֶ֫סֶד that is the subject again and again on the psalmist's lips. He is not regularly tooting his own horn in a psalm.

16. Brueggemann and Bellinger, *Psalms*, 206.

17. The use of legal language here has led some commentators to assume a formal accusation has been made against the psalmist in some court (see Longman, *Psalms*, 196). But the charge is said to come from an unfaithful people or even nation, and God could hardly be an actual defense attorney in a court. The language is surely metaphorical, just like most of the rest of the language in the psalm. Yes, someone has been mocking and troubling the psalmist, but we need not think of an actual legal situation.

18. Charry, *Psalms 1–50*, 223.

some sixteen or so times in these short stanzas. He is everywhere in the song.[19] The "religious value of the psalm is to be found in the fact that the longing for God which it depicts does not care about what it will get *out* of God but about what it will have *in* him, in other words, that it desires God for his own sake; and this is the secret of the power of man's longing for God."[20] In a sense, as Kidner say, the threefold refrain in this psalm portrays a person who feels called to live in eternity with his mind fixed on God, but also in time where mind and body are subject to pressures and difficulties. "The psalmist's refrain teaches us to take seriously both aspects of our existence."[21]

Mark 14:34 // Matthew 26:38 come at a crucial juncture in the passion narrative. It records the state of Jesus's heart as he enters the garden of Gethsemane. We need to back up a verse to get the full effect. It says Jesus "began to be distressed and agitated" and this is followed by his pronouncement to his inner circle that "I am deeply grieved even unto death." This is an odd thing to say, even with clear premonitions of what was likely to come, but remember Jesus is about to pray that the cup be removed from him, which did not happen. Let us start with the key phrase from Mark 14:33 // Matthew 26:37: ἤρξατο ἐκθαμβεῖσθαι καὶ ἀδημονεῖν ("he began to be deeply distressed and troubled"). This state of mind began when Jesus was taking Peter, James, and John to the garden with intent to pray, and it is manifested in what he says to the disciples, namely: Περίλυπός ἐστιν ἡ ψυχή μου ἕως θανάτου· ("My soul is overwhelmed with sorrow to the point of death"). Jesus is said to be deeply distressed and troubled, indeed so much is this the case, that he then tells the disciples that his *nepeš* is sorrowful even unto death.

The alert reader will immediately hear echoes of the threefold refrain of Psalms 42–43 and in fact much more than that, for Jesus is about to pour out his heart to God, about to be deeply disquieted within himself, basically to be in mourning and grieving ("sorrowful unto death"). In other words, Jesus is being cast in the role of the psalmist in Psalms 42–43 by the evangelist, and the basis for this is the allusion to this psalm on the lips of Jesus. This is the only time Jesus speaks of his "soul"/*nepeš*/ inner self in these Gospels, identifying with the plight of the psalmist who feels so very far away from God. In short, Jesus is depicted as just as deeply disturbed, even rattled, as the psalmist was—and that is not all.

19. See Goldingay, *Psalms: Volume 2*, 34.
20. Weiser, *Psalms*, 352 (emphasis original).
21. Kidner, *Psalms 1–72*, 167.

Just as Psalms 42–43 unveils the prayer life of a very distressed believer, so Mark 14 // Matthew 26 is about to reveal the inner prayer life of Jesus, and in Mark this is really the only glimpse of that inner spiritual life of Jesus. When one couples this with what is to come in Mark 15, where Jesus prays Psalm 22:1, an overall picture emerges of a Jesus who so identified with the distress of the psalmist that twice over in these two chapters he resorts to the Psalms to articulate what is on his heart. There may only be a few allusions to Psalms 42–43 in the NT, but this one proves crucial. That we are not alone in see- ing these allusions seems clear from Hebrews 5:7, "in the days of his flesh, Jesus offered up prayers and supplications with cries and tears to the one who was able to save him from death, and he was heard." This is surely a reference to the Gethsemane episode, especially in light of Hebrews 4:15. This tradition of interpretation of depicting Jesus as praying to God in deep distress and hoping to be delivered, just like our Korahite psalmist, is taken one step further in the famous addition found in Luke 22:43–44 which depicts Jesus in deep anguish, and pray- ing so earnestly to God that his sweat is dripping off of him like great drops of blood. We even find a trace of the influence of Psalms 42–43 in John 12:27, "now my soul is troubled. . . ."[22]

Particularly in the Synoptic accounts Jesus is clearly depicted as being like the deeply distressed psalmist who feels abandoned by God, and yet hopes in him. Maarten J. J. Menken is right that the text of the LXX makes the connection especially clear, for the LXX of Psalms 42:6, 12; 43:5 reads "why are you deeply grieved, O [my] soul."[23]

"Killed All Day Long": Psalm 44

Sometimes, the quoting of the OT by a NT author will seem very pecu- liar indeed, even when it is reasonably clear where the quotation comes from. The use of Psalm 44:22 in Romans 8:36 certainly qualifies. It interrupts the crescendo Paul is creating, as he builds to a climax at the end of Romans 8. One could leave the citation out altogether and never miss it. Yet clearly there has to be a reason why Paul inserts it

---

22. To his credit, Goldingay, *Psalms: Volume 2*, 26 is one of the few OT commentators to note this allu- sion to Psalms 42–43 in the Gospels. On the Johannine form of the allusion see Edwin D. Freed, "Psalm 42/43 in John's Gospel," *NTS* 29 (1983): 62–73.

23. Maarten J. J. Menken, "The Psalms in Matthew's Gospel," in Moyise, *Psalms in the New Testament*, 75. Amazingly, this allusion is missed entirely by all three of the commentators dealing with Matthew, Mark, and John, in Beale, *Commentary on the New Testament Use*. The allusion or echo is not missed however by Richard B. Hays, *Echoes of Scripture in the Gospels* (Waco, TX: Baylor, 2016), 77, although he takes the John 12:27 reference to be echoing Psalm 6:3–4 LXX on p. 326.

here, with the introductory formula "as it is written." So let us consider the psalm itself first and see if we can decipher why it shows up right in the middle of that great climactic portion of Romans 8.

It is instructive to compare this lament to Psalm 78. In the latter psalm, Israel is depicted as regularly fickle, unfaithful, rebellious, and God as regularly faithful and forgiving. By contrast in this lament, Israel is depicted as consistently faithful, but God seems to be missing-in-action.[24] If we are wondering how these two views are compatible we have to remember again that this reflects what's on the heart and mind of the psalmist and how things appear to him. These are sung prayers, not explorations of the mind of God, and of course in any case, both things could be true; God has sometimes rescued his people, and has sometimes allowed them to suffer, and sometimes it is unclear why there are these two different responses.

This lament in Psalm 44 toggles back and forth between an individual (vv. 4, 6, 15) and a group complaint about God's inactivity while Israel suffers. Once again this psalm is attributed to the sons of Korah, and once again it is called a particular kind of song, a *maskil*, and it is not clear what that means. The header in the LXX does not help us answer this question. In any case, this is the first largely corporate lament in the Psalter, and it has its surprising features, as we shall see.

MT Psalm 44	LXX Psalm 43
For the director of music. Of the Sons of Korah. A *maskil*. 1 We have heard it with our ears, O God; our ancestors have told us what you did in their days, in days long ago. 2 With your hand you drove out the nations and planted our ancestors; you crushed the peoples and made our ancestors flourish.	1 Regarding completion. For the sons of Kore. Regarding understanding. 2 O God, we heard with our ears; our fathers reported to us a deed which you wrought in their days, in days of old: 3 your hand destroyed nations, and them you planted; you distressed peoples, and cast them out;

24. See rightly, Charry, *Psalms 1–50*, 225.

3 It was not by their sword that they won
  the land,
nor did their arm bring them victory;
it was your right hand, your arm,
and the light of your face, for you loved
  them.

4 You are my King and my God,
who decrees victories for Jacob.

5 Through you we push back our enemies;
through your name we trample our foes.
6 I put no trust in my bow,
my sword does not bring me victory;
7 but you give us victory over our enemies,
you put our adversaries to shame.
8 In God we make our boast all day long,
and we will praise your name forever.

9 But now you have rejected and humbled us;
you no longer go out with our armies.
10 You made us retreat before the
  enemy,
and our adversaries have plundered us.

11 You gave us up to be devoured like
  sheep
and have scattered us among the nations.
12 You sold your people for a pittance,
gaining nothing from their sale.

13 You have made us a reproach to our
  neighbors,
the scorn and derision of those around
  us.
14 You have made us a byword among
  the nations;
the peoples shake their heads at us.
15 I live in disgrace all day long,
and my face is covered with shame

16 at the taunts of those who reproach
  and revile me,
because of the enemy, who is bent on
  revenge.

4 for not by their own sword did they
  inherit land,
and their own arm did not save them;
rather, your right hand and your arm,
and the illumination of your countenance,
because you delighted in them.
5 You are my very King and my God,
he who commands acts of deliverance for
  Jacob.
6 Through you we shall gore our enemies,
and through your name we shall despise
  our opponents.
7 For not in my bow shall I hope,
and my sword will not save me.
8 For you saved us from those who afflict
  us,
and those who hate us you put to shame.
9 In God we shall be commended all day
  long,
and in your name we shall acknowledge
  forever.

Interlude on strings

10 But now, you rejected us and put us to
  shame
and will not go out among our hosts.
11 You turned us back rather than our
  enemies,
and those who hate us kept snatching
  spoil for themselves.
12 You gave us like sheep for eating,

and among the nations you scattered us.
13 You sold your people without price,
and there was no abundance in their
  exchange.
14 You made us a reproach to our neighbors,
a mockery and laughingstock to those
  around us.
15 You made us into an illustration
  among the nations,
a moving of the head among the peoples.
16 All day long my embarrassment is
  before me,
and the shame of my face covered me
17 at the sound of one that reproaches
  and babbles,
from before enemy and pursuer.

17 All this came upon us,
though we had not forgotten you;
we had not been false to your covenant.
 	
18 Our hearts had not turned back;
our feet had not strayed from your path.
 	
19 But you crushed us and made us a
    haunt for jackals;
you covered us over with deep darkness.
20 If we had forgotten the name of our
    God
or spread out our hands to a foreign god,
 	
21 would not God have discovered it,
since he knows the secrets of the heart?
 	
22 Yet for your sake we face death all day
    long;
we are considered as sheep to be slaugh-
    tered.
23 Awake, Lord! Why do you sleep?
Rouse yourself! Do not reject us forever.
24 Why do you hide your face
and forget our misery and oppression?
 	
25 We are brought down to the dust;
our bodies cling to the ground.
 	
26 Rise up and help us;
rescue us because of your unfailing love.
	18 All this came upon us,
	and we did not forget you,
	and we did no wrong against your
	    covenant.
	19 And our heart did not stand back,
	and you diverted our paths from your
	    way,
	20 because you humbled us in a place of
	    ill-treatment
	and death's shadow covered us.
	21 If we had forgotten the name of our
	    God
	and if we had spread out our hands to a
	    foreign god,
	22 would not God search this out?
	For he it is that knows the secrets of the
	    heart;
	23 because for your sake we are being put
	    to death all day long,
	we were accounted as sheep for slaugh-
	    ter.
	24 Wake up! Why do you sleep, O Lord?
	Arise, and do not reject us totally!
	25 Why do you turn away your face?
	Why do you forget our poverty and our
	    affliction?
	26 Because our soul was humbled down
	    to the dust,
	our stomach clung to the ground.
	27 Rise up, O Lord; help us,
	and redeem us for the sake of your name.

The first stanza of the song in vv. 1–3 rehearses the fact that the oral tradition from the ancestors is all about how God drove out the nations from the promised land and planted his people there. The victory of Joshua and his cohorts is attributed purely to God's right hand, his arm, and the light of his countenance. A reason is given for why God did this: he delighted in his people.[25]

The second stanza in vv. 4–8 continues the historical review. God is king and he orders victories for Jacob, and again it is through God that Israel treads down their foes. The psalmist is clear about how the victories did and didn't come about, "for not in my bow do I trust, nor can my sword save me" (cf. Joshua 24:12, and this after using the sword).

---

25. As Goldingay, *Psalms: Volume 2*, 40 notes, the argument in this psalm would completely disintegrate if it was not true that Joshua and God's people entered the land from outside of it, and with God's assistance, took the land. The psalmist assumes these are past facts to which he can appeal to make his argument here.

No, it is God who saves Israel from its foes, and so it is in God that the psalmist boasts continually. Our psalmist would be in complete agreement with Zechariah, "not by might, nor by power, but by my spirit, says the Lord of hosts" (Zechariah 4:6).

In a sudden turn in the tenor of the psalm in vv. 9–12, the psalmist makes clear that "that was then, and this is now." The adversative particle in v. 9 אַף ('ap "yet") makes clear the dramatic disjunction. It "is exactly YHWH's *military effectiveness* that is celebrated in verses 1–8 and YHWH's *military failure* that is voiced in verses 9–16."[26] The facts on the ground now seem to be that God no longer goes into battle with Israel's armies and as texts like Joshua 7 (the debacle at Ai), or 1 Samuel 4 (defeat by the Philistines) or Lamentations 3 (defeat by the Babylonians), indicate, when Israel is left to its own devices, disastrous defeat is the outcome.[27] This is said to be the outcome one should expect, if Israel has breached the covenant (Deut 28:15–69), but the Psalmist says, "No way!" He is not claiming sinlessness, he is claiming basic loyalty to Yahweh and the covenant.[28]

Instead of winning, Israel has retreated from their enemies, leaving the spoils behind. God's people have become like sacrificial lambs, and have even been scattered among the nations, and some of them have even been sold into slavery for next to nothing, the very reverse of the exodus. Whether this reflects an exilic situation or a late monarchy situation where there had been military setbacks (cf. 2 Chr 20:7–12), in either case, the psalmist feels that God has abandoned his people. What is worse, according to vv. 13–16 they have become the laughing stock of their neighbors, a byword among the nations (cf. 1 Kgs 9:7; 2 Chr 7:20; Jer 24:9; Ezek 14:8; Joel 2:17). The psalmist himself has taken this personally; he has been shamed: "all day long my disgrace is before me, and shame has covered my face." But why?

The psalmist in vv. 17–19 protests that he and his fellow believers have not been false to the covenant, their hearts have not turned back or gone astray in terms of their loyalties to their God. Mays points out, following Franz Delitzsch, that this profession of innocence is unique among the psalms, and has only Job as a clear parallel.[29] He protests in vv. 20–21 that if they had forgotten their God or committed idolatry would God not know this, since he knows the secrets of all human

---

26. Rightly, Brueggemann and Bellinger, *Psalms*, 209 (emphasis original).
27. Longman, *Psalms*, 199.
28. Mays, *Psalms*, 178.
29. Ibid., 176.

hearts? Then comes the most painful accusation in v. 22: "because of you, God, we are being killed all day long, being accounted as sacrificial lambs", but the preposition here, עָלֶיךָ (ʿāleykā) can indeed be translated "for your sake" which is how Paul reads the text.[30] Kidner is very helpful here; he says, "suffering may be a battle-scar rather than a punishment; the price of loyalty in a world which is at war with God. If this is so, a reverse as well as a victory may be a sign of fellowship with Him, not of alienation."[31]

So it is that in the last stanza in vv. 23–26 the psalmist blows his bugle, calling God to wake up (cf. 1 Kgs 18:27, an accusation of sleep made of Canaanite gods), and not cast off his people! He asks rhetorical questions like, Why in the world are you hiding your face? Why do you forget the miseries we are going through, the suffering we are enduring? Israel is sinking down into the ground and is in danger of disappearing from the annals of history. So the psalmist cries out, "rise up, come help us, and redeem us if for no other reason than your own kindness/mercy" (חַסְדֶּךָ ḥasdekā once again). This song is nothing if not bold and does not pull its punches. In "the end Israel prays to the very God who has failed."[32] Why? Because the psalmist believes Yahweh is still capable of acting, still capable of helping, still capable of being kind and reliable, even if Israel is seen as undeserving of his help. But as for the psalmist, he thinks Israel has been holding up their end of the covenantal bargain, which is why he sees all suffering as inexplicable. The problem of theodicy raises its ugly head.

What are we to make of Paul's insertion of Psalm 44:22 into his dramatic crescendoing affirmation of God's love at the end of Romans 8? Longman suggests that "Paul cites verse 22 of our psalm as part of his strong affirmation that nothing can separate us from the love of Christ."[33] Is that really what is going on with this citation in Romans 8? Clearly, something important is happening because this is the first citation by Paul since Romans 4:23–25, and the last before a veritable forest of citations of the OT in Romans 9–11. Paul has not placed this quote from Psalm 44 here by accident or for no particular purpose. On the whole, his quotation follows the LXX except he has omitted the "because" at the beginning of the quotation, and he seems to know that the Hebrew preposition which follows "because" can be rendered "for

30. See Goldingay, *Psalms: Volume 2*, 47.
31. Kidner, *Psalms 1–72*, 170.
32. Brueggemann and Bellinger, *Psalms*, 210.
33. Longman, *Psalms*, 201.

your sake" just as easily as it could be rendered "on your account"—and it is the "for your sake" rendering that we should pay especially close attention to. Who is the "you" and who are the "we" in this new setting in Romans 8 for Psalm 44:22?

On the one hand, we have to bear in mind that Paul's audience in Romans seems to have been largely gentiles (see Rom 11:13) and the whole thrust of Romans 9-11 is explaining to gentiles why and how God has not forsaken Israel, his first chosen people, the Jews. We must also take into account that nothing in Romans suggests that the audience has undergone any particular suffering or persecution for their faith as of yet. This text was written somewhere around CE 57 and we are a long time before Nero began looking for scapegoats. Who is it then who are the "we" that are being offered as sacrificial lambs for "your sake?" In the context of Paul's letters, this is most naturally taken to mean that Paul, and his fellow apostolic workers (like Priscilla and Aquila, and Andronicus and Junia mentioned in Romans 16 as suffering with him) are the "we" who have been suffering and the "you" is the gentiles, whom Paul is primarily addressing here. Christ was led as a sheep to slaughter (cf. Isa 53:7 to Rom 8:17, 32-34) and so have been his apostles.[34] This reading of the use of Psalm 44:22 makes perfect sense in light of the litany of apostolic sufferings in a text like 2 Corinthians 11:23-29. Paul has done his sufferings for his converts and other gentiles who have become Christians. Who is it that has already suffered hardship, distress, persecution, famine, nakedness, peril, or the sword (Rom 8:35)? There is no evidence that the audience has already done that, with the exception of some of Paul's coworkers, but clearly Paul has done that, and he is trying to prepare his audience for the fact that they may one day face such abuse (and indeed did, beginning in CE 64 after the fire in Rome).

In what way is the creative use of Psalm 44:22 in contact with, and reflecting knowledge of the original psalm? First, in both cases the "we" referred to are Israelites or Jews who are suffering at the hands of gentiles, not just anyone but Jews. But quite unlike the psalmist in Psalm 44, Paul is quite confident and asserts in this very context that: (1) God works all things together for good for those who love him; and (2) no outside forces such as the list of abuses in v. 35 can separate such a believing person from the love of Christ. Far from complaining "where are you God, when we need you most" Paul is saying quite

---

34. See the helpful discussion by Seifrid, "Romans," 633 and 636-37.

the opposite here, and indeed he will go on in Romans 9–11 to make the case that *God has not abandoned his first chosen people*, despite what the psalmist in Psalm 44:22 is accusing God of. In other words, Paul has quite selectively picked this verse, a lament by an Israelite sufferer, to talk about the apostolic sufferings for gentiles, in this case gentile believers in Paul's audience, when he knows perfectly well that a good deal of that psalm does not fit and is not apt if applied to the current situation he is addressing in Romans.

In an interesting exposition, Keesmaat suggests that Paul's use of Psalm 44:22 is part of Paul's strategizing with his audience as to how to respond to the persecutions and suffering they are undergoing, just as Paul is.[35] While it true that some of the Jewish believers in Rome, in particular some of the few Jewish Christian leaders who are now back in Rome after the demise of Claudius in 54 CE, can be said to have suffered persecution at the hands of Romans, there is simply no evidence that the gentiles who likely make up the majority of that Christian community in Rome have done so. Indeed, Paul assumes that the community in Rome is doing well, is in good heart and their faith has become known in the Christian communities elsewhere (Romans 1). Nothing in the first eight chapters of Romans suggests otherwise.

Romans 13 would hardly have sounded like familiar and helpful advice, if the authorities were already harassing the Christian community in Rome when Paul was writing. It is Jews who have been suffering from Roman anti-Semitism and some Jewish Christians among them who were expelled by Claudius in the CE 40s (see Acts 18). We lack evidence that the Christian community writ large had endured such things in Rome, especially not if most of them were gentiles as the evidence suggests. So the "powers and principalities" Paul is talking about at the end of Romans 8 are not the human governing authorities who are part of "the evil Roman Empire," they are the angelic hosts who cannot separate the believer from the love of Christ. The people whom God may have seemed to cast off in both Psalm 44 and in Romans 9–11 are Jews, not gentile Christians, and not the Christian community in general either.

But Keesmaat is absolutely right that Paul, unlike the psalmist, does not see the solution to the suffering problem to be God intervening and grinding one's enemies into dust. On the contrary, Paul believes that both Christ and his followers are more than conquerors by committing

---

35. Keesmaat, "Psalms in Romans and Galatians," 149–52.

themselves to nonviolence and love, and suffering abuse, even to the point of death, and being vindicated by God thereafter. This is indeed part of the message of the end of Romans 8, and, unlike the psalmist, Paul is saying that if one is suffering unjustly it is no sign that God has abandoned him, rather since Christ suffered that way as well, as a sacrificial lamb at the hands of pagan executioners, it is clear that God's love is with such sufferers, because he in the person of his Son suffered the very same way and the Father did not abandon his Son.

This brings us to Hays's even more intriguing treatment of Paul's use of this text.[36] Hays does not wish to argue, as is sometimes done, that Paul is simply saying "it is ever thus for God's people, they suffered in the past at the hands of nonbelievers, and they still do today." In other words, Paul would be suggesting an analogy between the experience of Israel described in Psalm 44, and the experiences of Paul and his audience's experiences at the hands of pagans. No says Hays, "it would be more accurate to say . . . that Paul reads the Psalm as a prophetic prefiguration of the experience of the Christian church, so the text finds its true primary meaning in Paul's own present time."[37]

Hays is certainly right that in Psalm 44, the phrase "for your sake" is the psalmist talking about Israel's ongoing suffering for Yahweh. He is also right that Paul believes that suffering like Christ is a sign of a person's faithfulness to God, not a sign that they have been unfaithful. What is not the case is that Paul thinks the psalmist is addressing the church. He knows perfectly well that the psalmist is addressing Israel, and when Paul turns to address the Israel issue, he quite clearly means by the term "Israel" non-Christian Jews, not the church. The church is Jew and gentile united in Christ, but God is not finished with Israel yet, and Paul is arguing vigorously, and with many citations in Romans 9–11 that this is the case. He even foresees a day when "all Israel will be saved," when Christ returns from heavenly Zion and turns away the impiety of Jacob. For now however, Jews who have rejected Jesus have been temporarily broken off from the people of God. So in the eschatological logic of Paul there is Israel, there is the eschatological people of God, Jew and gentile united in Christ, and then there is Israel who will join in large numbers that people when Christ returns. How does this affect Paul's hermeneutics and his intertexuality?

Paul assumes that God's word is a living word, and so it addressed Israel in the past and it continues to address God's people in his present

---

36. See Hays, *Echoes of Scripture in the Letters of Paul*, 57–63.
37. Ibid., 58.

time, *not because the church had become the substitute for Israel, or even the extension of Israel for the rest of history.* He does think that the Psalms, like other parts of the OT, are prophetic in the sense that they have a surplus of meaning, and can be applied appropriately to the movement of Jesus, just as they were applied to Israel. Further, he believes the Scriptures can be used homiletically, using scriptural language, phrases, and verses to explain how God is working in the present, much as he had worked in the past, because God's character is consistent.

Paul is probably not using Psalm 44 metaleptically, by which I mean he is probably not suggesting the audience go back to Psalm 44, and try to apply the rest of the psalm to themselves. For one thing, some of the psalm would not suit either the Christian gospel or the situation of Paul's audience. The gospel is not urging God to get back on the job of grinding Israel's foes into dust. For another thing, we lack evidence that the church in Rome felt like God had abandoned them, or had allowed them to suffer in the horrific ways described in the psalm. Nevertheless, Hays may be right that Paul, like the psalmist, is indirectly rebutting the charge that the psalmist rebuts, namely that he had been unfaithful to the God of the Bible in his life or words or deeds, in this case by preaching the gospel which is good news for the Jew first as well as the gentile.[38]

David's Mea Culpa: Psalm 51

One of the problems with Psalm 51 is that it is too familiar to Christians. At the time of the Reformation, Luther appealed to this psalm to demonstrate his doctrine of justification by grace through faith.[39] The temptation is to see this psalm as about someone becoming a Christian, repenting of his sins, but actually it is no such thing. David, or the psalmist who wrote this, is a committed and devout Israelite who has also committed some major sins and is asking God for forgiveness. He's not asking to be "born again" and receive the Holy Spirit, he's asking that God not take his presence out of his life, which was already there. As Kidner puts it, this is not the prayer of the unbeliever at the point of

---

38. Ibid., 60. If Paul is attempting metalepsis in Romans 8–11, then the only ones likely to pick up the nuances in the Roman church are the minority Jewish Christians who knew the Psalms, or perhaps a few God-fearers, but not the majority gentile audience who readily distinguished themselves from Israel (i.e., non-Christian Jews). Paul is saying God has not abandoned Israel in Romans 9–11 even though they have been temporarily broken off from the people of God so those gentiles can be grafted into the people of God.
39. See Krauss, *Psalms 1–59*, 506–7.

conversion, this is the prayer of the backslider who has come to repentance, hence the use of the verbs "restore" and "renew" in the prayer.[40]

Part of the problem of course is that the terminology seems so familiar, not least of which is the reference to the Holy Spirit, the only such reference in the OT (except for Isa 63:10–11) where God's spirit is coupled with the word holy producing this specific noun phrase. True, the psalmist throws himself on the mercy of God, and believes that the only way forward is if God forgives his sin and restores him into right relationship. There is a *sola gratia* character to this psalm, but it is not about initial justification or "being born again." What it demonstrates is that OT writers also believed that they stood in positive relationship with God on the basis of God's grace. This is not just a NT or gospel notion. So it is all the more important in the case of this psalm that we hear it in its original setting and context as best we can before asking how the NT writers heard and used it. As it turns out, surprisingly, they did not use it much.

The story of the confrontation of David by Nathan the prophet, who tells a parable that leads to David's conviction about his serious sins with Bathsheba and in regard to her husband Uriah the Hittite, is told in 2 Samuel 12. The header for this psalm quite specifically relates this song to that situation. The psalm fits that occasion well, but it is written in generic enough fashion to suit other similar situations in the lives of other believers in later eras.[41]

The psalm according to formal categories is a lament, but on the basis of its content it has been associated with the psalms that came to be called penitential psalms, of which there are a goodly number in the Psalter (cf. Psalms 6, 32, 38, 102, 130, 143). The psalm at its end may show some evidence of later editing, for the last two verses (vv. 18–19) are suddenly not talking about the repentance and restoration of the individual psalmist, but rather about the restoration of the community of faith. However, as Goldingay points out, if this is truly a prayer of a leader of a community, a king even, then it is understandable that the leader would be worried about the effects of his sins on the community as a whole, and the need for the whole community to be restored as a result.[42]

The account in 2 Samuel 12 has some of the same language as we

40. Kidner, *Psalms 1–72*, 192.
41. See Longman, *Psalms*, 218.
42. Goldingay, *Psalms: Volume 2*, 125. There is still the issue about what it says about sacrifices and the walls of Jerusalem, which have suggested to most scholars that the end of the psalm is a later addition.

find in Psalm 51, for example, the acknowledgement of having done evil in God's eyes (2 Sam 12:9, 12 compare Ps 51:3, 6), and the words "I have failed Yahweh" (2 Sam 12:3 and Ps 51:4). Possibly the line "against you alone have I sinned" is an attempt to make the psalm more generally applicable to a wider audience, since of course David had sinned against Uriah and Bathsheba as well, not just against God.[43] The general movement or progression in this psalm is from confession in vv. 1–9 to anticipation of joy and a positive response in vv. 10–19, though no final word of pardon or assurance is offered at the close of this psalm.[44] More specifically, "the invocation . . . at once raises the theme of the forgiveness of sins (vv. 1–3), is followed by a confession of sin and a profound realization of its nature (vv. 4–6), this is followed by the worshipper's actual prayer for the forgiveness of his sins (vv. 7–9) and the renewal of the inner [self] (vv. 10–13), and ends in praise and thanksgiving (vv. 14–17)."[45] Verses 18–19 are often seen as a later addendum in the postexilic situation before the rebuilding of the temple, but this is not necessarily the case (see below). What makes this psalm stand out in some respects is that the general lament about sin in the Psalter has to do with the sin of the neighbor against the psalmist, not the sins or particular deliberate acts of wickedness the psalmist has personally committed.[46] Even though this psalm turns to a person's wrestling with his own personal sins, notice the generic way in which it is discussed.

The elasticity of the psalm is that while the superscription connects to David and to his very specific sins of coveting, adultery, and murder, the psalm itself does not, in fact describe any particular sin at all, and no particular time. Its language is very open and available to whoever knows the overwhelming sense of guilt for wrong-doing that is articulated in its words.[47]

MT Psalm 51	LXX Psalm 50
For the director of music. A psalm of David. When the prophet Nathan came to him after David had committed adultery with Bathsheba.	1 Regarding completion. A Psalm. Pertaining to David. 2 When the prophet Nathan came to him, after he had gone into Bersabee.

43. See ibid., 125–26 on all this.
44. Brueggemann and Bellinger, *Psalms*, 236.
45. Weiser, *Psalms*, 401.
46. See the helpful essay by Miller, "The Sinful and Trusting Creature," in his *Way of the Lord*, 237–49.
47. Ibid., 239. Miller is likely right that vv. 18–19 are a later addition to the psalm.

130

1 Have mercy on me, O God,
according to your unfailing love;
according to your great compassion
blot out my transgressions.

2 Wash away all my iniquity
and cleanse me from my sin.

3 For I know my transgressions,
and my sin is always before me.
4 Against you, you only, have I sinned
and done what is evil in your sight;
so you are right in your verdict
and justified when you judge.

5 Surely I was sinful at birth,
sinful from the time my mother conceived me.
6 Yet you desired faithfulness even in the
womb;
you taught me wisdom in that secret
place.
7 Cleanse me with hyssop, and I will be
clean;
wash me, and I will be whiter than snow.

8 Let me hear joy and gladness;
let the bones you have crushed rejoice.

9 Hide your face from my sins
and blot out all my iniquity.
10 Create in me a pure heart, O God,
and renew a steadfast spirit within me.
11 Do not cast me from your presence
or take your Holy Spirit from me.
12 Restore to me the joy of your salvation
and grant me a willing spirit, to sustain
me.
13 Then I will teach transgressors your
ways,
so that sinners will turn back to you.
14 Deliver me from the guilt of bloodshed, O God,
you who are God my Savior,
and my tongue will sing of your righteousness.
15 Open my lips, Lord,
and my mouth will declare your praise.
16 You do not delight in sacrifice, or I
would bring it;
you do not take pleasure in burnt offerings.

3 Have mercy on me, O God,
according to your great mercy,
and according to the abundance of your
compassion
blot out my lawless deed.
4 Wash me thoroughly from my lawlessness,
and from my sin cleanse me,
5 because my lawlessness I know
and my sin is ever before me.
6 Against you alone did I sin,
and what is evil before you I did,
so that you may be justified in your
words
and be victorious when you go to law.
7 For, look, I was conceived in lawlessness,
and in sin did my mother crave for me.
8 For, look, you loved truth;
the unclear and secret aspects of your
wisdom you made clear to me.

9 You will sprinkle me with hyssop, and I
shall be cleansed;
you will wash me, and I shall be whiter
than snow.
10 You will make me hear joy and gladness;
humbled bones will rejoice.
11 Turn away your face from my sins,
and all my lawless acts blot out.
12 A clean heart create in me, O God,
and an upright spirit renew within me.
13 Do not cast me away from your face,
and your holy spirit do not take from me.
14 Restore to me the joy of your deliverance,
and with a leading spirit support me.
15 I will teach lawless ones your ways,
and impious ones will return to you.

16 Rescue me from bloodshed, O God,
O God of my deliverance;
my tongue will rejoice at your righteousness.

17 O Lord, my lips you will open,
and my mouth will declare your praise,
18 because if you had wanted sacrifice, I
would have given it;
with whole burnt offerings you will not
be pleased.

17 My sacrifice, O God, is a broken spirit; a broken and contrite heart you, God, will not despise. 18 May it please you to prosper Zion, to build up the walls of Jerusalem. 19 Then you will delight in the sacrifices of the righteous, in burnt offerings offered whole; then bulls will be offered on your altar.	19 Sacrifice to God is a broken spirit; a broken and humbled heart God will not despise. 20 Do good to Zion in your good pleasure, and let the walls of Jerusalem be built; 21 then you will delight in a sacrifice of righteousness, in offering and whole burnt offerings; then they will offer calves on your altar.

This psalm has an enormous amount of repeated terms (wipe away, wash, rebellion, waywardness, failure, purify, acknowledge, faithfulness, like, crush, joy, heart and spirit, deliverance, sacrifice, whole offering, acceptance, truth), and not surprisingly uses Hebrew parallelism to drive home the seriousness of the matter by being emphatic. Rhetorically speaking repetition of terms is for *emphasis*.[48]

The appeal which comes immediately in vv. 1–2 is to God's gracious, committed, and compassionate character, as opposed to the character of the psalmist, which is said to be sinful, wayward, and involving moral failure. More specifically the appeal is for God to act according to his *ḥesed* (כְּחַסְדֶּךָ) which may either be speaking of his great and constant kindness or mercy, which couples nicely with the following reference to compassion, or some suggest one could translate it "loyalty," but this seems less apt here.[49] God's judging of the psalmist has nothing to do with disloyalty to him. Indeed, "the God who judges is shown to be the God who saves. God's righteousness is merciful and effects mercy as God combats and eliminates sin in its multiform wickedness and destructiveness."[50] The solution is said to involve washing, wiping away, and purifying, images of the cleaning of dirt, taint, or stain (cf. Leviticus 15).[51] This does indeed reflect sacramental ways of thinking about how sin is to be dealt with.[52] The word חָטָא (ḥaṭā') has as its root meaning a deep failure, in this case a moral failure, hence a sin.[53] If this really is a psalm David originally penned, we are talking about covet-

48. Goldingay, *Psalms: Volume 2*, 124.
49. See above on *ḥesed* and Longman, *Psalms*, 219.
50. Frank-Lothar Hossfeld and Erich Zenger, *Psalms 2: A Commentary on Psalms 51–100*, ed. Klaus Baltzer, trans. Linda M. Maloney, Hermeneia (Minneapolis: Fortress, 2005), 19.
51. For a pretty decisive refutation that this psalm is about a sickness rather than a moral failure, or even the belief that sickness is always caused by some sin, see ibid., 14–16.
52. On this whole subject, it is illuminating to work through Gary A. Anderson, *Sin: A History* (New Haven: Yale University Press, 2010). See the helpful discussion of this particular psalm in Miller, *Way of the Lord*, 237–43.
53. See Krauss, *Psalms 1–59*, 502.

132

ing, adultery, murder, misuse of royal power, sexual assault, conspiracy, and betrayal, an interwoven series of serious sins.[54]

As Goldingay suggests, in the Jewish way of thinking the effect of sin is comparable to the effect of coming in contact with death. It contaminates, defiles, and conveys a taint, which requires washing to eliminate.[55] But it is God himself who must do the purgation, though the psalm does not specify how God would do that. What is clear is "they need God to remove this defilement in order for it to be possible for God to have contact with them. Indeed they need God to remove it, in order for it to be possible for other human beings to have contact with them."[56] But, to be clear, the psalmist is by no means just talking about ritual defilement that could be ritually resolved. He is talking about profound moral defilement that only God can remedy.

Verses 3-6 explain why this cleansing is so needed. The speaker completely acknowledges his sin and rebellion, and the resulting moral failure is constantly on his mind. It weighs heavily on him. This is not just a confession of sin, this is a confession that God was absolutely correct in his guilty verdict on the behavior of the psalmist. Forgiveness alone does not remedy the problem. The person needs deep cleansing and reorientation, which only God's spirit can accomplish. What comes to light is that there are various kinds of confessions: confessions of faith, confessions of what God has done for a person, and confessions of sin; here we clearly have the latter. What the psalmist has done is not a mere error or mistake, it is a deliberate act of rebellion, of sin, characterized here as "I have done what is evil in your eyes." "Many of the prayers for help [in the Psalms] say 'Change my situation so I may praise you.' This one says 'Change me; I am the problem.'"[57]

There is a remarkable parallel to this song, found in the Akkadian psalms which reads as follows:

> Who is he who for all time has not fallen into sin against his god, who for all time observes the command? Human beings, as many as they are, know about sin. I, your servant, have sinned again and again in all things, stood before you, but again and again sought unrighteousness. Lies I spoke again and again, dismissing my sin lightheartedly, said harmful things again and again; all this you should know![58]

---

54. See Miller, *Way of the Lord*, 240.
55. Goldingay, *Psalms: Volume 2*, 126.
56. Ibid., 127.
57. Mays, *Psalms*, 202.
58. Quoted in Krauss, *Psalms 1–59*, 502.

The psalmist makes no excuses, and he acknowledges that God is wholly justified in his verdict. But is the psalmist not only saying God is justified in his verdict, but also, amazingly, the sinner is somehow justified in a different sense and set right by that same verdict? Let's be clear that the verdict is "guilty" as charged here, and the psalmist owns it. The verdict is not, "not guilty because of forgiveness or pardon." The verdict is one thing; what God does about the condition of the sinner is another here. God finds the sinner guilty, and then purely because of God's compassion and mercy, he cleanses and restores the sinner. This is an important point, and it becomes important in the discussion of what is going one with Paul's use of this material in Romans 3, as we shall see. In any case, "the true extent of grace is experienced only where the true depth of sin is grasped."[59]

There is plenty of evidence from elsewhere (e.g., Gen 39:9) that sins committed against other human beings are viewed as sins against God, and in the very story behind this psalm, 2 Samuel 12:13, David confesses he has sinned against God by committing adultery with Bathsheba. All sin is properly speaking against God, even if it is committed with or against another human being.[60] It is even probably possible to translate here "against you, the only God, have I sinned." Nevertheless, as Mays stresses, sin always has social implications:

> the notion that a person could sin without injuring others is inconceivable in the Old Testament. The Old Testament knows of hidden sins and unintended sins but not of private sins that neither concern nor affect others … apart from God's relation to all human acts, there would be no sin. Sin is essentially a theological category. … It is the divine oversight of human life that makes talk about sin meaningful and necessary. When there is no reckoning with the oversight of God, the vocabulary of sin becomes meaningless and atrophies.[61]

Notice the contrast between the David of 2 Samuel 11 who is essentially asking, "How can I cover my tracks?" and the David of 2 Samuel 12 after being confronted by Nathan. Human beings have an infinite capacity for self-justification and rationalization, and as a result are often blind,

---

59. Weiser, *Psalms*, 403.
60. As Miller, "Sinful," 241 points out, interestingly enough the claim "against you only have I sinned" connects this psalm directly to 2 Samuel 12; see 2 Sam 12:9–13. All sin is a deep betrayal of one's relationship with God, whatever else it may entail. Miller is right to insist that we "cannot speak about the human without first speaking about God and there is no dimension of human existence that is not first a matter of our relationship with and dependency on the one who created and redeemed us."
61. Mays, *Psalms*, 200.

even willfully blind to the consequences of their own actions, hence the need for a Nathan to uncover and expose the truth of the matter.[62]

Verse 5 suggests that the human problem goes much deeper than an occasional serious sin. The psalmist argues that he was born in sin or waywardness, that his mother even conceived him in sin.[63] It is sometimes argued that the OT does not have a doctrine of "original sin" or human falleness, but this is not really true. What is true is that it is not usually described in the same sort of global terms in the OT as we find, for example, in Romans 5:12–21 (but cf. Gen 8:21; Job 14:4, 15:14–15, 25:4; Ps 143:2; John 3:6). It is best to say that this verse supports the notion that "since the first human being's disobedience, sin is as natural to human beings as breathing, though it does not imply that this sinfulness somehow [necessarily] links with sex,"[64] though in David's case it manifested itself in that very way (and in other ways, including having some people murdered). At this point in his lament, David realizes "this crime . . . was no freak event: it was in character; an extreme expression of the warped creature he had always been."[65]

It may be however that this verse does convey the notion that sin is transmitted hereditarily, as it does not seem that the psalmist is claiming here that his parents were committing an act of sin, say adultery, which led to his conception. Notice that sin here is not limited to "a willful violation of a known law" or even to an action by the psalmist. Sin, it would seem, is a much broader category than just a list of forbidden actions. One can look at Genesis 8:21 or Isaiah 43:21, which seem to imply that sinfulness was brought about by the wrongdoings of the first human beings, and certainly texts like Genesis 6:5, 12; Psalms 130:3; 143:2; Proverbs 20:9; Jeremiah 17:9; and Ecclesiastes 7:20 acknowledge that all humans are and have been affected by sin and have unreliable, indeed devious hearts. They have all "fallen into shadow" ever since Adam and Eve and are indeed in need of divine intervention and help.[66]

As v. 6 indicates, God looks for and desires truthfulness and integrity right to the core of a human's being, truthfulness about self and the human condition in general, but what God finds is inward and outward

---

62. See Kidner, *Psalms 1-72*, 190.

63. I don't think these comments should be written off as mere hyperbole pace Longman, *Psalms*, 220. This does not mean that God couldn't have given him the grace to do various good things despite his endemic sinful inclinations, and periodic sinful actions.

64. Goldingay, *Psalms: Volume 2*, 129.

65. Kidner, *Psalms 1-72*, 190.

66. See K. Condon, "The Biblical Doctrine of Original Sin," *ITQ* 34 (1967): 20–36.

sin when he examines the psalmist, and others, closely; sin that is the very condition the psalmist has lived in since conception and then birth. This verse may also be about how one behaves behind closed doors, "in secret places" not just in one's inner being.

Verse 7 makes the heart-wrenching plea, "purge me with hyssop and I shall be clean, wash me and I will be whiter than snow." Hyssop was the plant used to sprinkle blood or water on various objects, including blood on the horns of the altar, but here since the parallel verb is "wash," the psalmist is probably thinking of water (cf. the ritual for cleansing a tent when someone has died; Num 19:6, 14–19; Lev 14:4–52). Hyssop also was the plant used to smear the blood on the door frames of the Israelites as an apotropaic act in anticipation of the coming of the angel of death at the first Passover. The use of the term "whiteness" is apt because it contrasts with "bloodiness" (Isa 1:18) and David, in various ways, was a man of blood, which is why he was not allowed to build the temple.

Verse 8 acknowledges that God has crushed the very "bones" of the psalmist, but the psalmist believes that the same God can make him hear of joy and gladness, with the result that he can actually rejoice despite the judgment on his sin. Second Samuel 12 tells of a verdict of Nathan that would lead to an "oh yes" and then an "oh no" response from David (2 Sam 12:13–14). On the one hand, there is "God has remitted your sin and you will not die" (for it), but on the other hand "the son who is born to you [as a result of your sin] will die." In a rather unique phrase in v. 9 the psalmist asks God to hide his face—from the psalmist's sin. Normally, the prayer is for God not to hide his face from the sinner. But here that request is accompanied by the sentence "and wipe away all my sinful acts" after which there would be no reason for God to hide his face.

It is not enough however for sin to be forgiven, or for God to hide his face when we sin. Sin can be forgiven and life can go on the same. Furthermore, forgiveness offered is not the same as forgiveness received; and so, rightly, v. 10 gives us the psalmist's plea for God to create a pure heart in this singer, and make a steadfast spirit dwell within him. The verb here is indeed בָּרָא (barāʾ) and every place it occurs in the OT, God is the subject (cf. Genesis 1). Only God can truly create, including creating a clean heart. The person in question needs not just forgiveness and cleansing from sin, he needs renewal in his inward being. It is not enough to just cleanse from past sin.

The psalmist knows that God needs to set up the conditions in the life of the sinner so that there will not be recurrence of sin again and again and again. Sinning is an addictive form of behavior and unfortunately one of the things that repeated sin does is deaden the conscience. So the psalmist is not just looking for a one-time quick fix to a serious past sin. He is looking for God to give him the inner strength of character to live a better life going forward. "Blessed are the pure in heart, for they shall see God," said Jesus. Verse 10b is not asking for God to merely repair something that is old or broken, the psalmist is asking for transformation, hence the verb "create," as in "create in me something that didn't exist before in me." Finally, in the Hebrew way of thinking, the "heart" (לֵב *lēb*) refers to the center of thought, will, and feeling in the human being (hence the phrase "the thoughts of my heart"), not just the source of feelings. It refers to the control center of a person's being. Thus the psalmist is asking for a comprehensive inner renewal that affects thoughts, will, feelings, and God's spirit, which can invade and permeate all such things, can get the job done.[67]

In v. 11 one could almost envision a scene in a royal court. People come in begging on bended knee for this and that from a king. But unless they are in the presence of the king, he cannot even hear their request, especially not in an ancient oral culture where documents were few and rare when it came to ordinary people. So it is that the psalmist pleads, "don't dismiss me from your presence, and please do not take your holy spirit from me." Kidner is likely right that if this psalm ultimately comes from David, he may well be flashing back to the horrors of what happened to Saul, from whom God did indeed take away his spirit, and he did not even know it.[68] If one is in the presence of the great king, one can at least plead one's case. Sin will separate a person from God unless: (1) the sinner repents, and (2) God takes action. The reference to the holy spirit, refers in this case to the pure presence of Yahweh in a person's life, not to the later Christian doctrine of the third person of the Trinity.[69] The surprise is that the psalmist believes God has not yet withdrawn his holy presence from him, despite his serious sin.[70] Verse 12 pleads that God not nullify the new joy of deliverance the psalmist is experiencing. It also pleads for God's divine spirit to so act on the psalmist's human spirit that it is

---

67. See Krauss, *Psalms 1-59*, 505.
68. Kidner, *Psalms 1-72*, 192.
69. Longman, *Psalms*, 221. He is right that this is not likely a reference to the human spirit, since it is said to be Yahweh's here and he is also right it is not a reference to a member of the Holy Trinity.
70. Mays, *Psalms*, 203.

upheld and becomes steadfast and even wholehearted in its embrace of what God wills for the psalmist.

If God will do all that, then the psalmist says in v. 13 that he will teach other sinners God's ways, and more sinners will turn to God as a result. One sin addict can now testify about deliverance to other sinners about how they can be set free. Verse 14 can be read and translated in several ways: Does it mean "rescue me from bloodshed," in which case the psalmist is fearing reprisals for past sins? It probably does not mean rescue me from blood guilt, though that is possible in light of David's previous sins (e.g., against Uriah),[71] but Goldingay suggests that what is meant is "rescue me from death" (cf. Ps 30:9) which would be about the same as "rescue me from bloodshed."[72] The psalmist believes if God will do the work of inward renewal then he will be able to praise God in a bolder and more clear and honest way. His tongue, his lips, his mouth will shout forth praise.

One of the real problems with some readings of this psalm is that it is assumed that vv. 16–17 offer an "anti-literal sacrifice" polemic, but this is probably mistaken. The kind of sacrifices the psalmist is referring to, a whole offering or a fellowship offering, in the first place did not have to do with atoning for sin, and if one had not repented, it would have been inappropriate to offer such a thing while still in a state of sin.[73] But more importantly, there was no sacrifice one could offer for premeditated sin of the sort David had done, the so-called sins with a high hand. Deliberate planned adultery or murder were such sins. This is why Yahweh would not look favorably on sacrifices after doing those types of sin.

One could only throw oneself on the mercy of God, which is exactly what the psalmist is doing. Here is a dramatic difference from what one finds in the NT; the death of Christ as a sacrifice for sin is viewed as covering any and all kinds of sins, including premeditated ones. This is why Paul in Acts 13:59 says what he does, "by this Jesus everyone who believes is set free from all those sins from which you could not be freed by the law of Moses." Goldingay is absolutely correct when he says that in David's condition and situation the "Torah had no sacrifice to prescribe. All one could do is turn from rebellion and shortcoming and cast oneself in repentance on God's mercy."[74] One could offer

71. In any case, as Mays, ibid., 201 points out, the Hebrew word דָּמִים,(dāmîm) literally "bloods," can be a comprehensive term for guilt (Isa 4:4; Ezek 18:13; 22:1–16; Hos 12:14).
72. Goldingay, Psalms: Volume 2, 136.
73. See ibid., 137.
74. Ibid., 138.

up one's broken and now more contrite heart to God, and hope for his mercy.

Verse 18 seems an odd follow-up to v. 17 on the surface, but again, it is possible the psalmist has now turned to the implications of God's accepting the leader's repentance, which had repercussions for the city of Jerusalem, so the psalmist says as you accept my broken and contrite heart please also help restore Jerusalem and its walls so that (v. 19) we can once again offer acceptable sacrifices to you. The proof that we should not have read v. 16 as "anti-literal sacrifice" in general is found in v. 19. It is possible in light of 1 Kings 3:1; 9:15; 11:27 that Solomon's building up of a Jerusalem wall that David had left unfinished could be seen as the answer to the psalmist prayer here.

In any case, the psalms ends on the note that when the people are "right with God" literal sacrifices should resume and are appropriate. We should note that words for sin occur some twelve times in vv. 1-9, and twice only in vv. 10-19, so there is a progression here in the psalm, which can also be seen in the opposite pattern where God is named only once in vv. 1-9, and some six times in vv. 10-19. The progression in the psalm is from sin to restoration, from self to community, and throughout only mercy and grace and transformation can solve the human dilemma.[75] But note there is no word of reassurance or pardon for the psalmist at the end of this psalm, as there is in other psalms.[76]

There are a variety of small allusions to this powerful Psalm 51 in the NT, though not as many as one might expect. For example, the cry of the penitent taxman in Luke 18:31 "Lord be merciful to me, a sinner" is an adaptation of the first line of this psalm.[77] Or again, the response of the authority before whom the man born blind has to appear in John 9:34 says "you were born entirely in sin" which of course alludes to Psalm 51:5. A more distant echo of the same verse can perhaps be found in Romans 7:14 in the phrase "sold under sin." Paul in any case is not the inventor of the concept of fallen human nature bound in sin.

A very faint echo of Psalm 51:12b can be found in Mark 14:38 in the reference to the willing spirit. Luke 15:18 also has a faint echo of Psalm 51:4 where the prodigal son says he will return and confess "Father I have sinned against heaven and before you," which in its directness is somewhat like "against you, you alone have I sinned" in

---

75. See the study of Seizo Sekine, "Psalm 51," in *Transcendency and Symbols in the Old Testament: A Genealogy of the Hermeneutical Experiences*, BZAW 275 (Berlin: de Gruyter, 1999), 157-214.
76. Brueggemann and Bellinger, *Psalms*, 239.
77. See Mays, *Psalms*, 199.

Psalm 51:4, except of course the psalm does not suggest a dual object that the individual has sinned against. Or again, the phrase "then I will teach transgressors your ways" (51:13) has a faint echo in the flattering remark made to Jesus in Mark 12:14 // Matthew 22:16, "you teach the way of God in accordance with the truth." All of these are faints echoes, and perhaps one clearer allusion. But much more needs to be said about what is going on in Romans 3 vis-à-vis Psalm 51.

Here we turn to the fascinating exposition of Hays.[78] He argues that behind the quick citation of Psalm 51:4b lies not only the rest of this psalm, but also the story behind the psalm in 2 Samuel 12, particularly the end of the story where David is angry about the stealing of the lamb, and Nathan responds, "you're the man." Hays puts the matter this way

> In this particular lineal linkage of texts, the rhetorical structure of Romans 1–3 recapitulates the narrative structure of its textual grandparent, the story of Nathan's confrontation with David. The reader of Romans stands in David's role, drawn by the invective of Rom 1:18–32 to pronounce judgment on pagan immorality, then unmasked and slapped by Paul's Nathan like pronouncement: "Therefore you have no excuse, O man, whoever you are, when you judge another; for in passing judgment upon him, you condemn yourself, because you, the judge are doing the very same things" (Rom 2:1). Romans 3, then like the denouement of the David story, sets forth a pattern of human guilt, met by divine judgment and mercy; for the reader of Romans, as for David, there is no escape from the righteousness of God.[79]

Hays goes on to say that probably these echoes are all at the subconscious level, not deliberately crafted by Paul, but that it is the parallel between Paul's overall message in Romans 1–3 and the Nathan-David encounter that led him to think that Psalm 51:4b was an appropriate text to cite.

> The point made explicitly by Paul's citation of Ps. 51:4 is that Scripture proclaims the justice of God's judgment. The point made implicitly is that Psalm 51 (and its narrative precursor in 2 Samuel 11–12) models the appropriate human posture before this righteous God: not challenging his just sentence of condemnation, but repenting and acknowledging desperate need. The allusion to the David tradition foreshadows Rom. 4:6–8 in which David (Ps. 32:1–2) is called as witness of the blessedness of those

---

78. Hays, *Echoes of Scripture in the Letters of Paul*, 46–51.
79. Ibid., 49.

whose sins are not "reckoned" by God (2 Sam. 12:13). In Rom. 3:4, however all these connections remain in the cave of echo. A reader unfamiliar with 2 Samuel and Psalm 51 would read right past . . . missing the more complex resonances between the Davidic psalm and Pauline kerygma.[80]

Hays is right on several points. He is right that this is probably too sophisticated an argument for most of the largely gentile audience to catch the echoes not only of Psalm 51, which is cited, but also of the narrative story behind it. He is also absolutely right that part of the reason Paul turns to Psalm 51:4 is because Paul's argument in Romans 3:1-20 "pivots on the contrast between God's blamelessness and human guilt"[81] He is right as well, that the "righteousness of God" theme of Paul has to do in the main with God's character and uprightness, rather than mainly about a legal status conferred on sinful humans. Psalm 51 is about the contrast between God, who is just, and a human who has been very sinful. Keesmaat in her study of the use of the Psalms in Romans basically follows Hays's lead at this point.[82] Of a different ilk altogether is Seifrid's treatment of Romans 3:4 and Psalm 51.

Seifrid argues, "Paul's opening declaration is thus rooted in Scripture, where the psalmist makes the startling confession to God that he sinned 'in order that you might be justified in your words, and triumph when you judge.'"[83] In other words, says Seifrid, Paul is talking about "God's reign in human sin"; that is, the psalmist is saying either that he sinned deliberately on his own initiative so God could demonstrate his just nature, or God had destined the psalmist to sin in order to demonstrate God's righteous character. Before critiquing these readings of Romans 3:4 // Psalm 51:4b it is important to ask whether Paul is following the MT or the LXX here.

The Greek of the relevant phrase in the LXX (v. 6b) reads ὅπως ἂν δικαιωθῇς ἐν τοῖς λόγοις σου καὶ νικήσῃς ἐν τῷ κρίνεσθαί σε. The Greek of Paul in Romans 3:4 reads Ὅπως ἂν δικαιωθῇς ἐν τοῖς λόγοις σου καὶ νικήσεις ἐν τῷ κρίνεσθαί σε. It seems clear enough that Seifrid is right that Paul is citing the LXX virtually verbatim. But the issue is what one does with the Ὅπως. True, it can be translated "in order that" and so introduce a purpose clause, but it can also mean "so that" in a sequence where one action prompts another, in this case the sin of the psalmist

---

80. Ibid., 50.
81. Ibid., 48.
82. Keesmaat, "Psalms in Romans and Galatians," 144-45.
83. Seifrid, "Romans," 615.

prompts a certain response of a just God. The Hebrew behind this verse suggests the latter rendering not the former.

In other words, the thrust of the sentence in its original psalm context is that the psalmist has confessed that he has sinned against God and accordingly, or so that, God is perfectly justified in his just judgment that what he did was profoundly wrong. There is no reason at all to take either the LXX rendering of this psalm verse, which at this point is following the Hebrew quite closely, or Paul's to mean anything other than what the original psalm meant. In other words, Paul is just saying God's is perfectly justified in condemning sin, and the psalmist is perfectly right in saying that God is justified in condemning his sin, a sin he is now confessing to God. There is nothing here that warrants the conclusion that Paul is arguing that God destined, or is reigning through, the sin of the person in question. That, of course, would make God the ultimate author of sin.

But what should we think of Hay's exposition? While I think he is right on the points I've mentioned above, if he is indeed arguing for metalepsis here *and* a highly tuned audience who will pick up the echoes and nuances all the way back to the story in 2 Samuel 12 and then go search the Scriptures and see the larger context in both Psalm 51 and 2 Samuel 12; I am dubious about that. Perhaps Paul is echoing both texts and quoting one of them, but whether he expected the audience to be adept enough to pick up the resonances beyond the bit he actually cites here can be questioned. After all, the cited text now is supposed to have a meaning in its new context in Romans and make sense where it is. The Romans text is meant to stand on its own two feet for the audience hearing it, and to make sense in its immediate context.

On the other hand, perhaps Paul *is* speaking over the vast majority of his audience's heads here. Goodness knows Romans is complex and dense as a text or, as the Corinthians would say, "his letters are heavy." It is well to keep in mind that Paul largely doesn't know the gentile majority in this audience. He has not converted most of them, nor has he met with them prior to writing this letter. My theory would be that possibly all sorts of intertextual things are going on here, but perhaps Paul is counting on the Jewish Christians in Rome mentioned in Romans 16 to help the pagan converts understand this tour de force argument in Romans. If so, it would take a lot of unpacking over a long period of time, and some real study of the OT. What is true is that Paul is arguing that all have sinned and lack the glory of God, and God is justified in condemning all such sin, and part of his righteousness is expressed in doing so, as Romans 1:18–32 makes clear. But God is also merciful, kind, and full of compassion, and he sets right the sinner who, like Abraham, trusts God, and that human trust is "reckoned as righteousness." But this is a subject for a more detailed discussion in a Romans commentary.[84]

"A Zeal for Thy House Has Consumed Me": Psalm 69

This psalm is a plea for help in two parts. Notice how the beginning and the end of the first part is a plea to be rescued (vv. 1 and 29), and in between we toggle between petitions (vv. 1, 6, 13–18, 22–28) and descriptions of trouble (vv. 1b–5, 7–12, 19–21, 26), which generate the petitions.[85] The psalm has the same first-person singular style as Psalm 22 and in the Christian lectionary has been read as a passion psalm of Christ for obvious reasons, namely that Jesus recites a line from this psalm in the midst of his temple cleansing. Or does he? The psalmist is in a life-threatening situation (not clearly specified) and he is mocked and shamed without good reason (vv. 4, 6–12, 19–21). In an honor and shame culture, that can be as problematic as being in physical danger, because one's honor, the honor of one's name, was widely seen to be as important, if not more important, than life itself. Better to die with honor than live with shame, which makes clear what is at the top of the ethical hierarchy of such a society.[86]

It is instructive to compare the second half of this psalm (vv. 30–36) to the very similar second half of Psalm 22. Praise is promised in response to being rescued, a praise that should encourage other oppressed and ridiculed needy persons, for it will make clear that God responds to those in need. "Then there is a prophetic hymn in praise of the Lord who will restore Zion and Judah as an inheritance for the servants of the Lord (vv. 34–36)."[87] The basic structure according to Hossfeld and Zenger is threefold: vv. 2–14b, vv. 14c–30, vv. 31–37 (following the Hebrew enumeration of the verses). The three parts follow

---

84. See Ben Witherington III, *Paul's Letter to the Romans: A Socio-rhetorical Commentary* (Grand Rapids: Eerdmans, 2004).

85. On the unity of the psalm rather than it reflecting several layers of editing see Leslie C. Allen, "The Value of Rhetorical Criticism in Psalm 69," *JBL* 105 (1986): 577–98.

86. The story of Judas is a perfect illustration of this honor and shame ethical priority. The ancient person reading his tale would conclude he could not live with the shame of what he did, so he did away with himself. Whatever shame might be attached to suicide in the ancient Near East, there was even more shame to go on living when one had publicly dishonored someone important, someone who did not deserve to be handed over or betrayed.

87. On all on of this see Mays, *Psalms*, 229–30; the quotation is on 230.

the prayer dynamic of lament–petition–praise.[88] Overall we seem to be dealing with a lament that ends in praise, as we find in Psalm 22.

Because this psalm is quoted, alluded to, and echoed in so many different contexts in the NT, it is again important to note that some of it certainly doesn't fit Jesus or his character. For example, most scholars would see v. 5 as a confession of *guilt,* something we never find on Jesus's lips; and then there are the imprecations or curses in vv. 22–25, which do not fit either the character of Christ, or the description of his passion, where far from calling down judgment on those who mock and deride him, he asks God to forgive them in their ignorance, or when abused before the Sanhedrin he does not respond in kind.

*For the most part, the psalms were used **selectively** to exegete Jesus and the Christ event, and it is mistake to think that it was a regular or normal practice to evoke the entire OT context of a cited verse, or follow the practice of letting the reader fill in the silences by backtracking to the OT and seeing how the rest of this or that psalm or passage, which is not quoted, provides further comment on Jesus. Yes, occasionally that sort of approach is in play, but no, it is not a regular practice of the writers of the NT. The NT writers were not, in the main, doing contextual exegesis of the OT, or urging their audiences to do so.*

None of this is problematic if we keep in mind two things: (1) the use of the OT by NT writers should be judged by what they are attempting to accomplish. If they are *not* doing or attempting to do contextual exegesis or for that matter metalepsis, then they should not be faulted for failing to do so; (2) the psalms in themselves are poetic, highly metaphorical, often generic in character, and only occasionally are intending to speak to a specific situation or about a specific person. To say that both Jeremiah and Jesus fit a good deal of the portrait of the righteous sufferer in this psalm is perfectly true, though not all of it in either case. This is because the psalm quite deliberately lacks specificity; it is intended to talk more generally about such experiences of a believing person. Jeremiah and Jesus were both such righteous sufferers who cared deeply about Jerusalem and its temple and the profound sin that always led to negative consequences one way or another because God is a righteous God. The mystery for many of course was why a righteous God would let his righteous servants suffer, while sometimes the wicked didn't seem to do so.

---

88. Hossfeld and Zenger, *Psalms 2,* 172.

MT Psalm 69	LXX Psalm 68
For the director of music. To the tune of "Lilies."[89] Of David.	1 Regarding completion. Over those that shall be changed. Pertaining to David.
1 Save me, O God, for the waters have come up to my neck. 2 I sink in the miry depths, where there is no foothold. I have come into the deep waters; the floods engulf me. 3 I am worn out calling for help; my throat is parched. My eyes fail, looking for my God. 4 Those who hate me without reason outnumber the hairs of my head; many are my enemies without cause, those who seek to destroy me. I am forced to restore what I did not steal. 5 You, God, know my folly; my guilt is not hidden from you.	2 Save me, O God, because waters came as far as my soul. 3 I was stuck in deep mire, and there is no foothold; I came into the depths of the sea, and a tempest overwhelmed me. 4 I grew weary of crying; my throat was hoarse. My eyes failed from hoping in my God. 5 They multiplied beyond the hairs of my head, those who hate me without cause; my enemies who persecuted me unjustly became strong. What I did not seize, I would then repay. 6 O God, you knew my folly, and the wrongs I did were not hidden from you.
6 Lord, the Lord Almighty, may those who hope in you not be disgraced because of me; God of Israel, may those who seek you not be put to shame because of me.	7 May those who wait for you not be put to shame because of me, O Lord, Lord of hosts; may those who seek you not be embarrassed because of me, O God of Israel,
7 For I endure scorn for your sake, and shame covers my face. 8 I am a foreigner to my own family, a stranger to my own mother's children; 9 for zeal for your house consumes me, and the insults of those who insult you fall on me.	8 because for your sake I bore reproach; embarrassment covered my face. 9 I became estranged from my brothers, and a visitor to the sons of my mother, 10 because the zeal for your house consumed me, and the reproaches of those who reproach you fell on me.
10 When I weep and fast, I must endure scorn; 11 when I put on sackcloth, people make sport of me. 12 Those who sit at the gate mock me, and I am the song of the drunkards.	11 And I bent my soul with fasting, and it became reproaches to me. 12 And I made sackcloth my clothing and became an illustration to them. 13 About me those who sit in a gate would gossip, and against me those who drink wine would make music.

---

89. The same tune is mentioned at the outset of Psalms 60 and 80, apparently a lament tune, but sadly we don't know what it is.

13 But I pray to you, Lord,
in the time of your favor;
in your great love, O God,
answer me with your sure salvation.

14 Rescue me from the mire,
do not let me sink;
deliver me from those who hate me,
from the deep waters.
15 Do not let the floodwaters engulf me
or the depths swallow me up
or the pit close its mouth over me.

16 Answer me, Lord, out of the goodness
of your love;
in your great mercy turn to me.

17 Do not hide your face from your servant;
answer me quickly, for I am in trouble.

18 Come near and rescue me;
deliver me because of my foes.

19 You know how I am scorned, disgraced
and shamed;
all my enemies are before you.
20 Scorn has broken my heart
and has left me helpless;
I looked for sympathy, but there was
none,
for comforters, but I found none.
21 They put gall in my food
and gave me vinegar for my thirst.

22 May the table set before them become
a snare;
may it become retribution and a trap.
23 May their eyes be darkened so they
cannot see,
and their backs be bent forever.
24 Pour out your wrath on them;
let your fierce anger overtake them.

25 May their place be deserted;
let there be no one to dwell in their tents.

26 For they persecute those you wound
and talk about the pain of those you hurt.

14 But as for me, with my prayer to you,
O Lord!
It is a time of favor, O God, in the
abundance of your mercy.
Hearken to me with truth of your deliverance.
15 Save me from the mud so that I shall
not get stuck;
may I be rescued from those who hate me
and from the depth of waters.
16 Do not let a tempest of water over-
whelm me
or a deep swallow me up
or a cistern close its mouth over me.
17 Listen to me, O Lord, because your
mercy is kind;
according to the abundance of your
compassion look upon me.
18 Do not turn away your face from your
servant;
because I am in affliction, quickly hearken to me.
19 Pay attention to my soul, and redeem
it;
for the sake of my enemies rescue me.
20 For you know my reproach
and my shame and my embarrassment;
before you are all those who afflict me.
21 Reproach my heart
A expected—and misery,
and I waited for one that would
sympathize, and none existed,
and for comforters, and I did not find.
22 And they gave gall as my food,
and for my thirst they gave me vinegar to
drink.
23 Let their table become a trap before
them,
and a retribution and a stumbling block.
24 Let their eyes be darkened so that they
cannot see,
and bend their back permanently.
25 Pour out upon them your wrath,
and may the anger of your wrath overtake them.
26 Let their steading become desolated,
and let there be no one who lives in their
coverts,
27 because they persecuted him whom
you struck,
and to the pain of your wounded they
added.

27 Charge them with crime upon crime; do not let them share in your salvation.	28 Add lawlessness to their lawlessness, and let them not enter in your righteousness.
28 May they be blotted out of the book of life and not be listed with the righteous.	29 Let them be blotted out of the book of the living, and let them not be enrolled among the righteous.
29 But as for me, afflicted and in pain— may your salvation, God, protect me.	30 Poor and in pain I am, and the deliverance of your face, O God, supported me.
30 I will praise God's name in song and glorify him with thanksgiving.	31 I will praise the name of God with an ode; I will magnify him with praise.
31 This will please the Lord more than an ox, more than a bull with its horns and hooves.	32 And it will please the Lord more than a young bull calf bearing horns and hoofs.
32 The poor will see and be glad— you who seek God, may your hearts live! 33 The Lord hears the needy and does not despise his captive people.	33 Let the poor see it and be glad; seek God, and your soul shall live, 34 because the Lord listened to the needy and his own that are in bonds he did not despise.
34 Let heaven and earth praise him, the seas and all that move in them,	35 Let the heavens and the earth praise him, sea and everything that creeps in them,
35 for God will save Zion and rebuild the cities of Judah. Then people will settle there and possess it; 36 the children of his servants will inherit it, and those who love his name will dwell there.	36 because God will save Zion, and the cities of Judea will be built, and they shall live there and inherit it. 37 And the offspring of his slaves shall possess it, and those who love his name shall encamp in it.[90]

It is appropriate to ask from the outset who is the person whose story and character is sketched in this song? Or perhaps one should ask, what *kind* of persons is being depicted here? Verse 17 tells us he is a servant of the Lord, and v. 29 adds he is a "lowly" one, and not just his own rescue but the salvation of other lowly persons is bound up in his salvation. Verse 26 seems clear in indicating that the psalmist has been smitten by God, but as one among "those who you have wounded." This may come as a surprise since the psalmist is emphatic that he is innocent, and he waits on God to rescue him (v. 3), but it will not just

90. As Hossfeld and Zenger, *Psalms 2*, 184 point out, there are not a lot of differences between the LXX and the MT in this psalm except the following: (1) the idea of a powerful windstorm that stirs up the water is referred to in vv. 3 and 16; (2) v. 5 reads "what I did not steal, I then repaid"; (3) in v. 23 the curse is intensified as follows: "may their sacrificial table be . . . and the occasion of falling and punishment for them."

be a personal humiliation if he is not rescued, no, anyone who hopes in Israel's God will be humiliated if he is not rescued. This person is a representative figure, and he is in mourning (fasting and in sackcloth), and in that context we have the saying about zeal for God's house. The implication seems to be that something has gone terribly wrong in, or in regard to, the temple. We have already come across this sort of temple piety in Psalms 42–43, and one may also compare Psalms 84 and 137. Notice how Zion's future figures into the last lines of the second part of this hymn (v. 36).

This person is clearly a public person subject to public scorn (vv. 19–20), but he is also alienated or rejected by members of his own family (v. 8). Here those familiar with the gospel will think of John 7:5. The sufferer looked to his own social group for support, but instead he became the butt of people's jokes and drinking songs (v. 12) and some cruel person, wanting to inflict anguish, gave him "gall for food and vinegar for drink" (v. 21). Again, the passion narrative comes to mind for the Christian reading this song. The psalmist believes that the reproaches and berating that he is enduring are for God's sake, and are indirectly aimed at God (vv. 7, 9 cf. Ps 22:6–8). The final rescue/salvation of the speaker will affect the lowly, the pious, the needy, the prisoners (vv. 32–33). "His salvation will also be a promise to the servants of the Lord who hope for the salvation of Zion and the restoration of Judah, a sign that the scenario of salvation proclaimed by the prophets of the exile will be completed (vv. 35–36). That will be significant for the whole universe (v. 34) because it will mean the coming of the Kingdom of God (cf. 22:27–28)" on earth as it is in heaven.[91]

Who again is this person? The description is generic enough that it could suit various sufferers in Israel's history, and not without reason some applied this psalm to Jeremiah (cf. Jer 7: 1–15; 11:18–20; 15:15–18; 17:14–18; 38:6). Lamentations 3 provides us with a very similar lament, but so does the psalm we treated earlier in this chapter, Psalm 44 (see vv. 13–22). Obviously, some have associated this psalm with Isaiah 53 as well. But there are *some* elements in the psalm that suit the passion narrative about Jesus particularly well, so well that the NT writers can talk about fulfillment of this or that portion of the psalm.

The first stanza of this psalm (vv. 1–3) is a plea for God to rescue a drowning man, if we were to take the words literally, which we shouldn't (cf. Pss 18:16; 29:3; 32:6; 42:7; 46:3). The drowning metaphor

---

91. Mays, *Psalms*, 232. Here I am simply following and amplifying May's helpful comments about the subject of this psalm.

depicts someone in a life-threatening situation, and that is not the whole problem.[92] He has been sending out the distress signal to his God, again and again, so many times that he is hoarse and his throat is dry, and his eyes have grown tired scanning the horizon, looking for and waiting for God to rescue him.

Even that is not the whole problem, because in the second stanza (vv. 4–8) we hear about the huge number of people who for no good reason hate the psalmist, accuse him falsely, and would like to destroy him. He asks God "What I did not steal, must I now restore?" though we cannot really tell what he is referring to. Verse 5 is equally vague, and perhaps should be seen as ironic. Goldingay puts it this way: "It is a hypothetical statement, or another ironical one. Whatever sin there is in the psalmist's life, God knows about it; the enemies do not. It is then God's business to expose it and do something about it. God is in a position to do so," but the detractors of the psalmist are not.[93] Above all, as vv. 6–8 indicate, the psalmist doesn't want either those who hope in God be put to shame because of the psalmist's actions or situation, and he says he has borne the shame himself, which "covers my face," for God's sake. These are surely the concerns of a leader of some sort. The psalmist has even become alienated from his own kin, his mother's children, his closest family. Goldingay reminds that the verb here connotes someone who has been disowned.[94]

According to vv. 9–12, what has really become the obsession of the psalmist is zeal for God's house. Apparently, there have been detractors of it, and the psalmist has been its defender, as he adds that the insults directed at God have fallen on him, even when he is practicing his faith by fasting and going around in mourning attire, regular behavior for those showing sorrow for sin. He has become a joke to some, a subject of malicious gossip for those siting in Jerusalem's gates, and drunkards make up satirical songs about him and sing them!

Verses 13–15 are odd in some respects as the psalmist prays, and the Hebrew suggests he says "at an acceptable or appropriate time God, intervene and answer my pleas" whereas the LXX indicates that now is the favorable time for such intervention. The psalmist returns to his

---

92. This might refer to the ancient water ordeal where someone has been suspected of committing some sin or crime and is tied to a weight and thrown in a large body of water with the assumption that if they survive they must be innocent, if they drown, they were not. See Longman, *Psalms*, 262–63 who also suggests that the reference to theft might allude to the accusation against David in 2 Sam 16:5–14 that he stole the kingship from Saul.
93. Goldingay, *Psalms: Volume 2*, 341; cf. Bruggemann and Bellinger, *Psalms*, 301.
94. Goldingay, *Psalms: Volume 2*, 343; cf. Weiser, *Psalms*, 494.

drowning metaphors in vv. 14–15, but what he is really talking about is being delivered from his enemies, which he likens to being swept away in a flood into a giant sinkhole called "the pit" or into the ocean itself. Terrien even suggests "a mythological memory may lurk behind the allusion to the feminine Pit who shuts her mouth over the miserable sufferer. The poet goes beyond the mere personification of a well or cistern. Descent into Sheol is thus demonized."[95]

The psalmist, in both vv. 13 and vv. 15–20 appeals to God's *ḥesed* (חֶסֶד), rightly rendered "mercy" in various Jewish translations, or it could mean kindness;[96] and in any case he pleads ever more urgently for God to hurry up and intervene. On the theme of the hiddenness of God's face the psalmists' often reflect (cf. Pss 13:2; 22:25; 27:9; 88:15; 102:3; 143:7). It needs to be stressed that the language "save," "redeem," "rescue" does not have their later Christian valence of spiritual salvation.[97] The psalmist is talking about actual rescue from foes and detractors. Verse 20 is poignant, "insults have broken my heart and [as a result] I am in despair." He looked for pity or comfort and found none; to the contrary, people gave him poison for food, and sour vinegar to drink. Gall is a poisonous herb that belongs to the carrot family (cf. Hos 10:4; Deut 32:33; Job 20:16, sometimes paired with wormwood due to its bitterness).[98] Vinegar, far from quenching thirst could even exacerbate it.[99] This reference to food and drink provides the transition to the next stanza.[100]

Verses 22–29 offer a series of curses or imprecations beginning with "let their table be a trap for them, and a snare for their friends" just like the food and drink he was offered. He asks that they may be blinded (see 2 Kings 6), that their "loins" might tremble as God's burning anger pours out on them (cf. Ps 79:6; Jer 10:25), and he adds "let no one live in their tents" (i.e., wipe them out). Verse 26 becomes important at this point; the psalmist accuses the enemies of piling on, so to speak. The psalmist indicates God has struck him down and wounded him, but they attack him on top of that. These are not Job's comforters, these are Job's enemies. The psalmist asks that they be found guilty, and blotted out of the book of the living! The psalmist wants God to kill them.

It should be obvious that this paragraph hardly applies to the depic-

---

95. Terrien, *Psalms*, 502.
96. See the discussion above.
97. See rightly Longman, *Psalms*, 264.
98. See Kidner, *Psalms 1–72*, 247n2.
99. Longman, *Psalms*, 264.
100. See Goldingay, *Psalms: Volume 2*, 349.

tion of Jesus's last day on earth in the Gospels. He did not respond to his enemies this way. He forgave them. Verse 29 says "let your salvation protect me," while his enemies are being blotted out. At least the psalmist leaves this matter of judgment in God's hands, as also is the matter of redemption or rescue. "An historical analogy might be seen at the time of the destruction of Jerusalem. Israel knew that God was behind the Babylonian attack, but they blamed Edom for taking unfair advantage of the situation (Lam. 4:21–22; Obad.)."[101] Perhaps the reference to "Lord YHWH of Armies" in v. 6 has prepared this way for asking God to judge the psalmist enemies by eliminating them. Kidner remarks that there is not simply an emotional difference between the psalmist's zeal and anger and Jesus's. "David's anger was fanned by his zeal for justice, which the Old Testament largely exists to keep before us; but Christ came to crown justice with atonement. Zeal for this, now it is accomplished, will stir us differently: cooling anger instead of kindling it; fostering rather than stifling compassion."[102]

In a dramatic change of tone in vv. 30–36 we are treated to a praise festival. The implication seems to be that if God intervenes, this is what the psalmist will do in response. He will praise and give thanks to God, which God will be more pleased with than literal sacrifices, even huge ones of oxen or bulls (see Leviticus 1). If God responds to the psalmist as requested, then the needy and oppressed and those in chains will see it and it will be a confirmation that there is a compassionate God who cares about them, and this will revive their spirits. The final stanza talks about all of creation praising God because God is going to save Zion and rebuild the Judean cities that have been destroyed (surely a reference to the situation after exile).[103] The final vision is of Jerusalem as once more fully inhabited by God's servants and their children and those who love God's name, much like the end of the book of Isaiah (chs. 65–66).[104]

Because there is such extensive use of this psalm in the NT, indeed it is second only to Psalm 22 among the laments for frequency of citation or allusion, perhaps a summary from Mays as to the diverse usage will be helpful:

It furnished a context for reflection of Jesus' rejection by his own people (John 15:25), on his motive for driving traders from the temple (John 3:17),

---

101. Longman, *Psalms*, 265.
102. Kidner, *Psalms 1–72*, 248.
103. See even Longman, *Psalms*, 262.
104. On which see Witherington, *Isaiah Old and New*, 320–38.

on the bitter treatment he was given instead of pity at the time of his death (Matt 27:34; Mark 15:23; Luke 23:36; John 19:19–30)[105] and on the meaning of his suffering (Rom 15:3). Even the harsh prayer against the persecutors (Ps 69:22–28), which seemed appropriate in the mouth of Jeremiah but not Jesus, took on meaning. Luke saw in it the prayer for vindication answered in the fate of Judas (Acts 1:20). Paul found here a clue to the hardening of those in Israel who rejected Jesus (Rom 11:9–10). For the prophet of Revelation, it pointed to the eschatological outpouring of wrath against the foes of the coming kingdom of God (Rev 16:1).[106]

The project of reading the OT backwards, by which I mean in light of the Christ event, is quite consciously advocated in the Gospel of John. More accurately, we are told that as the original disciples of Jesus were reading the OT, they remembered what Jesus said and how he used the OT, and then followed his lead. Not accidently both the key clues about this are in a context of discussing Psalm 69:9, "zeal for your house will consume me" in John 2. The first of these is John 2:17a just before the citation of that Scripture, "his disciples remembered that it was written." The second of these comes at the end of the pericope at John 2:22a, "after he was raised from the dead, his disciples remembered that he had said this and they believed the Scripture and the word that Jesus had spoken." Now the nearest saying of Jesus to this remark is Jesus's words "Destroy this temple and in three days I will raise it up."

There is, however, no OT Scripture that says *that*. Could it be referring to Psalm 69:9? Possibly, but in any case Jesus himself does not say "zeal for your house will consume me" here or in the Synoptics; indeed in the Synoptics a very different Scripture is found on Jesus's lips, one largely from Jeremiah (cf Mark 11:15–17 and parr.). Should we conclude here that the fourth evangelist is suggesting something that the author of Hebrews says explicitly, namely that Jesus is speaking in various OT texts, including the Psalms? Probably not. We've already seen how Psalms 69:5 and 69:22–25 are portions of Psalm 69 that Jesus would never have said (and didn't). So it is taking things much too far to say, as C. H. Dodd once did, "the intention of the New Testament writers is clearly to apply the whole [of Psalm 69] to the suffering and ultimate triumph of Christ."[107]

---

105. See Goldingay, *Psalms: Volume 2*, 356, speaking about the imprecatory stanza in vv. 22–29: "There is some irony in the fact that the point where the NT concentrates most of its use of the psalm is where commentators see it as unworthy of the NT."

106. Mays, *Psalms*, 232–33.

Did the NT writers apply a good deal of this psalm to Jesus? Yes, of course. But they used it *selectively*, as they did other psalms and other OT texts. While there are other OT texts that Jesus recites and uses to speak about his own experience and ministry, perhaps including Psalm 69, "zeal for your house . . ." is not one of them, though the evangelist thinks it appropriately comments on *why* Jesus did what he did in the temple; and this brings up another major point.

It would appear that the psalmist in Psalm 69 is *defending* temple piety as it then existed because it was being ridiculed by some cultured detractors. This is something very different from Jesus being upset with the corruption in and of the temple, and reacting with anger. In other words, zeal is involved in both the psalm and in the Gospel texts, but zeal and anger about two different things, it would appear. Here it is well to remember that the NT writers knew perfectly well that one could not simply replicate or follow all the words of the psalmist in this or other psalms, and continue to be a true follower of Jesus and his teaching. Even so conservative a commentator as Kidner has this to say on the matter:

> Can a Christian use these cries for vengeance as his own? The short answer must surely be no; no more than he should echo the curses of Jeremiah or the protests of Job. He may of course translate them into affirmations of God's judgment, and into denunciations of "the spiritual hosts of wickedness" which are the real enemy. As for the [persons] of flesh and blood who "live as enemies of the cross of Christ" or who make themselves our enemies, our instructions *are to pray not against them but for them*; to turn them from the power of Satan to God; to repay their evil with good; and to choose none of their ways. "As [persons] in need, who may yet be rescued, they are to be loved and sought; as [persons] who have injured us, they must be forgiven. But as [persons] to follow or to cultivate"—and here the psalms and the New Testament speak with one voice—"they are to be rejected utterly."[108]

We must be careful in our enthusiasm for figural or retrospective readings of the OT not to say more than the evidence warrants. Certainly the evangelist sees the *pattern* of the righteous sufferer who cares about the temple as depicted in Psalm 69 played out in Jesus's life.

---

107. C. H. Dodd, *According to the Scriptures: The Sub-structure of New Testament Theology* (London: Nisbet, 1952), 97; see the whole discussion in pp. 57–60 and pp. 95–97.

108. Kidner, *Psalms 1-72*, 32. He is actually quoting himself in this paragraph. I have substituted the word persons for men, since that is what he means in this passage. I have added the emphasis on the phrase about prayer.

This comports well with early Jewish expectations that the messiah would purge and reconstitute the temple (see Psalms of Solomon 17:21–22, 36).[109] It is also important to note that one of the things that distinguishes the Fourth Gospel from the Synoptics is more focus on the use of the Psalms than, say Isaiah, to characterize and depict the ministry of Jesus. Interestingly, Psalm 69 comes up early, middle, and late in the Fourth Gospel, and not just in the passion narrative itself, so there is no question but that this psalm was very important to the evangelist in the portrayal of Jesus and his life.

It is hard to know for sure whether the evangelist is following the LXX or the MT in this case because the two are quite close, but the one significant difference between the quote in John 2:17 and the LXX is that whereas the verb "consume" is in the aorist in the LXX, here the verb is future (possibly seeing the Hebrew as representing a prophetic perfect?), which has led Köstenberger and others, probably rightly, to suggest that this is pointing forward to the death of Jesus where he is "consumed" by his zeal for God.

Interestingly, despite the closeness of Psalm 22 and Psalm 69 on various fronts, both depicting the righteous sufferer, the evangelists use the material differently. The only saying of Jesus from the cross in Matthew and Mark is the quotation of Psalm 22:1, which is entirely absent from John and also from Luke's portrayal of the death. But it is John 19:24 that actually cites Psalm 22:18, whereas the Synoptics do not. On the other hand, all four Gospels allude to Psalm 69:21. Matthew 27:34 mentions the gall and 27:48 mentions the sour vinegar, whereas Mark 15:36 only mentions the latter, and Luke 23:36 follows suit. But in John 19:28–29 we have the story of the offer of wine vinegar, which is said to be in response to Jesus's saying "I am thirsty," which in turn is said to be a fulfillment of Scripture. But from where? In Psalm 69:3 we hear about the sufferer having a parched throat and in v. 21 there is the reference to being offered vinegar to drink, but no saying "I am thirsty."[110]

Is there a difference between a citation and claiming Scripture is fulfilled or brought to completion? The answer I think must be yes. Jesus in the broad sense is fulfilling the story of the righteous sufferer depicted in various psalms, especially Psalms 22 and 69. The reference

---

109. See the discussion in Köstenberger, "John," 431–32, and also Daly-Denton, "Psalms in John's Gospel," 123.
110. Notice that Köstenberger does not discuss John 19:28–29 as a Scripture citation despite detailed attention to all other citations and major allusions.

to the parched throat and the offer of gall to drink is enough for the evangelist to say that when Jesus said "I am thirsty," Scripture was being brought to fulfillment. We must remember again and again the point that Hays makes:

> There is a heavy concentration of Psalm texts within the group of Old Testament passages cited by John. More than 60 percent of John's quotations come from the Psalter. . . . This emphasis on the Psalter follows almost inevitably from John's concentration on the passion and death of Jesus as the center of gravity in his narrative. Because the Psalms foreshadow—or as John might prefer, *express*—the suffering of the crucified/exalted Jesus, it is understandable that a retrospective reading of Scripture as witness to Jesus would be drawn to these texts.[111]

Here perhaps is the right place to say something about the use of Psalm 69:4 in John 15:25. The quotation is said to come from "their law" and reads "they hated me without a cause." The context in John has to do with the hatred of Jesus and his followers by "the world," and in this case in particular by some Jews. We are told that in so hating Jesus they are fulfilling this particular scripture. Psalm 35:19 also has to be considered as a possible source of this quotation (cf. on the idea Ps 109:3 and Ps 119:161). Daly-Denton suggests "since all of these possible sources are in the Psalter, we are dealing here with what we might call a familiar phrase from the psalms of David that, in the evangelist's view, finds its full significance on the lips of Jesus."[112] As John 10:34 (and cf. 8:17) suggests as well, "law" here has the broader sense of the OT. The quotation seems to be from the LXX in view of the translation of the adverb here. As Köstenberger points out, there are multiple good reasons why this text is cited here in the context of Jesus's last warnings to his disciples of how they will face similar suffering that he is facing and will face it in full measure soon: (1) the reference to the large number of the sufferer's enemies; (2) the great power of those enemies; (3) the false charges leveled by the enemies; and (4) the righteous sufferer's trust in God.[113]

Hays is right that the fulfillment language reflects an apologetic motivation, "the Evangelist is explaining that the suffering and rejection experienced by Jesus in the passion story was not some unforeseen disaster; rather it was foreordained and played out in fulfillment of

---

111. Hays, *Echoes of Scripture in the Gospels*, 286–87. Emphasis original.
112. Daly-Denton, "Psalms in John's Gospel," 131.
113. Köstenberger, "John," 494.

God's will with Jesus' full knowledge and participation." As he says, it is instructive to compare the various citations where the fulfillment language comes up in John: John 12:37–40 (Isa 53:1; 6:10), John 13:18 (Ps 41:9), John 15:24–25 (Pss 35:19; 69:5), John 17:12 (Ps 41:9??), John 19:23–24 (Ps 22:19), John 19:28–29 (Ps 69:21) and John 19:36–37 (Ps 34:21, no bones broken but his side is pierced; see Zech 12:10).[114]

In John, the Psalms are not just cited and alluded to, they provide back stories, especially aspects of the back story of the righteous sufferer; they are taken over and used to depict the life, and especially, the death of Jesus. Jesus fulfills the role and story of the righteous sufferer, but this does not mean at all that the NT writers think *everything* that is said in a particular psalm is apropos of Jesus's story. They are *selective* in what they use when it comes to language, back story, citation, allusion, and echo.

The portrayal of Jesus as the sinless lamb of God and son of God requires such selectivity, as the psalmist often says things Jesus would never say and reports things Jesus would never do. The evangelists cite what suits, and they allude to what illuminates, and they appropriate stories which illustrate, and they use OT language that leads to understanding of Jesus, and this is because *the primary story they wish to tell is the recent story of Jesus,* and Scripture is used to illuminate it in various ways. The primary stories and texts are then *not* the OT ones and there is not a compulsion to try and conform Jesus to all sorts of OT material that does not fit.[115]

An extremely interesting use of Psalm 69, and one that underscores what I have just said, is found in Acts 1:20. Luke has Peter tell the story of Hakeldama, the field of blood, and why it is named such through its association with Judas and his death. Then Peter says "it is written in the book of Psalms: 'Let his homestead become desolate, and let there be no one to live in it' and 'let another take his position of overseer.'" Let's be clear that Luke tells a rather different story here about the demise of Judas than we find in the Gospels. In fact Luke says absolutely nothing about the demise of Judas after the betrayal in his Gospel, but then, neither does Mark, his source for some of his passion narrative.

It is Matthew 27:5 that briefly refers to Judas hanging himself. No

---

114. Hays, *Echoes of Scripture in the Gospels*, 286.

115. Obviously, there is *shaping* of the Jesus story on the basis of the OT and vice versa, but my point would be that the evangelists and other NT writers are creative in their handling of the OT *precisely because the main story* is the Jesus story. The Jesus story is not being created out of, or made up on the basis of, the OT. The blueprint is the remarkable story of Jesus, the interior decorating and explanation and correlation is done on the basis of the OT *where it suits the Jesus story.*

other Gospel mentions it. The account given in Acts 1:18 has a rather clear echo in part in the fragmentary material we have from Papias which reads, "Judas walked about in this world a sad example of impiety; for his body having swollen to such an extent that he could not pass where a chariot could pass easily, he was crushed by the chariot, *so that his bowels gushed out*" (*Exegesis of the Sayings of the Lord*, frag. 3.1742-44). We will not pause here to ask where Luke got the story in v. 18 (but see 2 Sam 20:10), but we need to ask about the use of the Psalms here.

First notice that in Luke 13:35 Jesus speaking in Jerusalem says "your house is left to you" referring to the temple and apparently speaking to Pharisees who have warned him Herod is after him (13:31). So before we ever get to Acts 1:20, have we already encountered Psalm 69:25 on the lips of Jesus? Probably not. Bear in mind that Psalm 69:25 is part of the imprecation passage in the psalm, and in fact the words of Jesus here are considerably closer to Jeremiah 22:5 "this house shall become a desolation," only Jesus is saying that this prophecy was now about to be fulfilled in light of their rejection of Jesus (cf. Jer 12:7; Ezek 8:6; 11:23; and Ps 69:25).[116] Turning to Acts 1:20, Peter says he is citing the Psalms. The citation from Psalm 69:25 here is fairly close to the LXX, except that there is a change from the plural to the singular, so the curse focuses on one particular person, Judas, and there is an omission of the reference to tents.[117] Matthew 27:7 may be of some relevance here, as we are told there that the property bought with the blood money was turned into a burial place for foreigners (see the whole story in 27:5-10). As Marshall say, Peter's version is more of a loose citation, or better said, a paraphrase. If we compare this material to the use of Psalm 69 to help interpret Jesus's story, it should be clear that the NT writers are not suggesting that we may hear just the voice of Jesus in such psalms, or even just the story of Jesus. No; it is being suggested that we also find prophetic words about the story of Judas and his demise. This is not a christological use of the psalm we find in Acts 1:20.

Even more intriguing is the use of Psalm 69:22-23 in Romans 11:9-10. In general it appears Paul is following a Greek version of the psalm, but if it is the LXX, he has omitted the words "before them" from "may their table become before them a snare and a recompense and a stumbling block [*skandalon*]" and he moves the reference to recompense to

---

116. See the discussion by Pao and Schnabel, "Luke," 336.
117. Marshall, "Acts," 530.

the final position for emphasis, and he adds the words "trap" after "snare." Notice first of all that Paul is applying this not to Jesus or his disciples, but to non-Christian Jews who, according to Paul, have been temporarily broken off from the people of God. This sort of application has some parallel in texts like Odes of Solomon 5:5 and Midr. Esther 7:9 where the psalm is applied to wicked Jews. Seifrid wrongly suggests that Paul is applying these terms to Israel as a whole. To the contrary, he very clearly distinguishes between the elect Jews (presumably the Jewish Christians) and "the rest" who were hardened.[118] Paul certainly wasn't talking about himself as a Jew when he refers to those hardened, nor other Jews who were followers of Jesus, whom Paul saw as "the righteous remnant" or "the elect" among the Jews.

In a helpful and detailed discussion of Paul's use of Psalm 69 in Romans 11, Wagner points out that Paul is saying that David himself mentioned by name, through the psalm, is calling Israel to account, adding his weight to Moses's and Isaiah's indictments. Wagner agrees that on the whole, Paul's citation, with the variations mentioned above, follows the LXX rather closely. He thinks however that the phrase "and a trap" comes from blending this citation with Psalm 35:8 (34:8 LXX), "let the snare/trap he does not recognize come upon him." Wagner points out the notable similarities between these two psalms, including the phrase "those who hate me without a cause," a reference to fasting and sackcloth, and becoming a byword because of one's piety. Further, both psalms have strong imprecations calling down darkness on the psalmist's foes. Also, both psalms are about a righteous sufferer. It is fair to conclude from the various ways Psalms 22 and 69 are used in the NT that the songs about the righteous sufferer aided christological readings of the OT. Wagner also thinks that Paul is drawing on Isaiah 8:14 as well, so that we have something of a gumbo of three texts in Paul's citations here in Romans 11.

Especially important is Wagner's observation that the likely reason Paul doesn't apply the rest of the imprecations in Psalm 69 to his fellow Jews is because it doesn't suit Paul's view in regard to those temporarily broken off from the people of God. As Wagner says, Paul immediately after this insists that Israel has not taken a fatal fall (Rom 11:11). God is not finished with Israel yet, as Romans 11:25–32 makes clear.[119] Notice again the selective use of some psalm verses by the NT writer, not a wholesale use of the psalm in question. Even when Paul places the

---

118. See Seifrid, "Romans," 670.
119. Wagner, *Heralds*, 257–65. See also Keesmaat, "Psalms in Romans and Galatians," 155.

words of the psalmist on the lips of Jesus himself as at Romans 15:9-11 (drawing on Pss 18:49 and 117:1), Paul is not suggesting Jesus would have endorsed or repeated all of the material in these psalms as his own views.[120]

Turning to Romans 15:3 we find a citation from Psalm 69:9b, "the insults of those who insult you have fallen on me." The citation here is a case where the LXX doesn't really deviate from the MT. This comes in the context of Paul's telling his mostly gentile audience that even Christ did not please himself, but put up with the failings of the weak. Christ is not merely a righteous sufferer, but he is a paradigm for Christians to follow, even when verbally abused.[121] While Seifrid suggests that Paul is addressing the Jewish Christians in Rome who should expect abuse from pagans for still associating with Jews, it seems far more likely in view of the main audience in this letter that Paul is telling his gentile converts that they should put up with the over-scrupulous Jewish Christians in their midst, indeed embrace them, and accept whatever abuse they would receive from pagans, in solidarity with their Jewish fellow believers.[122] In any case, Paul has Jesus cite the psalm here as apropos of Jesus's own situation: identifying with the weak and suffering abuse.[123] It is of course possible that Paul was also thinking of his own situation of abuse for the sake of the gospel.

Revelation 3:5 alludes to Psalm 69:28, only for John "the book of life" is the book of everlasting life, not the book of this life, so the threat is more dire than in the psalm, where the curse implies they ought to be killed. There is a definite difference between the book of the living and the book of (everlasting) life. As for the blotting out of a name from a book we may also compare Exodus 32:32-33 and Daniel 12:1.[124] The use of the term "erasure" in Revelation 3:5 points to Psalm 69 as the primary if not sole source of this allusion, and Moyise is absolutely right that there is no basis whatsoever for the suggestion by Beale and McDonough that John is only talking about people in Sardis who "thought" their names were in the book of life. This makes no sense, since it is Jesus himself who is threatening to blot out names that he says *are* in the book of life, names of some of those being addressed in

---

120. See Hays, *Echoes of Scripture in the Letters of Paul*, 162-63.
121. See the discussion in Keesmaat, "Psalms in Romans and Galatians," 156; Wagner, *Heralds*, 156.
122. See Seifrid, "Romans," 686.
123. While in the original psalm the "you" in question is probably God, and that may be the case here as well, it is also possible in view of the Pauline context that we are hearing about Jesus identifying with the abused weak.
124. See Gregory K. Beale and Sean M. McDonough, "Revelation," in Beale, *Commentary on the New Testament Use*, 1096.

Sardis who are provisionally in the book so long as they are faithful to the end and "conquer" in the sense John means. As Moyise comments, "one would expect such false-Christians to be warned of exposure rather than erasure."[125]

It is clear enough that the psalms influenced and were used by the writers of the NT in a myriad of ways to tell the good news about what God has done in Jesus. This is true even when we are talking about incidental or minor evidence of the impact of the Psalms on the NT. The impact is pervasive, even more so than Isaiah's impact in the sense of not just the direct and intentional use of the OT texts in quotes and allusions, but in the unreflective use of the language, images, and metaphors of the Psalms, as well as the quotes and allusions. Accordingly, we now turn to some of the less commented on or less obvious impact of the second book of the Psalter in the NT.

The Lexicon of Faith: The Broader Use of Psalms 42–72

Occasionally there are isolated quotations, a single verse quoted and used, for example, in a catena of quotations. A good example of this is the use of Psalm 45:6, "your throne O God endures forever and ever, your scepter is a scepter of equity." This psalm, which is paired with Psalm 102:25–27, is probably a celebration of a royal marriage, but the author of Hebrews has something very different in mind. Hebrews 1:8 as part of several quotations has "But of the Son he says 'your throne O God, is forever and ever, and the righteous scepter is the scepter of your kingdom.'" The original psalm is of course speaking about Yahweh, but in Hebrews, dramatically, Yahweh is speaking about his Son, Jesus, and calling him God![126] Since the Son belongs in the God category, his throne and rule can be said to be forever, and his superiority is clearly demonstrated. While this psalm was used of the messiah in early Judaism (cf. 4Q252 V,1–4; Testament of Judah 24:1–6), these examples fall short of calling the messiah God, taking "O God" as a vocative referring to Yahweh, whereas the messiah is the king in the passage. Not so the author of Hebrews. The LXX corresponds fairly exactly to the Hebrew text, except for small things like the Hebrew has the reverse subject and predicate order to that which we find in the LXX. The author of Hebrews generally seems to follow the LXX.[127]

Some echoes of the Psalms are very faint, and come more at the level

---

125. See rightly, Moyise, "Psalms in the Book of Revelation," 239.
126. See the discussion in Attridge, "Psalms in Hebrews," 202.
127. See the discussion by Guthrie, "Hebrews," 938–39.

of ideas and some at the level of actual verbal correspondence, but only involving a few words. For example, in Psalm 48:2 the phrase "the city of the great King" is used of Jerusalem in a praise hymn, and Jesus uses the phrase in Matthew 5:35, "Jerusalem, the city of the great King." There are so many of these kinds of subtle uses of phrases from the psalms, including often on the lips of Jesus, that it is hard to doubt it was part of his language of faith, one of the ways he articulated his piety.

Some have found in Psalm 50:12b, which reads "for the world and all that is in it is mine," an echo in 1 Corinthians 10:26 "the earth is the Lord's and the fullness thereof," but actually Paul is citing Psalm 24:1 there, not Psalm 50:12b. This is one of those cases where we are dealing with a common idea in the Psalter, and we should be cautious in claiming an allusion or partial quote of some specific verse on the basis of just a common idea. There needs to be some verbal correspondence.

There may be a slight allusion to Psalm 63:2, "I have looked upon you in the sanctuary, beholding your power and glory" in the final words of Stephen in Acts 7:55, where it is reported he looked into heaven and saw the glory of God and Jesus. There is a faint echo of Psalm 65:8, "you silence the roaring of the sea, the roaring of their waves" in several places in the Synoptic Gospels, only now applied to Jesus's stilling of the effects of the storm on the waves in the sea of Galilee (cf. Matt 8:26; 14:32; Mark 4:39; Luke 8:24; and cf. 21:25).

At the level of concepts, there is possibly an echo of Psalm 66:18 in John 9:31 where the man born blind starts preaching to the authorities saying, "we know God doesn't listen to sinners, but he does listen to one who worships him and obeys his will." The verse in the psalm is expressed as part of prayer suggesting that if indeed he had cherished sin in his heart, God would not have listened to him.

Psalm 68:18 reads, "you ascended the high mount, leading captives in your train, and receiving gifts from people" (MT), whereas the LXX has "you ascended on high, you led captivity captive, you received gifts from a person." By contrast we have in Ephesians 4:8, "Therefore it is said: 'when he ascended on high he made captivity itself a captive; he gave gifts to his people.'" What are we to make of this remarkable transformation of a psalm text? Even a cursory reading through a half dozen commentaries on Ephesians makes clear this is a crux. On the one hand, the first half of the quotation seems pretty clearly just to be following the LXX, except it has been put into the third person by Paul. On the other hand, neither the MT nor the LXX provide any encouragement for the translation "he gave gifts. . . ."[128] Nevertheless, there is some evidence from early Judaism that this verse was thought to refer to Moses going up on the mountain and *receiving* the ten commandments.[129]

Further, there are not many quotations from the OT in Ephesians at all; and when we notice that the formula "therefore it says" is used in Ephesians 5:14 to introduce something that certainly isn't a straightforward OT quotation[130], then we may need to consider that Paul is citing something else, perhaps a midrashic treatment on Psalm 68 similar to the use of it in early Judaism, only Paul has now referred it not to Moses going up on the mountain to receive the law and then coming back down and giving it to Israel, but rather to Christ ascending into heaven (having dealt with the powers and principalities) and giving the Holy Spirit thereafter to his followers. This seems to be the most likely explanation of what is transpiring here. Support for this reading can be found in the fact that Psalm 68 was used at the Pentecost festival to celebrate the giving of the law to humankind (cf. b. Meg. 31a; Jubilees 6:17–19; 1 QS 1.7–2.19).[131] One further point may be helpful, Psalm 68:29 says "because of your temple at Jerusalem, kings bear gifts to you," which suggests a further explication of v. 18 (see the echo in Rev 21:24). This makes rather certain that the original reading of the psalm had to do with the receiving, not the giving of gifts.

This partial citation or use of a "developed" version of Psalm 68:19 should serve as a reminder that: (1) the early Christians were creative in their use of their source material; and (2) we should NOT expect exegesis of the OT text when what we have is a sort of homiletical use of the OT, not unlike what we find elsewhere in early Judaism when a contemporizing midrash was attempted using an OT text as a starter kit.

Having said all that, there is one further possibility to consider in the use of that verse from Psalm 68 in Ephesians. Michael Heiser suggests the following: (1) placing the proper stress on captives, Paul is clearly not referring to followers of Jesus, but rather those over whom

---

128. The appeal to Targumic tradition (Midrash Tehillin on Ps 68:11) does provide a parallel where the word "give" rather than "receive" is used in the rendering of this psalm, but as Moritz rightly says, this targum comes from hundreds of years later, and could hardly be said to influence the writer of Ephesians. See the thorough discussion in Moritz, "Psalms in Ephesians and Colossians," 188–95.

129. See the discussion in Ben Witherington III, *The Letters to Philemon, the Colossians, and the Ephesians: A Socio-rhetorical Commentary on the Captivity Epistles*, (Grand Rapids: Eerdmans, 2007), 286–90.

130. See ibid., 310.

131. See the helpful discussion in Frank Thielman, "Ephesians," in Beale, *Commentary on the New Testament Use*, 821–24.

Christ has triumphed, namely the powers of darkness; (2) in the original psalm, the idea was Yahweh triumphing over the idols, the pagan demonic deities of Bashan; and (3) Christ put these deities in their jail cell beneath the earth—in Tartarus, the original prison of the Titans in the Iliad (*Il.* 8:1–3, "or I will hurl him down into dark Tartarus far into the deepest pit under the earth, where the gates are iron and the floor bronze, as far beneath Hades as heaven is high above the earth;" cf. 2 Pet 2:4).[132]

One of the reasons for oversight when it comes to a book like Revelation is that so much of the book reflects OT language in a more general way than one can see from obvious citations or allusions. The last psalm in book 2 of the Psalter, Psalm 72, is a good example of what I mean. The "Solomon" psalm (Ps 72:1–2) is used to characterize the rider on the white horse as one who will judge the world in righteousness, who is soon thereafter called the King of Kings (Rev 19:11 and 16), just as the outset of Psalm 72 talks about righteousness being bequeathed to the king and one who is also a king's son. Or, Revelation 21:26 tells the tale of how peoples will bring into the new Jerusalem the glory and honor of the nations, an echo perhaps of Psalm 72:10 and 15, where we hear about the gold and tribute being brought to Solomon in Jerusalem, a motif also found in Matthew 2:11 in regard to the magi.

This second book of the Psalter ends appropriately with a benediction, a good word about the good God from whom all blessing flow. The phrase "blessed be the Lord, the God of Israel" found at Psalm 72:18 is also found on the lips of Zechariah at Luke 1:68 in his *benedictio*. The language of the Psalms naturally springs to mind and occurs on the lips of the faithful, perhaps most especially when they want to praise God. While we are told in Psalm 72:20 that the sung prayers of David end here, in fact we will see this not quite accurate, as we turn now to the third book of the Psalter.

Conclusions

We have covered a considerable amount of ground in this chapter, and have learned quite a few things about both the nature of the psalms

---

132. Michael S. Heiser, *The Unseeen Realm: Recovering the Supernatural Worldview of the Bible* (Bellingham, WA: Lexham Press, 2015), 292–93. He also suggests that the gifts given were some to be apostles, prophets, etc. (Eph 4:11), which is possible, but some would see the Holy Spirit as the gift given when Christ ascended, however that is not referred to in the context of the discussion in Ephesians 4.

in this particular collection and about the various creative ways the NT writers were using this material. Some patterns become obvious: the righteous sufferer psalms were ready to hand and easy to use to talk about the righteous suffering of Jesus or his first followers. The patterns of sin, repentance, restoration and forgiveness were also easily transferrable from the psalmist's reflections to Christian reflections on "the human dilemma" and the seriousness of the sin problem for humanity. Because of the recognition of the universal scope of human sin, involving everyone, even pious leaders of God's people, it is also not surprising that when a term like *hesed* was used to characterize God's response, the word had the sense of mercy, undeserved kindness, not covenant loyalty. Mercy was not owed the sinner, but fortunately it characterized the God of the Bible. This readily transferred as well to descriptions of Jesus and his gospel message. What did not transfer were the imprecations against other human beings, however much they accurately and truthfully revealed what was on the hearts of various psalmists.

We have had a further reminder in this chapter about the *selectivity* in the use of psalm material by the NT writers, whether we are talking about quotes, allusions, echoes, or just key phrases and ideas. Indeed, reading the psalms through the lens of the Christ event *forced* the NT writers to be selective in what they chose to use to describe the life and teachings of Jesus, or to describe the lives and teachings of his earliest followers. It is saying too much that the NT writers, in their enthusiasm, hoped their audiences would apply *all* of the content of this or that psalm to Christ or their own situations. Definitely not. What this in turn meant as well is that even when there was encouragement or hints in some cases for the NT audiences to go back and read more of the psalm than just the bit quoted in a NT text and reflect on how it might further inform one's understanding of Christ and the gospel, this did not give a carte blanche to see if the whole psalm was fulfilled or filled out further by Christ or his disciples.

The psalms were to be read prayerfully, carefully, and *selectively* following the lead of the NT writers. Metalepsis was only occasionally in play and encouraged. Most of the time this was no more the case than that the NT writers were doing contextual exegesis of the OT. For example, the "zeal for thy house" saying meant one thing on the lips of David, but would mean something very different as applied to a Jesus who cleansed Herod's temple.

A further point to be emphasized is that the improvisations and creativity we see in the handling of the OT by the NT writers, often adopting and adapting it to new settings and offering previously unprecedented readings of OT texts, reflects a situation where a stable text is assumed, indeed a canonical text is assumed, which allows for paraphrase and improvisation from the baseline text, *without detracting from either the stable text or its original uses in its first contexts.*

In fact, we should *not* see the creativity of the NT handling of the Psalms as clear evidence that there were many OT Greek texts in play for the NT writers, or that there was textual chaos in general, or that the canon of the OT was not largely closed by Jesus's day. No, the creativity is brought to the stable text *by the NT writers themselves,* it does not likely reflect a bunch of different Greek versions of the OT from which the NT writers could choose.[133]

More than literal quotations or allusions of the Psalms, what we have encountered is the Psalms serving as the lexicon or source of the language the writers of the NT use to express the gospel story, their own faith, the way they articulate the human dilemma, and so much more. They speak "psalmese" if we can put it that way: it is the air they breath, the prayers they pray, the songs they sing, and the thoughts they have about Christ and the Christ event. This is why just studying the clear quotations or allusions to the Psalms in the NT could never get to the bottom of the influence that book has had on the NT writers, as the Lexicon of Faith section in each of these chapters will show again and again.

The use of the Psalms being fairly ubiquitous in the Gospels (especially in John), and in the retelling of the good news in the speeches in Acts, has raised the question of whether or not the gospel narrative *itself* has been constructed out of the OT. Raymond Brown's majesterial study of the death of Jesus led him to address this very question in some detail. In discussing the use of Psalm 22 in particular, he argues that at most that OT text led early Christian writers to do three things: (1) concentrate on certain details in the passion narrative (e.g., the piercing of Jesus's feet and hands); (2) dramatize the mockery and hostility toward Jesus from those critics observing the crucifixion at close hand; and (3) highlight the reversal in Jesus's abandonment in death and subsequent triumph.[134] The primary story was the Jesus tradition; the OT, including the Psalms, served to help interpret and express that

---

133. On this subject see Appendix B below.
134. Raymond E. Brown, *The Death of the Messiah: From Gethsemane to the Grave; a Commentary on the Passion Narratives in the Four Gospels,* ABRL (New York Doubleday, 1994), 1462.

story, but was not the basis for its composition. We have seen and will see confirmation that this is correct.

Brown was talking about the Synoptic portrayals, but Thompson is right that in John there is no abandonment by God nor a cry of dereliction. The presentation is different, including a use of *different portions* of Psalm 22 and other psalms than are used in the Synoptics. As she so helpfully points out, in the first major portion of his Gospel (1:1–12:16) the fourth evangelist introduces OT quotes with the phrase "as it is written," but in the second half some form of the formula of fulfillment (e.g, "that the scripture might be fulfilled") comes into play (in 12:16–19:42; there are no quotations in John 20–21).[135] The strong emphasis on the passion and triumph of Christ as a fulfillment of the Scriptures, particularly the Psalms, reflects the apologetic need to demonstrate how this unexpected outcome fulfills rather than disproves that Jesus is the Christ of Scripture. Thompson further notes that there is no mention of David, or that these quotations come from the Psalms, in John 12–19, but why?[136] Psalms 22, 34, 41, and 69 are all cited in the Johannine passion narrative but not attributed to David or the Psalter. Why? We will need to contemplate these sorts of questions further as we turn to book 3 of the Psalter, where yet more surprises now await us, not the least of which is that there is almost no mention of David at all in either the prescripts or the content of book 3 of the Psalms.

---

135. Thompson, "They Bear Witness to Me," 267–83.
136. Ibid., 269.

5

Psalter Book 3 (Psalms 73–89)

Asaph's Answers

The 89th Psalm is a prophecy of Christ and his Kingdom. The psalmist calls it a heavenly Kingdom (as Christ himself does in the Gospel). It takes up the prophecy of Christ given to David and emphasizes it with an abundant spirit. Particularly, the psalmist emphasizes that this kingdom shall never, for the sake of any sin, come to an end or be left behind. Accordingly, our salvation shall not be based on our piety.
—Martin Luther, "Preface to Psalm 89"[1]

The third and fourth books of the Psalter are quite brief compared to the others, containing seventeen and eighteen psalms respectively. There is exactly one "psalm of David" in book 3, namely Psalm 86. What this probably meant in practical terms is that those who were prone to read Davidic and royal psalms messianically found less material of use in book 3 of the Psalter. Sure enough, when we look at the lists of quotes, allusions and echoes what we discover is that only three or four songs in this collection, a collection mainly connected with Asaph, are used heavily in the NT, and we will look at each of these in detail: Psalms 78, 79, 80, and 89. There are several others of this collection that

---

1. Luther, *Reading the Psalms with Luther*, 210.

come in for a bit of important use, but on the whole the NT writers are not drawn to many of the seventeen psalms in this "book."

Of Dark Sayings and Parables: Psalm 78

Apart from Psalm 119, this is indeed the longest psalm in the Psalter, and unlike most everything else in the Psalter, it does not address God, it addresses the people directly with a teaching.[2] The Masoretes pointed out that Psalm 78:36 is the exact middle of the some 2,524 verses in the whole Psalter.[3] This salvation historical ode can be divided up into three sections: (1) a rather lengthy introduction in vv. 1–11 orienting the hearer and explaining what the song is about, namely, instructions on how not to be like one's ancestors (vv.8–9); (2) vv. 12–39, which beat the drum about the failures of the wilderness wandering generation; and (3) vv. 40–72, which dwell on the failures of the ancestors in Ephraim. There is a repeated theme throughout: God has done marvelous things for his people but they failed him; he responds by judging them, but nonetheless, he maintains his relationship with his people. Finally, an account is given as to how God did that. The function of this litany of grace and a lack of appropriate response to grace is to encourage God's people to both place their trust in their God and keep his commandments (v. 7).[4]

In short, this psalm is a form of *torah,* moral instruction, but it is not meant just to inform, it is meant to lead to doxology, the praise of God.[5] It is not a lament, not a praise song, not a hymn, but a teaching tune, and the singer or speaker of it has authority to address the specific audience he is lecturing.[6] The reciting of God's incredible works in vv. 12–16 and vv. 43–55 leads to particular examples of Israel's past failures, with the implicit message "go thou and do otherwise," very much like Paul's review of the same subjects in 1 Corinthians 10:1–11. The order of presentation in Psalm 78 is more logical than it is chronological.[7] "There is irony here; those who passed on the tradition also failed it. Every generation will have to reckon with the fact that the story tells

---

2. Goldingay, *Psalms: Volume 2,* 479.

3. See Hossfeld and Zenger, *Psalms 2,* 285 and contrast B.T. Kid 30a which insists that Ps 78:38 is the center because it counts 2,527 verses in the Psalter.

4. See Edward L. Greenstein, "Mixing Memory and Design: Reading Psalm 78," *Proof* 10 (1990), 197–218.

5. On the ethics in the Psalms, and the ethical use of the Psalms see especially Wenham, *Psalms as Torah.* Among other things, he is able to show that the psalmists knew, and were very keen on keeping, the Ten Commandments, and also had a strong influence on the ethic of various NT writers.

6. Hossfeld and Zenger, *Psalms 2,* 300.

of failure as well as faithfulness."[8] So what solution to the perfidies of Israel does the psalmist suggest? There is a focus on the temple and the Davidic monarchy. True worship and good godly rule can keep God's people on track and prevent some of the major sins and failures of the past, the narrative suggests. But perhaps most of all, they must remember their past, and stop putting God to the test.

MT Psalm 78	LXX Psalm 77
A *maskil* of Asaph. 1 My people, hear my teaching; listen to the words of my mouth. 2 I will open my mouth with a parable; I will utter hidden things, things from of old— 3 things we have heard and known, things our ancestors have told us. 4 We will not hide them from their descendants; we will tell the next generation the praiseworthy deeds of the Lord, his power, and the wonders he has done. 5 He decreed statutes for Jacob and established the law in Israel, which he commanded our ancestors to teach their children, 6 so the next generation would know them, even the children yet to be born, and they in turn would tell their children. 7 Then they would put their trust in God and would not forget his deeds but would keep his commands. 8 They would not be like their ancestors— a stubborn and rebellious generation, whose hearts were not loyal to God, whose spirits were not faithful to him. 9 The men of Ephraim, though armed with bows, turned back on the day of battle;	1 Of understanding. Pertaining to Asaph. Pay attention, O my people, to my law; incline your ears to the words of my mouth. 2 I will open my mouth in a parable I will utter problems from of old, 3 things that we heard, and we knew them, and our fathers told us. 4 They were not hidden from their children to a next generation, as they kept telling of the praises of the Lord and of his dominance and of the wonders that he did. 5 And he established a witness in Jacob and set a law in Israel, which things he commanded our fathers to make them known to their sons, 6 that a next generation might know them, sons that will be born, and they shall rise up and tell them to their sons 7 so that they should set their hope in God and not forget the works of God and seek out his commandments, 8 that they should not be like their fathers, a generation, crooked and embittering, a generation which did not set its heart aright, and its spirit was not faithful to God. 9 Ephraim's sons, though bending and shooting their bows, were turned back on a day of war.

7. A. F. Campbell, "Psalm 78: A Contribution to the Theology of Tenth Century Israel," *CBQ* 41 (1979): 54.
8. May, *Psalms*, 257.

10 they did not keep God's covenant
and refused to live by his law.

11 They forgot what he had done,
the wonders he had shown them.
12 He did miracles in the sight of their
ancestors
in the land of Egypt, in the region of
Zoan.
13 He divided the sea and led them
through;
he made the water stand up like a wall.
14 He guided them with the cloud by day
and with light from the fire all night.

15 He split the rocks in the wilderness
and gave them water as abundant as the
seas;

16 he brought streams out of a rocky crag
and made water flow down like rivers.
17 But they continued to sin against him,
rebelling in the wilderness against the
Most High.
18 They willfully put God to the test
by demanding the food they craved.
19 They spoke against God;
they said, "Can God really
spread a table in the wilderness?
20 True, he struck the rock,
and water gushed out,
streams flowed abundantly,
but can he also give us bread?
Can he supply meat for his people?"
21 When the Lord heard them, he was
furious;
his fire broke out against Jacob,
and his wrath rose against Israel,
22 for they did not believe in God
or trust in his deliverance.
23 Yet he gave a command to the skies
above
and opened the doors of the heavens;
24 he rained down manna for the people
to eat,
he gave them the grain of heaven.
25 Human beings ate the bread of angels;
he sent them all the food they could eat.
26 He let loose the east wind from the
heavens
and by his power made the south wind
blow.

10 They did not keep the covenant of
God,
and in his law they did not want to walk.
11 And they forgot his benefactions
and his marvels that he showed them
12 in the sight of their fathers, which
marvels he worked
in the land of Egypt, in Tanis' plain.

13 He broke asunder a sea and brought
them through;
he made waters stand like a wineskin.
14 And he led them with a cloud by day,
and all night long with an illumination of
fire.

15 He broke asunder a rock in a wilderness
and gave them drink as from a voluminous deep.

16 And he brought out water from a rock
and brought down waters like rivers.
17 And they added still to sin against him;
they embittered the Most High in a
waterless land.
18 And they tested God in their hearts
by demanding food for their souls.
19 And they spoke against God and said,
"Surely, God will not be able to spread a
table in a wilderness?
20 Even though he struck a rock and
waters
gushed out and wadis deluged,
surely, he cannot also give bread
or spread a table for his people?"
21 Therefore, the Lord heard and was put
out,
and a fire was kindled in Jacob,
and anger mounted against Israel,
22 because they had no faith in God
nor did they hope in his saving power.
23 And he commanded clouds above
and opened heaven's doors,

24 and he rained down manna for them
to eat,
and heaven's bread he gave them.
25 Bread of angels man ate;
provisions he sent them in abundance.
26 He removed a south wind from
heaven,
and he led on, by his dominance, a south-
west wind,

27 He rained meat down on them like
dust,
birds like sand on the seashore.
28 He made them come down inside their
camp,
all around their tents.
29 They ate till they were gorged—
he had given them what they craved.
30 But before they turned from what
they craved,
even while the food was still in their
mouths,
31 God's anger rose against them;
he put to death the sturdiest among
them,
cutting down the young men of Israel.
32 In spite of all this, they kept on sinning;
in spite of his wonders, they did not
believe.
33 So he ended their days in futility
and their years in terror.
34 Whenever God slew them, they would
seek him;
they eagerly turned to him again.
35 They remembered that God was their
Rock,
that God Most High was their Redeemer.

36 But then they would flatter him with
their mouths,
lying to him with their tongues;
37 their hearts were not loyal to him,
they were not faithful to his covenant.

38 Yet he was merciful;
he forgave their iniquities
and did not destroy them.
Time after time he restrained his anger
and did not stir up his full wrath.

39 He remembered that they were but
flesh,
a passing breeze that does not return.

40 How often they rebelled against him
in the wilderness
and grieved him in the wasteland!

41 Again and again they put God to the
test;
they vexed the Holy One of Israel.

27 and he rained upon them flesh like
dust
and winged birds like the sand of seas,
28 and they fell in the midst of their
camp,
all around their coverts.
29 And they ate and were well filled,
and what they craved he brought them;
30 they were not deprived of what they
craved.
While their food was still in their mouth,

31 God's wrath also rose against them,
and he killed among their sleek ones,
and the select of Israel he shackled.
32 Amidst all these things they still
sinned,
and they did not believe in his marvels.

33 And in vanity did their days end,
and their years with haste.
34 When he was killing them, they would
seek him out,
and they would turn to God and be early.
35 And they remembered that God was
their helper
and God the Most High was their
redeemer.

36 And they deceived him with their
mouth,
and with their tongue they lied to him.
37 And their heart was not upright with
him,
nor were they true to his covenant.
38 Yet he is compassionate
and will atone for their sins and not
destroy them,
and he will increase to turn away his
anger
and not ignite all his wrath.
39 And he remembered that they were
flesh,
a breath that passes and does not come
again.
40 How often they embittered him in the
wilderness;
they provoked him to anger in an arid
land!
41 And they turned about and tested God,
and the Holy One of Israel they provoked.

42 They did not remember his power—
the day he redeemed them from the
  oppressor,
43 the day he displayed his signs in
  Egypt,
his wonders in the region of Zoan.
44 He turned their river into blood;
they could not drink from their streams.

45 He sent swarms of flies that devoured
  them,
and frogs that devastated them.
46 He gave their crops to the grasshopper,
their produce to the locust.
47 He destroyed their vines with hail
and their sycamore-figs with sleet.

48 He gave over their cattle to the hail,
their livestock to bolts of lightning.
49 He unleashed against them his hot
  anger,
his wrath, indignation and hostility—
a band of destroying angels.
50 He prepared a path for his anger;
he did not spare them from death
but gave them over to the plague.
51 He struck down all the firstborn of
  Egypt,
the firstfruits of manhood in the tents of
  Ham.
52 But he brought his people out like a
  flock;
he led them like sheep through the
  wilderness.
53 He guided them safely, so they were
  unafraid;
but the sea engulfed their enemies.
54 And so he brought them to the border
  of his holy land,
to the hill country his right hand had
  taken.
55 He drove out nations before them
and allotted their lands to them as an
  inheritance;
he settled the tribes of Israel in their
  homes.

56 But they put God to the test
and rebelled against the Most High;
they did not keep his statutes.

42 They did not keep in mind his hand,
the day on which he redeemed them
from an oppressor's hand;
43 how he displayed in Egypt his signs,
and his wonders in Tanis' plain.

44 And he turned their rivers into blood,
and their pools, so that they could not
  drink.
45 He sent a dog-fly among them, and it
devoured them, and a frog, and it
  destroyed them.
46 And he gave their crops over to the
  rust,
and their labors to the grasshopper.
47 He killed their vine with hail
and their mulberry trees with the hoar-
  frost.
48 And he gave over their cattle to hail
and their property to the fire.
49 He sent among them his anger's
  wrath,
anger and wrath and affliction,
a dispatch through wicked angels.
50 He made a path for his wrath;
he did not spare their souls from death,
and their cattle he consigned to death.
51 And he struck every firstborn in
  Egypt,
first fruit of their labors in the coverts of
  Cham.
52 And he removed his people like sheep
and brought them up like a flock in a
  wilderness.
53 And he guided them in hope, and they
  were not in dread,
but their enemies a sea covered.
54 And he brought them to a territory of
  his holy precinct,
this mountain that his right hand
  acquired.
55 And he threw out nations from before
  them,
and he distributed to them shares by
  measuring line
and made the tribes of Israel encamp in
  their coverts.
56 And they tested and embittered God
  the Most High.
And his testimonies they did not observe

57 Like their ancestors they were disloyal and faithless, as unreliable as a faulty bow.	57 and turned away and were faithless as also their fathers; they were twisted into a crooked bow.
58 They angered him with their high places; they aroused his jealousy with their idols.	58 And they provoked him to anger with their hills, and with their carved images they moved him to jealousy.
59 When God heard them, he was furious; he rejected Israel completely.	59 God heard and disdained, and he treated Israel with utter contempt.
60 He abandoned the tabernacle of Shiloh, the tent he had set up among humans.	60 And he rejected his tent at Selo A covert where he encamped among human beings,
61 He sent the ark of his might into captivity, his splendor into the hands of the enemy.	61 and gave their strength over to captivity and their comeliness into an enemy's hands.
62 He gave his people over to the sword; he was furious with his inheritance. 	62 And he consigned his people to a sword, and his heritage he disdained.
63 Fire consumed their young men, and their young women had no wedding songs;	63 Their young men fire devoured, and their girls were not bewailed.
64 their priests were put to the sword, and their widows could not weep.	64 Their priests fell by sword, and their widows will not be lamented.
65 Then the Lord awoke as from sleep, as a warrior wakes from the stupor of wine.	65 And the Lord awoke as one that sleeps, like a strong man intoxicated with wine.
66 He beat back his enemies; he put them to everlasting shame.	66 And he struck his enemies backwards; everlasting disgrace he put them to.
67 Then he rejected the tents of Joseph, he did not choose the tribe of Ephraim;	67 And he rejected the covert of Joseph, and the tribe of Ephraim he did not choose,
68 but he chose the tribe of Judah, Mount Zion, which he loved.	68 and he chose the tribe of Judah, Mount Zion, which he loved.
69 He built his sanctuary like the heights, like the earth that he established forever.	69 And he built his holy precinct like that of unicorns, in the land—he founded it forever.
70 He chose David his servant and took him from the sheep pens;	70 And he chose David his slave and took him from the sheepfolds of the sheep;
71 from tending the sheep he brought him to be the shepherd of his people Jacob, of Israel his inheritance.	71 from behind the lambing ewes he took him to shepherd Jacob his people and Israel his inheritance.
72 And David shepherded them with integrity of heart; with skillful hands he led them.	72 And he shepherded them in the innocence of his heart, and by the cleverness of his hands he guided them.

This remarkable and lengthy salvation historical ode provides lots of material that the NT writers found congenial to their presentation of the good news. There are some twenty quotations, allusions, or echoes from Psalm 78 found in the NT. It deserves our close scrutiny. In the second half of the Psalter, there are more of these sorts of historical reminders (see Psalms 105, 106, and 136). Not surprisingly, these songs are meant to be mainly instructional, but the lesson varies from historical review to historical review. The review typically takes us from Genesis 1 through the exodus and up to King David, proclaiming the mighty acts of God and his faithfulness, and at the same time, the not infrequent infidelities of Israel. The obvious assumption is that a people who forget their past will neither know who they are, nor know who their God is either, nor will they behave better in the future if they forget their story. This of course is not secular history, but religious history that is being recounted, with the assumption not merely that there is a God, but that God is frequent in his interactions with and for his people. This is history retold and interpreted in a particular theological way.

From the outset, Psalm 78 comes across as a speech, a sung speech no doubt, somewhat like a medieval lay, though with more serious content. Verses 5-6 makes clear that every generation of Israelites had a responsibility to tell and own the story. In some ways this psalm is unique, as we shall see. It doesn't really resemble any of the other psalms, rather it is closest to the famous poetic speech of Moses in Deuteronomy 32. "The psalm does for those who hear it what Moses is portrayed as doing for Israel before they entered the land; it instructs Israel about the peril and promise of being the people of the Lord."[9] Memory is a repeated theme or refrain in the songs of Asaph in the collection of Psalms 73-83.[10] Here we may have a helpful clue as to the meaning of the term *maskil*; it seems to be derived from the Hebrew verb "to be wise" or "skillful," which would then suggest the meaning is a sung "instruction" or "sapiential" meditation.[11]

The opening of the song is especially important because it tells us that what follows is a parable or a riddle meant to convey some wisdom by means of metaphor and comparison. The word we translate "parable" is in fact *māšāl* (מָשָׁל) and the word for riddle is *ḥîdôt* (חִידוֹת). The latter term refers to puzzling or dark speech, whereas the former refers to various kinds of metaphorical comparisons that can be enig-

---

9. Ibid., 255; I am mainly following Mays in these introductory remarks.
10. Brueggemann and Bellinger, *Psalms*, 341.
11. Terrien, *Psalms*, 565.

matic. Ḥîdôt signals that the psalm will deal with deep or profound matters (cf. Ps 49:4–5; Prov 1:6; Ezek 13:34–35). It is a mistake to think of a parable simply as a short fictional narrative à la the parable of the Good Samaritan, when in fact even very short metaphorical comparisons, like the phrase "physician heal thyself" can be called a parable (see Luke 4:23 where the term παραβολή is used).[12] An aphorism, a riddle, a proverb, a maxim, or a short fictional narrative can all be called a māšāl or παραβολή. "The psalm's historical recital is a riddle in the sense that it reveals the continuing mystery of divine grace and human frailty. . . . The recitation is more than a description of the past; it is a rehearsal so the present and future might be wondrous."[13]

Some twelve times we are told in this psalm that the people have responded unfaithfully to God's wonders and gracious actions on their behalf. Verse 8 diagnoses the problem: God's people had not made their heart firm, and so their spirits were not true to God (so also v. 37).[14] This seems to mean something like, if you are not whole-heartedly committed to God's way, then your spirit can wander and be untrue to God (see the behavior of the Ephraimites in v. 9, and cf. v. 67; 2 Kgs 17; and 1 Chr 7:20–24).[15] This in itself, like God's grace continually extended to sinners, is something of a mystery from the psalmist's perspective. That perspective is clearly "southern," by which I mean that the major northern tribe, Ephraim, is singled out for special criticism for unfaithfulness. The southern perspective is also clear from the expressed view that Judah is the one God turned to, and that the temple in Jerusalem and the Davidic monarchy were important answers to the problem of perfidy.[16]

In an oral culture, where most people are not literate, the oral recitation of the tradition was critical, especially when one was talking about a long historical tradition, involving several hundred years since the exodus, and even much longer since Abraham. Parents, not surprisingly, were tasked with passing on the "instruction" to their children

---

12. See the detailed explanation of wisdom literature both in the OT and in the NT and how it works in Witherington, *Jesus the Sage.*
13. Brueggemann and Bellinger, *Psalms,* 341.
14. Goldingay, *Psalms: Volume 2,* 486.
15. Of a piece with the rejection of Ephraim is the rejection of the northern sanctuary at Shiloh (v. 60), in favor of the temple on Mt. Zion; see Hossfeld and Zenger, *Psalms 2,* 292.
16. Longman, *Psalms,* 293 is right to note that this psalm has some evidence of earliness, namely the reference to high places in Israel itself, something prohibited by the law of centralization according to Deuteronomy 12; this prohibition came into effect with Solomon and the building of the temple. When one couples this with the reference to the abandonment of the Shiloh tabernacle and the loss of the ark, which happened at the end of the period of the Judges (see 1 Samuel 4), it is hard to see this psalm as postexilic.

from generation to generation. When one stops singing the songs, when one stops telling the old, old story and passing along the old wisdom in one form or another, amnesia and moral and theological infidelity set in.

Thus, we note that from the outset the audience is told to "turn your ears to the words," the appropriate exhortation in an oral culture (v. 1). What is also notable from the outset is the use of the first-person plural (see e.g., vv. 3–4). This is not a mere finger-pointing to the past, saying "they did things wrong." It is an embracing of the history as a continuum saying, "we did things wrong."[17] One of the points of this song is to link the Sinai covenant with the Davidic one, and so vv. 9 and 67–68 become crucial, revealing the purpose. One may compare Deuteronomy 32, which also exhorts Israel to learn lessons from its own story.[18]

Some of the references in the song are shrouded in the mists of history, but the reference in v. 9 to Ephraim turning back seems to refer to their fleeing before the Philistines, even though Ephraim was well-armed (see 1 Sam 4:17); the result was the disastrous loss of the ark of the covenant (1 Sam 4:22). God didn't liberate Israel from Egypt, and provide gushing water from a rock in the desert (vv. 12–17) for that to be the outcome in the promised land itself, the singer implies. "God can split waters and make them like a cliff, or split a cliff and make it produce waters; it is all the same to God."[19] But where is the response of God's people to these stupendous miracles?[20]

Instead of trusting God, they kept testing God.

> We might think that God has no reason to test us, because God can look into our hearts, know what we are capable of, and know how we would respond to different pressures, whereas it is understandable for us to need to test God, because we cannot know what God will do. The OT sees this the other way around. Israel knows enough about God from God's acts such as those described in vv. 12–17 to make it reasonable to know what God can do and to trust God to look after them. To test God is to presuppose that we do not know enough about what God can and will do.[21]

It appears that two main sins of God's people are being criticized: their

---

17. Rightly, Terrien, *Psalms*, 366.
18. Goldingay, *Psalms: Volume 2*, 484.
19. Ibid., 491.
20. Notice again the hyperbole that is so typical of poetic language. According to Exodus, God did not make a river flow out of the rock, he simply provided good potable water. The function of rhetorical hyperbole is to emphasize and dramatize the importance and significance of what God has done.
21. Goldingay, *Psalms: Volume 2*, 492.

greed—not ever satisfied with what they had—and their idolatry. They spoke against God (v. 19) and the gushing water was never enough, they demanded bread and meat (v. 20). In effect, God in his anger said "you want bread, I'll give you bread" and "Israel was flooded with the manna from heaven, the food of angels" (vv. 23–28) but even then God's people didn't know when to say "enough" (vv. 29–30). Even the loss of youth through divine judgment, doesn't cure the sinning problem (v. 32), and even when they repented (v. 35) they still kept on breaking the covenant (v. 37). This section of the song ends, however, with God remembering that human beings are frail, mortal, "mere flesh and blood," and so with his having compassion.

Verses 41–51 recount the plagues in Egypt, and tell of the final disaster for a recalcitrant Egyptian leadership, the loss of firstborn sons, in other words the loss of their future. Verses 52–63 turn to the conquest of Canaan, but with the events of the exodus still lingering in memory. Notice how the psalmist skips over huge parts of the story, simply moving from the exodus to the entering of the land with the sentence, "God chased the nations before them" (v. 55). But having escaped the idolatries of Egypt, the Israelites ran right into the idolatries of Canaan: its high places and its graven images (v. 56). But all is not lost.

Verses 64–72 turn to God's choice of Mt. Zion as his "high place" and David as his king. Remarkably, vv. 64–66 describe God as waking from a long winter's nap, galvanized into action for his people.[22] But not for Ephraim, rather for Judah, the former replaced by the latter (vv. 67–68). Remarkably, God is likened to a drunken warrior who is suddenly woken up, and is both angry and dangerous.[23]

Then we are told that Zion will be tended by David, and God himself will aid in the building of the temple, and in so doing his people will be "rebuilt," restored. God personally took David from tending the sheep to instead be a shepherd of Jacob. He went from the sheep pen to the royal penthouse (v. 71). "With upright heart he tended them, and guided them with skillful hand." Thus ends the story, and much is left out. The selectivity is not accidental. As it turns out, hindsight is not always 20-20, but sometimes it is vital to mainly remember the best parts of the past if one is going to carry on in a positive direction. It gives hope that a good future is possible. "For the people of God, decid-

---

22. Actually, as Goldingay, ibid., 510–11 points out, we have the little word "like" here, because what he means is that God left inactivity behind and did something "like" a warrior who was suddenly aroused from sleep and snoring due to too much wine.
23. Longman, *Psalms*, 293.

ing to remember is . . . the key to faithfulness; deciding to forget is the key to failure."[24] So, enough of the sins of the past are recounted to help Israel avoid those mistakes in the future. God's anger at Israel's sin is intermittent and momentary, but his grace endures throughout the whole narrative.[25] The idealized memory of David at the end of the psalm probably suggests this song came to its final form in the time of the reforms of Josiah, or even Hezekiah. The *terminus ad quem* however is unlikely to be after the destruction of the temple in about 587 BCE and the disasters of the Babylonian exile.[26]

Matthew 13:35, a verse found only in Matthew, provides us with this quotation: "This was to fulfill what had been spoken through the prophet, 'I will open my mouth to speak parables, I will proclaim what has been hidden since the foundations of the world,'" about which Hays says, at least in regard to that last phrase, that the evangelist is freely quoting Psalm 78:2, "I will open my mouth in a parable [pl. in the LXX], I will utter dark sayings of old."[27] The key difference is of course the word *hidden*, which suggests that Jesus is unveiling what was hidden in the text all along, but just wasn't seen or understood prior to his coming. This is not an argument for a reading of something into the text that was never there. It is an argument that it was a meaning always there in the text, but could only be revealed by Christ and in light of the Christ event. Further, putting this saying on the lips of Jesus here is part of the Matthean portrayal of Jesus as the authoritative teacher of wisdom, indeed as wisdom come in the flesh, as I have demonstrated at length elsewhere.[28] As Kidner once said, both Asaph and Jesus "make the past hold up a mirror to the present . . . for the true pattern of history is not self-evident."[29] What we learn in Matthew 13:34–35 is that speaking in parables was a deliberate, chosen strategy by Jesus when he spoke openly, perhaps because, like the recalcitrant Israelites spoken of repeatedly in Psalm 78, figurative speech was all that could be used on such a people.

In her helpful study of the citations and allusions to the Psalms in

---

24. Goldingay, *Psalms: Volume 2*, 514.
25. Brueggemann and Bellinger, *Psalms*, 343.
26. See Terrien, *Psalms*, 569; Goldingay, *Psalms: Volume 2*, 481.
27. Hays, *Echoes of Scripture in the Gospels*, 359. The LXX rendering of the second clause "something put forward as an excuse" does not seem to be influencing the Matthean text here, but clearly the plural parables in the first clause follows the LXX; however the phrase "from the beginning" in the LXX may have led to the "from the foundations of the world" in Matthew. See Blomberg, "Matthew," 49. Contrast the use of Ps 78:2 in 1QS X, 23, which renders "parables" as "hymns."
28. See Ben Witherington III, *Matthew*, SHBC (Macon, GA: Smyth and Helwys, 2006).
29. Derek Kidner, *Psalms 73–150: An Introduction and Commentary on Books III–V of the Psalms*, TOTC (Downers Grove, IL: InterVarsity Press: 1975), 281.

John's Gospel, Daly-Denton draws this conclusion: "the precise verbal form of John's psalm quotations could be the result of intentional redaction or of spontaneous recollection."[30] She is right about this, and if it is a matter of recollection there can also be the further factor of combinations of texts in the person's memory, rather than a deliberate editing or piecing together of several texts.

What Daly-Denton doesn't really come to grips with is how a good deal of the OT was read through the filter of later Jewish literature, particularly in this case wisdom literature such as Sirach and the Wisdom of Solomon. In my commentary on the Gospel of John, I worked systematically through the Fourth Gospel, showing the influence of the later wisdom tradition in the Fourth Gospel, which is one of the reasons the Fourth Gospel is quite different from the Synoptics, though not the only reason.[31] This factor definitely comes into play in the discussion of the use of Psalm 78 in John 6.

For instance, Daly-Denton is right that Psalm 78:24 LXX is likely alluded to in John 6:31, "he gave them bread from heaven to eat," and again she is right that the particular phrasing "that which came down from heaven" is ambiguous enough to refer to either an object or a person (cf. John 6:33; 8:23, 42). She goes on to comment on the difficult passage in John 7:38 "from within him shall flow rivers of living water," and again rightly, she points to Psalm 78:16 and 20 as a possible source of the language here; both texts refer to the water that came forth from the rock according to Exodus 17. What she does not note or notice is that John's language here owes something to the retelling of the exodus-Sinai tale in Wisdom of Solomon 11 which tells of how Wisdom provided the water from the rock for the wilderness wandering generation. It will be worth quoting a bit of the text here:

"Wisdom prospered their works by the hand of a holy prophet.
2 They journeyed through an uninhabited wilderness,
and pitched their tents in untrodden places.
3 They withstood their enemies and fought off their foes.
4 When they thirsted they called upon thee,
and water was given them out of flinty rock,
and slaking of thirst from hard stone.
5 For through the very things by which their
enemies were punished,

---

30. Daly-Denton, "Psalms in John's Gospel," 136.
31. See Ben Witherington III, *John's Wisdom: A Commentary on the Fourth Gospel*, (Louisville: Westminster John Knox, 1995).

they themselves received benefit in their need.
6 Instead of the fountain of an ever-flowing river,
stirred up and defiled with blood
7 in rebuke for the decree to slay the infants,
you gave them abundant water unexpectedly,
8 showing by their thirst at that time
how thou didst punish their enemies.

Notice three things: (1) it is Wisdom who is called upon and provides the water; (2) there is a reference to a fountain of ever-flowing river; and (3) there is a further reference to abundant water. One of the things that John's Gospel has in common with Paul is the reading of the OT through the wisdom literature, and in particular Wisdom of Solomon which was seen to have all sorts of christological potential, if Christ was seen as wisdom in person, developing further the notion of the personification of wisdom found in Sirach and Wisdom of Solomon. We will say more about this in our treatment of 1 Corinthians 10 in a moment.

If indeed the Fourth Evangelist is influenced by the rereading of the history of Israel found in Wisdom of Solomon (and he is), then we probably have an answer to the old question about John 7:38: Jesus is talking about living water coming forth from himself, not from within the believer, a point already suggested by John 4:14—notice the reference to the gushing water, "the water I will give will become a spring of water in them gushing up to eternal life." But the point is that Christ is the ultimate source of this living water. You have to come to Christ and he gives the believer this water to drink, because he is the source of this infinite living water, not the belly of the believer! This becomes especially clear from the context of John 7:36-37 where Jesus says people have to come to him, and then believe in him and drink. Jesus is the subject and the source of this provision.

Then, we have "as the Scripture has said," which is meant to speak of where the water comes from, just as in Psalm 78:15-16 it is God who provides the abundant water from the rock, "and causes water to flow down like rivers" (cf. the reference to gushing in v. 20). There is much more that one could say along these lines, but here it must suffice to note that Wisdom 16:20-21 refers again to the time when God provided manna from heaven (cf. Philo, *Leg.* 3.169-176 and especially 2 Baruch 29:8 and Rev 2:17) and in terms that are echoed in the Gospel of John 6:48-51, 56. The bread that suits and permanently satisfies everyone is Christ, the true manna from heaven.[32] Paul in

1 Corinthians 10 will take this whole line of thought, again reading salvation history through the lens of later wisdom literature, a step further by stating clearly "the rock was Christ." This was a step taken out of the conviction of the preexistence of Christ, a conviction shared with the Fourth Evangelist.

Hays is right that in John 6 Jesus is, in a sense, teaching his audience how to read the OT. He is indeed suggesting that the manna was only a foreshadowing, or in this case, a foretaste, quite literally, of the future bread that was to come down from heaven. He correctly says of John 6:33: "the participial phrase . . . can be read either as attributive (thus: 'the bread of God is that which comes down from heaven') or as substantive ('the bread of God is the One who comes down from heaven'). We will surely be faithful readers of John's figural hermeneutic if we hear overtones of the latter interpretation."[33] True, but what makes this reading plausible is that by the time we get to the Fourth Gospel, many, including the Fourth Evangelist, were already reading their foundational narrative through the lens of later wisdom literature. The move from personification of wisdom to Wisdom in person had been facilitated through reflection on, for instance, Wisdom of Solomon 11.

In our previous volume in this series, *Isaiah Old and New*, we devoted an Appendix to demonstrating the influence of Wisdom of Solomon 11 on Paul's retelling of the exodus-Sinai events in 1 Corinthians 10, so we need not retread that ground here. [34] Here it is appropriate to point out the order of events in Psalm 78: dividing the Red Sea (78:13), cloud and pillar of fire (78:14), provision of water from the rock (78: 15–16), rebellion in the desert, testing of God demanding food (78:17–19), further reference to water from the rock (78:20), and God's angry response killing many (78:31). Paul's presentation is much more truncated, and shows more indebtedness to Exodus than to Psalm 78 at this juncture, though as the NA28 index suggests, there is some general indebtedness in 1 Corinthians 10:1–9 to Psalm 78:15–31, but like the use of Psalm 78 in John's Gospel, the reading of the OT text comes not directly but indirectly to the NT writer through the filter of later wisdom literature and its concept of the personified Wisdom that provides provisions for

---

32. See the discussion in Köstenberger, "John," 446 and in Maarten J. J. Menken, *Old Testament Quotations in the Fourth Gospel: Studies in Textual Form*, CBET 15 (Kampen: Kok Pharos, 1996), 52–54.
33. Hays, *Echoes of Scripture in the Gospels*, 322.
34. See Witherington, *Isaiah Old and New*, Appendix A, 361–70.

God's OT people as they journey to the promised land and beyond (cf. also Philo, *Leg.* 2.86).[35]

There are some incidental allusions to or echoes of Psalm 78 in the NT, for instance probably at Matthew 21:15 there is an allusion to Psalm 78:4 in the phrase "the wonders he has done," only in the Gospel it is Jesus's wonders in view. In John 21:15 Peter is commissioned to feed Jesus's lambs, which may echo Psalm 78:71, which speaks of David feeding and tending the ewe lambs and being taken by God to be the shepherd of his people Israel. Jesus is commissioning Peter to be such a shepherd, perhaps even *the* Davidic-type shepherd of his Jewish followers (cf. Gal 2:9). Another example of an allusion is Revelation 16:4, the reference to the Egyptian water polluted with blood has the double reference to rivers and streams, which probably owes something to Psalm 78:44.[36] Revelation 20:4 speaks of God's beloved city, Jerusalem, as does Psalm 78:68. On the whole, one may be surprised that there is not more influence of this psalm on the NT writers, but then the NT writers are mainly telling a new story, not doing a historical review of the story of God's people in the past. The old stories are used to serve and illustrate and illuminate the gospel story, rather than the other way around. This becomes very clear when we hear our earliest Christian witness, Paul, say things like the OT saints were "baptized into Moses," so to speak (1 Corinthians 10). It is the new story that has changed the reading of the old one. The new one is not *simply* an extension and completion of the old one, though in terms of fulfillment it is the latter in various ways.

Desolate Jerusalem and the Temple of Doom: Psalm 79

Some psalms were much better suited, by their very content, for appropriation for discussions about things apocalyptic, specifically about final judgment of both true believers and the adamant unbelievers. One such psalm is Psalm 79, which shows up in various ways, not surprisingly, mainly in the book of Revelation in the NT. "Psalm 79 is a poem of anger and grief at the loss of Jerusalem and its temple [in 587 BCE], a poem that lives in the context of the artistic limits of the book of Lamentations."[37] The back story here is important, for many Jews assumed, not least because Jerusalem survived the Assyrian inva-

---

35. But see the discussion in Ciampa and Rosner, "1 Corinthians," 724.
36. See rightly, Moyise, "Psalms in the Book of Revelation," 243.
37. Brueggemann and Bellinger, *Psalms*, 344.

sion in 721 BCE or so, and then survived the initial Babylonian incursion, that Jerusalem and its temple were inviolable, not least because of the presence of the only living God in the temple there. This is the sort of theology we see at play in Isaiah 37, for instance, but probably also in some of the early preexilic "songs of Zion" (Psalms 46, 48, 76). But sadly, Jerusalem was not impregnable nor subject to unconditional divine protection, and when the Babylonians came, they even burned the temple down (2 Kgs 25:8–21; Jer 39:1–10). The city was left in ruins as well. This song, a bitter song in many ways, reflects not merely disappointment, but the hard-won realization of what happens when bad theology is proved wrong. This is a communal or corporate lament in three parts: (1) complaint (vv. 1–5); (2) petition (vv. 6–12); and (3) anticipation of praise later when God answers the petition positively. It may be compared to the similar Psalm 74, also part of the Asaph collection.[38]

MT Psalm 79	LXX Psalm 78
A psalm of Asaph. 1 O God, the nations have invaded your inheritance; they have defiled your holy temple, they have reduced Jerusalem to rubble.	1 A Psalm. Pertaining to Asaph. O God, nations came into your inheritance; they defiled your holy shrine; they made Ierousalem into a garden-watcher's hut.
2 They have left the dead bodies of your servants as food for the birds of the sky, the flesh of your own people for the animals of the wild.	2 They placed the carcasses of your slaves as food for the birds of the air, the flesh of your devout for the wild animals of the earth.
3 They have poured out blood like water all around Jerusalem, and there is no one to bury the dead.	3 They poured out their blood like water all around Jerusalem, and there was no one to bury.
4 We are objects of contempt to our neighbors, of scorn and derision to those around us.	4 We became a reproach to our neighbors, mockery and derision to those around us.
5 How long, Lord? Will you be angry forever? How long will your jealousy burn like fire?	5 How long, O Lord, will you be utterly angry, will your jealousy burn like fire?
6 Pour out your wrath on the nations that do not acknowledge you, on the kingdoms that do not call on your name; 7 for they have devoured Jacob and devastated his homeland.	6 Pour out your wrath on nations that do not know you and on kingdoms that did not call on your name, 7 because they devoured Jacob and his place they laid waste.

38. Mays, *Psalms*, 260.

8 Do not hold against us the sins of past generations; may your mercy come quickly to meet us, for we are in desperate need. 9 Help us, God our Savior, for the glory of your name; deliver us and forgive our sins for your name's sake. 10 Why should the nations say, "Where is their God?" Before our eyes, make known among the nations that you avenge the outpoured blood of your servants. 11 May the groans of the prisoners come before you; with your strong arm preserve those condemned to die. 12 Pay back into the laps of our neighbors seven times the contempt they have hurled at you, Lord. 13 Then we your people, the sheep of your pasture, will praise you forever; from generation to generation we will proclaim your praise.	8 Do not remember our lawless deeds of long ago; let your compassion speedily preoccupy us, because we became very poor. 9 Help us, O God our savior; for the sake of the glory of your name, O Lord, rescue us, and atone for our sins, for the sake of your name, 10 so that the nations may not say, "Where is their God?"— and let the avenging of the outpoured blood of your slaves be known among the nations before our eyes. 11 Let the groaning of the prisoners come before you; according to the greatness of your arm preserve the sons of those put to death. 12 Return sevenfold into the bosom of our neighbors their reproaching with which they reproached you, O Lord! 13 But we, your people and sheep of your pasture, will acknowledge you openly forever; to generation and generation we will recount your praise.

Instead of sacrifice, sacrilege is what characterizes Jerusalem according to the psalmist. The city has been defiled by the foreign invaders, and the city is thus wide open, vulnerable, exposed to both shame and death. The prophecy in Micah 3:12 has been fulfilled (cf. Jer 26:18).[39] As Bruggemann and Bellinger point out, the word "you" keeps cropping up in the Hebrew text because the psalmist assumes that since this is YHWH's city, he himself has been attacked and logically should respond.[40] Indeed, Jerusalem and the temple are called "your inheritance" (i.e., Yahweh's). Were not the fall of the city and the temple enough, God's "servants," his people, including his priests, were killed, not given a proper burial, and then mocked to scorn by neighboring peoples (cf. Ps 137:7; Jer 49:7–22; Obad 10–14). In an honor and shame culture, the shame of all this is as hard to bear as the actual physical

---

39. On the closeness of this psalm to both Psalm 74 and Jeremiah see Hossfeld and Zenger, *Psalms 2*, 305.
40. Bruggemann and Bellinger, *Psalms*, 345.

disaster.[41] This is why the real climax of this psalm comes in v. 10a with the heartbreaking cry: "Why should they say to us 'Where is your God?'"[42] "When someone is killed, and their family cannot see the body, mourn over it, and bury it . . . in some ways this is worse than death itself. It means that people do not go to join their ancestors and rest in the family tomb."[43]

The complaint portion of the psalm ends with the familiar "how long, O Lord" cry for justice, one of the most constant refrains in the whole Psalter (cf. Pss 4:2-3; 6:3; 13:1-2; 35:17; 62:3; 74:10; 80:4; 89:46; 90:13; 94:3; 119:84). This reflects what a small and vulnerable country Israel was, being a land bridge caught as it was between large superpowers like Egypt, Assyria, Babylon, Syria, and Persia in the south, the east, and the north, to name but a few. Notice that already in v. 5 the Hebrew reads, "Until when Yahweh," almost a demand for God to set a limit on the amount of wrath he is inflicting on his own people.[44] Furthermore, we have the gruesome images of not only dead bodies in the streets of Jerusalem left unattended, but also blood being spattered around the city, and then, worst of all, what sounds like cannibalism: "because they have consumed Jacob" (v. 7). The use of this text in Revelation is of a piece with the horror show here. Notice also the complete absence of a recognition that God will take Israel's sin more seriously than that of foreigners, that "judgment begins with the household of the Lord."

Mainly, the psalmist petitions God for revenge against the destroyers of the holy city, but v. 8 is important as a confession of sin, for it means the psalmist is not being *purely* defensive. In fact, it is the only confession of sin in all the corporate laments in the Psalter.[45] He admits that Israel has sinned in the past and should be judged for her sins, but the main reason for mentioning this is rhetorical, to further motivate God's compassionate response for his people. The psalmist urges in v. 9 that God's compassion should hasten out and "meet" them, like an old friend who comes to comfort the bereaved who "are very low." Verse 9 is almost unique in its request for God to expiate the sins of his people himself (cf. Ps 78:38) and here the verb is in the imperative (cf. the only other example of such an imperative addressed to God, Deut 21:8).[46]

---

41. See Longman, *Psalms*, 295.
42. Mays, *Psalms*, 260.
43. Goldingay, *Psalms: Volume 2*, 521. He is of course referring to how many of them would have viewed the lack of proper burial in an honor and shame culture. This itself was a sacrilege.
44. Ibid., 522.
45. Mays, *Psalms*, 261.

This may reflect the fact that the temple sacrifices have stopped, and so Israel couldn't expiate its own sins, even if it wanted to do so.[47]

So bent is the psalmist on "vengeance," that, rather like Lamech, he speaks of a sevenfold revenge against the Babylonian "barbarians" (see Gen 4:23–24). How very different is this plea from the teaching of Jesus about sevenfold forgiveness in Matthew 18:21–35. Sadly v. 13, with its "then" assumes that praise can only whole-heartedly be given after God has unleashed his wrath on the Babylonians, and the praise will quite specifically be for that speedy delivery of "justice." Once again, we are reminded that this is a true revelation of what is in and on the psalmist's heart, not at all necessarily what God has in mind. The question is not "Is God on Our Side?" (cue the classic tune by Bob Dylan), but rather "Who is on the Lord's Side and is obeying his will?" Had he known it, the psalmist might well have recited the oracle pronouncing doom against Babylon found in Jeremiah 50–51.[48] This psalm should also be compared to Psalm 89 (on which see below) and Lamentations 5, as well as Jeremiah 10:25.[49] At least the psalmist leaves "vengeance" in the hands of God, and simply pleads for God to act. Perhaps he is not calling for irrational, emotional revenge-taking, but for a rational act of justice.[50]

In 1 Maccabees 7:17 the first few verses of this psalm are quoted to lament over the loss of the ḥasidim, the pious who were betrayed by rulers in about 162 BCE (cf. Ps 102:21 as well). After the fall of the Herodian temple, and when Judaism had become torah-centric, there was nevertheless a ritual using Psalm 79 and Psalm 137 on the anniversaries of the destruction of Jerusalem by Babylon in 587 BCE and by the Romans in CE 70 (cf. b. Sop 18.3).[51] So it may come as some surprise, that despite the tenor and content of this psalm, it continued to be seen as relevant and applicable long after the demise of the temple, twice over.

In the use of Psalm 79 in the NT, it appears clear that at least John of Patmos is following the Hebrew text, for the LXX of v. 1 doesn't have Jerusalem turned into a heap of ruins, but rather into a gardener's hut in a vineyard.[52] In John's portrayal of the temple being sized up for

46. Goldingay, *Psalms: Volume 2*, 526.
47. That would place this psalm somewhere between 587, and about 520 when they reinstituted the sacrifices and rebuilt the temple in Jerusalem, and probably while some of the captives are still in exile (see v. 11 on the captives).
48. Longman, *Psalms*, 297.
49. See Weiser, *Psalms*, 544.
50. Goldingay, *Psalms: Volume 2*, 529; Hossfeld and Zenger, *Psalms 2*, 307.
51. See Goldingay, *Psalms: Volume 2*, 520.
52. Hossfeld and Zenger, *Psalms 2*, 307.

judgment in Revelation 11, we find at v. 2 this description, "but do not measure the court outside the temple [or the outer court?] leave that out, for it is given over to the nations, and they will trample over the holy city for forty-two months." He goes on to speak of the two martyred prophetic witnesses in these terms at v. 8, "and their dead bodies will lie in the street of that great city . . . where also their Lord was crucified." This can only be a reference to the earthly Jerusalem, spoken of in terms that should sound familiar after a close reading of Psalm 79. At Revelation 16:6 we hear "because they shed the blood of the saints and prophets, you gave them blood to drink," which Beale and McDonough recognize is echoing Psalm 79:3, 10, 12.[53] The saints under the altar in heaven cry out to God in Revelation 6:10, "Almighty Lord, holy and true, how long will it be before you judge and avenge our blood on the inhabitants on the earth?"[54] Revelation 19:2 reassures the persecuted faithful that God's "judgments are true and just." John's vision of a tale of two cities, the harlot Babylon (Revelation 18) and the bride the new Jerusalem (Revelation 21–22), is of course speaking about Rome and a heavenly Jerusalem, but like with all other things in Revelation, he is speaking about them in the diction and with the names and labels of the OT, from a variety of OT sources, including Psalm 79.

Here is another case not of quotation or even in any full sense paraphrase, but of the use of the language of the Psalms that speak of the suffering of God's people, especially in Jerusalem, to address a contemporary situation after the temple has been destroyed and the city of Jerusalem conquered, with the dead lying in the streets, in short after CE 70, which John sees as much the same for the earthly Jerusalem as described in Psalm 79 and other such psalms. We may call these *echoes* of Psalm 79 and other psalms that urge God to unleash his justice on those who have persecuted and executed God's people and destroyed Jerusalem (in this case Rome which not accidentally is called Babylon in Revelation), and to fully redeem and restore his saints, which John thinks will not happen until Christ returns and resurrection happens (Revelation 20). Like the psalmist, John leaves vengeance in the hands of God, trusting his justice will come.

Interestingly enough, John is not the only one borrowing from Psalm 79 and other such laments. Even Luke is doing so. For example, in the apocalyptic discourse in Luke 21, and only in its Lukan form, Jesus predicts for Jerusalem that the city will be surrounded by armies,

---

53. Beale and McDonough, "Revelation," 1135.
54. Rightly seen as an echo of Ps 79:10 in ibid., 1104.

that it's desolation will come, the people of the city will "fall by the edge of the sword and be taken away as captives among all nations; and Jerusalem will be trampled on by the Gentiles" (vv. 20–25). This material did not come from Mark 13 or Matthew 24! Where did it come from? It came from Psalm 79 and other similar judgment psalms. Not accidentally, it is precisely in the segments of the NT that speak about future coming judgment involving the fall of the temple in Jerusalem and thereafter that Psalm 79 and other such material becomes readily serviceable to describe the future. Sometimes this is on the lips of Jesus himself, and sometimes on the lips of another prophet, such as John of Patmos, but in either case the Psalms are taken to adequately describe not only what is past, but what is to come.[55]

One of the main reasons we have focused here on Psalm 79 is to make a key point: you simply cannot judge the influence of a certain OT text by just studying clear quotations or obvious allusions and salient echoes. You have to go deeper into echoes, and indeed into the use of the lexicon of the psalmist in this case. At the level of similar ideas and the articulation of those ideas, both consciously and unconsciously, the Psalms are informing the writing of the NT authors and of the speech of Jesus himself. Even as helpful and huge a resource as the *Commentary on the New Testament Use of the Old Testament* is (and it is very helpful), and even though it describes a huge chunk of the visible OT appearances in the NT, there is still much more below the surface of the obvious quotations and allusions and echoes to be found. To mix my metaphors: the net needs to be cast not only more widely, but deeper, down at the level of diction, ideas, colorful language, types of rhetoric.[56]

The King Is Dead; Long Live the King: Psalm 89

Whatever else you say about the various songwriters of Israel, some of these psalmists, such as Ethan the Ezrahite, had considerable courage, accusing God of all kinds of infidelity and mayhem when it came to his relationship with his people. For instance, in Psalm 89:49 we hear the accusation "Where are your former deeds of loyalty which you

---

55. There are other minor echoes, e.g., in 1 Thess 4:5 Paul speaks of the gentiles who do not know God, which is possibly an echo of Ps 79:6, rightly noted by Jeffrey Weima, "1 & 2 Thessalonians," in Beale, *Commentary on the New Testament Use*, 877, 884.

56. It is telling that as large and helpful a study as Hays's recent *Echoes of Scripture in the Gospels* is, even he does not deal, for instance, with the influence of Psalm 79 on the unique parts of Luke's discourse in Luke 21. As for Moyise, *The Psalms in the New Testament*, there is only one brief mention of Psalm 79 in relationship to one verse in Revelation. That volume doesn't survey, it gives us samples and discussion of samples. This is helpful, but not adequate.

swore to David in your faithfulness?" Christian prayers in the NT are remarkably free of these sorts of broadsides against the Almighty. As for Ethan, he is probably the same person referred to in Psalm 88, and even more relevant is 1 Kings 5:11 which indicates he is a sage, and 1 Chronicles 6:29 (cf. 1 Chr 15:17, 19) which indicates that a person of this name was a singer, again presumably the same person.[57]

The problem is not so much theology as theodicy. If, as the psalmist believes, the living God is as advertised in the sacred texts, then how can God's people be in a position presently where even their ruler, their king, seems to have been abandoned to defeat and humiliation at the hands of Israel's foes? This is a very specific kind of complaint of the "why do bad things happen to God's people" sort. It is a complaint about God's apparent unfaithfulness to the Davidic monarchy. Here is a long royal song, with a difference. Is it a situation of "the covenant has been suspended until further notice" (vv. 38–45)? Is it a situation where the covenant was conditional from the start, and Israel broke the covenant, leaving God not having to fulfill his part of the bargain? Inquiring minds want to know.

Mays suggests that Psalm 89 is the counterpart to Psalm 2 that opened the Psalter. Psalm 89 leaves the listener where the end of 2 Kings leaves them—with the king and his people apparently in the hands and in the power of their enemies, going forward. In one sense this long song is like the drama in the *Lord of the Rings*, and where we are in the storytelling is at the end of the second part of the trilogy, waiting for the true king to make a comeback. Hope for the future, in this case, rests entirely on God's promise of faithfulness to David himself forever, because the psalmist understands, as vv. 30–32 shows, *that David's descendants, if they were unfaithful to God (and they were), were subject to the conditional covenant made at Sinai, subject to judgment and punishment in full measure.*[58] This may suggest that the psalmist was thinking that the solution would be a future righteous Davidic king to whom God would be faithful. This seems clearly enough to be Jeremiah's thinking in his prophecy about God raising up a righteous branch from the stump left of the Davidic monarch (Jer 23:5–6).[59] In the meanwhile, chaos threatens to engulf Israel and its monarchy.

The Israelites were not, by and large, a myth-making people, but they did adopt elements of ancient Near Eastern myths and demythol-

---

57. See Hossfeld and Zenger, *Psalms 2*, 407.
58. See Mays, *Psalms*, 286–87.
59. See Longman, *Psalms*, 326.

ogized them for their own purposes; we have a good example of that practice in this psalm, just as we do in the book of Revelation's stories about the evil dragon and the chaos waters. Now one of the recurrent ancient Near Eastern myths was a creation and combat myth, suggesting that there was a grand warrior god who prevailed over the chaos dragon, thereby creating, or restoring all of creation by his victory. The name Israel applied to the mythological chaos dragon or sea monster was Rahab (vv. 9–10; cf. Ps 74:13–14; Isa 51:9; Job 9:13, 26:12), not to be confused with the Rahab of the stories in Joshua. The story is relevant to this psalm for two reasons: (1) it establishes the great power of Israel's God, who made the heavens and the earth, the north and the south;[60] and (2) it therefore provides the basis for query as to why it is that God seems to be unable to sort out the chaos afflicting God's king and people to whom he has pledged allegiance. Why is it that God can sort out the whole of creation, but can't seem to help the Davidic king overcome his foes?[61] "The riddle of the *Heilsgeschichte* (salvation history) that here comes to light through the rejection of the bearer of the promise has not been solved in the Old Testament."[62]

The psalmist doesn't have a well-articulated answer to these puzzling questions, but what he needs more than an answer to his questions is a solution to the problem, and he is trusting God for that, as the opening of the psalm makes clear. God's great mercy and kindness is forever, but it needs to show up soon if it's going to help the psalmist and his generation of God's people. What starts out sounding like a royal psalm (vv. 1–37), turns into more of a community lament (vv. 38–51).[63] It is not necessary to see this dichotomy as the attempt to splice together two disparate psalms, for the recital in vv. 1–37 is necessary, indeed it is the basis of the complaint in vv. 38–51.

---

60. These are merisms, indicating "everything" by mentioning the two extremes or opposites. Longman, *Psalms*, 323.
61. Mays, *Psalms*, 284.
62. Weiser, *Psalms*, 593.
63. Longman, *Psalms*, 322.

MT Psalm 89	LXX Psalm 88
A *maskil* of Ethan the Ezrahite.	1 Of understanding. Pertaining to Aithan the Israelite.
1 I will sing of the Lord's great love forever; with my mouth I will make your faithfulness known through all generations.	2 Of your mercies, O Lord, I will sing forever; to generation and generation I will proclaim your truth with my mouth,
2 I will declare that your love stands firm forever, that you have established your faithfulness in heaven itself.	3 because you said, "Forever mercy will be built." In the heavens your truth will be prepared.
3 You said, "I have made a covenant with my chosen one, I have sworn to David my servant,	4 "I made a covenant with my chosen ones; I swore to David my slave:
4 'I will establish your line forever and make your throne firm through all generations.'"	5 'Forever I will provide offspring for you and will build your throne for generation and generation.' " Interlude on strings
5 The heavens praise your wonders, Lord, your faithfulness too, in the assembly of the holy ones.	6 The heavens will acknowledge your wonders, O Lord, indeed, your truth in an assembly of holy ones,
6 For who in the skies above can compare with the Lord? Who is like the Lord among the heavenly beings?	7 because who in the clouds shall be deemed equal to the Lord? And who among divine sons shall be compared with the Lord?
7 In the council of the holy ones God is greatly feared; he is more awesome than all who surround him.	8 God is glorified in a council of holy ones, great and awesome to all that are around him.
8 Who is like you, Lord God Almighty? You, Lord, are mighty, and your faithfulness surrounds you.	9 O Lord God of hosts, who is like you? You are powerful, O Lord, and your truth is around you.
9 You rule over the surging sea; when its waves mount up, you still them.	10 It is you who rule the might of the sea, and the surge of its waves you calm.
10 You crushed Rahab like one of the slain; with your strong arm you scattered your enemies.	11 It is you who brought low a proud one like one wounded; with the arm of your power you scattered your enemies.
11 The heavens are yours, and yours also the earth; you founded the world and all that is in it.	12 Yours are the heavens, and yours is the earth; the world and all that is in it you founded.
12 You created the north and the south; Tabor and Hermon sing for joy at your name.	13 The north and seas you created; Tabor and Hermon will rejoice in your name.
13 Your arm is endowed with power; your hand is strong, your right hand exalted.	14 Yours is the arm with dominance; let your hand be strong; let your right hand be exalted.

14 Righteousness and justice are the
    foundation of your throne;
love and faithfulness go before you.
15 Blessed are those who have learned to
    acclaim you,
who walk in the light of your presence,
    Lord.
16 They rejoice in your name all day long;
they celebrate your righteousness.

17 For you are their glory and strength,
and by your favor you exalt our horn.

18 Indeed, our shield belongs to the Lord,
our king to the Holy One of Israel.
19 Once you spoke in a vision,
to your faithful people you said:
"I have bestowed strength on a warrior;
I have raised up a young man from
    among the people.
20 I have found David my servant;
with my sacred oil I have anointed him.
21 My hand will sustain him;
surely my arm will strengthen him.
22 The enemy will not get the better of
    him;
the wicked will not oppress him.
23 I will crush his foes before him
and strike down his adversaries.

24 My faithful love will be with him,
and through my name his horn will be
    exalted.
25 I will set his hand over the sea,
his right hand over the rivers.
26 He will call out to me, 'You are my
    Father,
my God, the Rock my Savior.'

27 And I will appoint him to be my first-
    born,
the most exalted of the kings of the
    earth.
28 I will maintain my love to him forever,
and my covenant with him will never fail.

29 I will establish his line forever,
his throne as long as the heavens endure.

30 "If his sons forsake my law
and do not follow my statutes,

15 Righteousness and judgment are a
    provision of your throne;
mercy and truth will go in front of you.
16 Happy are the people who know a
    shout for joy;
O Lord, in the light of your countenance
    they will walk,
17 and in your name they will rejoice all
    day long,
and in your righteousness they will be
    exalted,
18 because you are the boast of their
    power
and by your favor our horn shall be
    exalted,
19 because support is of the Lord
and of the Holy One of Israel, our king.
20 Then you spoke in a vision to your
    devout ones and said:
"I added help to one who is powerful;
I exalted one chosen from my people.

21 I found David my slave;
with my holy oil I anointed him.
22 For my hand shall sustain him;
my arm also shall strengthen him.
23 An enemy shall not profit by him,
and a son of lawlessness shall not add to
    harm him.
24 And I will crush his enemies from
    before him,
and those who hate him I will rout.
25 And my truth and my mercy shall be
    with him,
and in my name his horn shall be exalted.
26 And I will set his hand in a sea,
and in rivers his right hand.
27 He shall call upon me, 'My Father you
    are,
my God and supporter of my deliver-
    ance!'
28 And I will make him a firstborn,
high among the kings of the earth.

29 Forever I will keep my mercy for him,
and my covenant with him will stand
    firm.
30 And I will establish his seed forever
    and ever
and his throne as the days of the sky.
31 If his sons forsake my law
and by my judgments do not walk,

31 if they violate my decrees
and fail to keep my commands,

32 I will punish their sin with the rod,
their iniquity with flogging;
33 but I will not take my love from him,
nor will I ever betray my faithfulness.

34 I will not violate my covenant
or alter what my lips have uttered.
35 Once for all, I have sworn by my holiness—
and I will not lie to David—
36 that his line will continue forever
and his throne endure before me like the
sun;
37 it will be established forever like the
moon,
the faithful witness in the sky."
38 But you have rejected, you have
spurned,
you have been very angry with your
anointed one.
39 You have renounced the covenant
with your servant
and have defiled his crown in the dust.
40 You have broken through all his walls
and reduced his strongholds to ruins.

41 All who pass by have plundered him;
he has become the scorn of his neighbors.
42 You have exalted the right hand of his
foes;
you have made all his enemies rejoice.
43 Indeed, you have turned back the edge
of his sword
and have not supported him in battle.
44 You have put an end to his splendor
and cast his throne to the ground.
45 You have cut short the days of his
youth;
you have covered him with a mantle of
shame.

46 How long, Lord? Will you hide yourself
forever?
How long will your wrath burn like fire?
47 Remember how fleeting is my life.
For what futility you have created all
humanity!

32 if my statutes they shall violate
and my commandments they do not
keep,
33 I will visit their lawlessness with a rod,
and with scourges their sins,
34 but my mercy I will never disperse
from him
nor be unjust in my truth,
35 nor will I violate my covenant
and set aside what proceeds from my lips.
36 Once and for all I swore
by my holiness, 'If I will lie to David.'

37 His seed shall remain forever,
and his throne is like the sun before me,

38 and like the moon, established forever.
And the witness in heaven is faithful."
Interlude on strings
39 But you, you spurned and rejected;
you put off your anointed.

40 You renounced the covenant with
your slave;
you defiled his sanctity in the dust.
41 You broke down all his defenses;
you reduced his strongholds to cow-
ardice.
42 All the way-farers plundered him;
he became a reproach to his neighbors.

43 You exalted the right hand of his enemies;
you made glad all his enemies.
44 You turned away the help of his
sword,
and you did not support him in battle.
45 You dismissed him from purification;
his throne you smashed to the ground.
46 You diminished the days of his time;
you covered him with shame.

Interlude on strings

47 How long, O Lord? Will you turn away
completely?
Will your wrath burn like fire?
48 Remember what my substance is.
For, surely, you did not create all the sons
of men in vain?

48 Who can live and not see death, or who can escape the power of the grave?	49 Who is the person who shall live and not see death, shall rescue his soul from the power of Hades?
	Interlude on strings
49 Lord, where is your former great love, which in your faithfulness you swore to David? 50 Remember, Lord, how your servant has been mocked, how I bear in my heart the taunts of all the nations, 51 the taunts with which your enemies, Lord, have mocked, with which they have mocked every step of your anointed one. 52 Praise be to the Lord forever! Amen and Amen.	50 Lord, where are your mercies of long ago, which you swore to David by your truth? 51 Remember, O Lord, the reproach against your slaves, which I bore in my bosom, from many nations, 52 with which your enemies reproached, O Lord, with which they reproached what had been exchanged for your anointed. 53 Blessed be the Lord forever. May it be; may it be

In some ways, the first thirty-eight verses of this psalm read like a reflection on 2 Samuel 7 and its implications, done in the context of praising God for his covenant with David. It should in any case be compared to the other "royal" psalms: Psalms 2, 18, 20, 21, 72, 110, and 132.[64] God showed great loving kindness[65] and also faithfulness to David. The Hebrew word for faithfulness, loyalty to what one has promised and agreed to do in the covenant, here is not *ḥesed* but rather אֱמוּן ('ēmūn). It is a mistake to read too much into the use of *ḥesed*, which various Jewish translations rightly render as "mercy."

Verse 3 speaks of a special agreement, a covenant God has made with David himself, who is called God's chosen one and his servant. A close reading of 2 Samuel 7:4–17 in fact shows that what God promised was that he would establish Solomon's kingdom, the one who, unlike David, is allowed to build God a house, "and I will establish the throne of his kingdom forever. . . . I will not take my loving kindness from him as I did from Saul." True, this is a promise made to David, but it is made *about* David's heir. And herein lies the problem. One of David's heirs, we cannot tell which one, is experiencing quite the opposite of God's favor, as we shall see. But notice as well that 2 Samuel 7 also says that

---

64. See the discussion in Hossfeld and Zenger, *Psalms 2*, 415. As they say, it is interesting to see how the LXX has modified the psalm by small changes so that what in the Hebrew is applied directly to David, in the LXX is applied more widely to the people of God (see p. 414).

65. See ch. 4 above on *ḥesed*.

when Solomon commits iniquity, he will be punished. Could this psalm be about Solomon? Possibly, but it seems more likely to be about one of Solomon's descendants, say a Rehoboam.[66] In any case, the psalm has been made generic enough that it could suit any king subsequent to David who is experiencing difficulties with enemies.

The psalmist says from the outset that God's loving kindness or mercy is established forever, and that his faithfulness is as firm and enduring as the heavens themselves. He illustrates this in vv. 3–4 by reciting what he sees as God's promise to David. His throne will hold up, last, be built for all generations.

In vv. 5–8 we hear about the heavenly court or council, "the assembly of the holy ones." In the ancient Near East outside of Israelite thought, this would be the council of the gods, since all of those other cultures were polytheistic. But the psalmist by קְדֹשִׁים (qedōšîm) probably is referring to the angels in Yahweh's heavenly court as in Isaiah 6 (cf. Psalm 82). Here they are simply called "holy ones," whereas in Psalm 8 they were called 'elōhîm. It is not just the psalmist on earth who should praise God, but the very heavens and the heavenly court should do so as well (see, e.g., Revelation 4). These beings are also called here literally "sons of might." The psalmist deliberately avoids calling them anything like "gods" here, and asks the self-evident rhetorical question "for who among the sons of might [אֵלִים בִּבְנֵי bibnê 'ēlîm] can be compared to the real God, Yahweh?" The answer of course is no one, not ever. God is revered by the entire heavenly council because he is so far above and greater than them all, no one is as mighty as he, which is why only he can be called "Lord of Hosts" (v. 8).

Verses 9–11 extol Yahweh as the creator God, who made the heavens and the earth and rules them both. He made great mountains like Mt. Hermon or Mt. Tabor in the north of the land (Hermon being on the border in the extreme north). Then too, God has scattered his enemies, whether celestial or terrestrial, with his mighty arm. Verse 14 goes on to make the point that not only did God create such things, but he rules with righteousness and justice and mercy or loving kindness and faithfulness. As a result Israel throws great parties and festivals in God's honor and extols his name. Blessed or happy those that walk in the light of God's countenance. It is only by God's favor, says v. 17 that

---

66. Hossfeld and Zenger, *Psalms 2*, 406 suggest postexilic, but this is an argument based on silence, namely the absence of mention of the temple. But this psalm is about a person David, not about the temple, and about his descendants. See Weiser, *Psalms*, 591 who points to the lack of mention of a king being deported, or of exile. The psalm speaks only of defeats by foreign armies, and this happened to various kings before the exile (see, e.g., Isaiah 36–39).

"our horn is exalted" and our king belongs to "the Holy One of Israel." "The point of this carefully drawn parallel between the kingship of God and that of David is to claim that the latter is integral to the former. It actualizes in the world what is reality in heaven. David's kingship is the agency through which the Lord's rule is extended from heaven to earth."[67]

Verse 19 is intriguing "you spoke in a vision to your faithful ones."[68] Who is the faithful one—the psalmist? A prophet like Nathan? It would not appear to be the king, since the revelation seems to be given to a third party to speak about what God has done for David: he has set a crown on him, exalted the one he has chosen, anointed him with holy oil, strengthened him with his arm, and his hand will always be with him with the result that David's foes have no chance of beating him, and David shall call God "father" (cf. 2 Sam 7:14; Ps 2:7) and the rock of his salvation (v. 26).

Verse 25 is interesting, using again a mythological motif. The idea is that the king controls chaos, emblemized by the chaos waters.[69] God promises to make David "the firstborn," which it would appear really just means preeminent, the highest of the earthly kings, or having firstborn status among the "sons of God," the people of Israel. Verses 30-31 warn that there will be punishment if David's offspring forsake God's law and ordinances. But God will never forsake David himself or violate the covenant he made with David. "His line shall go on forever" (v. 35). Only it didn't. The monarchy ended abruptly with Zechariah in 587 BCE. One must beware of taking too literally the poetic hyperbole of the psalmist. But the problem is, he seems to believe his own rhetoric, hence the lament in vv. 38-51.

Verse 38 is the fulcrum, or turning point in this psalm with וְאַתָּה (we'attâ), "but you," the psalmist now points his finger at his God.[70] Astonishingly, God has spurned, rejected, poured out his wrath on his anointed, renounced the covenantal agreement, and thrown the king's crown in the dustbin.[71] God has made him vulnerable, laid his strongholds in ruins, exalted his foes, and as a result he has become the laugh-

---

67. Mays, *Psalms*, 286.
68. The Hebrew is plural here, perhaps referring to the line of prophets who spoke to kings for God. See Mays, *Psalms*, 285.
69. Hossfeld and Zenger, *Psalms 2*, 410.
70. Brueggemann and Bellinger, *Psalms*, 387–88.
71. The terseness of the Hebrew is hard to render in English. As Goldingay, *Psalms: Volume 2*, 684 suggests, we have "a trio of confrontational verbs not exceeded in power anywhere in the Psalms": "you spurned, rejected, raged at your anointed." Especially the first of these verbs is telling because it is the one Samuel used to tell Saul he had been rejected by God (1 Sam 15:23, 26).

ingstock of the whole region. God has not supported the king in battle, even blunted his sword, snatched the scepter from his hand, hurled his throne to the ground, "cut short the days of his youth" (v. 45), and in general publicly shamed him. To the psalmist, this hardly sounds like covenant loyalty.

Thus the psalmist asks in v. 46, quite appropriately, if this is your judgment on him per the agreement in 2 Samuel 7, then it should come to an end at some point, could it happen please while I'm still breathing, says the psalmist, "remember how short my time is." Sheol is already calling my name, please don't hide your face much longer. "If God's steadfast love is forever, can wrath last forever?"[72] Only here is God accused directly of hiding.[73] As vv. 49-51 suggest, it is not just God's anointed that has been shamed, it is also his "publicist" so to speak, the psalmist, "remember how I bear in my bosom the insults of the people" (v. 50). Their taunts dog the very footsteps of God's anointed.

And then, all of a sudden, as if we had never heard vv. 38-51, the psalm ends: "Blessed be the Lord forever and forever." But this final doxology which closes the third book of the Psalter, is surely a later addition when the collection was being put together. The original psalm likely ended with v. 51.[74]

Not counting the final doxology, book 3 of the Psalter ends with a bang, and very differently from the more hopeful ending in book 2 at Psalm 72 in regard to the monarchy. Robert Cole has even suggested that Psalm 89 summarizes the essential message of the whole of book 3. He draws this conclusion by tracing the detailed links between Psalms 73-88 and Psalm 89. He may be right.[75] If so this is a sobering thought.

In early Judaism Psalm 89 shows up in messianic texts like Psalms of Solomon 17:4-44 (in particular vv. 4 and 43) and 18:1-5.[76] As Hays points out, what is significant is that in the LXX the title Χριστός is used of a Davidic king in contexts where the promise of an eternal Davidic line is reiterated. It shows up in Psalms 2:2; 19:7; 83:10; 88:39, 52; 131:10, 17 (remembering that the LXX numbering is one fewer than the MT numbering, so we are talking about Ps 89:39, 52).[77] Excerpts of

---

72. Mays, *Psalms*, 287.

73. Goldingay, *Psalms: Volume 2*, 687.

74. Longman, *Psalms*, 326; Brueggemann and Bellinger, *Psalms*, 385.

75. See Robert L. Cole, *The Shape and Message of Book III (Psalms 73-89)*, JSOTSup 307 (Sheffield: Sheffield Academic Press, 2000), 178-82.

76. See Wagner, *Heralds*, 320n51.

77. Hays, *Echoes of Scripture in the Gospels*, 380, and see John J. Collins, *The Scepter and the Star: The Messiah of the Dead Sea Scrolls and Other Ancient Literature*, ABRL (New York: Doubleday, 1995), 53-56.

our psalm show up as well at Qumran in 4QPsx, but oddly the verses are arranged with the distinctive order vv. 19–21, 25, 22, 26a, 27, and 30.[78]

Various NT writers were to answer some of the conundrums about the Davidic line by suggesting that God would choose a single and singular anointed one of Davidic descent to rule forever, rather than some perpetual hereditary succession of kings. The promises to David (and Solomon) would be fulfilled in a single figure, Jesus, who would be not merely David's son but David's Lord, and not merely a sage like Solomon, but Wisdom come in the flesh, who would personally rule forever. But the psalmist knows none of this and does not really foreshadow it either. "This remarkable dimension of the expectation of a coming king (messiah) is that as political possibility waned, the capacity for hope grounded in YHWH's fidelity persisted. Although our psalm has no answer to the question of verse 49, in the long run both Judaism and Christianity have bet on YHWH's ḥesed against the circumstances of lived history."[79]

While direct quotations of Psalm 89 are lacking in the NT, there are quite a few echoes and some allusions to take into account. It is no surprise that where the subject of Jesus being a promised royal son of David shows up, Psalm 89 comes to the mind of NT writers. For example, in the annunciation story in Luke 1:32–33 the angel tells Mary, "This one will be great, and he will be called the son of the Most High, and the Lord God will give to him the throne of his father David. And he will reign over the house of Jacob forever, and of his kingdom there shall be no end." It is customary of course to point to 2 Samuel 7:12–14 as being echoed here, but as we have already pointed out in this study, 2 Samuel 7 is quite specifically a promise about Solomon. It involves, for example, the promise that he will build the temple—which Solomon did. It promises a father-son relationship between God and Solomon. It is not a generic promise about Davidic descendants in general. But in the text of Luke 1:26–38 we are told that the son of Mary will be given the throne of David, "his father" and of his kingdom there will be no end. As Hays notes, Luke is not just dealing with 2 Samuel 7, he is dealing with the further elaboration of the promise to David in Psalm 89.[80]

The difference between 2 Samuel 7 and Psalm 89 is that, as vv. 38–45 make apparent, the psalmist is not talking about Solomon (notice the complete lack of mention of building the temple) he is talking about a

---

78. See Goldingay, Psalms: Volume 2, 665.
79. Brueggemann and Bellinger, Psalms, 390.
80. Hays, Echoes of Scripture in the Gospels, 195–96.

later royal descendant of David whom God seems to have abandoned. This is important, because the psalmist is calling for God to renew or redo his promises to David by upholding a latter day Davidic king. The psalmist expects God to do so at some juncture, preferably sooner rather than later. It is precisely this element in the story that made Psalm 89 useful for spurring later messianic hopes among Jews in a way that 2 Samuel 7, in its original context and meaning was not. Time and again in the NT what is echoed is the Davidic promise filtered through Psalm 89 or some other similar psalm. The NT writers were not alone in this because we find this same kind of influence of Psalm 89 in early Jewish texts like Testament of Simeon 7, Testament of Judah 24.1-6, and Testament of Naphtali 5.1-3, 8.2-3, and in the pesher of 2 Samuel 7:10-14 in 4Q174 II, 11-14 there is a focus on a particular singular Davidic descendant, further elaborated on in Psalms of Solomon 17.[81]

Further and even clearer evidence that Luke was reading the Davidic promises through the lens of psalms like Psalm 89 can be found in Acts 13:16-41 in Paul's inaugural synagogue sermon. Verses 22-23 read as follows: "When he had removed him [Saul] he made David their king. In his testimony about him he said: 'I have found David, son of Jesse, to be a man after my own heart who will carry out my wishes.' Of this man's posterity God has brought to Israel a Savior, Jesus, as he promised." It is in Psalm 89:21 and not in 2 Samuel 7, as Doble rightly points out, that we have the phrase "I have found my servant David." In other words, Acts 13 makes the connection between the Davidic promises and the coming savior primarily on the basis of the discussion in Psalm 89, which again is not about David, but about God being faithful to a latter day Davidic descendant. Doble is right to stress as well the word "promise" here in Acts 13. Psalm 89 harps on the theme of God's promise to David by repeatedly reminding God of what he had previously sworn to David, namely to establish his descendants forever (cf. vv. 3-4, vv. 19-37, vv. 49-51). As Doble notes: "It would be hard to find a more radical reflection on David's story than Psalm 88 [LXX, Psalm 89 MT], a psalm available to Luke, central to his major theme—rebuilding David's house—and the concluding psalm of Book III of a Greek Psalter."[82]

It will be remembered that the psalmist at the end of Psalm 89 demands to know *when* God would keep his promise to David

---

81. See the discussion in Pao and Schnabel, "Luke," 260.
82. Doble, "Psalms in Luke-Acts," 105, see also pp. 106-7 and especially the chart on p. 109.

(vv.46–51). He has stressed the covenant agreement again and again, reminding God of his obligations (see especially v. 28). "Where this psalmist demanded to know *when* God would keep his promise, Paul announced that God *had* kept it (Acts 13:23, 32). Further, the psalmist's question at Psalm 88:49 is linked by Paul with God's ancient promise (Acts 13:32). It's internal logic points to Psalm 88 setting Paul's sermon agenda."[83] As it turns out, one needs to probe deeper than simply looking for citations from the OT if one wants to understand the depth of influence of the Psalms on the NT writers. Some of the other earliest Christian writers certainly were sensitive to the need to read the foundational history stories through the lens of the Psalms' later perspectives. Notice for instance 1 Clement 18:1 for the combination of 1 Samuel 13:14 and Psalm 89:20.[84]

We can provide a further piece of evidence of the reading of the Samuel narratives through the Psalms, and in particular Psalm 89, if we turn to Revelation 1:5. Here Jesus is called both the faithful witness and the firstborn (of the dead), and the ruler of the kings of earth. Psalm 89:27 has the promise of God to David, "I will make him the firstborn, the highest of the kings of the earth" and this section of the psalm finishes in v. 37 with a reference to "an enduring witness in the skies." This last bit is of relevance to the discussion of Revelation since Christ is depicted there as being precisely a witness in the skies, that is in heaven. As Beale and McDonough acknowledge, all three phrases, faithful witness, firstborn, ruler of the kings of the earth uniquely occur in Psalm 89.[85]

Of course John is claiming more than the psalmist about the Davidic figure, for as Moyise stresses, "John does not think that Psalm 89 says all there is to say about Christ but neither is he contradicting. It is more that he wishes to bring the old and new into dialectical relationship where each affects the other."[86] Or should we rather say, John is simply appropriating the language of Psalm 89 and applying it to Christ? Much depends on who John's audience is in Asia Minor. If it is primarily Jewish Christians, like himself, then yes, he may well be urging them to search the Scriptures and hear the intertextual echoes he is creating.

Psalm 89 and its use in the NT goes in other directions as well. We

---

83. Ibid., 109 (emphasis original).
84. See Marshall, "Acts," 583.
85. Beale and McDonough, "Revelation," 1089. They point to Exod. Rab. 197 and possibly Pesiq. Rab. 34.2 as evidence this psalm was used messianically in early Judaism, but those sources are probably too late to be seen as background to the uses of Psalm 89 in the NT.
86. Moyise, "Psalms in the Book of Revelation," 237.

have not yet pointed out that calling the messiah God's son and the messiah calling God father, has a basis not just in 2 Samuel 7, which again is not in itself a messianic text, but in the royal psalms, for instance Psalm 2:7 and Psalm 89:26. Hays rightly points to John 1:49 where Nathanael exclaims that Jesus is "the Son of God" and in the same breath says "you are the king of Israel."[87] Not just one or the other, but both. Speaking of double titles, it is also in Psalm 89 that the royal figure is called God's servant and God's anointed one in synonymous parallelism (Ps 89:38–39 and vv. 50–52).[88] That these titles are closely associated in the NT probably owes something to the precedent in Psalm 89.

But some scriptural echoes are even more subtle than these. In the Psalms usually it is God who stills the raging chaos waters, for example, in Psalm 107:23–32. But we have something interesting going on in Psalm 89 in regard to this sort of theme. It is said clearly that God rules the raging seas at v. 9 and when the waves rise, God stills them. But what is also said, uniquely in Psalm 89, is this about God's Davidic ruler by God himself: "I will set his hand on the sea, and his right hand on the rivers." The context explains that this will show his power over both land and sea, over both his human enemies and the chaos waters. And this brings us to Mark 4:35–41 as Hays rightly suggests.[89]

What is most interesting is that the portrait of Jesus in that Markan text is of Jesus asleep in the stern of the boat when the storm and waves rage around him, which may echo Psalm 78:65 "then the Lord awoke as from sleep."[90] In the Markan account Jesus awakes, and rebukes the wind and says to the sea "peace, be still." Then the wind ceased and the water was dead still. In the Markan outline, the disciples are stunned and afraid, and importantly this is the first place where they directly ask the question, "Who then is this that even the wind and waves obey him?" The answer that Mark's account is working toward is not fully given until Peter proclaims Jesus to be the messiah at Mark 8:29, but already here in Mark 4, Mark is probably echoing Psalm 89, where the answer given is not merely God, but also God's anointed Davidic king. I am suggesting that the Mark 4 account echoes several of the psalms in book 3, in this case Psalm 78 and Psalm 89.[91] There are other small

87. Hays, *Echoes of Scripture in the Gospels*, 329.
88. Ibid., 380n68.
89. Ibid., 66–67.
90. See the discussion above.
91. Watts, "Mark," 158 misses this altogether. Speaking of missing altogether, Keesmaat, "Psalms in Romans and Galatians," 159–60 tries to suggest that Paul is drawing on Psalm 89 in Gal 3:16. Not a

echoes of Psalm 89 in the NT, for example in the remark in John 12:34, "we have heard from the Law that the Messiah remains forever." Probably "Law" here is simply a cipher for the OT Scriptures in general, and if so then Psalm 89:4, 36–37 could be in the background here, bearing in mind again that it is Psalm 89 that was interpreted of Davidic kings later than Solomon. But it is time to consider more broadly the third book of the Psalter and how the writers of the NT drew upon it.

The Lexicon of Faith: The Broader Use of Psalms 73–89

Psalm 73 begins the third book of the Psalter, and at v. 13 we hear these interesting words: "All in vain have I kept my heart clean and washed my hands in innocence." The psalmist is complaining about the wicked, among whom he is dwelling, though he is not one them. They seem to be prospering while "all day long I have been plagued and am punished every morning." If we ask where in the NT do we hear something similar, there is only one text of relevance, Matthew 27:24, "So when Pilate saw that he could do nothing, but rather that a riot was beginning he took some water and washed his hands before the crowd saying: 'I am innocent of this man's blood.'" There is some irony in this echo of the psalm because of course in the end Pilate was not "innocent" of Jesus's blood, since he had him executed, but at that juncture when he washed his hands, he was still innocent of Jesus's blood. The context of the two narratives is similar in that there is a stark contrast between the wicked and the innocent, of course in the psalm the innocent is the speaker, whereas in the Gospel the innocent is the man on trial before Pilate, whom Pilate is trying to avoid executing. Here we are simply talking about a use of similar biblical language, not a contextual exegesis of Psalm 73.

Scholars have long debated where the notions found in Acts 17:26 in Paul's famous Areopagus speech come from. He refers to God "allotting the times of their existence [i.e., the nations], and the boundaries of the places where they would live." An answer may in part be Psalm 74:16–17 which reads: "Yours is the day, yours also the night; you established the luminaries and also the sun. You've fixed all the bounds of the earth." The idea of God fixing limits on things is found in that psalm, and lest we think the psalmist is just talking about inan-

bit of it. He is talking about the promises to Abraham and his seed, and no connection whatsoever is made with the descendants of David in Galatians. *There is no mention of David in Galatians at all*, rather we have a contrast between the Mosaic and the Abrahamic covenants, the latter of which is connected to the new covenant, completely bypassing both Moses and David.

imate objects or seasons, he goes on to ask God to set limits on his and Israel's enemies (vv. 18–19), just as he did on the sea monsters (v.14). It is a faint echo, but the ideas in the psalm may have influenced the way the Areopagus speech was framed at that specific juncture.

Psalm 75:8 provides essential conceptual background for under-standing the cup saying of Jesus found in Mark 14:36 // Matthew 26:39 // Luke 22:42. Here in this psalm, and for that matter numerous places elsewhere in the OT (cf. Ps 60:3; Jer 25:15; Isa. 51:17; Ezek 23:31; Hab 2:16, et al.) the cup of wine is a metaphor for God's wrath against sin, poured out in judgment on the wicked. Confirmation that one is on the right track in interpreting Jesus's "let this cup pass" saying in light of this background can be found in Revelation 14:9–11 where we are told that the fate of the wicked will be, "they will drink the wine of God's wrath poured unmixed into the cup of his anger." The allusion to this OT idea is clearer because of the mention of mixed and unmixed in Revelation 14, which points very specifically to Psalm 75:8.[92]

In this sort of context, the incident in the garden of Gethsemane becomes an instance not of Jesus quailing before the prospective of dying prematurely in general, but rather not wanting to drink the cup of God's wrath on sin. It may be of relevance to this discussion that in Jesus's passion predictions, for instance in Mark 8–10, he refers to being killed, not being crucified, and he says nothing about facing God's wrath in the bargain. But in Gethsemane it is not just death, but God's dealing with sin that he is confronted with. It is God's cup of wrath that he asking to take a pass on, though he leaves the final deci-sion in the hands of the Almighty.

Psalm 82:6 reads "I say, 'You are gods ['elōhîm], children of the Most High, all of you; nevertheless you shall die like mortals, and fall like princes." Famously, this singular verse is cited in John 10:34 in the con-text of an argument Jesus is having with some Jewish officials who are complaining, not about Jesus's good deeds, but rather "because you, though only a human being, are making yourself God" (v. 33). Jesus answers with the quote cited above which he says is "written in your Law," again using law in the broad sense of Scripture (or if the word is not a mere label, in the sense of instruction, since this is what *torah* lit-erally means).

Jesus is looking for a precedent to show that human beings were on occasion called "gods" in the OT, and he finds it in Psalm 82. In fact

---

92. See Moyise, "Psalms in the Book of Revelation," 239–40. He is right that John seems to be following the LXX here again.

he insists that since the Scripture is inviolable and cannot be annulled, then it must be right to use such language. In its original context, Psalm 82, which begins with the heavenly council, may be referring to the end or mortality of all other so-called gods, namely the heavenly beings who are part of Yahweh's heavenly court, rather than referring to earthly princes.[93] The accusation is that they have not done their job of ruling the earth according to Yahweh's justice and mercy principles, and therefore Yahweh proclaims "the twilight of the gods," namely their death sentence.[94]

However, by Jesus's day, it was not unusual for Jews to interpret the reference to "the sons of the Most High" as a reference to Israel (see m. 'Abot 3.6), or as a reference to angels who were called upon to serve and rule the various nations (see 11Q13 II, 10–11 which takes this text to be referring to evil angels that needed to be judged), and Jesus seems to be operating with the former of these two assumptions in his rebuttal here.[95] Jesus then is rebutting the charge of blasphemy by not only pointing to scriptural precedent for calling someone "god" who is not Yahweh, but also by insisting that unlike those "gods" in Psalm 82, he is actually one whom God anointed and sent into the world to do good. He is arguing from the lesser to the greater, "if even they can be called gods, how much more can I be called God's very son."[96] If however Jesus is referring to the divine beings who are part of the heavenly council, then he would be making the even more shocking claim that he is indeed the divine Son of God, and has even more right than those "angelic" beings to be called such.[97]

Psalm 86:8–10 reads "There is none like you among the gods, O Lord, nor are there any works like yours. All the nations you have made shall come and bow down before you Lord, and shall glorify your name. For you are great and do wondrous things; you alone are God." This should be compared to Revelation 15:3–4, "Great and amazing are your deeds, Lord God the Almighty. Just and true are your ways, King of nations. Lord who will not fear and glorify your name? For you alone are holy. All nations will come and worship before you." As Moyise points out, John seems to be following the LXX of Psalm 86 quite closely here, as

---

93. See Weiser, *Psalms*, 560.
94. See Mays, *Psalms*, 269–70; cf. Goldingay, *Psalms: Volume 2*, 566–67.
95. On the early Jewish interpretation of Ps 82:1–6 see Daly-Denton, "Psalms in John's Gospel," 123–26
96. See the discussion in Köstenberger, "John," 465–66; and Hays, *Echoes of Scripture in the Gospels*, 299 and the notes there.
97. See now the argument of Heiser, *Unseen Realm*, 268–70.

there are some sixteen words taken verbatim from the LXX version of this psalm to compose the song in Revelation 15.[98]

In Psalm 88:11 we have a reference to Abaddon (which means destruction) and it is clear from the context that the psalmist is referring to the land of the dead, Sheol. In Revelation 9:11 interestingly it is the angel of the "bottomless pit" who is called Abaddon. There are more allusions and echoes one could comment on, but this must suffice. It's time to sum up what we've learned from book 3 of the Psalter and its use in the NT. Even sound-byte-sized phrases like "washed my hands in innocence" provided a precedent from the Psalms that gave a familiar ring to a phrase in the storytelling of the passion of Jesus. The more one studies even the incidental use of Psalm language the more one realizes it really was the lexicon for faith expression of the writers of the NT.

Conclusions

It cannot be said of the use of the material in book 3 of the Psalter that the writers of the NT must have turned to this material because of its Davidic connections and potential. There is not much material in this book with Davidic connections and only one psalm has a prescript with David's name, and yet Jesus quotes a verse of one of these psalms, and a key idea found in the psalms provides Jesus with the metaphor to talk about the unique nature of his coming death. Furthermore, several of these psalms provide eschatological language for the author of Revelation, including terms, phrases, and ideas, which John feels free to modify to suit his visions (e.g., Abaddon becomes an angel). The issue of justice/vengeance does come up in some of these psalms and this in itself provides some useful material for a book like Revelation, or the apocalyptic discourse of Jesus, for instance in Luke.

Sometimes we have a phrase that is used in the NT to characterize something important Jesus said or did. One such phrase is of course "parables and dark sayings" from Psalm 78, but there is more than just a phrase behind this reference, in this case in Matthew. It is meant to tell us that Jesus is a purveyor of God's wisdom, but it also suggests that

---

98. Moyise, "Psalms in the Book of Revelation," 235–36, and he is right that Beale is trying to damp down the universalistic thrust of this material, and wrongly suggests that Deuteronomy 28 lurks in the background here. See Beale and McDonough, "Revelation," 1134 and contrast Richard Bauckham, *The Climax of Prophecy: Studies in the Book of Revelation* (New York: T&T Clark, 1993), 306. I agree with Moyise that John is following the LXX and not translating the Hebrew here. He seems to have access to and a knowledge of both.

Jesus saw his audience as just as "hard of hearing" and recalcitrant as the psalmist did. Bringing up wisdom literature however is important for another reason, namely that the Psalms were read through the lens of later Jewish literature such as Wisdom of Solomon and Sirach, so that the form in which we see some of the ideas and phrases from the Psalms is the recycled form from one of these later sapiential works. This is no surprise since both of those sapiential works also have salvation historical reviews in them, like various of the psalms in this and other books of the Psalter.

The OT was seen as providing all sorts of precedents, including being used by Jesus in John to justify his being called a deity on the basis of a psalm verse that originally probably referred to either pagan deities, or somewhat later to angels in God's heavenly court. The point here is not exegesis, but precedent for the use of the term, it was meant to tease the audience's mind into active thought. Even Jesus is depicted as being creative in his handling of the Psalms.

Sometimes we need to talk about intentional echoes or overtones, for instance the use of psalm language about Yahweh stilling winds and seas to describe Jesus stilling the storm on the sea of Galilee, and one has to reckon with the probability that the evangelist is implying that Jesus was indeed divine, for the answer to the question, "Who then is this who controls wind and wave?" has only one answer in a Jewish context—God.

The Psalms provided the writers of the NT with both theological and ethical concepts, and it cannot be missed that one of the repeated themes is how Israel keeps going astray, and how God keeps having mercy on her, whether on her king, or on her as a nation. This stands in rather stark contrast to the message of some of the imprecatory portions of the same psalms, but the message of God's grace, kindness, compassion, mercy, and forgiveness was to be one Jesus and his disciples would emphasize again and again, while ignoring some of the other themes of these same psalms. Not surprisingly, the strong ethical orientation of the psalmists, including the recycling of various of the Ten Commandments in various forms, was to influence the teaching of Jesus and his followers, who like the psalmists placed the ethical teachings of torah inside the context of wisdom literature and expressed it as a form of wisdom, so, for example, the juxtaposition of beatitudes with imperatives in the Sermon on the Mount was already a part of the poetry and orientation of the Psalms. Law was just one more form of wise instruction.

Sometimes the key to unlocking an enigmatic saying of Jesus comes from seeing how the ideas are echoing something in the Psalms. We saw that the phrase in John 7:38 "from within him shall flow rivers of living water" in light of Psalm 78:16 and 20 surely is referring to living water coming forth from Jesus to those who become his disciples, not from within the believer herself. Jesus who is presented in John as wisdom come in the flesh, the very source of life, even everlasting life, can speak of a living water in John 4, and promise it to those who will receive him and his teaching. He is not only the rock from which water sprang for the wilderness wandering generation according to Paul, he is the source of the living water even for non-Jews like the Samaritan woman according to the fourth evangelist.

Sometimes the indebtedness to a psalm's way of presenting things is so stunning that one wonders how scholars have often missed just how strongly the NT is indebted to the psalmists. To give but one example from this chapter, it is in Psalm 89:21 and not in 2 Samuel 7 that we have the phrase, "I have found my servant David." In other words, Acts 13 makes the connection between the Davidic promises and the coming savior primarily on the basis of the discussion in Psalm 89, which again is not about David, but about God being faithful to a latter day Davidic descendant. The Psalms provide a crucial bridge between the historical narratives in the OT about the monarchy, and the way those institutions, ideas, and traditions were seen and understood as Jews looked forward to their coming king before and during the time of Jesus. They also provided Jesus with one of his sapiential self-images, that of the mother bird gathering her chick under her protective wings (see the next chapter). The Psalms were already pointing forward because even the preexilic psalms spoke of the failures of the Davidic monarchy, and the exilic and postexilic ones were hoping for a revival of the monarchy in a way that transcended the failures of the past.

And "when the time had fully come" it was time to sing a new song, even if the lyrics were familiar. We must never forget that the Psalms were the language of worship, not just private prayer. Jesus himself had been part of the crowds going up to Zion singing together the psalms of ascent, the psalms of going up. The Psalms were the language of devotion, the language of hopes and dreams, the language of emotional expressions of the joys and sorrows of life, the language of aspiration and inspiration, and the writers of the NT not only knew this, they embraced it. The Psalms were the language with which the devout reached out to God and unburdened their hearts and souls. It is how they prayed and thought about God. And in the NT, it is how they thought about and expressed their faith in Jesus. Yes, the prophets provided oracles, and previews of coming attractions, but the Psalms taught people how to embrace their faith and their God, even in the midst of suffering, sin, and sorrow. We will hear and explore more of this as we turn to the fourth book of the Psalter.

6

Psalter Book 4 (Psalms 90–106)

New Songs and an Old Law

> If you desire to establish yourself and others in devotion, to know what confidence is to be reposed in God, and what makes the mind fearless, you will praise God by reciting the Ninety-first Psalm.
> —Athanasius to Marcellinus[1]

Book 4 of the Psalter is almost as short as book 3, comprising only seventeen songs. The book begins with Psalm 90, called a prayer of Moses,[2] and contains exactly two Davidic psalms: Psalms 101 and 103. Unlike some of the other collections, this one does not have many laments (but see Psalm 90, a community lament and Psalm 102, an individual lament). Mostly what we have is hymns and praise songs of the familiar sort, and at least one royal psalm, Psalm 101. Though the size of this collection is a little larger than the one in book 3, it seems to have had less overall impact in some ways on the writers of the NT, as we shall see. In any case, Brueggemann and Bellinger are perhaps right that the song with Moses in the superscript may be placed first in this fourth collection of songs in order to

---

1. Cited in Mays, *Psalms*, 296, but without the specific reference.
2. As Mays, *Psalms*, 294 suggests, the prescript probably comes from the fact that vv. 1–2 seem to echo Deut 33:27.

take readers back to the time prior to the kingdom of David, to the time prior to the building of the Jerusalem Temple, to the time of "Moses, the man of God." . . . Connecting the prayer to Moses suggests that the psalm responds to the question of the fall of Jerusalem by going back to a time when the community's relationship with YHWH shaped the life of Israel but was not mediated by temple and king.[3]

This may well explain the placing of this psalm here, especially after the royal shock of the latter part of Psalm 89. It would not however explain the whole of this collection, since two of the psalms have David's name in the prescript. Notice as well that several of the hymns in this collection celebrate God's kingship over his people (Psalms 93, 95, 99), as opposed to David's.

At the other end of book 4 of the Psalter, it is perhaps significant that in the last three psalms in this collection, the word "hallelujah" shows up (Psalms 104–106), which seems to anticipate the conclusion of the whole book of Psalms in Psalm 150.[4] In addition, the doxology at Psalm 106:48 separates this book from the following one, just as we saw at Psalm 89:52. If the use of the Psalms at Qumran is any clue, it would appear that the assembling and ordering of the last two books of the Psalter was still somewhat open to change, for Psalms 90–150 are arranged at Qumran differently from our canonical ordering.[5] On the other hand, this could just reflect the idiosyncratic nature of that community and its handling of the Psalms.

In their discussion of the composition of book 4 of the Psalter, Hossfeld and Zenger make some salient points that are worth repeating: (1) Psalms 90–92 are transitional as the Psalter moves away from the messianic psalms to the God is king psalms in Psalms 93–100; (2) Psalms 90–92 need to be taken together as they share words and themes; (3) from Psalm 90 on to the end of the Psalter as a whole, the superscripts become irregular and they differ considerably; (4) possibly the superscript about Moses in Psalm 90 is meant as a header for the whole fourth book of the Psalter because all of the references to Moses in the whole Psalter save one (Ps 77:21) come in this book of the Psalter (cf. 99:6; 103:7; 105:26; 106:16, 23, 32, noticing how there is an emphasis in the last psalm in the collection on Moses, just as the beginning of Psalm 90 leads with that thought); (5) it is possible that the original entire Psalter concluded with Psalm 100, which in any case

3. Brueggemann and Bellinger, *Psalms*, 393.
4. See Mays, *Psalms*, 17.
5. Ibid., 14.

takes up some of the themes and trajectories of Psalms 95, 96, and 98: (6) the four-book Psalter ending with Psalm 100 was probably complete about the fourth century BCE[6] Some of this is pure conjecture, but some of it seems to be accurate. In any case, we must evaluate psalms on an individual basis because none of the prehistory of the composition of the Psalter affects the way the NT writers use the material, searching the whole of the Psalter for material germane to talking about the Christ event and Christ's followers thereafter. The NT writers assume it is all God's Word, Holy Scripture, and can be studied together in various combinations and permutations.

Angelic Aides: Psalm 91

> If anyone thinks . . . that Psalm 91 contradicts the NT and is even an argument for the "lesser value" of the OT, he or she should read Rom 8:28-31, a text that is, in effect, a summary of Psalm 91.[7]

This psalm falls rather neatly into two parts: (1) vv. 1-13; and (2) vv. 14-16.[8] As Goldingay points out, vv. 1-2 seem to be the psalmist's opening words of commitment, insisting God is his refuge, and the rest of the psalm is a response to that, moving from a first- to a third-person voicing.[9] The basic thrust of the psalm has to do with trusting God for protection, hence vv. 3-13, which describe the many dangers from which God can and will protect the faithful.[10] One of the major themes of the whole Psalter comes to light when one does a study of both the noun and verbal forms of the word translated "refuge." As a noun it expresses confidence in God's protection (cf. Pss 14:6; 46:1; 61:3) and as a verb it can be used to urge people to "take refuge" in God (cf. Pss 2:11; 5:11; 11:1, et al.). These words belong to the semantic field and are often used in tandem or as synonyms for words like fortress, stronghold, shelter, even dwelling place. The metaphorical image of God as a giant bird under whose wings his children may hide when necessary is also part of the same imagery (cf. Pss. 91:4, 17; 36:7; 57:1; 63:7).[11]

What the use of this sort of language implies is that life was difficult and dangerous on an ongoing basis for God's people, even when foreign enemies were not busy attacking, conquering, or carting them off to

---

6. Hossfeld and Zenger, *Psalms 2*, 6-7.
7. Zenger, ibid., 433.
8. See, rightly, Weiser, *Psalms*, 605.
9. Goldingay, *Psalms: Volume 3; Psalms 90-150*, BOTCWP (Grand Rapids: Baker Academic, 2008), 42.
10. Mays, *Psalms*, 296.
11. See ibid., 297 on all this.

exile. There were accidents, natural disasters, and dangerous animals to deal with as well, not to mention the fragility of human life in general, with many children and their mothers dying in childbirth. This psalm certainly discusses supernatural help, even in the form of angels, and may also allude to supernatural dangers. There were many things to produce anxiety in that world and age. Verses 14–16 provide a sort of divine oracle of reassurance for those who trust God.[12] As with so many of these psalms, the descriptions of things, in this case dangers, while quite vivid, are nevertheless generic enough that they could suit many difficulties and settings. This psalm has no superscript in the Hebrew text, but the LXX says the psalm pertains to David. It is like various other songs of trust in Yahweh.

Goldingay thinks the psalm may well have been meant to address the king, like Psalm 20, though it is generic enough that it could be used more broadly. The battle imagery favors having the king in mind, but there doesn't seem to be anything pressing militarily at the time of this poetic reflection.[13] This is one of those psalms that shows up in the manuscripts from Qumran, in this case 11Q11 (i.e., 11Q Apocryphal Psalms) and the quotations are part of a larger document giving help to those plagued by demons. Psalm 91 has been adapted to deal with that theme. This is one of those cases where either through adaptation or looseness of quotation, there are quite a number of textual differences from the MT in the Qumran citations.[14]

MT Psalm 91	LXX Psalm 90
	1 A laudation. Of an Ode. Pertaining to David.
1 You who live in the shelter of the Most High,	He who lives by the help of the Most High,
who abide in the shadow of the Almighty,	in a shelter of the God of the sky he will lodge.
2 will say to the Lord, "My refuge and my fortress;	2 He will say to the Lord, "My supporter you
my God, in whom I trust."	are and my refuge; my God, I will hope in him,"
3 For he will deliver you from the snare of the fowler	3 because it is he who will rescue me from a trap of hunters
and from the deadly pestilence;	and from a troublesome word;

---

12. Brueggemann and Bellinger, *Psalms*, 395.
13. Goldingay, *Psalms: Volume 3*, 39–40.
14. See ibid., 40.

4 he will cover you with his pinions, and under his wings you will find refuge; his faithfulness is a shield and buckler.	4 with the broad of his back he will shade you, and under his wings you will find hope; with a shield his truth will surround you.
5 You will not fear the terror of the night, or the arrow that flies by day,	5 You will not be afraid of nocturnal fright, of an arrow that flies by day,
6 or the pestilence that stalks in darkness, or the destruction that wastes at noonday.	6 of a deed that travels in darkness, of mishap and noonday demon.
7 A thousand may fall at your side, ten thousand at your right hand, but it will not come near you.	7 At your side a thousand will fall, and ten thousand at your right, but it will not come near you.
8 You will only look with your eyes and see the punishment of the wicked.	8 Only with your eyes will you perceive, and the requital of sinners you will see.
9 Because you have made the Lord your refuge, the Most High your dwelling place,	9 Because you, O Lord, are my hope, the Most High you made your refuge.
10 no evil shall befall you, no scourge come near your tent.	10 No evil shall come before you, and no scourge shall come near your covert,
11 For he will command his angels concerning you to guard you in all your ways.	11 because he will command his angels concerning you to guard you in all your ways;
12 On their hands they will bear you up, so that you will not dash your foot against a stone.	12 up on hands they will bear you up so that you will not dash your foot against a stone.
13 You will tread on the lion and the adder, the young lion and the serpent you will trample under foot.	13 On asp and cobra you will tread, and you will trample lion and dragon under foot.
14 Those who love me, I will deliver; I will protect those who know my name.	14 Because in me he hoped, I will also rescue him; I will protect him, because he knew my name.
15 When they call to me, I will answer them; I will be with them in trouble, I will rescue them and honor them.	15 He will call to me, and I will listen to him; I am with him in trouble; I will deliver and glorify him.
16 With long life I will satisfy them, and show them my salvation.	16 With length of days I will satisfy him and show him my deliverance.

Verse 1 provides us with two interesting titles for Yahweh: *Elyon* and *El Shaddai*, regularly translated as "Most High" and "Almighty," but you will notice the LXX renders the second title as "God of the Sky." Weiser suggests that the two dominant or most notable images here have the sense "dwelling in the hiding place of the Most High" and "staying overnight in the shadow of the Almighty."[15] Ancient Near Eastern people had interesting ideas about the effects shadows of important people, prophets, priests, kings, healers could have (see Acts 5:15 on Peter's shadow). In this case we are talking about God's shadow, which could truly protect someone from harm, for God could be anywhere when help was needed.[16] No sooner had words of trust come out of the psalmist's mouth than he speaks in vv. 3–4 about the dangers of a hunter's trap (cf. Hos 9:8) or some dread disease or pestilence. Verses 5–6 speak of "night terrors," or a pestilence that stalks in the darkness, or arrows and destruction that can show up in the daytime. On the image of God as like a giant mother bird see also Deuteronomy 32:11, Ruth 2:12, Psalm 17:8.[17] From the very first, this psalm exudes the language of personal piety and trust in God.[18] The verb בָּטַח (beṭaḥ) here is a loaded term for "rely on," or better "rely on someone known to be reliable." It connotes an ongoing dynamic relationship with the person who "trusts" having come to depend on the reliable one.[19] Notice as well that in v. 4c we are told that God's truthfulness shields the psalmist. "In a battle out in the open country, God's truthfulness is like a big freestanding shield that hides the whole person."[20]

The reference to the arrow foreshadows the reference to a major battle in v. 7 where thousands of people "may fall at your side," but it will not reach the psalmist as he looks on from afar and sees the punishment of the wicked (cf. 2 Kings 18–19). These verses have suggested that a king who observes his troops fighting from afar is in view. But the real reason that danger doesn't come near the psalmist's tent is divine protection (see vv. 7–10). Were this not enough, vv. 10–11 say God will provide angels to even guard one's step so one won't even stumble over a rock in one's path.[21] Verse 13 concludes the "witness protection plan" with a promise of protection from lions and snakes.

It is interesting that in some cases the protection amounts to divine intervention (God will deliver, v.3, God will cover you, v. 4, God will command his angels to guard you, v. 11) but in other cases the verbs indicate things the psalmist will do ("you will not fear," v. 5, "you will only look from afar," v. 8, and finally "you will trample snakes under-

---

15. Weiser, *Psalms*, 606, both of which convey the sense of total protection from serious danger of some sort.
16. See Goldingay, *Psalms: Volume 3*, 41.
17. See Terrien, *Psalms*, 650.
18. Hossfeld and Zenger, *Psalms 2*, 429.
19. See ibid. It is not clear at all to me that the psalmist here is talking about the temple as a sanctuary where one is safe. It seems clear that he is talking about God himself as the psalmist's refuge and protection.
20. Goldingay, *Psalms: Volume 3*, 44.
21. Brueggemann and Bellinger, *Psalms*, 396. It is possible as well that demons are alluded to in vv. 5–6, as later Jewish interpreters thought. See Goldingay, *Psalms: Volume 3*, 44–47.

foot," v. 13). The ethos of this psalm may suggest we are talking about a prayer for those serving in the military, involved in the dangers of battle, disease in the camp, and wild creatures where they are camping. This would also explain metaphors like "refuge" or "stronghold" in psalms like this.[22] It might also explain the reference to angels, since angels of nations were thought to fight for and with the people of that nation (see e.g., Dan. 10:13–21 and 12:1 [Michael]; and cf. Dan. 3:28 and Gen 24:7).[23] The verb translated "rescue" "meant originally 'to equip for war' and its cognates include fortifications and military belts."[24] Notice in v. 4b the word for shield refers to the large standing shield behind which one could completely hide from incoming arrows (cf. Psalm 60).[25]

Verses 14–16 present us with a rapid-fire series of verbs spoken by Yahweh promising "I will deliver," "I will protect," "I will answer," "I will be with them," "I will rescue," "I will honor,"[26] "I will satisfy," and finally "I will show them my salvation." [27] Verse 14 is interesting because it says literally "because I am the one he [presumably the king?] is attracted to." It is crucial to bear in mind once more that the word "salvation" in these OT contexts does not refer to the same thing as Christians later meant by the term. Weiser is right to speak of the "this-worldliness of the OT faith."[28] The word "salvation" has a more mundane sense of rescue, protect, heal, defend—as the first portion of this psalm makes clear. It is not about conversion, or some specific spiritual experience, though of course it is about the piety of the psalmist trusting God for protection and the like. The psalmist reassures "you will see it with your own eyes" because he is talking about a visible, tangible, physical rescue or protection from disease, danger, death.

Finally, "according to the views held in antiquity the *name* includes [or indicates] the *nature* of the person in question, and 'to know' signifies in Hebrew more than merely 'being informed' about something; it comprises at the same time 'to be on terms of intimacy' with someone

---

22. See Longman, *Psalms*, 330–31.
23. Terrien, *Psalms*, 650 also points to the images of God's shield and buckler, part of the larger continued portrait of God as a warrior who fights alongside his people.
24. Ibid., 651.
25. Hossfeld and Zenger, *Psalms 2*, 430.
26. As Terrien, *Psalms*, 651 says, it is rare to hear about God honoring human beings, but see 1 Sam 2:30; Ps 15:4; Prov 4:8. Usually of course the term is applied to God: 1 Sam 2:30; Ps 22:24; Isa 24:15; 43:30.
27. Hossfeld and Zenger, *Psalms 2*, 432 say of vv. 14–16: "This section, which explicitly cites the great divine discourse of Psalm 50 (cf. 50:15, 25), is a summary of biblical theology."
28. Weiser, *Psalms*, 610.

and to be devoted to someone."[29] When we hear about the Most High God, or the Almighty God this is not just colorful language, or even just an assertion that Yahweh is at the top of the pantheon of deities. It tells us the most vital things about the nature of the living God in regard to the specific issue of whether or not God can protect his children from everything wicked or dangerous that could come their way—and the answer is yes.

Notice how the psalm makes clear that this protection is not for just anyone, it is for "Those who call on me," "those who love me" (cf. Rom 8:28), "those who know my name." In other words, for those who have a close relationship with God, even an intimate one. But a word of caution is necessary even when it comes to those who love God, "the psalm is a poetic affirmation of God's trustworthiness. . . . It is not a theological treatise that attempts to answer all the challenges to its confession and portrayal of divine protection."[30]

The deliberate use of poetic hyperbole to reassure the frightened was sometimes wrongly taken to assure that nothing bad would *ever* happen to the faithful, which led to superstitions both in Judaism and early Christianity. Portions of this very text were rolled up and placed in amulets and worn by Jews and Christians, believing that *the text itself* could provide a sort of magical protection for those wearing it (91:5–6 or vv. 10–13 were used).[31] This psalm was even the stimulus for the belief that God provided guardian angels for each one of the faithful and helped lead to angels becoming a focus of piety, especially in Christianity leading up to the Middle Ages.

But as we shall learn in examining the NT use of this psalm, even the devil can quote and use this Scripture, even in dialogue with someone like Jesus. The text itself can be used or misused but it is not in itself a talisman that provides automatic protection. There is a difference between the belief in magic, and the belief in miracle. Magic is the attempt to manipulate or control the supernatural through particular religious practices, such as wearing amulets. Miracle is top down, and in the control of God. It cannot be conjured even by pious practices. Rather it requires trust in God and a letting go of control over one's life.[32]

There are both minor and major ways Psalm 91 shows up in the

---

29. Ibid., 612.
30. Brueggemann and Bellinger, *Psalms*, 397.
31. Hossfeld and Zenger, *Psalms 2*, 433.
32. See Mays, *Psalms*, 297–98.

NT, especially in the Gospels. We will attend to these various citations, allusions, and echoes, working progressively through the psalm itself. First of all comes the use of Psalm 91:4 in Luke 13:34. Hays remarks on how Jesus uses the language of this verse to refer to his own ministry, whereas in the original psalm, it is Yahweh himself who is speaking.[33] What he does not note or notice is that Jesus has modified the thought in the psalm, which does not depict Yahweh as a female creature, so that on Jesus's lips it now reads "Jerusalem, Jerusalem . . . how often have I desired to gather your children as a hen gathers *her* brood under *her* wings, and you were not willing!" Contrast this with "his pinions under his wings" in the psalm. This is because Jesus is presenting himself as Wisdom/Ḥokmâ, a female figure here, in contrast to Yahweh, a male figure. There is another difference as well. In the psalm it is all about God protecting his children, but here Jesus is saying that the children are refusing such protection, despite the gathering storm, which within a generation would destroy the temple and much of the city with it. Jesus is using the psalm's imagery, but to convey a different message with a different effect. Why is it the chicks don't seek shelter under the protection of Wisdom's wings?[34]

At Matthew 26:53 Jesus states boldly that if he wished, he could ask God to send him twelve legions of angels to defend him and protect him, but to do so would prevent the Scripture being fulfilled. A legion, strictly speaking had 5,120 men in it, and twelve legions would be well over 61,000 angels! I bring this up because the psalmist talks in terms of numbers: a thousand may fall on one side, ten thousand at your right hand, but you will be untouched in the fray. Why? Because God will send his angels to protect the person the psalmist is speaking of. Jesus is refusing the protection the psalmist assures the hearer of, "so the Scripture may be fulfilled"; but clearly it is not Psalm 91 he is thinking of as being fulfilled in his capture and later the trial.

More importantly than either of these allusions is the direct quotation of Psalm 91 in the Synoptic portrayal of the middle or last temptation of Jesus, depending on whether you go with the Matthean or Lukan version of the story. Here it will be useful to lay out the parallels in a table.[35]

---

33. Hays, *Echoes of Scripture in the Gospels*, 261.
34. Pao and Schnabel, "Luke," 336 are right that Jesus identifies with the care of God for his people, but they miss the interesting wisdom allusions and nuances here. On Jesus as wisdom see Witherington, *Jesus the Sage*, passim.
35. Here I am following the helpful example in Michael Labahn, "The Psalms in Q," in Moyise, *Psalms in the New Testament*, 51. I still think that it is more probable than not that there was a sayings

Psalm 91:11–12	Matthew 4:6	Luke 4:10–11
For he will command his angels concerning you *to guard you in all your ways* On their hands they will bear you up, so that you will not dash your foot against a stone.	for it is written "He will command his angels concerning you" and "On their hands they will bear you up, so that you will not dash your foot against a stone."	for it is written "He will command his angels concerning you, *to guard you*" and "On their hands they will bear you up, so that you will not dash your foot against a stone."

What makes this whole scenario especially intriguing is several things. First of all we have here a battle of the Bible verses, and it is Satan, no less, who is quoting bits of Psalm 91 (and other psalms) with Jesus rebutting with various verses from Deuteronomy. Satan is using the citation to try and tempt Jesus into being what Menken calls "some kind of Messianic stunt man instead of the obedient Son of God."[36] Even more to the point, Jesus reminds Satan that no one should put God to the test, which implies at least a particular image of how Jesus viewed himself in this encounter.

Some have tried to suggest that Jesus is presented here as Israel in the wilderness passing the test that the Israel in Exodus failed. The problem with this analysis is fourfold: (1) Jesus says he is being tempted as "God" and Satan should not tempt God; (2) the issue is whether or not Jesus is "the Son of God" not whether he is true Israel or the Son of David; (3) the temptations are not like those of the Israelites in the wilderness, who did indeed put God to the test (cf. Psalm 106). These are temptations only a divine Son of God would find even remotely tempting, because they were possible for him, not for mere mortals; (4) Satan is playing the role of Israel here putting God's Son to the test like the wilderness wandering generation did to Yahweh![37]

There are further interesting aspects about the citation of Psalm 91:11 by Satan. He omits the phrase "in all your ways" from the psalm. Is this significant? Commentators have been divided on this point and the answer is not clear. Even more intriguing is the fact that this Scripture is being cited as a justification to get Jesus to jump off

source of "Jesus's greatest hits" used by both Matthew and Luke, though I am less certain of this than I used to be due to the arguments of Mark Goodacre.

36. Menken, "Psalms in Matthew's Gospel," 65.

37. But see Hays, *Echoes of Scripture in the Gospels*, 119 for the Jesus = Israel gone right argument. Blomberg, "Matthew," 15–16 does not weigh in on these matters. Pao and Schnabel, "Luke," 286–87 take a more nuanced approach and recognize that, "Satan is using Scripture to tempt Jesus to test the presence of God, as Israel did in times of old." (p. 287).

the pinnacle of the temple to demonstrate he is the Son of God. Now the word for pinnacle (τὸ πτερύγιον) in Greek is a variant of the word for pinions in Greek (πτέρυγας, Ps 90:4 LXX). Further, the temple was of course seen as the locale where God's presence could especially be encountered. Is jumping off the pinnacle like rejecting the protection of the pinions of Yahweh, and so putting God to the test?[38]

Second, and perhaps just as fascinating is the fact that it is this very verse from Psalm 91 that was used in apotropaic collections and in the magical papyri *to protect people from Satan and demons!!* "The tempter quotes a word from Scripture which is intended against him."[39] The irony of this would be lost on anyone who did not know about the later use of this text in amulets and for other superstitious purposes, but then the text as used in the Synoptics is already loaded with irony.

The psalm text is about good guardian angels that would not let a believer's foot stumble on the path, whereas Satan is using it to, so to speak, lead Jesus down the garden path. Third, because the LXX has an accurate rendering of the MT at this point, it is not clear which version the NT writers are following. Matthew leaves out the phrase "to guard you in all your ways" Luke simply leaves out "in all your ways." There are no other major differences, and, in any case, they don't affect the thrust of the text.

This pericope presents a Jesus who resists the temptation to be a Son of God that performs gratuitous miracles for his own benefit, which, had he done so, would have not incidentally violated his having accepted the normal human limitations of time, space, knowledge, power, and mortality which other human beings could not avoid. He would have obliterated his true humanity, and the divine condescension that was part of the incarnation (see Phil 2:5–11, "he limited himself"). In short, the temptations Jesus faced here were not normal human temptations.[40] They were temptations that only a divine, yet human person, a true Son of God, might face, and conquer. Clearly, much more is going on here than a cursory examination of the text would bring to light. At the end of the day, as Blomberg humorously suggests, we are not being encouraged to follow the hermeneutic of Satan and twist the text of the psalm in question because the psalm is not about angels catching someone who deliberately jumps off a

---

38. See Pao and Schnabel, "Luke," 287 on this point.
39. See Labahn, "Psalms in Q," 51 on this point.
40. I've known people who could turn bread into stones, but I've never met a sane person who thought he could or was tempted to try and turn stones into bread.

precipice, it's about protecting a person from stumbling along the road.[41] Furthermore, far from it being a text about *tempting* God to act, it is a text about *trusting* God whom the psalmist says can protect the believer.

Psalm 91:13 promises that the one trusting God will "trample under foot the serpent." We have an allusion or direct echo of this in Luke 10:19 (cf. Luke 9:1–2) where Jesus promises his seventy emissaries, "see, I have given you authority to tread on snakes and scorpions and over all the power of the enemy."[42] I agree with Hays, in his comment on this verse that "Jesus is said to confer powers and blessings that no one but God could confer."[43] Just so, which makes it puzzling as to why Hays didn't see Jesus speaking as God in the Luke 4 passage (see above).

Totally missed out by the NA28 index is Romans 16:20: "The God of peace will shortly crush Satan under your feet," which is followed immediately with the offer of the grace of Christ. The mixed metaphor in Romans 16:20 is fascinating. On the one hand there is a reference to the God of peace, and on the other hand this God of peace is crushing the life out of Satan, elsewhere depicted in the NT as the serpent or dragon (see Revelation). And who exactly is this God of peace? The context suggests that it is Jesus himself, since he is the only person mentioned in this paragraph (16:18, 20b) who seems a reasonable antecedent. Finally, note that Satan is being crushed under the *believers'* feet. An echo of perhaps both Psalm 91:13 and Luke 10:19 seems likely. Clearly, a lively and diverse use of Psalm 91 is in evidence in various NT texts.

Romans 8:28–30 should be read in tandem with this psalm, as a further development of one of its main themes. The difference is this: What may be mostly poetic hyperbole (since things didn't always work out in this life even for believing kings) in the psalm and for the psalmist's day, became more substantive promises in the NT era when a much more robust view of the afterlife and of everlasting salvation, including life on earth in the final kingdom, was in play. What was poetry in the psalm became prose in the light of the Christ event, giving new more substantive opportunities for a somewhat literal application of the psalm to Christian life.

---

41. Blomberg, "Matthew," *Commentary on the Use of the OT in the NT*, 15–16.
42. See Pao and Schnabel, "Luke," 318, who think Deut.,8:15 may also be in view here.
43. Hays, *Echoes of Scripture in the Gospels*, 261.

No Rest for the Wicked: Psalm 95

Psalm 95 is the second (Psalm 93 was the first) in a series of praise songs that laud God as king (see Psalms 96–99). There are a variety of psalms in the Psalter that have dramatic shifts in them, and Psalm 95 is one of them, for at v. 7c suddenly we are hearing a prophetic oracle of warning from Yahweh himself. These sorts of dramatic shifts have led to various theories about the splicing together of several songs, or, as a better explanation, the idea that different voices are speaking as part of the temple liturgy, the congregation in vv. 1–7b and the priest or song leader or a prophet speaking for Yahweh in the rest of this song.[44] If we were to draw an analogy, it is like a contemporary worship scene in which one has opening hymns followed by a sermon or exhortation where God's word is read and spoken.[45] It is the endless repeating of the sin of the wilderness wandering generation that is being warned against in the oracle, otherwise those who make that mistake will not enter God's rest.

The LXX adds the superscript telling us that the psalm pertains to David, but some scholars have suggested this psalm probably dates to the renewal of Yahwism under Josiah's reforms (ca. 622 BCE).[46] The psalm is generic enough that the dating doesn't particularly help us with or affect the interpretation of the psalm's meaning. God's people have always been struggling with fidelity issues, not to mention willingness to participate in whole-hearted worship. The LXX also alters the way the psalm may be perceived by translating "let us kneel" in v. 6 as "we will weep," turning the whole thing into a penitential psalm, as a response to the infidelity of God's people past and present.[47]

---

44. On theories of multiple psalms originally see Brueggemann and Bellinger, *Psalms*, 412; and especially the discussion in Hossfeld and Zenger, *Psalms 2*, 459–60: "the stylistic connections, literal repetitions, and logical conception of Psalm 95 all favor its unity." (p. 460). On the speaker in v. 7c–11 see Weiser, *Psalms*, 626.
45. See, e.g., Goldingay, *Psalms: Volume 3*, 88, who sees the basic structure as: (1) exhortation (vv. 1–2); (2) reasons (vv. 3–5); (3) exhortation (v.6); and (4) reasons (vv. 7a–c), followed by a very different sort of exhortation in vv. 7d–11. The first half is about God's authority as creator, the second about God's unique relationship with Israel.
46. Terrien, *Psalms*, 672.
47. See Hossfeld and Zenger, *Psalms 2*, 462. The LXX also renders Meribah in a unique way as "provocation."

MT Psalm 95	LXX Psalm 94
	1 A laudation. Of an Ode Pertaining to David.
1 O come, let us sing to the Lord;	O come, let us rejoice in the Lord;
let us make a joyful noise to the rock of our salvation!	let us make a joyful noise to God our savior!
2 Let us come into his presence with thanksgiving;	2 Let us anticipate his face with acknowledgment,
let us make a joyful noise to him with songs of praise!	and with melodies let us make a joyful noise to him,
3 For the Lord is a great God,	3 because the Lord is a great God
and a great King above all gods.	and a great King over all the gods,
4 In his hand are the depths of the earth;	4 because in his hand are the ends of the earth
the heights of the mountains are his also.	and the heights of the mountains are his,
5 The sea is his, for he made it,	5 because his is the sea and he made it
and the dry land, which his hands have formed.	and the dry land his hands formed!
6 O come, let us worship and bow down,	6 O come, let us do obeisance and prostrate
let us kneel before the Lord, our Maker!	ourselves before him,
	and let us weep before the Lord, who made us,
7 For he is our God,	7 because he is our God
and we are the people of his pasture,	and we are people of his pasture
and the sheep of his hand. O that today you would listen to his voice!	and sheep of his hand!
	Today if you hear his voice,
8 Do not harden your hearts, as at Meribah,	8 do not harden your hearts, as at the embittering,
as on the day at Massah in the wilderness,	like the day of the trial in the wilderness,
9 when your ancestors tested me,	9 where your fathers tried;
and put me to the proof, though they had seen my work.	they put to the proof and saw my works.
10 For forty years I loathed that generation	10 For forty years I loathed that generation,
and said, "They are a people whose hearts go astray,	and said, "Always do they stray in heart, and they did not know my ways."
and they do not regard my ways."	
11 Therefore in my anger I swore,	11 As I swore in my wrath,
"They shall not enter my rest."	"If they shall enter into my rest!"

The call for praise and a joyful noise from the congregation opens this psalm, and God is called: (1) the rock of our salvation (i.e., the protector who rescues us from calamities); and (2) the king above all gods (cf. Ps 96:4; Ps 97:9; 136:2; Exod 15:11). Notice that the psalmist is not denying there are other supernatural beings out there (Psalm 82). Paul, in 1 Corinthians 8:4–13 and 10:20–21, was later to argue that while these beings are not gods, they are also not nothing, he calls them δαιμόνιον, demons, and insists they are dangerous and not to be fraternized with. Some scholars have seen here a joyous procession into God's presence (v. 2), but nothing is said here about processing, only about kneeling and bowing down.[48] The joyful noise may be a reference to a "ritual shout that mobilizes the attention and the cooperation of the whole assembly" (cf. Pss 47:2; 81:2; 98:4;100:1–2).[49] As Goldingay points out, mere "heart praise" is not enough because, for one thing, it is not a community act, which is what worship is supposed to be mainly about, and second, it is not praise with the whole person, it does not use our physical voice and bear witness outwardly.[50]

Verse 4 turns to the usual praising of God as creator and sustainer of all creation who formed the earth, the sea, and all that is in it. The point is that Yahweh is not a local deity who has this or that piece of land as his turf; it all belongs to him for he made it. Notice the merism: depths of the earth and heights of the mountains. The point is, he made and governs it all and everything in between as well.[51] The claim to control the sea is an implicit claim to control chaos, symbolized by the chaos waters (cf. Ps 93:3–5).

> It is not without good reason that besides the sea and the dry land, the depths of the earth and the tops of the mountains are specifically mentioned as belonging to the sphere of God's influence; for popular belief regarded the underworld as the realm of other powers (Amos 9:2; Pss 65; 30:9; 88:10f.; 115:17) and the high mountains as the abode of the gods (Pss. 68:15f.; 89:12). The psalm deliberately destroys this belief; God's power knows of no limitations—this is the unshakeable foundation of his salvation.[52]

Verse 6 exhorts the congregation that before such a God the appropriate response of his creatures is to worship and bow down, precisely because he is our maker and the psalmist includes himself in the action, "let us bow down. . . ." There are in fact three verbs here with essentially the same action in mind, "let us bow low," "let us bow down," "let us kneel," all actions involving lowering oneself and showing fealty to the true God. What we do with our bodies expresses our real identity. "If there is no physical self-lowering, there can hardly be inner self lowering."[53]

---

48. But see Mays, *Psalms*, 305.
49. Terrien, *Psalms*, 669.
50. Goldingay, *Psalms: Volume 3*, 91.
51. Longman, *Psalms*, 339.
52. Weiser, *Psalms*, 626.

The psalmist then draws on the familiar image of God's people as sheep, "the people of his pasture." On God as shepherd, see Psalms 23 and 100 (cf. Pss 77:20; 78:52; 80:1; 100:3). The shepherd image for God, which is an image regularly applied to kings in the ancient Near East, deals with how he leads and feeds, guards and guides his people. Sheep are not notably bright creatures, and they do not see very well either, hence the need for constant supervision and care.[54] Notice that along with vv. 1–2 this is the second call for the congregation to rouse themselves and begin truly worshiping God. Notice also that we have both a summons to worship and the reason for doing so in both cases.[55] In the first case, the reason given is that God is the creator of us all, but in the second case the reason given is that Israel is God's people and has a special relationship with God. God is both creator and sustainer of his people.

Verse 7c suddenly exclaims, "oh that today you would listen to his voice!" This is very much like the summons at Sinai (Exod 19:5) and also the more familiar one at Deuteronomy 6:4.[56] That Israel has to be exhorted in strong terms to listen intently to God suggests they are too often focused on themselves or are distracted with mundane things. The psalm then goes directly into a divine oracle with Yahweh speaking, urging his people, "don't harden your heart like they did at Meribah and at Massah in the wilderness, where Israel put God to the test." In fact the name Meribah means quarreling and Massah means testing. This is in reference to what the wilderness wandering generation did according to Exodus 17:1–7 // Numbers 20:1–13 (the latter account refers only to Meribah), where they were worried that they would not have sufficient water. They grumbled, "Is the Lord among us or not?" The complaint says that they did this even though they had already seen God's mighty works in person.[57] This seems to have a close affinity to Psalms 50 and 81. "Putting God to the test is a self-centered demand for signs and wonders for me and us in the present, as though the signs and wonders of God's creation and salvation were not enough reason to trust him, and him alone."[58] "The failure to trust YHWH is

---

53. Goldingay, *Psalms: Volume 3*, 93.

54. There may be a very faint echo of Ps 95:7 in John 10:2–3, though the psalm is not about leading anyone anywhere, or about gates or gatekeepers. In fact it is about the true flock, about thieves who want to steal sheep, and so the thrust of the material is quite different, and in any case the image of God/Jesus as shepherd is very common, and need not depend on Ps 95:7.

55. See Brueggemann and Bellinger, *Psalms*, 411.

56. Ibid., 411. Cf. S. Dean McBride, "The Yoke of the Kingdom: An Exposition of Deuteronomy 6:4–5," *Int* 27 (1973): 273–306.

57. Longman, *Psalms*, 340.

the central motif of these narratives, the voice in the psalm summons contemporary Israel in its own 'today' *not* to replicate that ancient infidelity."[59]

Verse 10 turns to the emotions of Yahweh, where we hear that for forty years God positively despised/detested that generation muttering to himself, "they are a people whose hearts keep going astray, and have no regard for my ways." The Hebrew verb קוּט (*qût*) is a very strong verb and is used only here in the OT of God (cf. Ps 119:158 which speaks of the sinner's revulsion over sin). God decided something must be done about this despicable state of affairs and so God in his anger swore an oath, "They shall not enter my rest," by which what *seems* to be meant originally is "enter the place where they could actually find some rest, the promised land, where they would have to travel no more and could continually experience my *shalom*." On Jerusalem specifically being God's place of rest, see Psalm 132:8, 14 (and cf. Deut 12:9).[60] In fact, only Joshua and Caleb entered the promised land and the reason they did so as the only exceptions to the rule is because they did listen to, trust, and obey God (Num 14:22-24). Later, as we shall see, in Hebrews this verse seems to be used to speak about heavenly rest or even eschatological rest, but that does not seem to be the case here in this psalm. Notice that it is called "my rest," not "your rest," a comment that probably alludes to God ceasing from creation (Gen 2:2) and admiring his handiwork.[61]

There is in Hebrews 3-4 a sustained use of the second portion of Psalm 95, with Psalm 95:7c-11 being quoted at Hebrews 3:7-11, Psalm 95:7c again quoted in Hebrews 3:15, Psalm 95:11 quoted in Hebrews 4:3, and Psalm 95:7c quoted in Hebrews 4:7, all the while juxtaposing these references with allusions and reference to Genesis 2:1-4a.[62] The psalm is used in the service of exhorting the wavering Jewish Christians in Rome not to commit apostasy under pressure as the wilderness wandering generation did.[63] Because this is the longest commentary on any psalm in the NT, it will be worthwhile to do some extended reflection on what is going on in Hebrews, and how the author is using Psalm 95. I suggest this will provide us with an impor-

58. Mays, *Psalms*, 307.
59. Brueggemann and Bellinger, *Psalms*, 411 (emphasis original).
60. Goldingay, *Psalms: Volume 3*, 97.
61. For reflections by non-NT scholars on the use of Psalm 95 in Hebrews see Peter E. Enns, "Creation and Recreation: Psalm 95 and its Interpretation in Hebrews 3:1-4:13," *WTJ* 55 (1993): 255-80; H. Weiss, "*Sabbatismos* in the Epistle to the Hebrews," *CBQ* 58 (1996): 674-89.
62. Brueggemann and Bellinger, *Psalms*, 413.
63. Mays, *Psalms*, 307.

tant clue for understanding the NT use of the OT and how we should evaluate it in general.[64]

In Hebrews 3:7-11 we have a quotation of what is for our author a crucial psalm, Psalm 95:7-11, introduced as the living voice of the Holy Spirit speaking directly to our author's Jewish Christians in Rome "today." The word "today" which introduces the quotation makes it easy to contemporize the text and apply it directly to the audience, but the reference to the Holy Spirit has the same contemporizing effect. Our author has previously introduced such quotations as the voice of God (1:5-9, 13) or of Christ (2:12-13) speaking directly to the audience. There can be little doubt that he sees all three as personal expressions of the one God he worships, and so we must recognize the implicit Trinitarianism here. "The effect of such attribution is to allow no discontinuity between the past and present people of God."[65] This hermeneutical move is made easier because it was David himself, in 2 Samuel 23:2, who claimed that the Spirit of the Lord spoke through him and, as Hebrews 4:7 will make evident, David is assumed to be the author of our Psalm 95. There is also little doubt that our author believes that he and his audience are living in the age called "today." This quotation of the psalm will set off a chain of linked comments and we need to notice that the opening verse of the quotation is reiterated at 3:15 and in 4:7, and the final part of the quotation recurs in 4:3 and 5. Clearly the discourse is ongoing and we should not set a hard division at the end of Hebrews 3.

As we have seen in this psalm, the psalmist is alluding to the experience of Israel as recorded in Exodus 17:1-7 and also Numbers 14:20-35. One of the effects of not directly using the story from the Pentateuch, but rather using the psalm, is that we see that our author is in good company, for he is doing for his own audience what the psalmist did for his audience, contemporizing, or doing what the French call *relecture*, "making a past word a present word."[66] There is a certain incompleteness to the quotation as well. Notice how in v. 11 it actually reads "if they enter my rest," offering the protasis but not the apodosis of a conditional statement. This incompleteness is reflected in the Hebrew text, the LXX, and the quotation in Hebrews, and it probably is done deliberately. What would normally follow in the second half of the

---

64. See a more detailed version of this discussion in Witherington, *Letters and Homilies for Jewish Christians*, 171-91.
65. Fred B. Craddock, "The Letter to the Hebrews," *NIB* 12:47.
66. Ibid., 48.

statement would be a curse (see e.g., Ps 7: 4–5 or 137:5–6). But neither the psalmist in his homily, nor our author is comfortable with leaving the audience with a curse sanction, perhaps in the case of our author because Jesus said "no oaths."

Verses 12 and 19 form a sort of rhetorical *inclusio* with key terms like "see to it" and "unbelief" being repeated, and these terms are only found here in Hebrews. If we compare v. 12 to v. 1 we see how the exhortation becomes more strident—there the imperative was "closely consider," here it is "see to it" but both exhortations are qualified by the word "brothers," making clear this is an in-house matter. There is an urgency to the exhortation in v. 12.

Scholars have often compared the use of the OT here to Paul's use of the story of the wilderness wandering generation in 1 Corinthians 10:1–11. There are of course similarities between 1 Corinthians 10 and Hebrews 3 since in both cases we have a typological sort of use of the OT, but Paul's reading of the OT text is more overtly christological, whereas our author here, writing to Jewish Christians does not merely say, "it happened to 'them' so it could happen to 'you,'" as Paul does for his largely gentile audience. No, our author is more direct: the Holy Spirit *says*, "do not harden your hearts as *you* did in the rebellion." There is an ethnic and religious continuity between this audience in Rome and the rebellious Israelites of long ago.

Our author sees their story as the continuation of the story of Israel, not merely analogous to it; and our author's concern is that the audience might act like their actual forefathers, giving way to unbelief and turning away, hardened by sin and going astray. Thus at v.13 our author picks back up the first verse of the psalm quotation and urges "exhort one another every day, as long as it is called 'today.'" Every day is a test, and every day the call to faithfulness needs to ring out and be positively responded to. The reference to "sin" in v. 13 refers to apostasy and unfaithfulness, not moral aberrations such as sexual sin. The verb ἀπιστέω is the root for both the terms unbelief and disobedience in vv. 18–19. Notice the insistence in this verse that the audience should "keep exhorting one another."

Our author is very adept at handling the interpretation technique known as Midrash *pesher*. The word *pesher* means interpret, and this procedure is already in evidence in Hebrews 2:6ff. in the way our author handled Psalm 8.[67] The way a pesher works is by taking up

---

67. See ch. 3 above on Psalm 8.

certain key words from the cited text and incorporating them in an address or argument to one's audience. It does also involve a molding of the quotation to fit the situation being addressed to make it more apropos. This form of use of Scripture is well known to us now from Qumran and elsewhere in early Jewish literature; it is only puzzling if one assumes that the author is citing the text as a proof text for an argument that is coherent without the citation.

In point of fact, the argument is not coherent apart from the citation and the way the citation is woven into the discussion. It also sometimes presupposes an understanding of the original setting and significance of the original text, something a Jewish Christian audience would be more likely to have than a gentile one. As we have already noted, the textual base that is cited in our case is Psalm 95 (94 LXX), which is cited first extensively and then in pieces no less than five times between 3:7 and 4:7. This particular psalm basically has two major parts, vv. 1–7a are a call to worship, while vv. 7b–11 are a warning against disobeying God, reinforced by a reminder of what happened to Israel in the wilderness.

It is the second half of the psalm that our author uses. He, like the psalmist, is concerned with the events the psalm alludes to which are recorded in Exodus 17 and especially Numbers 14:20ff., which is important to understanding the argument here. Our author wishes to draw an analogy between the situation of the wilderness wandering generation and the fate that befell them of not entering the resting place (i.e., Canaan), and the situation of his audience who were in danger of not entering a more ultimate form of God's promised rest. In due course, he will also bring into the argument the story in Genesis 2:2 about God resting from his creation labors (at Heb 4:7).

These Scriptures plus the intertestamental ideas about the "rest" provide the grist for our author's mill. The key assumption of our author is that the situation of that wilderness wandering generation and his audience are *analogous* in some ways. The trials are seen as the same (cf. 3:12, 19; 4:1–2, 6) and also Hebrews 4:1 suggests that the same promise of rest is extended to both groups of God's people. In both cases we are talking of the pilgrim people of God, and here in this subsection is where our author introduces this theme, which becomes increasingly major in the homily and climaxes in Hebrews 12.

The way our author's argument will proceed is as follows: (1) Psalm 95 makes quite clear that the wilderness wandering generation didn't enter God's promised rest, that is, the resting place of Canaan;

but (2) furthermore, since the psalmist still is extending the promise in his own time using the word "Today if you hear this promise," it is clear that the promise is still outstanding, that one can still enter the rest, even though David lived so much later than the time of Moses and Joshua. There is one further stage in the argument; (3) Genesis 2:2 indicates that the rest to be entered is God's own. This means it has existed since he ceased from creating and is continuing even now (in part this is based on the fact that the Genesis text mentions no evening and morning, and thus in early Jewish exegesis it was assumed that God's rest was still ongoing, since it was not said to end, that is, he is still in his seventh day so far as rest is concerned).

There is a major debate among scholars as to whether our author actually believes that those who are Christians can and do enter the rest prior to death, or whether they, like the OT saints, simply have the promise that they shall later enter it. In part this issue is determined by whether one thinks that "rest" means resting place in Hebrews, or is speaking of an eschatological *condition* believers may participate in here and now.

What is clear is that our author stands in a long line of expositors, including Christian expositors (cf. 1 Corinthians 10), who use the exodus/Sinai typology to enforce a vital exhortation on his present audience. Notice at v. 7 the reference to the Holy Spirit speaking in the OT, which means the Spirit is seen as not merely the one who inspires it, but is the one who *speaks* in these words. This is important, for our author believes that this is a living word of God for his audience, not least because the same Holy Spirit that believers have in their lives speaks throughout the Scriptures.

Sometimes it has been argued by some scholars that our author would never accuse those lapsing back into Judaism of falling *away* from the living God, but that depends on whether our author thought a response to Christ was ultimately essential to salvation and entering that eschatological rest. If he did, then for him to turn back to a shadow when we have the substance that revelation foretold is in fact a sin against the light, a form of apostasy. This, it seems to me, is clearly our author's view—Christ is essential in the "today" age to having a relationship with the living God, he is the mediator of that relationship, the old has passed away, the new has come in this regard.

One of the interesting aspects of using the LXX instead of the Hebrew text of Psalm 95 is that the place names in the MT (Meribah and Massah) become human experiences in the LXX (rebellion and testing) where the names are translated. But the place names may have come from the experiences of God's people in those places in the first instance. In any event, our author is highlighting the potential parallels between the wilderness wandering generation and his own audience. Another interesting aspect of our author's choice of citing the psalm instead of the original story in the Pentateuch is that it tips his hands, it shows his homiletical purposes. Craddock puts it this way: "by using the psalmist's account and not that of the historical books themselves, the author has appropriated a piece of liturgy for a homily that is liturgical in nature. Psalm 95 is a call to enter God's presence with praise, and in that setting it urges the people to fidelity, avoiding Israel's ancient failure."[68]

At vv. 15–16 our author deals with the terrible irony and tragedy that it was the very ones Moses led out of Egypt that were the ones who rebelled in the wilderness. They had every evidence of God's love and grace, and indeed had been miraculously rescued from Egypt, and yet they still went on and committed apostasy. This is a sobering story, a sort of a wake-up call, to tell to an audience under pressure and thinking of defecting.

Just because one is part of God's chosen people does not mean that a particular individual will be saved, and particularly not if they are unfaithful. Notice how unbelief and disobedience are virtually synonymous for our author. "There seems to be a shift from exhortation to exposition through v. 19 but this only appears to be the case. Both the quotation and the comments that follow are clearly hortatory; the move is simply from direct to indirect. The writer is speaking *about* Israel but in so doing is speaking *to* the readers. Rhetoricians understood that relief from confrontational style was often more effective than continuous confrontation."[69] Just so, and the rhetorical technique our author is following in miniature here is called *insinuatio*, the indirect way of exhorting an audience by telling someone else's story, and letting the parallels with the audience's situation come gradually into view.

Near the end of this section, in v. 18, our author introduces what will be a major theme of his ongoing discourse: the theme of rest, which is a multivalent term for him ranging in meaning from the rest God experienced when he "ceased" from creating, to the arriving in the promised land and resting from traveling, to the actual taking control

68. Craddock, "Hebrews," 48.
69. Ibid., 50 (emphasis original).

of the promised land and putting an end to hostilities during the reign of David in that land, to the rest one has from harm in the sanctuary or tabernacle when one grasps the horns of the altar, to entering into the Shabbat shalom here and now, to entering into eternal rest in heaven or at the eschaton. Verse 19 concludes the section on the note that disbelief and disobedience work hand in hand, or we could call it mistrust and misbehavior. By the same token so do real trust and real obedience to God.

At the outset of Hebrews 4 we have the concluding section of the portion of the discourse based on an interpretation of Psalm 95, which began as early as 3:7. Probably we should see an *inclusio* with the two exhortations in 4:1 and 4:11 framing the section ("let us be afraid/careful . . . let us be eager"). This in turn means we should see 4:12–13 as a transitional piece that takes us into the next segment of the discourse, which begins at 4:14. This is clearly one of the more complex portions of our author's discourse as he continues to unpack the meaning of Psalm 95 for his audience, and deals with the concept of God's rest and how believers can and should enter into it. It should be noticed that he is not arguing that they have already entered into it and should beware of losing it. His concept is clearly eschatological.

There is then something *incomplete*, at present, about the salvation and final rest of believers. Notice as well that our author believes that the Israelites already had a proleptic form of the good news preached to them about God's rest (v. 6). There is continuity of message as well as people of God in our author's way of thinking about salvation history. "Despite differences due to the progress of revelation in history, a basic continuity exists between what the Old Testament saints experienced in their time frame and what is now experienced in the church."[70] Notice as well the already and not yet dimension to our author's eschatology, the audience "are entering" (present continual tense) the rest, but they must eagerly strive to enter it as well.

In order to instill in an audience the need to do as they are exhorted to do, there must at some juncture be an appeal to the deeper emotions, such as fear. Sometimes this is withheld until the peroration, but in an epideictic discourse such as this, deeper emotions tend to be appealed to throughout the discourse. Here we have in v. 1 a strong appeal to fear. The fear has to do with failing to "enter his rest," as 4:1 will make clear, and as David deSilva stresses, this fear is appealed to

---

70. Donald A. Hagner, *Encountering the Book of Hebrews: An Exposition*, EBS (Grand Rapids: Baker Academic, 2002), 73.

repeatedly in this whole section by repetition of the theme of "entering his rest," hammering home the importance of keeping going in the direction they had been heading in since conversion (3:18–19; 4:1, 3, 5, 6, 10, 11).[71]

Our author's concept of rest is a complicated one. For a start it refers to God ceasing from his creating activities, and then by extension to his enjoying the ongoing rest he has had ever since that time. "Rest" in this more extended sense refers to a positive state of being, not just the absence of creative activity. Since God's rest is continuing, it continues to be a possibility that believers may enter it, especially since many in the past who were offered the chance to enter it failed to do so due to unbelief. Thus the opportunity still exists in part due to the disobedience and disbelief of some of God's people in the past. One needs to stress as well that unlike what we find in the later Gospel of Thomas, our author is not primarily talking about rest/peace *entering the believer*, but rather the believer entering "rest," an eschatological rather than psychological view of things. Our writer does not evaporate "Israel's history in some grand allegory of the pilgrimage of the soul. History remains history; neither past nor present is consumed by the other."[72] Herein lies an essential difference between the way our author treats the OT and the way Philo does (cf. Philo *Leg.* VIII, 52, 60).

Our author is not an allegorizer, but is he a spiritualizer—turning physical rest in a land into eternal rest in heaven (cf. Joseph and Aseneth 8.9; 22.13)? One must be careful in suggesting such a view. While our author does believe that dying and going to be with the Lord is a blessing and a rest from trials, ultimately he sees the consummate rest as not in heaven but rather on earth at the eschaton. In this he is like Paul, though our author places more stress on what is true now in heaven, for the very good reason that the time focus of epideictic rhetoric is "today," speaking about what is true in the present. History is moving toward a goal of sabbatical, but our author also thinks "there is rest in movement and movement in rest."[73]

There is nothing static or stultifying or stilted about our author's view of rest. If we must be precise, our author is saying that "today" we must embrace the promise of rest and continue to move faithfully forward to it. He is not suggesting believers enter that rest in any full

71. David deSilva, *Perseverance in Gratitude: A Socio-rhetorical Commentary on the Epistle "to the Hebrews"* (Grand Rapids: Eerdmans, 2000), 153.
72. Craddock, "Hebrews," 55.
73. Ibid., 56.

sense in the present, as the exhortations in 4:1 and 4:11 stress, unless one counts the observance of Shabbat as a foretaste. The parallels with the wilderness wandering generation are only persuasive and apt if the present audience is still *in medias res* and on the way to the rest, but in danger of missing it. This means that the verb "enter," here in the present, should be seen as a futuristic present tense as in Matthew 17:11, John 14:3, and 1 Corinthians 16:5. Striving to enter, and already entering are two different things. We would have expected a perfect tense here if "entering" has already been completed.[74]

Rather, believers are in the process of crossing the threshold and so of entering, but it is only after finishing entering that one has complete "rest." It is still possible to hesitate or waver or fall back from the threshold. To stand at the entryway to the promised land and be in the process of filing in is not the same as "having entered." Our author draws the analogy between the wilderness wandering generation "treading the verge of Jordan" and in the process of crossing over, with Joshua being the pioneer going before them into the promised land, and the Jewish Christian audience following their own Joshua/Yeshua/Jesus into the "rest." It is the pioneer, Jesus, who has fully crossed the threshold into "his rest," not those who still must strive to follow his example (Heb 12:1–2).

What do we learn from this more detailed attention to the use of a psalm in the NT? For one thing, we learn that at least some writers of the NT not only knew the OT well, but knew the context of the quotations and allusions they drew upon. They were not likely always drawing upon collections of proof texts or catenae. Secondly, we learn that the OT is being handled in a thoroughly Jewish manner, even with all the new christological insight and readings. They were of course not alone in reading the OT in a contemporizing manner, nor were they alone in reading it in an eschatological and messianic manner. What we *find almost never* in the NT is a use of the Psalms or other portions of the OT in the manner we find it so often used by Philo, the great allegorizer of the OT. Galatians 4 is the remarkable exception to this rule.

The relentlessly historical orientation, including a focus on future history (eschatology) of the NT handlers of the OT is apparent again and again, even in Hebrews. In our particular text under scrutiny, the author of Hebrews makes the argument, on the basis of the assumption that if David (as the LXX suggested) was the author of this psalm, then

---

74. Rightly, deSilva, *Perseverance in Gratitude*, 154–55.

obviously since David lived well after the time of Joshua and the initial entering of the promised land, then he could not have been referring to that event when he talks about entering into God's rest. Rather, he was looking mainly to the future, though through catchword connection based on the word "rest," he is able to connect Psalm 95 with the story of God's original resting in Genesis 2.[75] It is interesting that Rabbi Eliezer, according to b. Sanh. 110b, in discussing whether the wilderness wandering generation would have any portion in the world to come, countered the exegesis of some of his contemporaries who suggested that Psalm 95 ruled out their "entering his rest," but Eliezer argued that God "swore" in his wrath, but then later changed his mind! Along the same lines is Num. Rab. 14:19 where in a comment on Psalm 95:11 the rabbi suggests that it means that when God's anger ceased or turned away, "then" they could enter the rest.[76]

The NT writers also show precious little interest in Greek-styled philosophical reflection on the OT as did Philo. The principles of historical analogy and typology are in play again and again, and within those parameters we find a good deal of creativity in the handling of the OT. Like the good preachers that they were, they were eager to get to the application of the OT text for their "today" and beyond. This I call the homiletical use of the OT, and the term *relecture* is also apt. With a Jewish audience knowledgeable of the OT, such as at least some of the audience of Hebrews were, we might expect a good deal *more* along the lines of intertextual echo and metalepsis, with an assumption that the audience might know or seek out the larger OT context. It is surprising perhaps that there is not as much of this as one might expect, even in Hebrews.

But this is because the writer assumes that the OT is the living word of God and just as applicable for his audience as for the original one, even in new and unprecedented ways. He is less concerned with contextual exegesis and exposition or with his audience doing that, than with the use of the language of the psalms and other parts of the OT to make his own points, note how he simply enfolds Psalm 95 into his rhetorical discourse (see above). The psalm material is enfolded into a whole new presentation. Psalm 95 is not viewed or treated as merely a glorious anachronism from the past that is worth studying out of historical curiosity. Indeed, our writer is concerned with the ongoing spiritual well-being of his charges and trying to make sure they avoid

75. See, rightly, Attridge, "Psalms in Hebrews," 207.
76. See the discussion by Guthrie, "Hebrews," 954.

apostasy. The psalms provided salient and sobering reminders of what can happen to those who go down that dark road, a road that leads back to Egypt and bondage.

Guthrie helpfully summarizes this way:

> [T]he author understood Ps. 95 as a perennially pertinent word from God to people. Rather than being primarily concerned with the wilderness generation, the author uses that generation as an exemplar on how people should not respond to God and his revelation. The force of the example works by way of analogy and consists of people in relationship with God, to whom God speaks his word, and who will respond in some way; but this also, therefore is an analogy of potential situation. They have the potential of following the bad pattern, and the challenge to choose another path constitutes the exhortation. The analogous nature of the wilderness situation to the experience of Hebrews' addressees is clearly expressed in places such as 4:2—"just as those" (*kathaper kakeinoi*)—and it works because there is both continuity and discontinuity between the old- and new-covenant situations.[77]

Psalm 95, and the Christian use of it, renews the struggle to understand not merely why evil exists in the world, a more abstract academic debate, but why it affects and infects God's own people, leading to sin and apostasy, the breaking away from an intimate relationship with God. Terrien, reflecting on Psalm 95, shares some of his own wisdom on this matter:

> It has been said for a long time, and rightly, that the problem of evil is the creation of monotheism. A positivist humanist looks at natural or biological mysteries but does not try to find any transcendental cause. A polytheist will speak mythologically of a fight between gods or goddesses and let his inquiries end there. A pantheist will enter into the vast horizon of the worlds and avoid digging into the question of cosmic injustice by embracing the forces of good and evil and communing with life in its terrestrial fullness. But the theist, a Hebrew monotheist, who affirms both the omnipotence and the goodness of God, faces an insoluble scandal of theology.[78]

The God of Mercy and Forgiveness: Psalm 103

This is that rare psalm in book 4 of the Psalter that has a superscript connecting it to David both in the MT and in the LXX. The psalm begins

---

77. Ibid., 955; his whole discussion is worth consulting.
78. Terrien, *Psalms*, 671.

and ends with imperatives calling for praise of the forgiving God, more particularly in vv. 1–2 and in the final four lines for the "blessing" of God, and so we have an *inclusio*. In fact the opening and closing lines are identical. "Rhetorically the psalm moves from 'you' (the self; vv. 1–5) to 'they' (Israel of the past; vv. 6–9) to 'we' (Israel of the past and present; vv. 10–14) to humanity (vv. 15–18), to the heavenly and earthly cosmos (vv. 19–22)."[79]

It is an unusual praise song in that the psalmist is addressing and exhorting himself to praise, which of course he does in this very song.[80] There are in addition twenty-two lines in the psalm, the same number as letters in the Hebrew alphabet, which may be a further indication of the psalmist's desire to be comprehensive, lauding the merciful God from beginning to end. Furthermore the term "all" shows up five times in the first six verses and four times in the last four verses. Notice as well the warning not to forget in the second line of the psalm, so that the psalm becomes "a recollecting, remembering, reminding."[81] Scholars are in disagreement about when this psalm originated, possibly in the postexilic period since it has some telling Aramaisms and some parallels with Isaiah 40–66.[82]

Not surprisingly in a psalm that emphasizes the merciful and forgiving nature of God, the psalm rings the changes on all three Hebrew words for sin, regularly translated "iniquity," "sin," or "transgression." The issue is how God relates to his sinful people, and how grateful they should be as a result. We also have in this psalm a comparatively rare thing: the citing of another Scripture, in this case Exodus 34:6–7 is drawn on to reveal the character of God, "the Lord is compassionate in nature, slow to anger and abounding in *ḥesed*," a word which refers to God's loving kindness and mercy.[83] This text from Exodus is in fact quoted also in Psalm 86:15 and 145:8 and alluded to in Psalms 78:38–39, 99:8, and 111:4. "Psalm 103 reads like a hymn based on study and reflection on the proclamation [of Exod 34:6–7] in its original context."[84] Weiser is prepared to say: "this psalm is one of the finest blossoms on the tree of biblical faith."[85] Finally, if we are wondering about this regular toggling back and forth between individual personal remarks, and

79. Goldingay, *Psalms: Volume 3*, 165.
80. Brueggemann and Bellinger, *Psalms*, 440.
81. See Mays, *Psalms*, 326 on all of this.
82. See Goldingay, *Psalms: Volume 3*, 165.
83. See above, ch. 4 on *ḥesed*.
84. Mays, *Psalms*, 328.
85. Weiser, *Psalms*, 657.

corporate remarks in so many of these psalms, Longman is probably correct in concluding that it is because worship in Israel was primarily public, and even when the song leader spoke in profoundly personal terms, this was not just a matter of private devotions but rather he was testifying to the worshipers and in some case speaking for them as well.[86]

MT Psalm 103	LXX Psalm 102
Of David. 1 Bless the Lord, O my soul, and all that is within me, bless his holy name. 2 Bless the Lord, O my soul, and do not forget all his benefits— 3 who forgives all your iniquity, who heals all your diseases, 4 who redeems your life from the Pit, who crowns you with steadfast love and mercy, 5 who satisfies you with good as long as you live so that your youth is renewed like the eagle's. 6 The Lord works vindication and justice for all who are oppressed. 7 He made known his ways to Moses, his acts to the people of Israel. 8 The Lord is merciful and gracious, slow to anger and abounding in steadfast love. 9 He will not always accuse, nor will he keep his anger forever. 10 He does not deal with us according to our sins, nor repay us according to our iniquities. 11 For as the heavens are high above the earth, so great is his steadfast love toward those who fear him; 12 as far as the east is from the west, so far he removes our transgressions from us.	1 Pertaining to David. Bless the Lord, O my soul, and all that is within me, his holy name. 2 Bless the Lord, O my soul, and do not forget all his repayments— 3 who is very conciliatory toward all your acts of lawlessness, who heals all your diseases, 4 who redeems your life from corruption, who crowns you with mercy and compassion, 5 who satisfies your desire with good, your youth will be renewed like an eagle's. 6 One who performs acts of pity a is the Lord and judgment for all who are being wronged. 7 He made known his ways to Moses, to the sons of Israel his will. 8 Compassionate and merciful is the Lord, slow to anger and abounding in mercy. 9 He will not be totally angry, nor will he keep his wrath forever. 10 Not according to our sins did he deal with us, nor according to our acts of lawlessness did he repay us, 11 because, as the sky is high above the earth, he strengthened his mercy toward those who fear him; 12 as far as east is from west, he has removed from us our acts of lawlessness.

86. Longman, *Psalms*, 356.

13 As a father has compassion for his children, so the Lord has compassion for those who fear him. 14 For he knows how we were made; he remembers that we are dust. 15 As for mortals, their days are like grass; they flourish like a flower of the field; 16 for the wind passes over it, and it is gone, and its place knows it no more. 17 But the steadfast love of the Lord is from everlasting to everlasting on those who fear him, and his righteousness to children's children, 18 to those who keep his covenant and remember to do his commandments.	13 As a father has compassion for sons, the Lord has had compassion for those who fear him, 14 because he knew our makeup. Remember that we are dust! 15 As for man, his days are like grass; like a flower of the field, so it will bloom, 16 because a breath passed through it, and it will be gone, and it will no longer recognize its place. 17 But the mercy of the Lord is from everlasting even to everlasting on those who fear him, and his righteousness on sons' sons, 18 for those who keep his covenant and remember his commandments, to do them.
19 The Lord has established his throne in the heavens, and his kingdom rules over all. 20 Bless the Lord, O you his angels, you mighty ones who do his bidding, obedient to his spoken word. 21 Bless the Lord, all his hosts, his ministers that do his will. 22 Bless the Lord, all his works, in all places of his dominion. Bless the Lord, O my soul.	19 The Lord prepared his throne in the sky, and his kingdom rules over all. 20 Bless the Lord, O all you, his angels, powerful in strength doing his bidding, to obey the voice of his words. 21 Bless the Lord, all his hosts, his ministers doing his will. 22 Bless the Lord, all his works, in every place of his dominion. Bless the Lord, O my soul.

There is a problem, in the case of both vv. 1 and 22, namely how to translate the word נַפְשִׁי (napšî) rendered in older English translations "my soul." The word does not refer to the whole self, much less the Greek concept of the immortal soul. Brueggemann and Bellinger helpfully suggest "the inner person."[87] Notice the reference to "all that is within me" in v. 1; the psalmist wants what we would call "wholehearted" praise. The psalmist is probing the depths of God's character, and what he finds is a holy and just God who nonetheless is also merciful and compassionate. His vision of God's character is much the same as that of Hosea 11:8–9, where God says "my heart recoils within me, my compassion grows warm and tender, I will not execute my fierce wrath, I will not again destroy Ephraim, for I am God and not a mere human being, the Holy One in your midst." The psalmist assumes it is

---

87. Brueggemann and Bellinger, *Psalms*, 441.

238

normal to have an internal dialogue with oneself, and even to exhort oneself (cf. Pss 42:5, 11; 43:5; 62:5; 116:7; 146:1).

In vv. 3–5 the reason to "bless the Lord" are enumerated: because he forgives, heals, redeems, crowns, and satisfies. Here the psalmist testifies of his own experience of mercy and grace and in vv. 6–13 he will move on to the evidence of God's mercy in tradition and in history.[88] The reference to healing in close conjunction with sin may be because the psalmist saw a connection between the two (see Ps 38:1–8).[89] Sometimes sickness is brought on by sin. But also, it was often assumed that when someone was sick it *must have been* because someone had sinned. You will notice that Jesus in John 9 rejects the idea that there is a necessary and universal connection between sickness and sin; you can't necessarily tell the state of someone's heart from the condition of their body. In any case, the psalmist thanks God for healing and bringing him back from death's door, here called "the pit" (i.e., the gaping hole known as Sheol). Not only did the psalmist get well, he was rejuvenated as if young once more. The eagle was a symbol of virility and strength.[90]

Three key terms come up in this context for sin, first of all עָוֺן (ʿawôn), which can refer to iniquity or the guilt caused by iniquity. A bit later in v. 10 we hear the familiar term "sin," חֵטְא (ḥēṭ') and then in v. 12 we have פֶּשַׁע (pešaʿ), transgression. The middle of these terms is the most generic, covering offenses against God in general, the former term focuses on the wickedness of the misdeeds in question, and the latter term refers to willful violation of a known law or moral principle. The point of citing the traditional passage from Exodus in v. 8 is to make clear that God's gracious character has always been the same, from the time of Moses until the present. Notice the use of the term רַחוּם (raḥûm) here, translated compassion. This root can appear as an adjective, a verb, or a noun. In some more secular contexts it refers to someone who restrains their anger and acts in a kind fashion, someone with power such as a military conqueror (see 1 Kgs 8:50; Jer 42:12). Not surprisingly, in the Psalms this word comes up in contexts where sin is discussed, indicating God's gracious reaction to his people's misdeeds.[91] But note that there is a threefold reminder that God's mercy and loving kindness are "for those who revere him" (vv. 11, 13, 17). As Psalm 130:4 will make clear, the revering of God comes from knowing

---

88. Weiser, *Psalms*, 658.
89. See Longman, *Psalms*, 356.
90. Ibid. In some contexts it was also considered an impure bird; see Lev 4:13; Deut 14:12; and Terrien, *Psalms*, 703.
91. See the helpful discussion in Mays, *Psalms*, 328.

that one's sins have been forgiven. God does not forgive in a *quid pro quo* exchange for reverence or "fear."

In vv. 9–10 we hear not only that God is famously slow to anger, but also that God's anger against sin does not last forever, and that in fact God does not deal with the believer according to his or her sins.[92] There is mention of God's justice, but clearly the emphasis in this particular psalm is on mercy. Verses 11–12, making comparisons, suggest that as far as east is from west is how far God removes the sinner's transgressions from him, and then we are told that God is like a merciful parent dealing with a child. The poetry here in vv. 12–13 is sublime in the Hebrew, involving alliteration (*kīraḥōq . . . keraḥēm*). Verse 14 indicates that God knows we are frail and mortal and is accordingly taking that into account, and so is compassionate (cf. Ps 90:5; Isa 40:6–10; Job 7:7–10). The term *ḥesed* crops up in vv. 4, 8, 11, and 17 indicating God's loving kindness, and ongoing mercy. Indeed, the psalmist wants to say it fills all time and space.[93]

Verses 19–22 suggest that praise of God should ring out from heaven to earth, from the angels to the humans, in fact from all of creation: sun, moon, stars, earth, and had he known it, he could have quoted Isaiah 55 where we hear of trees clapping their hands. Everything alive should praise this God of mercy and compassion.[94] And once more at the end, the psalmist exhorts himself to join the heavenly chorus. Because God rules over all, he has the power and ability to separate the sinner from his sin, as far as the east is from the west.[95]

The story of the healing of the paralytic in Mark 2:1–12 is a story that raises the issue of the relationship of sin to disease or disability. When Jesus first says to the paralytic "your sins are forgiven," quite naturally some present asked the question, "Who can forgive sins but God alone?" This question may well be an echo of Psalm 103:4a, but Jesus responds in a way that implies they should have read both halves of that verse which reads "who forgives all your iniquity and heals all your diseases." Jesus replies that in order that they may know that he has the authority to forgive sin, he will heal this man. If you are going to question Jesus's right to forgive you on the basis of Psalm 103:4 and its clear statement that forgiveness *and* healing comes from God, then

92. Goldingay, *Psalms: Volume 3*, 170–71.
93. Mays, *Psalms*, 328.
94. On the relationship of justice and mercy in Israel's God and in Psalm 103 see D. F. O'Kennedy, "The Relationship between Justice and Forgiveness in Psalm 103," *Scriptura* 65 (1998): 109–21.
95. Goldingay, *Psalms: Volume 3*, 175 points out that the image of a throne established in the heaven implies ruling over the whole cosmos.

you should have also questioned his right and ability to heal the man. The two things go together, and the remedy for both come from God according to Psalm 103:4. What Mark intends for this to imply about Jesus's identity becomes clear.

The belief that God had exclusively revealed his will and his ways and his character to his people, through the person of Moses and the prophets was a common belief in early Judaism, and one that Paul affirms in Romans 3:2: "for . . . the Jews were entrusted with the oracles of God." Paul is not quoting or directly alluding to Psalm 103 here, but he is assuming that Psalm 103:7 is true when it says, "He made known his ways to Moses, his acts to the people of Israel." This is even clearer in the list of things God has blessed Israel with in Romans 9:4–5. Again, we are not dealing with a quotation or a direct allusion, but a shared idea that was disseminated widely through the praying, singing, memorizing, teaching, and preaching of the Psalms.

The combination "God is compassionate and merciful" that we find in Psalm 103:8, which in turn is an echo of the original character statement about Yahweh in Exodus, is found in James 5:11. Of importance here is that James takes the word *hesed* whether in the original statement in Exodus, or in its reaffirmation in Psalm 103, to refer to God's mercy, not his covenant loyalty. Notice as well that James is commenting on Job and his endurance. God allows suffering even when it comes to the upright and God-fearing, but can be still be said to be merciful and compassionate in such cases. This combination of ideas is also found in Psalm 103, for in v. 6 we hear about God's justice and vindication of the oppressed, and surely Job qualified.

Luke 1:50 says in the song we know as the Magnificat that God's mercy is for those who fear him from generation to generation. This should be compared to Psalm 103:17, "but the *hesed* of the Lord is from everlasting to everlasting on those who fear him." This is certainly an allusion to the psalm text, and once again it brings up the point that *hesed* means something other than "in-group" love or covenant love and loyalty, a love Yahweh has obligated himself to give. Rather, it means mercy. In no OT covenant document that I know of is God "obligated" to show mercy when someone has violated the covenant. This is not part of the contract. It just isn't. It's part of God's nature, as the psalmist says, but it's not part of what he is *obligated* in the covenant to do. The old KJV of course translated the word "loving kindness," but the more I look at this, the more I think it just means mercy or kindness. Note that from the outset in the paradigmatic text in Exodus it is paired with the word for compassion. Covenant keepers don't need compassion, sinners do; and Psalm 103 is about how God responds to his people's sinning. One more point about Luke 1:50: it talks about generation to generation whereas the psalm text is talking about everlasting to everlasting. The former has to do with people, the latter with time, though both are indicating something infinitely extended.

Psalm 103:19 tells us God has established his throne in heaven. Revelation 4:2 speaks of the creator God sitting on a throne in heaven. It is interesting to compare this to what Jesus says in Matthew 5:34, namely that heaven itself is God's throne. This is not even an echo of Psalm 103:19, but rather a related concept, which assumes God is a king, and therefore must have a throne, whether in heaven or as heaven itself since heaven by definition is "high and lifted up."

What we have seen in these associations of Psalm 103 with the NT is that it mostly comes at the level of concepts, language, or, in one case, as a probable allusion in Luke 1:50. But this hardly tells the whole story. What is more important is that the concept of the character of God which front-lights his mercy and compassion, with his justice becoming a subdominant note, is precisely the character of God that is stressed in the NT over and over again, not at the expense of God's justice, and sometimes even in tandem with it. By this I mean that when God vindicates the oppressed it is as an expression of his mercy on them. The only book in the NT that places more emphasis on the justice of God than on his love is Revelation, and even there it is mostly about vindicating the martyrs and the oppressed believers. Psalm 103 and texts like Hosea 11 pointed the way toward the sort of emphasis we find on God's love and compassion in the NT, including in the teaching of Jesus.

The Lexicon of Faith: The Broader Use of Psalms 90–106

The notion that God's conception of time (or at least the way time works in eternity) is different from a human perspective on time is an idea that crops up from time to time in the Scriptures. Psalm 90:4 says "a thousand years in your sight are like yesterday when it is past, or like a watch in the night." What seems like a long period of time to humans seems like a very brief period to God. This can be compared to 2 Peter 3:8, "that with the Lord one day is as a thousand years, and a thousand years as one day." This may be said to be a partial allusion, if we match up the second half of 2 Peter 3:8 with the first half of

Psalm 90:4. But the author of 2 Peter also wants to say that for God a brief period of time can be extended to a very long period of time, or at least in the mind of God it can seem that way.

While Keesmaat has suggested that Psalm 94:1 lies in the background of Romans 12:19, it surely is more likely to be Deuteronomy 32:35 which has the exact words "vengeance is mine, and retribution in due time." Keesmaat is also unlikely to be correct in assuming that Paul is addressing a situation of the empire persecuting the Christian church in Rome, but she is right that Paul is saying that God has not rejected his first chosen people. Romans 12:19–20 addresses the issue of personal animus and "enemies" in a reciprocity and honor challenge society, not the issue of governmental persecution.[96]

We have a quotation by Paul in 1 Corinthians 3:20 of some form of Psalm 94:11 which in the MT reads, "the Lord knows the thoughts of humankind, and they are but empty breath," while the LXX has, "the Lord knows the thoughts of human beings, that they are futile." Interestingly, Paul has "the thoughts of the wise," but otherwise seems to be following the LXX. Paul has in fact combined a citation of Job 5:13 in 1 Corinthians 3:19 with this citation of Psalm 94:11 LXX. Paul seems to have adapted his citation to the subject of his discourse, namely the difference between human wisdom and God's wisdom, an argument which is coming to a close at this juncture in 1 Corinthians 3.[97] The function of the citation is to make clear that the wisdom of this world is futile, vain, and foolishness in God's sight (cf. 1 Cor 1:18–25 and 3:19). The word μάταιοι in the LXX while it can be translated "empty breath" indicating something ephemeral, is rightly rendered "vain" or "futile" (cf. LXX Pss 5:10; 11:3; 23:4; 59:13; 61:10; 107:13). The Hebrew in Psalm 94:11 of course is הֶבֶל (hābel), made famous as the opening cry of Qoheleth in Ecclesiastes.[98] The Hebrew word הֶבֶל can be rendered either as "empty" or "vain." Paul however has not simply substituted the word "wise" here. A close reading of Psalm 94 shows that there is a sapiential contrast between the fool and the wise person in the psalm itself, and the person described in the verse quoted is seen as a fool by the psalmist, and so Paul can be using the word "wise" in an ironic or sarcastic manner here, which makes very good sense in the larger context of his critique of worldly wisdom in 1 Corinthians 1–3.[99] Paul has

---

96. Keesmaat, "Psalms in Romans and Galatians," 153–54.
97. See the discussion in Ben Witherington III, *Conflict and Community in Corinth: A Socio-rhetorical Commentary on 1 and 2 Corinthians* (Grand Rapids: Eerdmans, 1995).
98. See the helpful discussion of Williams, "Psalms in 1 and 2 Corinthians," 164–67.

occasion to allude to this psalm again at Romans 11:2 only this time it is Psalm 94:14.

Psalm 94:14 in the MT reads, "for the Lord will not forsake his people, he will not abandon his heritage." The LXX is much the same, "for the Lord will not reject his people, and his heritage he will not abandon." As Wagner points out, the concept of Israel being God's inheritance is an important one in the OT, and also for Paul. Thus when we get to Romans 11:1–2 we will not be surprised that the emphatic answer to the rhetorical question "has God rejected his κληρονομία?" (v. 1)[100] is no, as v. 2 goes on to insist, "God has not rejected his people whom he foreknew."[101] The notion in play is that since God chose Israel to be his portion, his people, his particular possession, then Israel is his inheritance, so to speak (see Deut 32:8–9).

In Revelation 9–19 we find a whole series of allusions to Psalm 96, which is worth quoting at this point.

O sing to the Lord a new song; sing to the Lord, all the earth. 2 Sing to the Lord, bless his name; tell of his salvation from day to day. 3 Declare his glory among the nations, his marvelous works among all the peoples. 4 For great is the Lord, and greatly to be praised; he is to be revered above all gods. 5 For all the gods of the peoples are idols, but the Lord made the heavens. 6 Honor and majesty are before him; strength and beauty are in his sanctuary. 7 Ascribe to the Lord, O families of the peoples, ascribe to the Lord glory and strength. 8 Ascribe to the Lord the glory due his name; bring an offering, and come into his courts. 9 Worship the Lord in holy splendor; tremble before him, all the earth.	"and they sing a new song" Rev. 14.3 "idols of gold and silver" Rev 9:20

---

99. On which see Witherington, *Conflict and Community in Corinth*; and Ciampa and Rosner, "1 Corinthians," 704.

100. There is a textual problem here. Most manuscripts read "the people" here, but p46, G, and a few others read κληρονομία. Wagner thinks the latter is original, and I'm inclined to agree with him, not least because in Romans 10:19 he has already drawn on Deuteronomy 32:21.

101. Wagner, *Heralds*, 224–28.

10 Say among the nations, "The Lord is king! The world is firmly established; it shall never be moved. He will judge the peoples with equity." 11 Let the heavens be glad, and let the earth rejoice; let the sea roar, and all that fills it; 12 let the field exult, and everything in it. Then shall all the trees of the forest sing for joy 13 before the Lord; for he is coming, for he is coming to judge the earth. He will judge the world with righteousness, and the peoples with his truth.	"rejoice then, you heavens, and those who dwell in them" Rev 12:12 "the rider is called faithful and true And in righteousness he judges" Rev 19:11

Some of these echoes are closer than others, and notice that often it is in the *songs* in Revelation that we find echoes of the Psalms. This is part of the larger pattern of allusion and echo that indicates just how saturated John's brain was not only with Isaiah, but also with the Psalms, using its lexicon to articulate his visions and their meaning. But it is not just Psalm 96, it is also Psalms 97–98 that are used this way by John. For example, in Revelation 19:6 in the song of joy we hear, "For the Lord our God Almighty reigns, let us rejoice and exult and give him the glory." This echoes "The Lord is king, let the earth rejoice, let the many coastlands be glad" in Psalm 97:1. Or compare even more convincingly Revelation 11:5, "And if anyone wants to harm them, fire pours from their mouth and consumes their foes" to Psalm 97:3 "fire goes before him, and consumes his adversaries" (only in this case it is the prophets who are fire-breathing!).

Psalm 97:7 reads "all אֱלֹהִים ['*elōhîm*] bow down before him,"[102] which the LXX renders "worship him all his angels," which in turn must be compared to Revelation 7:11 "and all the angels . . . fell on their faces before the throne and worshiped God, singing." That we are on the right track here is shown by the direct citation of Psalm 97:7 in Hebrews 1:6, "let all God's angels worship him."[103] Revelation 15:4 reads, "Lord who will not fear and glorify your name? For you alone

---

102. On אֱלֹהִים ('*elōhîm*) as used of angels, see ch. 5, Psalm 89, above.
103. Attridge, "Psalms in Hebrews," 201 points out that we have here some impressive evidence that the author of Hebrews was following the Greek psalter, in particular like the one appended to Codex Alexandrinus, which is the closest to this form of citation of Ps 97:7 in Heb 1:6. In a *tour de force* presentation, the author of Hebrews refers the text to the angels worshiping the Son, the firstborn of God, rather than Yahweh. But see the discussion in Guthrie, "Hebrews," 931.

are holy. All nations will come and worship you, for your judgments have been revealed." Psalm 98:2 says, "he has revealed his vindication in the sight of the nations." Revelation 11:18, again in a poetic song text, says, "the nations raged, but your wrath has come"; and the LXX of Psalm 99:1 reads, "The Lord became king, let peoples grow angry . . . it was you who executed justice and righteousness."[104]

Psalm 98:3 reads, "he has remembered his *hesed* and his faithfulness to the house of Israel," which in the LXX reads, "he has remembered his mercy and his truth to the house of Israel," and in Luke 1:54, again in a song, we have, "he has helped his servant Israel, in remembrance of his mercy." In the second half of Psalm 98:3 we have, "all the ends of the earth have seen the victory of our God" whereas the LXX has "salvation" (σωτήριον) instead of "victory," and in Luke 3:6 we have, "and all flesh shall see the salvation of God" (the same text is probably echoed in Acts 28:28). Here we run across the problem we have seen many times, namely that whereas Jewish translators are rendering *hesed* as mercy, as are the translators of the LXX, who are followed in this by Luke and others in the NT, *nevertheless* the English translation of the MT is rendered time and again as "steadfast love" or the like. But this is not what the word in question means in these contexts (cf., e.g., Ps 100:5 to Luke 1:50). It means mercy, and so Luke rightly has at 1:54 "in remembrance of his mercy." The whole verse of Psalm 98:3 in the LXX reads, "he remembered his mercy to Jacob, and his truth to the house of Israel; all the ends of the earth saw the deliverance of our God." The use of these psalms is fluid, sometimes a citation, sometimes an allusion, sometimes an echo, sometimes a key phrase, sometimes simply a main idea. Psalm 100:5 reads, "for the Lord is good, his *hesed*/mercy endures forever, and his faithfulness to all generations," and the LXX has, "his mercy endures forever, and unto generation and generation is his truth." Luke 1:50 reads, "his mercy is for those who fear him, from generation to generation." Luke 1:50 seems to be closer to this psalm, than the one previously mentioned.

Hebrews 1:10-12 reads, "in the beginning, Lord, you founded the earth, and the heavens are the work of your hands. They will perish, but you remain; they will all wear out like clothing; like a cloak you will roll them up, and like clothing they will be changed. But you are the same, and your years will never end." It will be useful to quote the psalm at this juncture:

104. Here, as in various other places, we see further evidence that John follows a Greek text of the Psalms regularly, not the Hebrew.

246

MT Psalm 102:25–28	LXX Psalm 101:26–29
25 Long ago you laid the foundation of the earth, and the heavens are the work of your hands. 26 They will perish, but you endure; they will all wear out like a garment. You change them like clothing, and they pass away; 27 but you are the same, and your years have no end. 28 The children of your servants shall live secure; their offspring shall be established in your presence.	26 At the beginning it was you, O Lord, who founded the earth, and the heavens are works of your hands. 27 They will perish, but you will endure, and they will all become old like a garment. Like clothing you will change them, and they will be changed. 28 But you are the same, and your years will not fail." 29 The sons of your slaves shall encamp, and their offspring shall prosper forever.

The author of Hebrews of course has now applied this to the son, which in the psalm was applied to Yahweh and his eternality (cf. Heb 13:8).[105] The text as quoted in Hebrews generally follows the LXX, but with a few wrinkles or variations. The future "you will remain" is changed to the present tense in Hebrews 1, and the verb "change" is replaced in Hebrews with the more vivid, "you roll up" (cf. Isa 34:4). At Hebrews 1:12 the author adds the phrase "as a garment" which is a rerun from the previous verse. The temporary usefulness of clothes is seen as analogous to the temporal and temporary nature of the created order.[106] Psalms 45 and 102 here serve the function of demonstrating the eternality of the Son compared to the nature of the angels, but there is also the thought that the Son was involved in the creation of everything and all of it will be subjected to him in the end as well.

Psalm 104:4, which reads in the LXX "who makes angels his messengers and flaming fire his ministers," is quoted in Hebrews 1:7 as "of his angels he says 'He makes his angels winds, and his servants flames of fire,'" which seems closer to the MT, at least in the first phrase for it reads, "you make the winds his messengers, fire and flame his ministers."[107] But there is ambiguity in the Hebrew because while רוח (rûaḥ) could refer to winds, it could also mean "spirits" which is perhaps why

---

105. See the discussion in Attridge, "Psalms in Hebrews," 202–3; and especially the detailed analysis in Guthrie, "Hebrews," 941–43. Guthrie is right that the author of Hebrews is following the LXX, but tailoring it to his own context and in order to make it fit together with these other quotations from the psalms and elsewhere.
106. See Guthrie, "Hebrews," 941.
107. The Hebrew has "his," despite the many English translations, which for consistency with vv. 1b–3, have "you" as the subject of the verb.

the LXX renders it "angels." Targum Onqelos, Psalm 104:4 reads, "Who made his messengers as swift as the wind, his servants as strong as burning fire." There is the further point that in Hebrew thinking angels were associated with the elemental forces anyway, in particular air and fire (cf. Ps 103:20–21). It is just possible that the author has picked this text because of the ephemeral nature of angels—they can be transformed into winds and lightning and fire—compared to the unchangeable nature of the Son.[108]

There has been considerable debate in the guild of NT scholars about where exactly some of the information came from that Stephen is passing on in Acts 7 in his "salvation historical" review. One possible source insufficiently explored by some is the salvation historical review material in the Psalms, in this case in Psalm 105. Too often the discussion has gone from "this is not in the Pentateuch" to "it must have come from some early Jewish oral traditions or literature that's not part of the canon." This may well be true in some cases, but the Psalms, which often have salvation historical reviews, should have been scrutinized first.

Take for example Psalm 105:21. Speaking about Joseph and his experience in Egypt the psalmist says, "He [Pharaoh] made him lord of his house and ruler of all his possessions, to instruct his officials at his pleasure and teach his elders wisdom." Acts 7:10 says, "God was with him and rescued him from all his afflictions and enabled him to win favor and to show wisdom when he stood before Pharaoh, king of Egypt, who appointed him ruler over Egypt and over all his household." If one compares this to Genesis 41:37–45 you will notice that there is nothing about Joseph showing or teaching wisdom to the court officials there. But the psalm wants to stress this.

Or consider Psalm 105:24, 42, which says, "and the Lord made his people very fruitful and made them stronger than their foes . . . for he remembered his holy promise and Abraham his servant," and compare Acts 7:17, which says, "as the time drew near for the fulfillment of the promise that God had made to Abraham, our people in Egypt increased and multiplied." The point here is not that Stephen is directly citing the psalm version of the story, the point is that the psalm version of the story *has influenced the way he tells the story*. The stories of the patriarchs have been processed through a psalms filter or lens.

Psalm 106:10 LXX reads, "and he saved them from the hand of people

---

108. See the helpful discussion in Guthrie, "Hebrews," 934–36.

that hate, and redeemed them from an enemy's hands," which is rather clearly echoed in Luke 1:71, "that we would be saved from our enemies and from the hand of all who hate us." Though the clauses are reversed, this is a direct allusion to the LXX rendering (contrast the MT and cf. 4Q174 11).[109]

Paul uses these psalms in terms of allusions and echoes, not in the creation of more songs, but as part of his discourses. A couple of examples will have to suffice. Romans 1:23 provides us with a partial citation of Psalm 106:20, "they exchanged the glory of God for the image of an ox that eats grass" (MT). The Romans text has, "and they exchanged the glory of the immortal God for images resembling . . . four footed animals." Here Paul is surely following the MT rather than the LXX, which has, "they exchanged their glory." Paul, unlike some of the other writers of the NT (e.g., Luke), seems to have had a choice of which version of the OT he would follow. You will notice there is no citation formula here however. Paul is simply incorporating the phrases and thoughts into his own argument.[110]

This is not all; Romans 1:18–32 in general seems to reflect a real indebtedness to Psalm 106 in regard to the universal scope of sin.[111] Hays rightly noticed the allusion to Psalm 106 in Romans 1:23 and helpfully points out that while the psalm was talking about the sin of Israel, here Paul is using the language to discuss the sin of gentiles, in service of eventually making clear that all have sinned and fall under the judgment of God on sin—Jew and gentile alike. But this rhetorical switch serves another purpose as well. In Romans 2:1–3:20 he will make plain that Jews have no basis to criticize the idolatry of gentiles when they long ago did the same thing: "the golden calf story becomes a parable of the human condition apart from the gospel, a condition of self-destructive idolatry."[112]

Psalm 106 is able to help us with one further Pauline conundrum as well. It is well known that Paul, apart from 1 Corinthians 10, doesn't really mention demons, at least by that term. But there is a verse

---

109. See the discussion of Pao and Schnabel, "Luke," 264. Much could also be made of how many times the language of the telling of salvation history by Stephen in Acts 7 seems to be indebted to the Psalms retelling of that story, for instance in Psalms 105–106. See, e.g., Acts 7:17 and 7:41.

110. Because this use of the OT is close enough, it raises the question whether Paul saw what he was writing as a continuation of Holy Writ, or at least just as inspired as Holy Writ. Certainly, he viewed his proclamation of the gospel that way (see 1 Thess 2:13).

111. See Mays, Psalms, 342. Some Greek manuscripts of Psalm 106 apparently have the reading "the glory of God," but the Hebrew in any case is such that "their glory" in the MT might not refer to human glory, but rather Yahweh being Israel's glory.

112. Hays, Echoes of Scripture in the Letters of Paul, 93–94; the quotation is on p. 94.

where, in his argument about avoiding temple meals where food sacrificed to "idols" (false gods in Paul's view), he says this "I imply that what pagans sacrifice, they sacrifice to demons" (v. 20). Where does this idea come from? Why not just say they sacrifice to nonexistent gods, or aspects of creation? Why this formulation? The answer can be found in Psalm 106:36–37 MT: "They served their idols, which became a snare to them. They sacrificed their sons and daughters to the demons."[113] Paul's whole discussion is about idols, and sacrifices to idols, and he is saying just as the psalmist did that they were really sacrificing to demons!

An interesting study in the different way Paul can use an OT phrase from the way it was meant in its original context is found at Romans 4:3 where Paul is discussing Abraham and how his "faith was reckoned as righteousness." Clearly the story in mind is the grand saga in Genesis 12–25, and specifically Genesis 15:6 LXX is in play, but the specific phrase "something reckoned as righteousness" is *also* found in Psalm 106:11, where after Phineas in his zeal interceded with the Lord on behalf of idolatrous Israel, this faith act of his "was reckoned to him as righteousness from generation to generation." In one case it is trust in God that is so reckoned, in another case it is interceding with God that is so reckoned. It is important to consider all the parallels or indebtedness when one is dealing with as important a phrase as this in the NT.[114]

Finally, in Psalm 106:48 we have the exhortation or acclamation, "blessed be the Lord God of Israel," which we also find almost verbatim in Luke 1:68 in Zechariah's speech. In any case, we are seeing a definite pattern emerge. *The Psalms of book 4 of the Psalter are used by Luke, the author Hebrews, and John who wrote Revelation especially in their framing of song material, sometimes quoting, sometimes alluding to, and sometimes simply borrowing the language of the psalms to compose something new, and with no qualms, applying things to Jesus previously said only of Yahweh.* Paul how-

---

113. Though he may also be indebted to the LXX of Ps 106:37 which has τοῖς δαιμονίοις, to some degree, but the LXX of v. 36 is quite different from the MT, and does not use the word "idol," but rather carved image and talks about people becoming subject to carved images.

114. See the discussion in Seifrid, "Romans," 622 who uses the phrase "legal fiction." But neither Abraham nor Phineas are in any law court or negotiating with the Almighty. It would be better to notice that this language is the language of barter and business—credits and debits. We are not talking about a legal fiction here, we are talking about an exchange, and even more importantly, we are talking about one aspect of the person in question being reckoned as another thing. Abraham's faith is reckoned as Abraham's righteousness, just as in the case of Phineas it is his intercession that is so reckoned. There is nothing here about an external righteousness of someone else being imputed or imparted to the person in question. The issue is something the person in question has is credited as or for something else in God's eyes.

ever enfolds the psalm material into his discourse and makes them serve and bolster his arguments.

Conclusions

Sometimes it takes repeated encounters with the evidence before the light dawns on us. We have seen yet more evidence in this chapter that the NT writers read the foundational stories through their retellings in the Psalms. What is happening in the Psalms is that a liturgical use is being made of those historical narratives, and in the case of the more didactic psalms, a homiletical use is being made of the earlier material. This should have tipped us off that the latter is what is going on in the NT most of the time as well: a homiletical use of the OT, in this case of the Psalms. That sort of use tends to be improvisational and creative and should not be seen as an attempt to do straight exegesis in a "this is that" kind of manner. It's more like "this is *analogous* to that" or "this is an *illustration* of that sort of thing." We have seen how this plays out in the use of Psalm 95; the psalmist was probably talking about "rest" from traveling by dwelling in the Holy Land, but the author of Hebrews is talking about eschatological rest, or heavenly rest. What is foreshadowed in the psalm becomes something much grander in the later reality.

We learned some things about the devil and demons as well. There's no doubt that the writers of the NT believed in both, but the writers of the NT had a theology of demons in league with a head devil that went well beyond what the psalmists were talking about when they alluded to other gods. The latter foreshadowed the former, but these things were not viewed in the same way. In short, thought about Satan and his minions evolved over time, and this affected how the Psalms and other portions of the OT were used to discuss such matters. It is interesting that Job 1 does not come up directly anywhere in the NT.

We have seen in the use of Psalms 91, 95, and 103 just how rich these psalms were for the use of NT writers in a plethora of ways, in both theological and ethical ways. Sometimes it takes no more than a phrase, such as "enter his rest" for a psalm to spawn a whole line of thinking about the afterlife and whether and how one can become a part of it. Sometimes a whole series of lines in a psalm like Psalm 91 is evocative, prompting reflections on everything from angels to demons to metaphorical images of a divine redeemer to providing content for a Bible face off between the devil and Jesus. One wonders if Jesus's resort to Deuteronomy rather than the Psalms reflects his attempt to combat insinuation based on poetry and song lyrics with a "laying down of the law" to the nefarious one.

We saw how Psalm 95 could be enfolded into a lengthy discourse by the author of Hebrews in the service of an exhortation about avoiding apostasy, avoiding a repeat performance of what the wilderness-wandering generation did, a story also fueling the arguments of Paul in 1 Corinthians 10. But in both cases it was the sapiential rereading of the ancient pentateuchal narrative that proved most useful to these writers. The Psalms not merely prompted such "wise" rereadings of the story in the salvation historical reviews in these songs, they promoted it!

Or consider how Psalm 103 in just a few phrases can provide Jesus with material to show that after all, both healing and forgiveness come from God; so why object to Jesus doing the former when there is little or no objection to his doing the latter, indeed there is a desperate need for it, as almost all would admit in Galilee. Which is the bigger problem, sickness or sin? What exactly is the connection, if any, between the two? Neither Psalm 103 nor Jesus makes it all clear. What mattered most was not who got the clarification but who got the cure.

We have been accumulating considerable evidence in the final section of each chapter of just how much of the influence of the Psalms on the NT writers would be and is regularly missed by only focusing on clear citations and certain allusions to that corpus of literature. More often than not, these are not the main ways the language, phrases, and ideas, of the Psalms show up in the NT. What may seem incidental on first glance is important because it is not accidental that most of the psalm material in the NT shows up in this fashion. The tune that especially the Jewish writers of the NT and Jesus himself were humming regularly and brought into speech in a myriad of ways were the songs they heard and learned in worship that helped them articular their faith, hope, and love.

Not all the use of the Psalms was christological, sometimes it was just logical. Not all the use of the Psalms was exegetical or alluded to larger OT contexts, sometimes it was just homiletical. Often the language of the psalms was appropriated to address some very different subjects than the psalmist addressed. When that happened, it was not because the author took a cavalier approach to interpreting the Psalms; it is because he found the generic and multivalent character of much of the Psalms poetic language open to all sorts of reuse and *relecture*. Its very openness, universalness, evocativeness, metaphorical character fairly begged for a variety of applications and repurposing.

One more thing. The early Christian evangelists were mission-minded, evangelistic to the core. Their faith was that the good news should be offered to all. It was the more universal language about mercy and forgiveness for all in the Psalms, rather than some sort of exclusive covenant love and loyalty, that proved most service-able—especially when the audience increasingly became more and more gentile for Paul and his coworkers. We will see considerably more examples of the christological and apologetical use of the Psalms in our final full exegetical chapter on book 5 of the Psalter, to which we shall now turn.

7

Psalter Book 5 (Psalms 107–150)

Songs of Praise and Pilgrimage

> It is not that every sentiment expressed by a psalmist is admirable, but that in praying the Psalms, we confront ourselves as we really are. The Psalms are a reality check to keep prayer from becoming sentimental, superficial, or detached from the real world.
> —Richard H. Schmidt[1]

The final book of the Psalter, book 5, is enormous compared to the previous two books, with some forty-three psalms included. Of these forty-three psalms, only ten of them, other than the songs of ascents, have superscripts. Book 5 seems on the surface to be something of a catchall for whatever songs were still not included in the previous collections, with numerous songs of ascent (Psalms 120–34), a gigantic torah psalm (Psalm 119) and all kinds of other psalms as well. The final collection ends as Psalm 1 began with songs of *praises* (hallelujahs, Psalms 146–150), which of course is what *tehillim*, the title for this whole book in Israelite tradition, meant (*mizmor* literally means to sing praises) in the first place. If we take seriously Psalm 102:18, the primary motive for recording the psalms was "so that a people yet unborn may praise the Lord."[2]

---

1. Richard H. Schmidt, *Glorious Companions, Five Centuries of Anglican Spirituality,* (Eerdmans, 2002)

The final editor of the whole collection must have wanted the collection of collections that became our book of Psalms to be known primarily as a collection of praise songs, even though the laments, both individual and corporate, are the most common psalms in the Psalter. There is some reason to think that book 4 and book 5 were assembled at about the same time because when it comes to the names of God, these books are very similar; in fact Yahweh occurs some 339 times in books 4 and 5, but Elohim only 7 times. We cannot of course be sure about this.

The organization of the Psalms into five books suggests not merely a parallel with the Pentateuch, but also that these songs themselves should be seen as torah, instruction, like the Pentateuch, an idea that gains further traction from the fact that the Psalter is introduced in Psalm 1 by a torah song, and the longest psalm of all, Psalm 119, the crown of this final collection, is also a torah song.[3] What we know for sure is that the Psalter had been divided into five books before the close of the OT canon.[4] The Psalter was not just tunes for singing, it was for instruction.

It is probably also important to remember that in an age before the codex, books rolls of texts copied on papyri and glued together, were the order of the day, and book rolls could only be so large and still be practical. The famous Qumran Isaiah scroll shows that some of them could be quite long, but we have no evidence of a single roll as long as the whole Psalter, and certainly not during OT times.

I would suggest then that there may well have been five separate books of the Psalter to begin with, or five separate collections, later grouped together and then combined by scribes. Again Psalm 72:20 encourages us to think along these lines about earlier individual collections that eventually were enfolded into the Psalter as a whole. We should be wary as well of assuming that book 5 was necessarily the last book of the Psalter to be collected, as if the Psalms current ordering could be assumed to be a chronological order. The final editor might be surprised to hear this, especially since there are some Davidic psalms, some probably preexilic in book 5.

The Psalter in its present form is not the result of one single act of collecting, nor has it been compiled throughout by the same people. . . . The final compiler produced the present Psalter from various earlier collec-

---

2. See rightly the comments of Weiser, *Psalms*, 95.
3. See especially Wenham, *Psalms as Torah*, 119–37.
4. See Longman, *Psalms*, 36.

tions. This follows, first from the psalms that occur twice in the Psalter (Psalm 14 = Psalm 53; Ps 40:13–17 = Psalm 70; Pss 57:7–11 and 60:5–12 = Psalm 108), a phenomenon which would hardly have been possible if all the psalms had been grouped together all at once, and by the same compiler.[5]

For our purposes, what should be noted about this remark is that the last book of the Psalter, book 5 includes portions of two earlier psalms, namely Psalm 108, which suggests it at least is older than those two previous psalms.

Weiser points out, "the way in which Psalms 90–150 have been collected is quite obscure. The 'Book of the Pilgrim Songs' (Psalms 120–134) is a smaller collection in which each psalm carries the title 'a song of ascents' . . . but it contains only one genuine pilgrim song (Psalm 122)."[6] Goldingay is able to point to Psalms 113–118 as the Egyptian Hallel psalms, Psalms 135–36 as the great Hallel psalm, and Psalms 146–50 as more Hallel songs. There is a lot of praising going on in book 5 of the Psalter.[7] Psalm 137 reflects back on the exile. Perhaps more importantly, Goldingay shows that there seems to be some close connections between Psalms 105–6 and Psalm 107 which in turn suggests that the division into separate books is artificial and not a major clue to interpretation.[8]

Whatever the vagueries of the compilation process, there seems little doubt that the placing of praises songs at the end and the final doxology in Psalm 150 marked book 5 and the Psalter as a whole as a songbook to be used in worship. Furthermore, the very existence of the LXX, which involves all these 150 psalms and a little more, suggests that the whole Hebrew Psalter must have been completed by at least 200 BCE. The prologue to Sirach from about 132 BCE presupposes the threefold division of the Greek OT canon, and clearly the Psalms of Solomon from the time of Pompey, never mind the new Qumran psalms, were too late to be included in our Psalter. This means that the Psalter, which shows no trace of later Hellenistic influence, must have reached something close to its final form "in the Second Temple period, in Persian or early Greek times."[9]

This discussion is important to us because almost without exception

---

5. Weiser, *Psalms*, 99.
6. Ibid., 100.
7. Goldingay, *Psalms: Volume 1*, 36.
8. Goldingay, *Psalms: Volume 3*, 247.
9. Goldingay, *Psalms: Volume 1*, 35.

all of the 150 psalms in the Psalter are used in some way in the NT, and none of the later material from Qumran or the Psalms of Solomon are. The 150-psalm Psalter is treated as Scripture by the NT writers.[10] We must turn now to a select few psalms from book 5 that are of relevance to the discussion of the use of the Psalter in the NT. It will be seen that the most frequently used of all the psalms in the NT is in fact a psalm from book 5, Psalm 110, and not the whole psalm, but simply Psalm 110:1 and v. 4.

The Trials and Tribulations of the Redeemed: Psalm 107

In regard to the structure of Psalm 107 there seems to be a prelude and postlude (vv. 1–3, 43) in between which we have a two-part song: (1) vv. 4–32; and (2) vv. 33–42. The former part has repetitions or refrains, the second does not. The thread that connects the various parts is the sovereignty of God over nature and circumstances.[11] There is no attempt at balance, as the first major part of the psalm is considerably longer than the second major part. The echoes of themes in Isaiah 40–66 may suggest a postexilic setting where reflection back on the exile and the return was possible.[12]

MT Psalm 107	LXX Psalm 106
1 O give thanks to the Lord, for he is good; for his steadfast love endures forever.	1 Halleluia. Acknowledge the Lord, because he is kind, because his mercy is forever.
2 Let the redeemed of the Lord say so, those he redeemed from trouble	2 Let those redeemed by the Lord say so, whom he redeemed from an enemy's hand.
3 and gathered in from the lands, from the east and from the west, from the north and from the south. 4 Some wandered in desert wastes, finding no way to an inhabited town;	3 From the lands he gathered them in, from east and west and north and sea. 4 They wandered in the wilderness in a waterless region; a way to a city of habitation they did not find,
5 hungry and thirsty, their soul fainted within them.	5 being hungry and thirsty; their soul fainted within them.

10. On the problems with assuming too much pluraformity when it comes to the numbers of variant Old Greek texts of the OT, as well as in regard to the Hebrew Bible, not to mention the failure to realize that the OT canon was basically closed in the NT era when it comes to a text like the Psalms, see Appendix B below.
11. See Terrien, *Psalms*, 737–38.
12. Goldingay, *Psalms: Volume 3*, 248.

6 Then they cried to the Lord in their
trouble,
and he delivered them from their distress;
7 he led them by a straight way,
until they reached an inhabited town.
8 Let them thank the Lord for his steadfast love,
for his wonderful works to humankind.

9 For he satisfies the thirsty,
and the hungry he fills with good things.

10 Some sat in darkness and in gloom,
prisoners in misery and in irons,

11 for they had rebelled against the
words of God,
and spurned the counsel of the Most
High.
12 Their hearts were bowed down with
hard labor;
they fell down, with no one to help.

13 Then they cried to the Lord in their
trouble,
and he saved them from their distress;
14 he brought them out of darkness and
gloom,
and broke their bonds asunder.
15 Let them thank the Lord for his steadfast love,
for his wonderful works to humankind.

16 For he shatters the doors of bronze,
and cuts in two the bars of iron.
17 Some were sick through their sinful
ways,
and because of their iniquities endured
affliction;
18 they loathed any kind of food,
and they drew near to the gates of death.
19 Then they cried to the Lord in their
trouble,
and he saved them from their distress;
20 he sent out his word and healed them,
and delivered them from destruction.
21 Let them thank the Lord for his steadfast love,
for his wonderful works to humankind.

6 And they cried to the Lord when they
were being afflicted,
and from their anguish he rescued them

7 and led them by a straight way,
to go to a city of habitation.
8 Let them acknowledge the Lord for his
mercies
and for his wonderful works to the sons
of men,
9 because he fed an empty soul
and a hungry soul he filled with good
things,
10 when they sat in darkness and death's
shadow,
imprisoned in poverty and iron,
11 because they had embittered the sayings of God,
and the counsel of the Most High they
had provoked.
12 And their heart was brought low by
exertion;
they became weak, and there was no one
to help.

13 And they cried to the Lord when they
were being afflicted,
and from their anguish he saved them,
14 and he brought them out of darkness
and death's shadow,
and their bonds he broke asunder.
15 Let them acknowledge the Lord for his
mercies
and for his wonderful works to the sons
of men,
16 because he shattered bronze gates
and iron bars he crumpled.
17 He aided them from their lawless way,
for on account of their lawless acts they
were brought low;
18 any kind of food their soul loathed,
and they drew near to the gates of death.
19 And they cried to the Lord when they
were being afflicted,
and from their anguish he saved them;
20 he sent out his word and healed them
and rescued them from their corruption.
21 Let them acknowledge the Lord for his
mercies
and for his wonderful works to the sons
of men.

22 And let them offer thanksgiving sacrifices,
and tell of his deeds with songs of joy.
23 Some went down to the sea in ships,
doing business on the mighty waters;

24 they saw the deeds of the Lord,
his wondrous works in the deep.

25 For he commanded and raised the
  stormy wind,
which lifted up the waves of the sea.
26 They mounted up to heaven, they
  went down to the depths;
their courage melted away in their
  calamity;
27 they reeled and staggered like drunkards,
and were at their wits' end.
28 Then they cried to the Lord in their
  trouble,
and he brought them out from their distress;
29 he made the storm be still,
and the waves of the sea were hushed.

30 Then they were glad because they had
  quiet,
and he brought them to their desired
  haven.
31 Let them thank the Lord for his steadfast love,
for his wonderful works to humankind.

32 Let them extol him in the congregation of the people,
and praise him in the assembly of the
  elders.
33 He turns rivers into a desert,
springs of water into thirsty ground,
34 a fruitful land into a salty waste,
because of the wickedness of its inhabitants.
35 He turns a desert into pools of water,
a parched land into springs of water.

36 And there he lets the hungry live,
and they establish a town to live in;

22 And let them sacrifice a sacrifice of
  praise
and tell of his deeds with rejoicing.
23 Those who used to go down to the sea
  in ships,
doing business on many waters—
24 it was they who saw the deeds of the
  Lord
and his wondrous works in the deep.
25 He spoke and the tempest's blast
  stood,
and its waves were raised on high.
26 They mount up as far as the heavens,
and they go down as far as the depths;
their soul would melt away in calamity;

27 they were troubled; they staggered
  like the drunkard,
and all their wisdom was gulped down.
28 And they cried to the Lord when they
  were being afflicted,
and out of their anguish he brought
  them,
29 and he ordered the tempest, and it
  subsided to a breeze,
and its waves became silent.

30 And they were glad, because they had
  quiet,
and he guided them to a haven of their
  want.
31 Let them acknowledge the Lord for his
  mercies
and for his wonderful works to the sons
  of men.
32 Let them exalt him in an assembly of
  people
and in a session of elders praise him.

33 He turned rivers into a wilderness
and channels of water into thirst,
34 a fruitful land into a salt marsh,
due to the evil of its inhabitants.

35 He turned a wilderness into pools of
  water
and a parched land into channels of
  water.
36 And there he settled hungry ones,
and they established a city for settle-
  ment,

37 they sow fields, and plant vineyards, and get a fruitful yield.	37 and they sowed fields and planted vineyards and produced a fruit of a yield.
38 By his blessing they multiply greatly, and he does not let their cattle decrease.	38 And he blessed them, and they were multiplied greatly, and their cattle he did not decrease.
39 When they are diminished and brought low through oppression, trouble, and sorrow,	39 And they were diminished and mal-treated through affliction, wrong and sorrow.
40 he pours contempt on princes and makes them wander in trackless wastes;	40 Contempt poured down on rulers, and he a made them wander in an impassable and trackless region,
41 but he raises up the needy out of dis-tress, and makes their families like flocks.	41 and he helped a needy one out of poverty and made their paternal families like sheep.
42 The upright see it and are glad; and all wickedness stops its mouth.	42 The upright will see it and be glad, and all lawlessness will stop its mouth.
43 Let those who are wise give heed to these things, and consider the steadfast love of the Lord.	43 Who is wise and will keep these things?— and will they take note of the mercies of the Lord?

This song starts in vv. 1–3 not unlike others telling us that God's ḥesed endures forever, and the proof of this is that he has brought back Jews from exile, from all points of the compass (cf. Isa 56:8, where the term "gather" is used in the same way).[13] Here again, since exile was a pun-ishment, it makes sense to translate ḥesed, as the Jewish translations do, with the word "mercy." This also matches with the calling of God's people the "redeemed", he redeemed them from trouble and foreign lands.[14] A rather clear clue that we are on the right track about ḥesed is that we find it in both the singular (v. 1) and in the plural (v. 43). It does not mean covenant loves (plural) in v. 43, it means "mercies." Further support for this view is the rather universal terms used in the psalm, this is not *exclusively* about Israel but rather about all the sons of Adam. What sets God's redemption in motion is his mercy, and the sincere cry of the needy to the Lord, whether sinner or pious Israelite, not some obligation God has bound himself to, by means of a covenant.

The story of where and what the "redeemed" were rescued from is told in vv. 4–32 with the repeated refrain "some . . . some . . . some." The first group was wandering in desert wastelands and could find no way to an inhabited place. They were starving and thirsty and their

13. See above, ch. 4 above on the meaning of this key term. See Brueggemann and Bellinger, *Psalms*, 464, on gathering from exile.
14. On the setting of this psalm as postexilic see Longman, *Psalms*, 376.

inner-being and sense of well-being was at the point of fainting. Why it took so long is not clear, but at the point of desperation they cried out to God and he delivered them by a straight path to an inhabited town. Perhaps the old saying is true, one has to come to the end of one's self and one's resources sometimes to turn to God for help. The psalmist in v. 8 exhorts those rescued in this manner to thank God for showing his mercy and for his wonderful works for "the sons of Adam," which is how the Hebrew reads. God slakes the thirst of the parched and fills the hungry with good food.

The second story line is about prisoners, rotting in the darkness and misery of leg irons in a gloomy place. In fact the word ṣalmāwet probably means "deathly shadow" or the shadow of death hovering over these persons (cf. vv. 10 and 14).[15] But this group of persons was there because they had rebelled against God's word and wise counsel, a confession regularly made about Judah and why it was sent into exile.[16] As prisoners they had been forced to do hard labor to the point of exhaustion and "their hearts were bowed down." Again we have the refrain, here at v. 13 "then they cried to the Lord." In this case we are told God saved them from their distress by bringing them into the light, having broken their shackles. So once more we have the exhortation from the psalmist at vv. 15–16, "so let them thank the Lord for his mercy," and clearly here it is mercy that is involved as these were violators of God's Law. But the exhortation remains identical in its first line, again mentioning his wonderful works for the sons of Adam. The second line however is distinct, "for he shatters the doors of bronze, and cuts in two the bars of iron."

Verses 17–22 presents us with yet another scenario. The Hebrew calls this group "fools," but because of the word healed in v. 20, some translations have "some were sick because of their sinful ways." This is probably wrong because we are also told that because of their iniquity, they endured affliction, came to loath any sort of food, and as a result "drew near to the gates of death." But . . . "then they cried to the Lord in their trouble and he saved them." Verse 20 is interesting, for it says God sent out his word and healed them, and delivered them from self-destruction. Once again at v. 21 the psalmist thus exhorts this group to thank the Lord for his mercy and for his wonderful works for the sons of Adam. As Brueggemann and Bellinger suggest, "wonderful works" refer to miracles that lie "outside the capacity and understand-

15. Goldingay, Psalms: Volume 3, 251.
16. Longman, Psalms, 376.

ing of Israel."[17] For the first time, in v. 22 the psalmist also exhorts that they should offer sacrifices of thanksgiving and tell of their rescue in songs of joy.

Verses 23–32 is about sailors who do business on the seas (cf. Isa 42:10), but unfortunately encountered a great storm on the sea, wrought by God himself, indeed it says, "they saw the deeds of the Lord," for it was God who brought the mighty winds and caused the great waves, and the ship went up and down with the great swells, and the crew staggered around on deck like drunken sailors. When finally they were at their wits end, "they cried to the Lord in their trouble . . . and he made the storm to be still, and the waves of the sea were hushed" (cf. Jonah 1:11–12). They were thankful for the peace and quiet, and on top of that God led them into a safe haven. Cue the identical refrain (cf. vv. 8, 15, 21, 31) with the additional new line, "let them extol him in the congregation of the people, and praise him in the assembly of the elders."

Mays is right to point out that while other psalms deal with prayers for help with a terminal illness (cf. Psalms 6, 38, 88), and possibly one other for imprisonment (Psalm 142), none but this one includes prayer caused by hunger and thirst during a journey or peril at sea. In other words, this variety seems to especially suit the experiences of exiles dispersed all over the place. In addition, "the language of God as redeemer and the returnees as the redeemed is characteristic of Isaiah 40–66 (e.g., Isa 51:10; 62:12; 63:4, 35:9)."[18]

Through with human tales of woe, the psalmist in vv. 33–42 turns to talking about God's almighty actions. He can turn rivers into a desert, fruitful land into a salt waste "due to the wickedness of its inhabitants" (see Sodom and Gomorrah, Genesis 18–19). But he can do the reverse, turning deserts into pools and springs of water, a place where the hungry can build a town and live, sowing fields, planting vineyards, increasing their herds of cattle. Does all this happen simply because these people are hard workers? No, the psalmist insists. Even in the case of the cattle, "by his blessing they multiply greatly and he does not let their cattle decrease." Even if (vv. 39–41) these same people are oppressed and brought low by wicked rulers (cf. Job 12:21a, 24b), God makes those princes wander in trackless wastes and raises up the needy out of their distressing situation and "makes their families like flocks," presumably meaning he makes them multiply.

17. Brueggemann and Bellinger, *Psalms*, 465.
18. Mays, *Psalms*, 345–46.

How should one react to the mighty responses of God to the prayers of a person in distress? The psalmist says that the upright see it and are glad, whereas the wicked say, "well hush my mouth"—their bad mouthing is stopped (cf. Job 5:11–16; 22:19a; 1 Sam 2:4–8). The psalm concludes with one final exhortation to everyone in v. 43, "Let those who are wise give heed to these things, and consider the mercy of the Lord." The call for meditation at the end is important. The psalmist believes that if one recognizes the pattern of God responding positively to urgent, earnest prayer, it should teach his audience a lesson, no matter how grave their circumstances, malady, danger, sins.[19] God will even rescue those who have grievously sinned against him, if they genuinely turn to him and ask for rescue.[20]

There is a balance in this psalm between God's almightiness and the human freedom to either respond positively or negatively to God. God's control over nature does not appear to mean he has predestined human nature and human responses to his overtures. "The accent on divine freedom in vv. 33–43 and on divine responsiveness in vv. 4–32 are both the subject of Israel's thanks and praise. Neither responsiveness without freedom, nor freedom without responsiveness would lead to gladness. But Israel, in its thanksgiving and doxology bears witness to this convergence that makes for life."[21] This psalm explodes the myth of human self-sufficiency, again and again.

Psalm 107 seems to have been especially important to Luke, for his speakers draw on several different verses of this psalm in its LXX form in the Gospel of Luke and Acts. We find evidence of Psalm 107:9b–10 in Luke 1:53a, 79; Psalm 107:3 at Luke 13:29 (a Q saying); and Psalm 107:20 at Acts 13:26.[22] We will start with the last reference first.

It makes perfect sense that Paul would draw on the LXX in a diaspora synagogue, and Psalm 107:20 (106 in the LXX) reads: "he sent out his word and healed them and rescued them from their corruption." The Hebrew is different as it has "destruction" as the last word in the verse. Notice that the word "corruption" occurs some four times at the heart of Paul's sermon (13:34–37) with v. 35 being especially crucial (see Psalm 15:10) because it is talking about Jesus not decaying in the grave, much as we heard in Peter's Pentecost speech in Acts 2. So when Paul refers in 13:26 to his message of salvation (a phrase alluding to

19. Terrien, *Psalms*, 740.
20. Longman, *Psalms*, 378.
21. Bruggemann and Bellinger, *Psalms*, 467.
22. See Doble, "The Psalms in Luke-Acts," 110.

God sending out his word/message) the real punch line comes in v. 35, which Psalm 107:20 in the LXX has prepared us for. God is one who rescues people from corruption.[23] *The argument really only works on the basis of the LXX rendering.*

Psalm 107:3 speaks about God gathering the diaspora from the east and the west and the north and the south, and interestingly, it is the Lukan rather than the Matthean form of the so-called Q saying found in Matthew 8:11 // Luke 13:29 that is closer to the original text in the Psalms. Luke has, "then people will come from east and west, from north and south and will eat in the Kingdom of God." Luke has already mentioned that Abraham and the prophets will be there for the big dinner (v. 35). The Matthean form of the saying lacks the "north and south" phrase. In neither Gospel version of this saying does the concept of God gathering people come up, rather they come on their own.[24] In both of the cases just discussed we are talking about an adaptation of Psalm 107, not a quotation; perhaps we can call it an echo.

Psalm 107:9b is basically quoted in Luke 1:53, which reads, "he has filled the hungry with good things," which in fact is closer to the Hebrew text, because the LXX focuses on the feeding of one person, not a broader application. The same can be said about Luke 1:79, which like Psalm 107:10 speaks of those who sit in darkness, those whom God brought out into the light of day.

The speech of Peter in Acts 10 alludes at v. 20 to the message that God sent to his people (see Ps 107:20a), and then he speaks about Jesus healing all who were oppressed (v. 38), which echoes Psalm 107:20b, "and healed them and delivered them from corruption." The echo in Acts 10 reveals that Peter, like Paul, regularly draws on the language of the Psalms to describe Christ and his ministry.

The account of Jesus asleep in a boat in a storm is found in Mark 4:35–41 // Matthew 8:23–27 // Luke 8:22–25. It seems apparent that this particular story owes more than a little to Psalm 107:23–32 (and perhaps other psalms), in fact Hays even suggests that the Markan version of the story reads like a midrash on that passage in Psalm 107. He points out that Mark provocatively leaves the rhetorical question, "Who then is this that even the wind and the sea obey him?" unanswered.[25] Who indeed.

The Markan story does not rush to answer the query, nor does Mark

---

23. See the discussion in ibid.
24. See Labahn, "The Psalms in Q," 58.
25. Hays, *Echoes of Scripture in the Gospels*, 66–67.

want his audience to do so. Mark intends to let the "who" question be raised in several forms, leading up to the great confession of Peter at the end of Mark 8. It is not so much that he expects his audience to hear the overtones of Psalm 107 and race back to the psalm to find that the answer is none other than God. No, from a narratival point of view, he is dropping hints that will not become answers for several more chapters in this Gospel, not least because this is the Gospel that is apocalyptic in character. Only divine revelation can make some things clear, like for instance the identity of Jesus.

But of course it is also true that those who knew the psalms well would likely find an allusion or echo here to Psalm 107, especially in the lines about his stilling the storm and hushing the wind and the happiness of the sailors when things quieted down and "he brought them to their desired haven."[26] The Markan story, and for that matter the Matthean parallel, raises the who question, but does not yet provide the answer.[27]

There is one final story which is a bit tantalizing and may owe something to Psalm 107. I am referring to the famous story of Paul and Barnabas singing psalms in jail in Philippi, and then an earthquake (presumably we are meant to think sent by God) leads to their release. We might also compare the angelic jailbreak of Peter in Acts 12:17, where Peter says directly that it was the Lord who extracted him from the prison. This of course is reminiscent of this passage, "some sat in darkness and in gloomy prisons in misery in irons . . . then they cried to the Lord in their trouble and he saved them from their distress, he brought them out." Acts 12:25 tells us that the apostles were both praying and singing hymns to God and the prisoners were listening to them. Could they have been praying and singing Psalm 107? Luke does not tell us, but the possibility might come to the mind of anyone in Luke's audience who knew the Psalms well. I am not suggesting that any of these gospel or Acts stories are created out of an imaginative reflection on the Psalms rather than on the basis of the Jesus and early Christians traditions. What I am suggesting is that the gospel writers definitely

---

26. There may be a slight echo of this in the somewhat different storm tale in John 6:16–21, particularly in the conclusion of it where it reads, "and immediately the boat reached the land towards which they were going."

27. It is something a shock that neither Watts nor Blomberg in the *Commentary on the New Testament Use of the Old Testament* have anything at all to say about the echoes of Psalm 107 in Mark 4 or Matthew 8. Oddly, Pao and Schnabel, "Luke," 308 in the same volume discuss a possible allusion to Jonah 1 (which they are unconvinced by), then they say that the Psalms are closer in character, often revealing Yahweh's mastery of the sea and wind, but completely fail to mention Psalm 107. Strange.

266

drew on the language of the Psalms again and again to articulate their narratives in biblical terms, including stories about both Jesus and his earliest followers. The Psalms provided a major source and resource for their lexicon of faith and the articulation of the gospel.

Whose Lord, Which Priest? Psalm 110

Certainly one of the briefest, but also most debated, of the psalms is Psalm 110. The psalm contains two divine oracles at v. 1 and v. 4, the very same two verses that show up in the NT in numerous places. Perhaps we are meant to think of a prophet who spoke these two oracles in worship that were later incorporated into this song.[28] In its original context the Lord who is speaking would be Yahweh, and "my lord" would be either king David or one of his successors, or in the postexilic period, the hope for a successor, which led to the messianic use of this psalm, both in the NT and elsewhere.

The superscript connects this psalm with David and makes clear that not just any kind of Israelite king from any ethnic extraction was in view. What is distinctive about these proclamations is the connection of the king with a priesthood, not the Aaronic priesthood, or the Levitical priesthood or any other familiar Israelite priesthood, but with a priesthood of the mysterious and shadowy figure of Melchizedek, whose very name means righteous king. It is well to remember that this is a song, but it is a song that contains prophetic oracles in it, which made it a natural candidate to be treated as a prophecy as well as a song. The action in the psalm is largely taken by Yahweh on behalf of the king spoken of and his people.

The psalm basically divides into four parts: (1) initial oracle (v. 1); (2) action based on the installation of the king (vv. 2–3); (3) second oracle (v. 4); (4) action based on the promises made to the king (vv. 5–7). It should be noted that there is a concern about not only establishing the monarchy, but also establishing some sort of priesthood. Israel's kings were of a separate order from Israel's priests, indeed a separate tribe, whether we think of the Aaronic or Levitical or Zadokite priesthoods. David was of none of these tribes, which is presumably why he or his successor in his hereditary line is associated with a priesthood that never had a role before in the Davidic monarchy. The language of the first oracle, and indeed of much that follows it, is very much like the language of the oracle in Isa 45:1–2, "thus says Yahweh to his

---

28. See Goldingay, *Psalms: Volume 3*, 291.

anointed one, whom he holds by the hand . . . he will throw down the nations before him."[29]

The story of Melchizedek is of course found in Genesis 14 and is a story connected with the patriarchal period, and specifically with Abraham in a tumultuous period in his life where there is much fighting and Abraham's relatives have to be rescued. In exactly three verses, Genesis 14:18–20, Melchizedek the king of Salem (possibly Jerusalem well before it was David's capital city; see Josh 18:21) appears, brings out bread and wine, blesses Abraham, and Abraham tithes to him, giving him one-tenth of all the booty taken in the military conflict with Chedorlamer, and the kings of the east allied with him (v. 17). We are told nothing about Melchizedek's background and with v. 20 he disappears entirely from the pages of the narrative. This very way of telling the story led to all sorts of speculation as to who indeed he might have been (on which see below). His sudden appearance in Psalm 110:4 comes as something of a shock. What was the need to connect the Davidic king with this specific mysterious priest-king Melchizedek? Inquiring minds want to know.

As Brueggemann and Bellinger suggest, the fact that Psalm 110 appears after Psalm 89, which seems to reflect the fall of the Davidic monarchy, made it natural to see this psalm as reaffirming hopes for the restoration of the Davidic monarchy.[29] But who would have been speaking the two divine oracles, and to whom? To the king? To the postexilic community as a whole as a promise of restoration? It is hard to answer these questions. Was there a prophet who spoke in the worship service, a prophet whose oracles were incorporated later into a song, and then repeated by the worship leader as part of the song? According to Longman, recent research has provided evidence, precedents, where in the Assyrian royal situation a prophet would speak at the temple to the king.[30] Was there a prophet like Nathan who regularly spoke in temple worship? It is possible. Besides those who have suggested this is a coronation ode, à la Psalm 2,[31] others have suggested that it is a "battle hymn" sung in preparation for battle. The latter seems more plausible. In any case, the writers of the NT were no doubt thankful for this brief song, as it would appear Jesus was as well, since he cites the beginning of it as a word from David himself.

---

29. Brueggemann and Bellinger, *Psalms*, 479. See also Mays, *Psalms*, 353.
30. Longman, *Psalms*, 381.
31. See e.g., Weiser, *The Psalms*, p. 693, and see 2 Kgs 11:14, 23:3.

MT Psalm 110	LXX Psalm 109
1 The Lord says to my lord, "Sit at my right hand until I make your enemies your footstool." 2 The Lord sends out from Zion your mighty scepter. Rule in the midst of your foes.	1 Pertaining to David. A Psalm. The Lord said to my lord, "Sit on my right until I make your enemies a footstool for your feet." 2 A rod of your power the Lord will send out from Zion. And exercise dominion in the midst of your enemies!
3 Your people will offer themselves willingly on the day you lead your forces on the holy mountains. From the womb of the morning, like dew, your youth will come to you. 4 The Lord has sworn and will not change his mind, "You are a priest forever according to the order of Melchizedek." 5 The Lord is at your right hand; he will shatter kings on the day of his wrath.	3 With you is rule on a day of your power among the splendors of the holy ones. From the womb, before Morning-star, I brought you forth. 4 The Lord swore and will not change his mind, "You are a priest forever according to the order of Melchizedek." 5 The Lord at your right shattered kings on day of his wrath.
6 He will execute judgment among the nations, filling them with corpses; he will shatter heads over the wide earth. 7 He will drink from the stream by the path; therefore he will lift up his head.	6 He will judge among the nations, will make full with corpses he will shatter heads on the land of many 7 From a wadi by a road he will drink; therefore he will raise head high.

This song, in both its parts, promises that God will deal with the king's enemies. Only here in the OT do we find the phrase "oracle of the Lord" at the beginning of a sentence, though we do find something similar at the end of a poem in Isa 56:8 and Num 24:3, 4, 15, 16.[32] Two lords though will be involved: Yahweh and his king, who is his earthly representative. The promise to make the human king's enemies his footstool probably refers to placing them in the posture of submission, having been conquered by the king. It was the practice of antiquity for a conquering king to symbolize his victory by having the conquered general or king kneel, bow down, and the king would put a foot on the neck of the conquered one, a symbol of complete domination, involving the shaming of the opponent. For example, we have images of the Assyrian king doing this very thing (see below).[33] The Romans had a simi-

---

32. Terrien, *Psalms*, 751.

lar practice called *sub iugum missum* in which the conquered would bow down and pass under a low bar made of a spear, indicating their submission.

That God will act did not mean the king was *not* to act against his enemies, it meant that God would be with him when he went into battle. The king is still to lead his forces (v. 3) into the fray. Verse 3 also suggests that the ruler (and his troops?) will suddenly feel as he did in the days of his youth, adrenaline pumping as he leads the troops into battle.[34] Notice that clearly the message is for and about the Davidic king because "the Lord sends out from Zion, your mighty scepter." As Brueggemann and Bellinger point out, the king does not have independent authority and power, he himself has a lord and his own power and authority is derived from the most high king, Yahweh.[35]

Whereas the first oracle simply has "the Lord says" (v. 1), the second one says "The Lord has sworn and will not change his mind" (cf. Amos 4:2; 6:8). The person being addressed is told he will be a forever priest, but surprisingly according to the order of Melchizedek. This has confused many, since 1 Sam 13:8–15 suggests that kings should not meddle in priestly matters, but perhaps that is why God swears an oath in this case, because the demand is unexpected. Yes, occasionally David acted like a priest (2 Samuel 6) but it was rare, and not his regular task.

While v. 1 has the king sitting at God's right hand, in v. 5 we are told that the Lord is at "your right hand" or, as we would put it, "your right hand man," with the king in all things, making sure judgment is

---

33. See rightly ibid., 752; Weiser, *Psalms*, 694. This image is of Tiglath-pileser III standing over an enemy. (Bas-relief from the Central Palace at Nimrud).
34. In view of the mention of "youth" I think it is unlikely this verse has to do with the birth and origins of the king, though clearly that is how the LXX takes it, because it translates it "from the womb . . . I brought you forth." Weiser, *Psalms*, 695 suggests that it refers to the youthful volunteers for the army, but the grammar suggests it is the king who is being referenced.
35. Brueggemann and Bellinger, *Psalms*, 479–80.

executed on the enemies of the ruler, indeed on their nations. Verse 7 is very interesting, for in all of vv. 5–7 God (or is it the king?) is portrayed as the divine warrior, who, like the warriors Gideon picked in Judges 7:4–8, is always scanning the horizon for trouble even when he leans down to slake his thirst from a clear stream by the path. Terrien suggests that the two clauses in the final verse are causal in nature, "he drinks from the stream along the way, *therefore* he raises up his head."[36] He is probably right that the last gesture has to do with victory, and so the phrase "lifting up the head" would be a sign of honor like "lifting up the face."

It was possible that on occasion the Davidic king would assume some priestly functions, but apparently not on a regular basis, perhaps, for instance, on Yom Kippur, the day of national mourning for sins, but notice the whole rest of the second part of this psalm is not about the king and his priestly duties, but more about the king and Yahweh as warriors.[37] What might be overlooked is that since the Davidic king would indeed be the king who reigns from Jerusalem, and since he also might on occasion fulfill a priestly role, it was not all that shocking to suggest that the Davidic king, like Melchizedek who was *once the ruler in Salem*, would also be a priest like that ancient figure from the time of Abraham. "There are things that are achieved by the combining of powers in one person. Politics and war are not allowed to escape from the context of the people's relationship with God."[38]

Some have thought that v. 7 refers to a ritual of drinking from the Gihon spring (1 Kgs 1:38) in Jerusalem as a part of a coronation ritual, but this ill-suits the context in which the remark is made—a military context.[39] The other possibility is that the image in v. 7 is of the king, after the heat of battle, pausing to drink because his foes had been vanquished and he did not need to be vigilant any more, but rather could now "raise his head high" instead of ducking for cover.[40]

Finally, it is important to note the universalizing of the context in v. 6: God will give the king victories not just over local tribal enemies, but "among the nations" and across "the wide earth." This is poetic hyperbole if this was originally directed to David or even the later Davidic monarchy, but as so often with the universalizing language, the

---

36. Terrien, *Psalms*, 753 (emphasis original).
37. Goldingay, *Psalms: Volume 3*, 296–97.
38. Ibid., 299.
39. But see Hans-Joachim Kraus, *Psalms 60–150: A Commentary*, CC (Minneapolis: Augsburg, 1989), 352.
40. Weiser, *Psalms*, 697, realizes that the logical antecedent here is the king, though he is confused about the verse's meaning. More insightful is Mays, *Psalms*, 352.

early Christians were able to make good use of such verbiage to make clear that Jesus was David's greater son, indeed even David's Lord.

In OT times this might be thought to refer to the Yom Yahweh, the day of God's final judgment of the nations, whereas in the NT it was referred to the second coming of Christ for final judgment.[41]

To say that Psalm 110:1 comes up a lot in the NT, and its various occurrences have been scrutinized and analyzed many times, is an understatement. This is so not least because it shows up all over the NT (Matt 22:44; Mark 14:62; Luke 22:69; Acts 2:34–35; 7:55; Rom 8:34; Eph 1:20, Col 3:1; Heb 1:3, 13; 8:1; 10:12; 1 Pet 3:22; and more). It is obviously important not least because it has been said to be the *only* OT passage of any kind that directs a human being to sit at God's right hand.[42] In every case, the psalm is put to christological use.[43] Luther even calls it the main OT messianic text that deals with Christ.[44]

To understand some of the significance of this material, one needs to realize that in antiquity the symbolism of right hand and left hand, a symbolism that lasted well into modernity, was as follows: to be on someone's right hand was a place of favor and blessing, and if you were to the right of a king or lord of some sort, that was the highest position of honor and authority and power other than that held by the king, or deity, himself. Literally on the other hand, "left hand" had a negative valence, indeed being on the left in general had a negative valence (cf., e.g., the parable of the sheep and goats in Matt 25:31–46). Indeed this symbolism still exists today in the cliché "my right hand man." The word *sinistra* in Latin (and Italian) means "left" and it is the word from which we get the English term "sinister." So when Yahweh invites the king to sit at his right hand, or later Christians talk about Christ being at the right hand of God the Father in heaven, they are ascribing the highest possible position and status to that person other than the status of the one who made the invitation in the first place. The person at the right hand of a king was empowered to carry out the king's will and policies.

---

41. See Weiser, *Psalms*, 696. For an argument that takes the hyperbole as actually meant literally with the psalm involving David musing about a future messianic king see Blomberg, "Matthew," 83. While I would not completely rule this out, it seems to fail to take into account the nature of this poetic language, which is definitely and regularly prone to hyperbole, as we have seen in various places in this study.

42. See, rightly, Pao and Schnabel, "Luke," 391.

43. Two useful places to start to see how Ps 110:1 has been discussed in NT studies are David M. Hay, *Glory at the Right Hand: Psalm 110 in Early Christianity*, SBLMS 18 (Nashville: Abingdon Press, 1973); and Martin Hengel, *Studies in Early Christology* (Edinburgh: T&T Clark, 1995), 185–214.

44. See Mays, *Psalms*, 350.

Let us first consider the numerous uses of Psalm 110:1 in the Gospels and Acts, where a pattern emerges.[45] We must begin with the use in the Synoptics, particularly in Mark 12:46 (and 14:62) // Matthew 22:44 (and 26:64) // Luke 20:42 (and 22:69) // Acts 2:34. In each case the quotation appears in speech material. The pericope in the Gospels reveals Jesus going on the offensive after having waded through a barrage of queries and barbed comments in what have been called the four temple controversies. Jesus decides to question his interlocutor's understanding of Psalm 110:1 vis à vis the issue of the messiah.

The citation in Mark seems to be following the LXX version except that it deletes the phrase "the footstool of" and instead has "under" possibly under the influence of Psalm 8:9, which may have affected the Pauline and Petrine renderings as well (see below).[46] A further rather clear sign that the LXX is being followed is because the Hebrew text distinguishes the speaker from the one spoken to by using two different words, whereas in the Greek κύριος is used in both cases, the difference between the two lords being signaled through the syntax rather than the word choice.[47]

However, and it is a big however, if Jesus was speaking in Aramaic he could easily have quoted Psalm 110:1 and included the word play (*'amar marya lemari*).[48] The assumption being made by Jesus in regard to his interlocutors is that they would both agree or at least allow that one of these lords is likely to be the messiah, in particular the second one whom the psalmist, assumed to be David here (not some prophet talking to David on behalf of Yahweh), calls "my lord." Thus Jesus asks the inevitable question, If David himself calls the messiah his lord, how is it adequate to merely talk about the messiah being the descendant of David? This suggests a much more exalted role for the messiah than

---

45. See Dale Brueggemann's helpful chart in Appendix C below. Goldingay, *Psalms: Volume 3*, 292, is right that the whole of this psalm cannot be applied to Christ, and to their credit, the NT writers do not attempt to do so. However, when he claims that the NT use of this psalm requires a meaning that would not correspond to its meaning in any OT context, this is not quite correct or fair. The psalm speaks of the king in an exalted way, and while the NT use goes beyond what we find here in the psalm, it certainly doesn't go *against it* in significant ways, as the messianic use of the psalm in early Judaism also makes evident. In both Psalm 110 and in the NT "the Lord" is Yahweh. That the "my lord" in the former case is the ancient Davidic king as addressed by a priest or prophet, and that in the NT it is Jesus is again just an extension of the royal treatment to a latter day Davidide. What gives the use by Jesus in Mark 12 an ironic twist is that Jesus is stressing that it is David himself who has composed this psalm, so "my lord" indirectly becomes David's lord, rather than referring to David himself.

46. See Menken, "The Psalms in Matthew's Gospel," 74.

47. See Attridge, "The Psalms in Hebrews," 197–99.

48. See the discussion in Pao and Schnabel, "Luke," 372 who is following the suggestion of Joseph Fitzmyer.

just being the descendant of King David. Watts is however probably right that Jesus is not querying the Davidic descent of the messiah, he is simply saying that seeing the messiah that way is inadequate, not inaccurate.[49] But there is an important difference between the implications of this discussion and those in Acts (see below). In Acts one can conclude Jesus is David's lord now because he has been raised from the dead and ascended to the right hand of God. But here in the first such discussion of Psalm 110:1, Jesus seems to be implying that the messiah is inherently David's lord, with or without resurrection and ascension.[50]

The "seated at the right hand" portion of Psalm 110:1 also shows up in those other texts listed above. In the case of Mark 14:62 and parallels, Psalm 110:1 is combined with the son of man material from Daniel 7:13–14 to explain not only that Jesus will be at God's right hand after his death, but he will coming back to judge the Jewish authorities, and indeed the world, in the future. Possibly one impetus that led to this sort of combination of texts is the possible reference to the Yom Yahweh in Psalm 110, now predicated of Jesus in the Gospels. Note that it is not Jesus's claim to be "the son of the blessed" that leads to the charge of blasphemy in Mark 14. Jews didn't think of the messiah as a divine figure. No, it was the claim to be the Son of Man who sits at God's right hand in heaven and will come on the clouds for judgment, taking the role predicated of God in all those Yom Yahweh traditions in the Psalms and the prophets.

Acts 2:32–35 is of course different because it is speaking about a situation after the death, resurrection, and ascension of Jesus, the latter of which is so prominently featured in both Luke 24 and Acts 1.[51] Peter's speech assumes the exaltation of Jesus to God's right hand happened as a result of the ascension of Jesus to heaven, and so he is able to make a further contrast with David: not only was David not "my lord" in that psalm, neither did he ascend bodily into heaven as Jesus did. Thus, a further theological point could be made about Jesus after his death and the events that ensued thereafter. Romans 8:38 also has this sequence: raised, now sits at the right hand of God in heaven, as does Ephesian 1:20, which goes so far as to say that God seated him at his right hand, indicating God's value judgment on Jesus.[52] Different is 1

49. Watts, "Psalms in Mark's Gospel," 39.
50. But see the discussion in Hays, *Echoes of Scripture in the Gospels*, 233, on the Acts discussion.
51. See the discussion in Marshall, "Acts," 542.
52. See Thielman, "Ephesians," 815.

Corinthians 15:25, where Paul suggests that after Jesus returns to earth at the parousia, he must reign on earth until he puts all his enemies under his feet (cf. similarly 1 Enoch 51:3; 55:4; 61:8; 62:2 and especially 11QMelch 13, which says Melchizedek will return to preside over the final judgment of the nations).[53] Thus Psalm 110:1b suddenly is given a christological twist in this text with the aide of Psalm 8:9.[54]

We must deal at some length with the way the author of Hebrews spins out his unique christology chiefly on the basis of Psalm 110:4, but it is in order first to notice his use of Psalm 110:1 and the structural role it plays in his arguments. Here Attridge is of assistance. Psalm 110:1 appears as a theme verse, as it were, signaling Christ's exaltation to the right hand of God the Father in heaven. This is alluded to in Hebrews 1:3 ("took a seat at the right hand of the Majesty on high"), appears again at Hebrews 1:13 in explicit citation as part of a catena of citations ("sit at my right hand until I make your enemies a footstool for your feet"), a further allusion shows up at Hebrews 8:1 in a summary statement about what preceded in the discourse, and in another summary passage at 10:12 there is a further allusion to Psalm 110:1. Finally, at the climax of his discourse in Hebrews 12 we hear at v. 2 "having endured the cross, despising its shame, he took a seat at the right hand of the throne of God." By contrast, the use of Psalm 110:4 is mainly clustered in Hebrews 5–7, though the idea is further developed in Hebrews 8–10.[55] It is assumed that both the divine oracles in Psalm 110:1 and 4 are addressed by the Father to the Son. And our author is clearly enough drawing on a long tradition of Jewish reflection on the meaning of the Melchizedek story, including the assumption that since we are not told where he came from or what happened to him after meeting Abraham, these silences may suggest he was an eternal priest (see Heb 7:3).[56]

The use of Psalm 110:4 requires extended treatment, not least because the author of Hebrews has used that Scripture as a major jumping off point to develop his whole christological vision of Jesus.

53. See Ciampa and Rosner, "1 Corinthians," 745.
54. See Williams, "Psalms in 1 and 2 Corinthians," 170–72. 1 Pet 3:22 also has the reference to being seated at the right hand of God, but in addition the mention is made of angels, authorities, and powers being already subjected by God to him. This is different from the subjection of the enemies after Jesus returns to earth. See Woan, "Psalms in 1 Peter," 226. The *Commentary on the New Testament Use of the Old Testament* does not deal with this allusion in 1 Pet 3:22.
55. See Attridge, "Psalms in Hebrews," 209.
56. See Fred L. Horton, *The Melchizedek Tradition: A Critical Examination of the Sources to the Fifth Century A.D. and in the Epistle to the Hebrews*, SNTSMS 30 (Cambridge: Cambridge University Press, 1976). On all this see the discussion in Attridge, "Psalms in Hebrews," 197–99.

Let's be clear that he was hardly the only learned early Jew in the first century CE wondering about and reflecting on the Melchizedek story (cf. Josephus, *Ant.* 1.180; Philo *Leg.* 3.79–82).[57] In fact, there were some stunningly creative things written in early Judaism about the story in Genesis 14, for example b. t. San. 108b tells us that it was Abraham, no less, that sat at God's right hand while he defeated the kings opposing the patriarch!

The one truly unique concept in this document called Hebrews which makes it stand out from all other NT documents is our author's vision of Christ as the heavenly high priest of the Melchizedekian order. If one has an understanding of this major issue most of the rest of the homily falls into place rather readily. It is difficult to say what sparked our author to write about Christ in this way. It may have been his penetrating study of the OT and its institutions. He may have been looking for a way to say that Christ fulfilled their intention and indeed eclipsed and replaced them. But it is also possible that he was familiar with the varieties of messianic speculation in early Judaism, which at Qumran and perhaps elsewhere included the idea of a priestly messiah.[58]

Whatever his state of knowledge of the speculation about a priestly messiah, our author certainly goes beyond what we know of these concepts from these other sources, for he is going to insist not only that messiah died, but that he was both the perfect high priest and unblemished sacrifice offered by the priest. There was also, of course, a Melchizedek speculation before the time of Jesus, as the Qumran documents show clearly enough. There was then certainly a Jewish speculation about messiah being a priest before our author wrote.

When our author wishes to describe Jesus as high priest he uses as his basis the messianic interpretation of Genesis 14 and Psalm 110:4. Now it must be understood that the whole idea of priesthood in the OT is dependent on the idea of covenant. The shape that a priesthood takes depends on the shape and stipulations of the covenant or treaty that God's people are called upon to live by. The way our author is going to show that the Levitical priesthood is obsolescent is by showing: (1)

---

57. On this see Watts, "The Psalms in Mark's Gospel," *The Psalms in the NT*, 37.

58. Not surprisingly the literature on this subject is vast, most of it focusing on Hebrews 7. See, e.g., Robert H. Culpepper, "The High Priesthood and Sacrifice of Christ in the Epistle to the Hebrews," *TTE* 32 (1985): 46–62; Horton, *Melchizedek Tradition*; Jerome H. Neyrey, "'Without Beginning of Days or End of Life' (Hebrews 7.3): Topos for a True Deity," *CBQ* 53 (1991): 439–55; Deborah W. Rooke, "Jesus as Royal Priest: Reflections on the Interpretation of the Melchizedek Tradition in Heb. 7," *Bib* 81 (2000): 81–94.

there was a higher and prior priesthood in the case of Melchizedek, and Jesus is connected to that sort of priesthood, which is an eternal one; (2) the very fact that the Levitical priesthood is linked to heredity (and thus is dependent on death and descendants to determine who will next be priest) is in our author's mind a clear sign of the inadequacy of the Levitical priesthood; (3) the inferiority of the Levitical priesthood is also shown by the fact that Abraham the forebear of Levi was blessed by and tithed to Melchizedek.

In all of this our author, like Jesus before him, operates with the idea that the earlier idea or institution has precedence and thus higher claim to authority. But a text like Hebrews 7:27 or 9:28 makes quite clear that our author is no slave to previous concepts, for he goes on to talk of Jesus voluntarily offering himself up as sacrifice. Hebrews 9:28 seems to refer to Isaiah 53:12, and perhaps more than any other NT writer, except perhaps the author of 1 Peter, our author has been affected by reflection on Isaiah 53.

It is quite true also that from texts like 4 Maccabees 6:29 there was the idea that a martyr such as a Maccabee could offer an atoning sacrifice, and in the case of Eleazar he was a priest. Yet there is a difference here, for a death as atonement is not quite the same as a deliberate sacrifice of atonement, and more to the point, the Maccabean concept is tied up with the idea of the suffering of the righteous, which doesn't seem to be in the foreground here. Our author operates out of the concept of cultic sacrifice, not martyrdom for a cause, per se.

One of the essential elements in understanding the high priestly concept in Hebrews is that the Son of God had to be a human being to be a priest. In other words, all of this reflection on Christ as high priest tells us a lot about his perfect humanity and his human roles, but very little if anything about his divinity. The latter ideas are bound up with our author's presentation of Jesus as also God's unique and preexistent Son and Word. Jesus is the perfect human being, and thus is the perfect candidate to be a perfect sacrifice. But he is also a perfect high priest and thus is the perfect one to freely offer such a sacrifice, and when he does, so he himself is perfected in his intended vocation. It is not that his going to heaven perfects him in any moral sense, but what is meant is that he completes his vocation to perfection. The language of perfection in application to Christ is sometimes thought to be cultic (i.e., in terms of consecration rather than moral sanctification) but I am not at all convinced on this score. Yet it is also true that in this homily we learn of Jesus's moral perfection as well, for he was tempted like all humans in every regard save without sin. This resistance to sin is conceived of as part of the way he fulfilled his vocation and so could be both perfect high priest and sacrifice.

But there is more to this than one might imagine, for in fact Christ is able to forgive sins and be the perfecter/completer of faithfulness for believers, leading them on to maturity/completion in their vocation not only because he was in a position to have compassion knowing their temptations, but also because he successfully passed such tests so that he was in a position to judge sin and offer forgiveness, which he himself did not need to receive.

Now the claim that Jesus was sinless is not very meaningful unless it includes the notion that he voluntarily and willingly resisted temptation, that is, that it was possible for him to have done otherwise. By definition temptation is not tempting unless one is actually inclined and could attempt to do what one is tempted to do. Thus we must take seriously statements such as we find in Hebrews 2:17 or 4:15 and assume that Jesus was subject to all the common temptations, including sexual ones, that we are, yet he had the victory over them.

We are also told at Hebrews 5:8 that Jesus learned obedience. This of course means he learned through experience, and it may be that he knew it prior to that conceptually, but the point is that Jesus as a human learned things through experience just as we do. His life manifested a normal development and progressive consciousness. What is the connection between learning obedience through death and being made perfect through suffering? Simply this: that Jesus fulfilled God's will for his life that he die on Golgotha and so he completed the task that would not have been made perfect and complete without that death.

Now our author is able to talk of Jesus as a human being having faith (12:2), indeed being our pioneer or model for faith and faithfulness. One of the key things that sets apart Jesus's work as high priest from all previous such attempts is the unique character of his sacrifice. It is said to be *once for all time*, unlike the previous repeated sacrifices (which shows that they at most only had temporary and limited efficacy, and in fact it appears our author would dispute they even had that value). There is a great deal in Hebrews that could lead one to the conclusion that our author was antiritual, and or that he has spiritualized the very material promises in the OT about rest, land, and other things. Against this sort of conclusion it must be argued that our author in fact maintains that there is only one sacrifice that is and was truly cultic, the sacrifice of the human will of Jesus, and by extension the call for believers to make that same sort of sacrifice through the praise of their lips and lives (cf. Hebrews 13). It is not the abolition of ritual but its perfection in human form that our author is about, for God ultimately wants the obedience and self-giving of humans, the highest form of his creation, the only form of it that can be in personal relation with its maker, the only form of it which could have Psalm 8 spoken about it. Furthermore, our author does not simply spiritualize the OT like say, Philo does in the service of his higher philosophy. Quite the contrary, our author believes that God's promises are now fulfilled in heaven, but that *that* reality will one day come to earth as well and transform earth. Nor is our author's perspective simply that the OT merely has to do with externals and imperfection. Our author says nothing of the OT being imperfect, he does say it is partial, piecemeal, shadow, and inadequate finally to deal with human sin. But one must also remember he sees the essential spiritual promises of God such as those found in Jeremiah 31 in the OT, and furthermore there is the whole matter of the eternal priesthood of Melchizedek who is more than a mere shadow, he is a likeness of Christ.

Our author's complaint is not with the OT per se nor with ritual per se but with a particular ritual system, the Levitical one, which was inadequate. He never says it was bad or incorrect in its intent, just inadequate to meet human needs. Our author's terminology when he discusses old and new is comparative, not merely positive: the old is a shadow in comparison to the new reality in Christ. Yet there is of course the matter of discontinuity as well, the once for all aspect (Heb 9:12). This means that Jesus not only fulfills all the OT priesthood, but he goes beyond it and overcomes its inadequacy.

What is striking about all this high priest language is that our author in this one concept has a way to bridge both the earthly and heavenly work of Christ, for Christ offers the sacrifice on earth, then takes the blood into the heavenly sanctuary, and intercedes for believers on an ongoing basis, as well as proclaiming sins forgiven. Herein we see the picture of the OT priest sacrificing the animal outside the temple, then taking the blood and pouring it on the altar, and going into the holy of holies on Yom Kippur, and then coming back out and pronouncing forgiveness of sins and reconciliation between God and his people.

It is the genius of our author's conceptualizing of things that he is able to bridge the past and the ongoing work of Jesus for believers, as a human being. Our author does seem to operate with the well-known ancient concept of the earth as the vestibule of the heavenly sanctuary. One enters the heavenly sanctuary by passing through the earthly one, and he envisions the sacrifice of Christ as offered in that earthly portico of the heavenly sanctuary, after which he enters into the sanctuary with the blood to sprinkle. Of course the analogy with OT practice should not be pressed too far. Does our author really think Jesus took a bowl of his blood with him to heaven? Is there really an altar or curtain in heaven where he sprinkled it? Probably not, but the point is that Jesus affected on earth and in heaven what these ritual acts symbolized: atonement for sin, placation of God's wrath, cleansing of the sinner, reconciliation with God. He conveys these profound concepts by using the OT picture language.

In contrast to earthly priests Jesus is a priest forever, thus forestalling anyone else ever being, or needing to be a priest in this sense. Christ is a priest forever because he lives forever, and as 7:25 says, he always lives to make intercession for believers. Oscar Cullmann sums up his masterful investigation of Christ as high priest in Hebrews by saying the following: "the High Priest concept offers a full Christology in every respect. It includes all three fundamental aspects of Jesus' work: his once for all earthly work, his present work as the exalted Lord, and his future work as the one coming again. Yesterday, today and forever."[59]

In closing one might wish to ask how the second coming fits into this schema. The answer intimated by our author is that the high priest had to come forth again from the temple to proclaim to the people the results of his work and the benefits. So also Christ will come again from the heavenly sanctuary. Thus we see the single most comprehensive christological concept in the NT, which exalts the perfect human work of Christ, the believer's high priest. What was the font of all this remarkable conceptualization? Psalm 110:1 and 4.[60]

The Torah From A to Z: Psalm 119

Psalm 119 is by far the longest song in the Psalter. It has no prescript and some may be forgiven for saying it has no end, as it just keeps ringing the changes of a series of Hebrew words related to the word com-

---

59. Oscar Cullman, *The Christology of the New Testament*, rev. ed. (Philadelphia: Westminster, 1964), 103–4.
60. For a full discussion of Richard Bauckham's important treatment of the implications of predicating Ps 110:1 of Christ in terms of his place in the divine identity see Appendix D.

mandment (מִצְוָה *miṣwâ*): word (דְּבָר *dābār*), decree (עֵדוּת *ʿēdût*), statute (חֹק *ḥōq*), precept (פִּקֻּד *piqûd*), law (תּוֹרָה *tôrâ*), judgment (מִשְׁפָּט *mišpāṭ*), even promise (אִמְרָה *ʾimrâ*).[61] Of all these terms the term *tôrâ* is the most general (appearing twenty-five times in the psalm, with judgments second at twenty-three times and commandments third most frequent at twenty-two times), and the rest refer to sentences, sayings, commands of various sorts that provide instruction.[62]

This poem is an alphabet acrostic, by which I mean there are twenty-two sections of eight verses each, matching the twenty-two letters in the Hebrew alphabet, and the first word of each line of each section begins with the appropriate letter of the alphabet: paragraph one with *aleph*, paragraph two with *bet*, and so on. If you are going to do eight lines on each letter of the alphabet, then inevitably you end up with 176 lines or verses. What might seem like redundancy to us is meaningful repetition meant to help the listener memorize and learn the meaning and purpose of torah. It is to be studied, learned, memorized, chewed over, meditated on, discussed, debated, shared, proclaimed, lived. This is a long song, but then learning God's ways and precepts is a lifetime journey because there is so much to learn and to do. It is possible, as Longman suggests, that each stanza has eight lines because of the eight different words used to speak about this subject.[63] Note however that just five of these twenty-two stanzas employ all eight Hebrew words, but none of them use less than six of these words. As Goldingay says, the psalmist is not interested in creating perfectly symmetrical stanzas, showing once again "OT psalmody's preference for leaving poetic patterns not quite perfectly realized rather than absolutely complete."[64] I would suggest that this lack of symmetry is because content was more important than mere form to the psalmist. He is trying to teach something, not merely create something with per-

---

61. Brueggemann and Bellinger, *Psalms*, 519 say, "it is also notoriously rated to be boring, repetitious and without plot development" (cf. the complaint by Weiser, *Psalms*, 739). This is forgetting that repetition is the hallmark of music that wants to be remembered. It is also forgetting that not all songs are story songs, many are concept songs, and this is one of those. The psalm should not be criticized for things it's not trying to be, e.g., a story or a discourse. These scholars however know this and say that the psalm is attempting comprehensiveness on the issue of torah piety. For a better assessment of this psalm's merits see James L. Mays, "The Place of Torah-Psalms in the Psalter," *JBL* 106 (1987): 3–12. Also see Patrick D. Miller, *Israelite Religion and Biblical Theology: Collected Essays*, JSOTSup 267 (Sheffield: Sheffield Academic, 2000), 319–36.
62. Mays, *Psalms*, 382. Terrien, *Psalms*, 804, has an answer for those complaining there is no story or "salvation history" in this long song, "Truth anticipates all stories of revelation in Israel: no Sinai, no Moses, no Samuel, no prophet. Just God's word at creation." On the number of times these various terms related to torah occur in the psalm, see ibid., 806.
63. Longman, *Psalms*, 403.
64. Goldingay, *Psalms: Volume 3*, 378.

fect form. This psalm is rightly seen as a wisdom psalm like Psalm 1 and Psalm 19, but perhaps it will be helpful to say that at this juncture, commandments were seen as one form of God's wisdom and wise instruction and by no means the only form.

When the Hebrew text was translated into Greek, and *tôrâ* was rendered as νόμος, the semantic range narrowed to something more like a "law" laid down, and sometimes the wisdom context and content got lost—all the more so after the destruction of the Temple in CE 70, when the Jewish focus necessarily narrowed from territory, temple, and torah, to simply torah. It is safe to say that for this psalmist the notion of onerous dictatorial rules or legalism is nowhere in sight when he extols God's instruction and teachings. Indeed, for him ruminating on torah was like eating a piece of bread with the very best honey on it. The later Christian stereotypes about law and legalism as opposed to grace and faith should not be imposed on our reading of a text like this. The psalmist sees the law as potentially life-giving, not death-dealing, *if one keeps it*, but he also recognizes that when one of the people of God sins, sin becomes transgression, a very serious matter, because it was forbidden by God's commandments and the transgressor knew it. He also knows there are negative moral consequences for breaking God's precepts or rules.

This of course is a poem meant to be sung, not a theological treatise. It is meant to celebrate God's perfect word and will and ways as revealed in his instructions. It does not really deal with the issue of human fallenness, which we have seen mentioned elsewhere in the Psalter, nor, of course, does it deal with the issue of what life would be like after the messiah comes, saves God's people, and inaugurates a new covenant that makes obsolescent a good deal of the old.

For the era in which the psalmist is writing, the Mosaic covenant, and its law, was indeed the law of God's people, meant to keep them on track, in line, and striving for a closer relationship with God. Paul will later say that the Mosaic law served the good function of being the legal guardian of God's people "until the time had fully come and God sent forth his Son, born of woman, born under the Law, in order to redeem those who were under the Law." (Gal 4:4–5). But that day was many lifetimes away when this beautiful psalm was written, which was completely apropos for its day and age. Finally, as Goldingay notes, this psalm looks more like a compendium of things one might pray to God about rather "than a prayer for someone to pray as a whole at the same time with the same immediacy."[65]

MT Psalm 119	LXX Psalm 118
	1 Halleluia.
	1 alph.
1 Happy are those whose way is blameless, who walk in the law of the Lord.	Happy are the blameless in way, who walk in the Lord's law.
2 Happy are those who keep his decrees, who seek him with their whole heart,	2 Happy are those who search out his testimonies; wholeheartedly they will seek him.
3 who also do no wrong, but walk in his ways.	3 For those who practice lawlessness did not walk in his ways.
4 You have commanded your precepts to be kept diligently.	4 It is you who commanded your Commandments to keep diligently.
5 O that my ways may be steadfast in keeping your statutes!	5 O that my ways may be directed to keep your statutes!
6 Then I shall not be put to shame, having my eyes fixed on all your commandments.	6 Then I shall not be put to shame, as I regard all your commandments.
7 I will praise you with an upright heart, when I learn your righteous ordinances.	7 I will acknowledge you with uprightness of heart, when I have learned the judgments of your righteousness.
8 I will observe your statutes; do not utterly forsake me.	8 Your statutes I will observe; do not utterly forsake me.
	2 beth.
9 How can young people keep their way pure? By guarding it according to your word.	9 How shall the young keep his way straight? By observing your words!
10 With my whole heart I seek you; do not let me stray from your commandments.	10 With my whole heart I sought you; do not thrust me aside from your commandments.
11 I treasure your word in my heart, so that I may not sin against you.	11 In my heart I hid your sayings so that I may not sin against you.
12 Blessed are you, O Lord; teach me your statutes.	12 Blessed are you, O Lord; teach me your statutes.
13 With my lips I declare all the ordinances of your mouth.	13 With my lips I declared all the judgments of your mouth.
14 I delight in the way of your decrees as much as in all riches.	14 In the way of your testimonies I delighted as much as in all riches.
15 I will meditate on your precepts, and fix my eyes on your ways.	15 In your commandments I will ponder and put my mind to your ways.
16 I will delight in your statutes; I will not forget your word.	16 In your statutes I will meditate; I will not forget your words

65. Ibid., 380.

17 Deal bountifully with your servant,
so that I may live and observe your word.
18 Open my eyes, so that I may behold
wondrous things out of your law.

19 I live as an alien in the land;
do not hide your commandments from
me.
20 My soul is consumed with longing
for your ordinances at all times.
21 You rebuke the insolent, accursed
ones,
who wander from your commandments;
22 take away from me their scorn and
contempt,
for I have kept your decrees.
23 Even though princes sit plotting
against me,
your servant will meditate on your
statutes.
24 Your decrees are my delight,
they are my counselors.

25 My soul clings to the dust;
revive me according to your word.
26 When I told of my ways, you answered
me;
teach me your statutes.
27 Make me understand the way of your
precepts,
and I will meditate on your wondrous
works.
28 My soul melts away for sorrow;
strengthen me according to your word.
29 Put false ways far from me;
and graciously teach me your law.
30 I have chosen the way of faithfulness;
I set your ordinances before me.
31 I cling to your decrees, O Lord;
let me not be put to shame.
32 I run the way of your commandments,
for you enlarge my understanding.

33 Teach me, O Lord, the way of your
statutes,
and I will observe it to the end.

3 gimal.

17 Requite your slave;
I shall live and observe your words.
18 Uncover my eyes,
and I will put my mind to the
wondrous things out of your law.
19 I am a resident alien in the land;
do not hide your commandments from
me.
20 My soul was consumed with longing
for your judgments in every situation.
21 You rebuked arrogant ones;
accursed are those who deviate from
your commandments;
22 take away from me reproach and contempt,
because I sought your testimonies.
23 Indeed, rulers sat and kept railing at
me,
but your slave would ponder in your
statutes.
24 Indeed, your testimonies are my meditation,
and your statutes are my counsels.

4 delth.

25 My soul clung to the ground;
quicken me according to your word.
26 I told of my ways, and you hearkened
to me;
teach me your statutes.
27 Your statutes' way make me understand,
and I will ponder in your wondrous
works.
28 My soul was drowsy from exhaustion;
confirm me in your words.
29 Injustice's way put far from me,
and by your law have mercy on me.
30 Truth's way I chose;
your judgments I did not forget.
31 I clung to your testimonies;
O Lord, do not put me to shame.
32 I ran the way of your commandments,
when you made my heart spacious.

5 he.

33 Make the way of your statutes, O Lord,
my law,
and I will seek it continually.

34 Give me understanding, that I may
    keep your law
and observe it with my whole heart.
35 Lead me in the path of your command-
    ments,
for I delight in it.
36 Turn my heart to your decrees,
and not to selfish gain.
37 Turn my eyes from looking at vanities;
give me life in your ways.
38 Confirm to your servant your promise,
which is for those who fear you.
39 Turn away the disgrace that I dread,
for your ordinances are good.

40 See, I have longed for your precepts;
in your righteousness give me life.

41 Let your steadfast love come to me, O
    Lord,
your salvation according to your
    promise.
42 Then I shall have an answer for those
    who taunt me,
for I trust in your word.
43 Do not take the word of truth utterly
    out of my mouth,
for my hope is in your ordinances.

44 I will keep your law continually,
forever and ever.
45 I shall walk at liberty,
for I have sought your precepts.
46 I will also speak of your decrees before
    kings,
and shall not be put to shame;
47 I find my delight in your command-
    ments,
because I love them.
48 I revere your commandments, which I
    love,
and I will meditate on your statutes.

49 Remember your word to your servant,
in which you have made me hope.
50 This is my comfort in my distress,
that your promise gives me life.

34 Make me understand, and I will search
    out your law
and observe it with my whole heart.
35 Guide me in a path of your command-
    ments,
because I wanted it.
36 Incline my heart to your testimonies
and not to greediness.
37 Turn my eyes from looking at vanity;
in your way quicken me.
38 Establish for your slave your saying,
for fear of you.
39 Take away my scorn, which I sus-
    pected,
for your judgments are kind.
40 See, I longed for your commandments;
in your righteousness quicken me.

6 ouau.

41 And may your mercy come upon me, O
    Lord,
your deliverance according to your say-
    ing.
42 And I shall have a word for those who
    reproach me,
because I hoped in your words.
43 And do not remove a word of truth
    utterly from my mouth,
because I pinned my hopes on your judg-
    ments.
44 And I will keep your law continually,
forever and forever and ever.
45 And I would walk in spaciousness,
because your commandments I sought.
46 And I would speak of your testimonies
before kings, and I was not ashamed.

47 And I would meditate on your com-
    mandments,
which I loved very much.
48 And I raised my hands to your
commandments, which I loved,
and I would ponder in your statutes.

7 zai.

49 Remember your word to your slave,
by which you buoyed me with hope.
50 This comforted me in my humiliation,
because your saying quickened me.

51 The arrogant utterly deride me,
but I do not turn away from your law.

52 When I think of your ordinances from
of old,
I take comfort, O Lord.
53 Hot indignation seizes me because of
the wicked,
those who forsake your law.
54 Your statutes have been my songs
wherever I make my home.
55 I remember your name in the night, O
Lord,
and keep your law.
56 This blessing has fallen to me,
for I have kept your precepts.

57 The Lord is my portion;
I promise to keep your words.
58 I implore your favor with all my heart;
be gracious to me according to your
promise.
59 When I think of your ways,
I turn my feet to your decrees;
60 I hurry and do not delay
to keep your commandments.
61 Though the cords of the wicked
ensnare me,
I do not forget your law.
62 At midnight I rise to praise you,
because of your righteous ordinances.

63 I am a companion of all who fear you,
of those who keep your precepts.

64 The earth, O Lord, is full of your steadfast love;
teach me your statutes.

65 You have dealt well with your servant,
O Lord, according to your word.

66 Teach me good judgment and knowledge,
for I believe in your commandments.

67 Before I was humbled I went astray,
but now I keep your word.

51 Arrogant ones would blatantly transgress the law,
but from your law I did not deviate.
52 I remembered your judgments from of
old, O Lord,
and I took comfort.
53 Despondency beset me due to sinners,
those who keep forsaking your law.
54 Your statutes were musical to me
in my place of sojourn.
55 I remembered your name at night, O
Lord,
and kept your law.
56 This fell to me,
because I sought your statutes.

8 heth.

57 You are my portion, O Lord; I said
that I should keep your law.
58 I implored your face with all my heart;
have mercy on me according to your saying.
59 Your ways I considered,
and I turned my feet to your testimonies;
60 I was prepared and not troubled
to keep your commandments.
61 Cords of sinners ensnared me,
and your law I did not forget.
62 At midnight I would rise to acknowledge you,
because of your righteous judgments.
63 I am a partner with all who fear you
and with those who keep your commandments.
64 The earth, O Lord, is full of your
mercy;
teach me your statutes.

9 teth.

65 You practiced kindness with your
slave,
O Lord, according to your word.
66 Kindness and discipline and knowledge teach me,
because in your commandments I
believed.
67 Before I was humbled I was in error;
therefore I kept your saying.

68 You are good and do good;
teach me your statutes.

69 The arrogant smear me with lies,
but with my whole heart I keep your precepts.

70 Their hearts are fat and gross,
but I delight in your law.
71 It is good for me that I was humbled,
so that I might learn your statutes.

72 The law of your mouth is better to me
than thousands of gold and silver pieces.

73 Your hands have made and fashioned
me;
give me understanding that I may learn
your commandments.
74 Those who fear you shall see me and
rejoice,
because I have hoped in your word.

75 I know, O Lord, that your judgments
are right,
and that in faithfulness you have humbled me.
76 Let your steadfast love become my
comfort
according to your promise to your servant.
77 Let your mercy come to me, that I may
live;
for your law is my delight.
78 Let the arrogant be put to shame,
because they have subverted me with
guile;
as for me, I will meditate on your precepts.
79 Let those who fear you turn to me,
so that they may know your decrees.
80 May my heart be blameless in your
statutes,
so that I may not be put to shame.

81 My soul languishes for your salvation;
I hope in your word.

68 You are kind, O Lord, and in your kindness
teach me your statutes.
69 Injustice of the arrogant filled out
against me,
but I, with my whole heart, I will
examine your commandments.
70 Their heart was curdled like milk,
but I, on your law I meditated.
71 It was good for me that you humbled
me
so that I might learn your statutes.
72 Better to me is the law of your mouth
than thousands of gold and silver.

10 ioth.

73 Your hands made and fashioned me;
give me understanding, and I will learn
your commandments.
74 Those who fear you shall see me and
be glad,
because on your words I pinned my
hopes.
75 I knew, O Lord, that your judgments
are righteousness
and that with truth you humbled me.

76 Do let your mercy come to comfort me
according to your saying to your slave.

77 Let your compassion come to me, and I
shall live,
because your law is my meditation.
78 Let arrogant ones be put to shame,
because they acted unjustly and lawlessly
against me,
but as for me, I will ponder in your commandments.
79 Let those who fear you turn to me,
and those who know your testimonies.
80 Let my heart become blameless by
your statutes
so that I may not be put to shame.

11 chaph.

81 My soul fails for your deliverance,
and on your word I pinned my hopes.

82 My eyes fail with watching for your
    promise;
I ask, "When will you comfort me?"
83 For I have become like a wineskin in
    the smoke,
yet I have not forgotten your statutes.
84 How long must your servant endure?
When will you judge those who persecute
    me?
85 The arrogant have dug pitfalls for me;
they flout your law.
86 All your commandments are enduring;
I am persecuted without cause; help me!
87 They have almost made an end of me
    on earth;
but I have not forsaken your precepts.

88 In your steadfast love spare my life,
so that I may keep the decrees of your
    mouth.

89 The Lord exists forever;
your word is firmly fixed in heaven.
90 Your faithfulness endures to all gener-
    ations;
you have established the earth, and it
    stands fast.
91 By your appointment they stand
    today,
for all things are your servants.
92 If your law had not been my delight,
I would have perished in my misery.

93 I will never forget your precepts,
for by them you have given me life.
94 I am yours; save me,
for I have sought your precepts.
95 The wicked lie in wait to destroy me,
but I consider your decrees.
96 I have seen a limit to all perfection,
but your commandment is exceedingly
    broad.

97 Oh, how I love your law!
It is my meditation all day long.
98 Your commandment makes me wiser
    than my enemies,
for it is always with me.

82 My eyes failed for your saying,
saying, "When will you comfort me?"

83 Because I became like a wineskin in
    hoarfrost,
your statutes I did not forget.
84 How many are the days of your slave?
When will you do me right against those
who persecute me?
85 Transgressors of the law told me tales,
but not so your law, O Lord.
86 All your commandments are truth;
unjustly did they persecute me; help me!
87 They almost made an end of me on the
    earth,
but as for me, I did not forsake your com-
    mandments.
88 In your mercy quicken me,
and I will keep the testimonies of your
    mouth.

12 labd.

89 Forever, O Lord;
your word endures in the sky,
90 your truth to generation and genera-
    tion;
you founded the earth, and it endures.

91 By your arrangement the day endures,
because all things together are slaves of
    yours.
92 If it were not for the fact that your law
    was my meditation,
then I would have perished in my humili-
    ation.

93 Your statutes I will never forget,
because by them you quickened me.
94 Yours I am; save me,
because your statutes I sought.
95 Sinners waited for me to destroy me;
your testimonies I considered.
96 I saw a limit to all perfection;
your commandment is exceedingly spa-
    cious.

13 mem.

97 Oh, how I loved your law, O Lord!
All day long it is my meditation.
98 Wiser than my enemies you made me
regarding your commandment,
because it is mine forever.

99 I have more understanding than all my teachers,
for your decrees are my meditation.

100 I understand more than the aged,
for I keep your precepts.

101 I hold back my feet from every evil way,
in order to keep your word.
102 I do not turn away from your ordinances,
for you have taught me.
103 How sweet are your words to my taste,
sweeter than honey to my mouth!

104 Through your precepts I get understanding;
therefore I hate every false way.

105 Your word is a lamp to my feet
and a light to my path.
106 I have sworn an oath and confirmed it,
to observe your righteous ordinances.
107 I am severely afflicted;
give me life, O Lord, according to your word.
108 Accept my offerings of praise, O Lord,
and teach me your ordinances.

109 I hold my life in my hand continually,
but I do not forget your law.
110 The wicked have laid a snare for me,
but I do not stray from your precepts.

111 Your decrees are my heritage forever;
they are the joy of my heart.
112 I incline my heart to perform your statutes
forever, to the end.

113 I hate the double-minded,
but I love your law.

---

99 More than all who were teaching me, I understood,
because your testimonies were my meditation.

100 More than the aged, I understood,
because I sought out your commandments.

101 From every way of evil I held back my feet
in order to keep your words.
102 From your judgments I did not deviate,
because you legislated for me.
103 How sweet are your sayings to my throat,
beyond honey and honeycomb to my mouth!

104 Due to your commandments, I understood;
therefore I hated every way of injustice.

14 noun.

105 Your word is a lamp to my feet
and a light to my paths.
106 I have sworn an oath and confirmed,
to observe your righteous judgments.

107 I was deeply humbled;
O Lord, quicken me according to your word.
108 With the freewill offerings of my mouth do
be pleased, O Lord,
and your judgments teach me
109 My soul was in my hands continually,
and your law I did not forget.
110 Sinners laid a snare for me,
and from your commandments I did not stray.

111 Your testimonies were my heritage forever,
because they are my heart's joy.
112 I inclined my heart to perform your statutes
forever on account of an exchange.

15 samch.

113 Transgressors of the law I hated,
and your law I loved.

289

114 You are my hiding place and my
    shield;
I hope in your word.
115 Go away from me, you evildoers,
that I may keep the commandments of
    my God.
116 Uphold me according to your
    promise, that I may live,
and let me not be put to shame in my
    hope.
117 Hold me up, that I may be safe
and have regard for your statutes contin-
    ually.
118 You spurn all who go astray from
    your statutes;
for their cunning is in vain.
119 All the wicked of the earth you count
    as dross;
therefore I love your decrees.
120 My flesh trembles for fear of you,
and I am afraid of your judgments.

121 I have done what is just and right;
do not leave me to my oppressors.

122 Guarantee your servant's well-being;
do not let the godless oppress me.
123 My eyes fail from watching for your
    salvation,
and for the fulfillment of your righteous
    promise.
124 Deal with your servant according to
    your steadfast love,
and teach me your statutes.
125 I am your servant; give me under-
    standing,
so that I may know your decrees.
126 It is time for the Lord to act,
for your law has been broken.
127 Truly I love your commandments
more than gold, more than fine gold.

128 Truly I direct my steps by all your
    precepts;
I hate every false way.

129 Your decrees are wonderful;
therefore my soul keeps them.

114 You are my helper and my supporter;
I pinned my hopes on your word.

115 Go away from me, you evildoers,
and I will examine the commandments of
    my God.
116 Support me according to your saying,
    and I shall live,
and do not put me to shame due to my
    expectation.
117 Help me, and I shall be saved
and shall meditate on your statutes con-
    tinually.
118 You despised all who stood aloof
    from your statutes,
because their notion was wrong.
119 All the sinners of the earth I counted
    as transgressors;
therefore I loved your testimonies.
120 Nail down my flesh from fear of you,
for I was afraid of your judgments.

16 ain.

121 I did what was just and right;
do not hand me over to those that do me
    wrong.
122 Accept your slave for good;
let not arrogant ones extort from me.
123 My eyes failed for your deliverance
and for the saying of your righteousness.

124 Deal with your slave according to
    your mercy,
and teach me your statutes.
125 Your slave I am; give me understand-
    ing,
and I shall know your testimonies.
126 It is time for the Lord to act;
they scattered your law.
127 Therefore I loved your command-
    ments
beyond gold and topaz.
128 Therefore I would set myself straight
    by all your commandments;
every wrong way I hated.

17 phe.

129 Your testimonies are wonderful;
therefore my soul searched them out.

130 The unfolding of your words gives light;
it imparts understanding to the simple.
131 With open mouth I pant,
because I long for your commandments.

132 Turn to me and be gracious to me,
as is your custom toward those who love your name.
133 Keep my steps steady according to your promise,
and never let iniquity have dominion over me.
134 Redeem me from human oppression,
that I may keep your precepts.

135 Make your face shine upon your servant,
and teach me your statutes.
136 My eyes shed streams of tears
because your law is not kept.

137 You are righteous, O Lord,
and your judgments are right.
138 You have appointed your decrees in righteousness
and in all faithfulness.
139 My zeal consumes me
because my foes forget your words.
140 Your promise is well tried,
and your servant loves it.
141 I am small and despised,
yet I do not forget your precepts.
142 Your righteousness is an everlasting righteousness,
and your law is the truth.
143 Trouble and anguish have come upon me,
but your commandments are my delight.
144 Your decrees are righteous forever;
give me understanding that I may live.

145 With my whole heart I cry; answer me, O Lord.
I will keep your statutes.
146 I cry to you; save me,
that I may observe your decrees.

130 The exposition of your words will enlighten
and will impart understanding to infants.
131 I opened my mouth and drew breath,
because I was longing for your commandments

132 Look upon me, and be merciful to me,
as is your judgment toward those who love your name.
133 Direct my steps according to your saying,
and do not let any lawlessness exercise dominion over me.
134 Redeem me from extortion of human beings,
and I will keep your commandments.

135 Make your face shine upon your slave,
and teach me your statutes.
136 My eyes shed streams of water,
since they did not keep your law.

18 sade.

137 Righteous you are, O Lord,
and upright is your judgment.
138 You commanded your testimonies
to be righteousness and truth, very much.
139 Zeal for you wasted me,
because my enemies forgot your words.
140 Your saying was well tried,
and your slave loved it.
141 Rather young I am and of no account;
your statutes I did not forget.
142 Your righteousness is righteousness forever,
and your law is truth.
143 Affliction and anguish found me;
your commandments are my meditation.

144 Your testimonies are righteousness forever;
give me understanding, and I shall live.

19 koph.

145 I cried with my whole heart; hearken to me, O Lord.
Your statutes will I seek.
146 I cried for you; save me,
and I will observe your testimonies.

147 I rise before dawn and cry for help;
I put my hope in your words.

148 My eyes are awake before each watch
　　of the night,
that I may meditate on your promise.
149 In your steadfast love hear my voice;
O Lord, in your justice preserve my life.

150 Those who persecute me with evil
　　purpose draw near;
they are far from your law.
151 Yet you are near, O Lord,
and all your commandments are true.
152 Long ago I learned from your decrees
that you have established them forever.

153 Look on my misery and rescue me,
for I do not forget your law.

154 Plead my cause and redeem me;
give me life according to your promise.
155 Salvation is far from the wicked,
for they do not seek your statutes.
156 Great is your mercy, O Lord;
give me life according to your justice.
157 Many are my persecutors and my
　　adversaries,
yet I do not swerve from your decrees.
158 I look at the faithless with disgust,
because they do not keep your com-
　　mands.
159 Consider how I love your precepts;
preserve my life according to your stead-
　　fast love.
160 The sum of your word is truth;
and every one of your righteous ordi-
　　nances endures forever.

161 Princes persecute me without cause,
but my heart stands in awe of your
　　words.
162 I rejoice at your word
like one who finds great spoil.
163 I hate and abhor falsehood,
but I love your law.
164 Seven times a day I praise you
for your righteous ordinances.

147 I got a head start at an unseemly
　　hour, and I cried;
on your words I pinned my hope.
148 My eyes got a head start at dawn,
that I may meditate on your sayings.

149 Hear my voice, O Lord, according to
　　your mercy;
by your judgment quicken me.
150 Those who persecute me with law-
　　lessness drew near,
but they were put far from your law.
151 You are near, O Lord,
and all your commandments are truth.
152 Long ago I learned from your testi-
　　monies
that you established them forever.

20 res.

153 Look on my humiliation, and deliver
　　me,
because your law I did not forget.
154 Plead my cause, and redeem me;
because of your word quicken me.
155 Deliverance is far from sinners,
because they did not seek your statutes.
156 Your compassion is great, O Lord;
by your judgment quicken me
157 Many are those who persecute me
　　and afflict me;
from your testimonies I did not deviate.
158 I looked at faithless ones and wasted
　　away,
because they did not keep your sayings.
159 See how I loved your command-
　　ments;
O Lord, by your mercy quicken me.
160 The beginning of your words is truth,
and forever are all the judgments of your
　　righteousness.

21 sen.

161 Rulers persecuted me without cause,
and my heart was in dread of your words.

162 I will rejoice at your sayings
like him who finds much spoil.
163 Injustice I hated and abhorred,
but your law I loved.
164 Seven times a day I praised you
for the judgments of your righteousness.

165 Great peace have those who love your law; nothing can make them stumble. 166 I hope for your salvation, O Lord, and I fulfill your commandments.	165 Great peace have those who love your law, and nothing can make them stumble. 166 I kept waiting for your deliverance, O Lord, and your commandments I loved.
167 My soul keeps your decrees; I love them exceedingly. 168 I keep your precepts and decrees, for all my ways are before you.	167 My soul kept your testimonies, and it loved them exceedingly. 168 I kept your commandments and your testimonies, because all my ways were before you, O Lord.
	22 thau.
169 Let my cry come before you, O Lord; give me understanding according to your word.	169 Let my petition come before you, O Lord; according to your saying give me understanding.
170 Let my supplication come before you; deliver me according to your promise. 171 My lips will pour forth praise, because you teach me your statutes. 172 My tongue will sing of your promise, for all your commandments are right.	170 May my request come before you; according to your saying rescue me. 171 May my lips pour forth a hymn, when you teach me your statutes. 172 May my tongue articulate your saying, because all your commandments are righteousness.
173 Let your hand be ready to help me, for I have chosen your precepts. 174 I long for your salvation, O Lord, and your law is my delight. 175 Let me live that I may praise you, and let your ordinances help me. 176 I have gone astray like a lost sheep; seek out your servant, for I do not forget your commandments.	173 Let your hand be ready to save me, because your commandments I chose. 174 I longed for your deliverance, O Lord, and your law is my meditation. 175 My soul shall live and praise you, and your judgments will help me. 176 I went astray like a lost sheep; seek your slave, because I did not forget your commandments.

It is impossible with the space we have in this study to deal with every line and detail of such a huge psalm, so we will deal with it stanza by stanza starting with stanza one in vv. 1–8. From the first we have a signal that this should be seen as a wisdom psalm, as it begins with a beatitude, the first of several in this song, "Blessed are those whose way is blameless" (v. 1; cf. Psalm 1 and Psalm 112 both of which are also wisdom psalms, and Prov 8:32; Deut 28:11, 14; Hos 1:2; 2:2).[66] Sometimes blameless is confused with the concept of "perfect" or "sinless" but

<hr>

66. Ibid., 380–81 insists this is simply a torah psalm not a wisdom psalm, but that is ignoring that "instruction" *is* a form of wisdom in ancient Israel, and the various wisdom forms in this psalm, such as the opening beatitude, make clear that the psalmist is framing what he says about torah as wisdom for the young, much like the opening chapters of Proverbs. The fact that the term wis-

these ideas are not synonymous. To be blameless means one has not broken any law. Sin is a much bigger category than transgression—a violation of a known law. Thus when the psalmist speaks of someone being blameless, he means that they are not a lawbreaker. This hardly means that they are fulfilling to the full extent all the positive things God requires of his people, such as loving him with their whole hearts. Blameless simply means avoiding blameworthy conduct, transgressions, and of course Paul says that when he was a Pharisee, "in regard to a righteousness which comes from the Law, I was blameless," by which he meant no one could accuse him of violating the "thou shalt nots." As such he was like Job (Job 1:1). Psalm 119:1–2 strongly echoes Psalm 1:1, and both affirm that keeping the commandments is the path to a good, godly, whole, and even joyous life, despite life's trials and tribulations.[67]

Stanza two (vv. 9–16) begins with a question, the only stanza to do so, "How can a young man keep his way pure?" The Hebrew word *na'ar* can refer to anyone up to about the age of forty, interestingly enough (see 1 Kgs 12:10), but we must remember that the ancient Near East was full of senior-dominated cultures, where "the elders" were the most honored, looked up to, and who made the rules. Calling someone "young" who could be up to forty years of age reflects the perspective of a senior person. Notice that wisdom literature is often addressed to the young (cf. Proverbs 1–8). And the dominant image used is the "two ways" or "two paths" discourse, trying to steer the young person down the right path, with God's word as a lamp to illuminate the way. Not surprisingly, the dominant ethical language is that of walking, walking on this path rather than that one, this way or road, rather than that one. The advice is normally dyadic, there are two major ways to go, the way of the wise and the way of the foolish. How does a young man stay on the right track? By obeying God's word, his statutes, his commands. But this requires knowing God's word, hence, memorization: "I have hidden your word in my heart." No one can steal it from that location.

The third stanza (vv. 17–24) makes clear that the psalmist needs ongoing illumination to both understand and keep God's word. He expresses his earnest desire to do so again and again in this psalm, but he recognizes he needs ongoing help from God to accomplish the goal.

---

dom/wise shows up but once is not a good counterargument since various sorts of other wisdom language occur in this psalm, including synonyms for the terms wise and wisdom.
67. See Brueggemann and Bellinger, *Psalms*, 520.

It is not as though he could learn things at one point in life, and then be set for life. No, he needs ongoing guidance.

The fourth stanza (vv. 25–32) makes clear that even for someone who desires God and longs to obey him as much as the psalmist does, he has troubles in life and has been "laid in the dust," presumably by some suffering, and he calls for God to rescue him. He is suggesting perhaps that he is as good as dead if God doesn't raise him up from the mire.[68] The psalmist protests that he is indeed obeying God, and so perhaps he doesn't quite understand why he is suffering. His plea in v. 25 is "quicken me" or even "keep me alive."[69] Interestingly, he speaks of running in the way of God's commands, rather than "walking," the usual verb for such an activity. This may suggest energetic and enthusiastic following of God's word. This is one of those verses that suggests we are dealing with an enthusiastic young person.[70]

The fifth stanza (vv. 33–40) tells us that the psalmist promises to keep the law fully, to its full extent, to the nth degree as we might say, although the Hebrew could mean "to the end," which might mean "until I receive the promised reward" (see Deuteronomy 27–28). The psalmist is honest about his ability to get distracted, even indulge in selfish desires and get off track. He longs however to obey God's word and doesn't want to endure the shame that comes from disobedience. A couple of the assumptions underlying the whole psalm include: (1) *torah accurately* reveals the character and will of God, which God desires to replicate in his people; (2) God is true to his word. What he says he will do, he will do, and so God is as good as his word and can be trusted. Obedience to God's word results in character formation, "trust and obey for there's no other way, to be happy/blessed." Notice that what is elsewhere predicated of God—instruction, protection, life, comfort, joy—is here predicated of torah. "What the hymns and prayers in the Psalter usually say about the Lord is said here about all forms of *torah* . . . in dealing with the teaching one deals with the teacher."[71]

The sixth stanza (vv. 41–48) again tells us that the psalmist is in some distress, and so he asks for God's mercy (*hesed*) and salvation to come his way. The psalmist believes that keeping God's word, far from being restrictive, is freeing (v. 45). How so? Well for one thing one doesn't have to live with the negative consequences of doing immoral things,

68. Goldingay, *Psalms: Volume 3*, 393.
69. Terrien, *Psalms*, 800.
70. Goldingay, *Psalms: Volume 3*, 396.
71. Mays, *Psalms*, 383–84.

which always have negative consequences, nor does he want to live with the shame of being a wrongdoer. But there is a second way in which knowing and keeping the law sets one free: one doesn't have to figure out what is right and wrong on one's own. That saves a lot of reflection, soul-searching, consciousness-raising, and saves having a conflicted conscience on some matters.

The seventh stanza (vv. 49–56) tells us that this person has been harassed for his piety (v. 53), made fun of. So he calls on God to remember his word to him (v. 49) and do what he promised if one keeps his commandments. The psalmist even says that he has turned God's word into a song, which of course helps him keep it in mind and on his heart (v. 54), and presumably he means this alphabet acrostic poem we are now examining. The reference to a "house" in v. 54 could be taken as a reference to the temple, and Terrien suggests that perhaps the psalmist is one of sacred singers in the temple.[72]

The eighth stanza (vv. 57–64) is a reaffirmation of the psalmist's commitment to keep God's word, in spite of the obstacles others, the wicked, are putting in his way. He even says in v. 61 that people are tying him down to keep him from obeying. Nevertheless, when no one is looking, he rises at midnight and gives thanks to God for his precepts.

In the ninth stanza (vv. 65–72), instead of blaming someone else, the psalmist comes clean and says that his affliction was caused by his own going astray (v. 67), though v. 69b tells us that he has been urged on in the wrong direction by the arrogant. He now pledges allegiance again and says God and his law are the most precious things in the world to him (v. 72). He also says that the hearts of the arrogant are clogged with fat (v. 70)![73] Hardening of the spiritual arteries is a dangerous condition.

The tenth stanza (vv. 73–80) calls for the punishment of the arrogant, those who led him astray before. It also advances the logic that since God made him, God has every right to make demands on him and undoubtedly knows the right way for him to live his life. We are a very long way from the late Western notions of individual autonomy, and the idea that it is always best to "do it my way as I see best." "Wrong!" says the psalmist. It is always best to do it God's way, "for he has made us." Brueggemann and Bellinger put it this way: "it is clear that Torah piety in general and in this psalm in particular view adherence to

---

72. Terrien, Psalms, 801.
73. Ibid.

Torah instruction as the alternative to a life of autonomous self-serv-ing and self-sufficiency that can only end in self-destruction."[74]

Notice that one of the major themes of this wisdom psalm is the request for "life"; "the psalmist regularly petitions YHWH for the gift of life, which is given through YHWH's promise (vv. 17, 25, 37, 40, 50, 88, 93, 107, 149, 159, 175). It is clear that obedience to Torah is not an automatic trigger for 'life' but that 'life' is a gift of YHWH's own self in faithful commitment to Israel and to this psalmist."[75] The theme of how to have and live a good life is a constant one in wisdom literature (see both Proverbs and Ecclesiastes), and the subject of considerable debate. We do need to make clear that the subject in question here is life in this world and how it can be good and godly, not everlasting life in heaven or some other form of the afterlife.

The eleventh stanza (vv. 81–88) tells us that the psalmist is now in extreme distress, his inner self is ready to give up, his eyes are failing to see the right path, and in a vivid image at v. 83 he says he is like a wineskin in smoke—the notion is that the wineskin, which to remain flexible needs to be in contact with liquids, is in danger of shriveling up and becoming useless.[76] Verse 87 warns that he has nearly been wiped out by his enemies.

The twelfth stanza (vv. 89–96) is another dramatic statement about God's law, here said to be eternal and always relevant. As a generaliza-tion this is true enough, especially in a fallen world, but of course law comes in specific forms in specific law codes and covenants and so spe-cific laws come and go depending on the age and the audience. There is no need today for the law prohibiting parking one's horse in front of the courthouse in Lexington, Kentucky, even though this is still the horse capital of America. That law is obsolete because the times have changed. The psalmist is simply saying that there is always a need and relevance for God's law in general and for our obedience. Interestingly, in v. 96 the definition of perfection is one who is eager to keep the law. About this verse Mays stresses, "verse 96 makes the amazing state-ment that while every perfection has its limits, the commandment of the Lord is broad beyond measure. Clearly, it is not the limitedness but the inclusiveness of the Lord's instruction that the psalm celebrates."[77]

The thirteenth stanza (vv. 97–104) sounds like a young person, not

---

74. Brueggemann and Bellinger, *Psalms*, 520.
75. Ibid.
76. See, rightly, Longman, *Psalms*, 406.
77. Mays, *Psalms*, 383.

only in his many professions of his eagerness to obey, but a little pride seems to creep in at v. 99 where he suggests he is smarter than his teachers! He loves, and meditates on the law, its like honey in his mouth. "To say the Law 'is mine' is to use the language of the lover rather than the language of the ethicist (v. 97)."[78]

The fourteenth stanza (vv. 105–12) tells us that a life should not be characterized by aimless wandering; it's a journey, and it should be going in a certain purposeful direction following a path illuminated by God's word. That's how one avoids many potholes and pitfalls and problems. Nevertheless, the psalmist tells us that his life has been characterized by suffering (v. 107) and so once more he calls on God for help.

The fifteenth stanza (vv. 113–20) talks more about the threat to the psalmist from "double-minded" wicked people. Double-minded seems to mean someone who appears to be following God's way, but really isn't, perhaps someone who is skeptical or has doubts.[79] In any case, the psalmist needs help to fend off such people.

The sixteenth stanza (vv. 121–28) indicates that the psalmist needs protection by God because he is not merely being berated or browbeaten or ridiculed, he is being oppressed by his enemies. He is applying to be in God's witness protection program.

The seventeenth stanza (vv. 129–36) cries out for mercy, for better understanding of God's word, for clear guidance as to the way forward, and he pleads for God's presence to shine upon him, which seems to be a rather clearly allusion to the priestly prayer found in Numbers 6:22–37. He is weeping when he examines those around him and discovers they do not keep God's law.[80]

The eighteenth stanza (vv. 137–44) makes the observation that the law reflects God's character, in particular, his righteousness. The psalmist indicates he has been teaching God's law, and it has brought him trouble rather than reward or success. Nevertheless, he will keep doing it, because he believes it is true, but he admits he needs to understand it better.

The nineteenth stanza (vv. 145–52) is much like several of the immediately preceding ones. The psalmist is being threatened, attacked, and so he calls for rescue, in part because he has been devout and a

78. Terrien, Psalms, 802.
79. See ibid., 802–3.
80. See Longman, Psalms, 407.

defender of God's word. Here in v. 151 he says that at least God is near, even if the situation is dire.

The twentieth stanza (vv. 153–60) again involves calling on God to rescue him from the wicked, and again the basis for his making this request is that he has kept God's law. The word for compassion in v. 156 is *raḥamîm* which indicates a deep emotion prompting action.

At stanza twenty-one (vv. 161–68) we finally learn that among his enemies are "the rulers, the powerful of this earth." Notice v. 164, "seven times a day I praise you"—seven being the number of perfection or completion. The psalmist portrays himself as utterly devout.

The psalm finally concludes in stanza twenty-two (vv. 169–76) with further supplications asking for God to hear (in fact he says "let my cry come near to your face"),[81] answer, rescue, and the psalmist asks for stamina to continue worshiping for at the very end he admits, "I have gone astray like a lost sheep." It should be stressed that the psalmist is not talking about "how to obtain right-standing with God." He is already a devout Jew, who believes that keeping torah is what God requires of his people whom he has chosen and blessed. Obeying the law then is seen as a way of maintaining a right relationship with God, but not without the constant grace and help of God.

Even as devout as this psalmist is, he has to admit that he has gone astray, has made some bad choices, has had wandering thoughts, and has weakened under temptation and persecution. The psalm is both earnest, but also honest, and as we have said from the start, it is a truthful revelation of the human heart poured out to God, like all these psalms. What we learn is that the human heart can be wayward, and is not any more a reliable guide to right and wrong than the human conscience, hence the need for a revelation from an all-knowing, all-wise, and omnibenevolent God. This psalm "allows no piety that takes the form of legalism, nor any that takes the form of fideism," it involves a living relationship with God that calls for both trusting and obeying.[82] In the words of Anselm, it involves *fides quaerens intellectum*—faith seeking understanding—so that obedience and wise living is possible.

Despite the importance of Psalm 119 to early Jewish torah piety, and despite the fact that NA28 in its index tells us there are fourteen places in the NT where this psalm comes into play, surprisingly, the psalm is not discussed by those deeply interested in the issue of intertexuality between the OT and the NT, by which I mean all of the writers save

---

81. Terrien, *Psalms*, 805.
82. The quotation is from Mays, *Psalms*, 385.

one (who gives only a passing reference to one verse in Revelation and Psalm 119) in *The Psalms in the New Testament* and also Hays and Wagner. There is a bit more in the *Commentary on the New Testament Use of the Old Testament,* as might be expected, but not a lot more. And yet "law," particularly the Mosaic law, is a major subject of discussion in the NT, as are the Psalms. So let us see what can be learned from the references in the psalm index in NA28.

The first verse that is echoed in the NT is Psalm 119:29 at 2 Peter 2:2. It will be remembered that a good deal is said by the psalmist about falseness, including false teachers, and about the psalmist being maligned. Here is what 2 Peter 2 says, "But false prophets also arose among the people, just as there will be false teachers among you, who will secretly bring in destructive opinions. They will even deny the Master who bought them—bringing swift destruction on themselves. Even so, many will follow their licentious ways, and because of them *the way of truth will be maligned.*" (emphasis added). The audience of 2 Peter seems to be afflicted in a similar way to the psalmist, and there is a concern about false ways, bad teaching, and the way of truth being maligned (noting how often the words "path"/"way" come up in the psalm). There is a shared ethos and concern in these two documents.

Psalm 119:32 includes a request to make wide my heart (the Hebrew text followed by the LXX). This is the phrase Paul chooses to use when he appeals to his Corinthians in 2 Corinthians 6:11 which reads literally, "our mouths are wide open to you, Corinthians, make wide our[83] hearts." This seems a clear enough echo of our psalm, or even an allusion to a specific phrase. The phrase "the word of truth" occurs at Psalm 119:43 and the same exact phrase is used by James in James 1:18.

Psalm 119:46 says, "I will speak of your decrees before kings, and shall not be put to shame," which could be compared not only to what we are told in Acts 9:15 where Jesus says to Ananias about Saul, "Go, for he is an instrument whom I have chosen to bring my name before gentiles and kings and all the people of Israel," as well as Paul's own statement in Romans 1:16, "for I am not ashamed of the Gospel, it is the power of God for salvation to everyone who has faith, to the Jew first, and also to the Greek." What the psalmist avers about torah, Paul avers about the gospel.

Psalm 119:57 says, "the Lord is my portion; I promise to keep your words." Luke 10:38–42 tells the story of Jesus in the home of Martha

---

83. Possibly "your" hearts, as the two Greek words were regularly confused and looked very much alike in *scriptio continua* and all capital letters.

and Mary. We are told at v. 39 that Mary is sitting at Jesus's feet listening to the Lord's word. Martha objects and wants more help in the kitchen to which Jesus replies, "there is only one thing necessary, Mary has chosen the good portion."

Psalm 119:89 says, "the Lord exists forever, your word is firmly fixed in the heavens," whereas the LXX has, "forever O Lord, your word endures in the heavens, your truth to generation and generation." Luke 21:32–33 has on the lips of Jesus, "Truly I tell you this generation will not pass away until all things have taken place. Heaven and earth will pass away, but my words will not pass away." The reference to generations in the LXX coupled with the reference to the enduring word seems to make evident the echo here of Psalm 119. Pao and Schnabel recognize the echo of Psalm 119 in Luke 21:33b, but suggest that 21:33a echoes Psalm 102:25–26, which is possible.[84]

In Psalm 119:103 we hear that God's word is "sweeter than honey in my mouth," and in Revelation 10:9 John is told to eat the scroll and the angel promises, "it will be bitter in your stomach, but in your mouth as sweet as honey." Notice that in the LXX it speaks of throat and mouth, and in both cases the sweetness of God's word, sweet as honeycomb, is in the mouth. Now the Greek word στόμα can sometimes mean mouth (see 2 Cor 6:11, mentioned above), but it is also the word for "stomach" (the English word derives from the Greek at this point). The word κοιλία however means "belly," "womb," the innermost part of the person. It surely does not mean "mouth" in Revelation 10:9, whereas, as I said the word στόμα can most certainly mean mouth, as well as stomach. So I am suggesting that the proper reading of Revelation 10:9 involves a direct parallel to the key phrase in Psalm 119:103, so Revelation reads, "it will be bitter in your stomach, but in your mouth sweet as honey" with the last half very close to the "sweeter than honey in my mouth" (in this case closer to the Hebrew than the LXX).[85]

Psalm 119:120 reads, "my flesh trembles for fear of you, and I am afraid of your judgments." Jesus in Luke 12:5 says, "But I warn you whom to fear; fear him who after he has killed, has authority to cast into Gehenna," and in this case Jesus is likely referring to the same person the psalmist is talking about—Yahweh.

Moyise mentions that Psalm 119:137 has the phrase "God's judgments are just," which we also find in Revelation 15:3, "God's judgment are true and just," and also in Revelation 16:7 where we have the

---

84. Pao and Schnabel, "Luke," 379.
85. Beale and McDonough, "Revelation," 1117, mention, just in passing, the parallel.

reverse, "God's judgments are just and true," which is closer to the psalm (and see Ps 19:9). I agree with Moyise that Beale is likely wrong that the main allusion here is to Deuteronomy 34:2.[86]

The psalmist in Psalm 119:160 says in sequence that God's torah is truth, and then that "the head [r'oš] of your word is truth," which presumably means the start or beginning of it. In any case Jesus also affirms the end of v. 160 in John 17:17 where he agrees with the psalmist in saying "your word is truth." Jesus is praying to God and so presumably he too is referring to the OT. This would be one more example of how widespread, even down to small echoes, is the influence of the Psalms on the Fourth Gospel.

Whereas Psalm 119:164 speaks of praising God seven times a day, Jesus in Luke 17:4 speaks of someone who sins against a disciple seven times a day and then repents the same number of times. This is probably not an echo of the psalm because seven times a day is a conventional number indicating a complete set, or in the case of the psalmist, total devotion.

In Psalm 119:105 there is the familiar word about God's word being a light unto one's path, and then in 119:165 he goes on to say that for those who love God's torah nothing can make them stumble. In a general way this may lie in the background of 1 John 2:7–11 where the contrast between darkness and light is stark. The writer says he is writing them a new commandment and the light is already shining in the darkness. He affirms that whoever loves a brother or sister is living in the light and in that person there is no cause for stumbling. The imagery of commandments, light, paths, stumbling, and darkness and how God's word can prevent one from stumbling is shared.

Finally the common imagery of a lost sheep who has gone astray is found in both Psalm 119:176 and in Matthew 18:12, but the image is too common to suggest any direct connection. While there are not a great deal of allusions or echoes to Psalm 119, there are more than commentators usually realize, and it is a useful reminder that the influence of the Psalter is much broader than just examples of clear citations or allusions.

The Praise of the Gracious God: Psalm 145

This psalm has had a long and interesting history of reception and use.

---

86. Moyise, "Psalms in the Book of Revelation," 244.

To give but two examples, v. 15 was used in the early church at mid-day meals as a sort of blessing.[87] The Talmud (b. Ber. 4b) says of this psalm, "Everyone who repeats the *tehillah* of David three times a day may be sure he is a child of the world to come." Here we have another alphabet acrostic, like Psalm 119, only much shorter this time, and it is the last such poem in the Psalter.[88] Unlike Psalm 119, this one is said to be Davidic in some sense in the prescript to both the MT and LXX versions of this song. This song is most definitely a praise song (see the prescript in both Hebrew and Greek), praising the name and the nature and the mighty deeds of God for his people. In fact this psalm is the only one in the whole Psalter that simply has the one word "praise" (תְּהִלָּה *tehillâ/αἴνεσις*) to describe what follows.

The basic structure of the song is that the psalmist declares his intention to praise God the king, followed by a characterizing of God's attributes. Verses 1 and 21 form an *inclusio* with the same beatitude. There may be a textual problem however with this psalm, namely that the *nun* line in the acrostic is missing from the MT (v. 13b in most English translations), but this has been supplied by an array of other witnesses to this psalm.[89] "The psalm . . . concludes the final collection of Davidic psalms in the Hebrew Psalter. It is likely that the psalm concludes Book V, with Psalms 146–50 providing a fivefold doxological conclusion to the Psalter."[90] Along a similar line Mays suggests Psalm 145 is the overture to the final movement of the psalter, a sort of prelude to the final "Ode to Joy."[91] Note that the final five psalms echo various themes and language of Psalm 145, with the conclusion of Psalm 150 matching up well with the conclusion of Psalm 145.

Finally, this psalm is a perfect example of the rhetorical device known as "accumulation," the piling up of words with similar meanings for the sake of emphasis and effect. Goldingay brings this to light clearly:

It refers to exalting, worshipping, praising, lauding, murmuring, talking, proclaiming, pouring forth, resounding, confessing, and speaking. . . . It refers to YHWH's greatness, mighty acts, majesty, glory, splendor, wondrous acts, might, awesome acts, reign and rule. It refers to YHWH's goodness, faithfulness, grace, compassion, long-temperedness, commit-

---

87. See Weiser, *Psalms*, 826.
88. It is missing the *nun* line, but as Goldingay, *Psalms: Volume 3*, 695 points out, it is not unusual in alphabet acrostic poems to have a line missing.
89. Mays, *Psalms*, 437.
90. Brueggemann and Bellinger, *Psalms*, 603.
91. Mays, *Psalms*, 439.

ment, and trustworthiness. It describes YHWH upholding, lifting up, giving, opening the hand, filling, being near, listening, delivering, watching, and destroying.[92]

MT Psalm 145	LXX Psalm 144
Praise. Of David. 1 I will extol you, my God the King, and bless your name forever and ever. 2 Every day I will bless you, and praise your name forever and ever. 3 Great is the Lord, and greatly to be praised; his greatness is unsearchable. 4 One generation shall laud your works to another, and shall declare your mighty acts. 5 On the glorious splendor of your majesty, and on your wondrous works, I will meditate. 6 The might of your awesome deeds shall be proclaimed, and I will declare your greatness. 7 They shall celebrate the fame of your abundant goodness, and shall sing aloud of your righteousness. 8 The Lord is gracious and merciful, slow to anger and abounding in steadfast love. 9 The Lord is good to all, and his compassion is over all that he has made. 10 All your works shall give thanks to you, O Lord, and all your faithful shall bless you. 11 They shall speak of the glory of your kingdom, and tell of your power, 12 to make known to all people your mighty deeds, and the glorious splendor of your kingdom.	1 Praise. Pertaining to David. I will exalt you, my God, my King, and bless your name forever and forever and ever. 2 Every day I will bless you and praise your name forever and forever and ever. 3 Great is the Lord, and very much praiseworthy, and to his greatness there is no limit. 4 Generation and generation shall commend your works, and your power they shall declare. 5 Of the magnificence of the glory of your holiness they shall speak, and your wondrous works they shall recount. 6 And the power of your awesome deeds they shall relate, and your greatness they shall recount. 7 Mention of the abundance of your kindness they shall gush forth, and at your righteousness they shall rejoice. 8 Compassionate and merciful is the Lord, slow to anger and abounding in mercy. 9 Kind is the Lord to all things together and his compassion is over all his works. 10 Let all your works acknowledge you, O Lord, and let all your devout bless you. 11 Your kingdom's glory they shall relate, and of your dominance they shall speak, 12 to make known to the sons of men your dominance and the glory of the magnificence of your kingdom.

92. Goldingay, *Psalms: Volume 3*, 697.

13 Your kingdom is an everlasting kingdom, and your dominion endures throughout all generations. The Lord is faithful in all his words, and gracious in all his deeds. 14 The Lord upholds all who are falling, and raises up all who are bowed down. 15 The eyes of all look to you, and you give them their food in due season. 16 You open your hand, satisfying the desire of every living thing. 17 The Lord is just in all his ways, and kind in all his doings. 18 The Lord is near to all who call on him, to all who call on him in truth. 19 He fulfills the desire of all who fear him; he also hears their cry, and saves them. 20 The Lord watches over all who love him, but all the wicked he will destroy. 21 My mouth will speak the praise of the Lord, and all flesh will bless his holy name forever and ever.	13 Your kingdom is a kingdom of all the ages, and your dominion is in every generation and generation. 13a Faithful is the Lord in his words, and devout in all his works. 14 The Lord upholds all who are falling and sets upright all who are cast down. 15 The eyes of all hope in you, and it is you who give them their food in due season. 16 You, you open your hand and satisfy every living thing with good pleasure. 17 Just is the Lord in all his ways, and devout in all his works. 18 Near is the Lord to all who call on him, to all who call on him in truth. 19 The will of all who fear him he will do, and to their petition he will hearken and will save them. 20 The Lord watches over all who love him, and all the sinners he will destroy. 21 Praise of the Lord my mouth will speak, and let all flesh bless his holy name forever and forever and ever.

This psalm lauds God as king from the outset, and so not surprisingly it also talks a lot about God's kingdom. Notice the definite article before the word king in the Hebrew (הַמֶּלֶךְ hammelek). Notice as well that the opening line speaks of "my God THE King' not 'my God and King' as some translations have it. This is unique to this psalm and a way of being emphatic about God's kingship.[93] Terrien wonders if there is some polemic here against the human Davidic monarchy, but clearly whoever added the prescript didn't think so.[94] The psalmist promises to praise and bless God's name ad infinitum and every single day. The first stanza ends at v. 3 with the explanation for all this praise: God is great, but his greatness is beyond full comprehension.

The psalmist says in the second and third stanzas (vv. 4–9) that the older generation will pass on the praise duties to the younger generation having proclaimed God's mighty acts (unspecified at this point),[95]

93. Mays, Psalms, 438.
94. Terrien, Psalms, 904–5.
95. Longman, Psalms, 467 suggests the exodus events are alluded to, perhaps those in Exodus 14–15.

and God's character, his righteousness and his goodness, his generosity and grace, his love and compassion (cf. Exod 34:6; 2 Chr 30:9; Neh 9:17; Pss 86:15, 103:8, 111:4; Joel 2:13). "God's power is good, and God's goodness is powerful."[96]

There was an obligation in an oral culture to pass on the sacred tradition about God and his deeds for his people, something Psalm 78:3–4 explains as follows: the psalmist saying he will tell "of things we have heard and known, things our ancestors have told us. We will not hide them from their descendants; we will tell the next generation the laudable deeds of the Lord, his power and the wonders he has performed." As the listing of attributes mounts, the praise gets louder and louder. The psalmist is groping for words big enough to praise such a God. Notice how personal the psalmist is, Yahweh is "my" God the king.[97]

Verses 8–9 are a rehearsal of Exodus 34:6 to some extent, and I would again draw attention to the fact that the LXX rightly translates *hesed* not as covenant love and loyalty, but rather as mercy and so the verse quite properly reads, "the Lord is merciful and compassionate, slow to anger and abundant in mercy. The Lord is good to the whole of creation, and his mercies are over all his works." Indeed, these two verses make clear that God's *hesed* is not limited to those whom he has a covenant relationship with, rather his mercy is over all his works.[98]

In vv. 10–12 we are told that all God's people will extol him not just to each other, but to all "the sons of Adam" and will explain what a great and glorious king God is. In the following stanza in vv. 13–15 it is made clear that Israel's God is king for all time everywhere, not just in one place, not just for one age, not just for one people (cf. Dan 2:44 and 4:3).

The psalmist says God is trustworthy in his promises, faithful in his deeds, and he pays special attention to those "who are bowed down," lifting up those who stumble. "There is particular praise for the fatherly care of God, and for the help and comfort which those who have gone astray and those who are bowed down find in God (v. 14)."[99] God has both an open hand and a readily available presence especially for his people in need.

This provides a natural transition to the next stanza in vv. 16–18, where we are told that all eyes are on God and they all hope in him, in the first place because he is the one who provides food in due season.

---

96. Mays, *Psalms*, 439.
97. Rightly, Brueggemann and Bellinger, *Psalms*, 604.
98. See again the translation at http://www.mechon-mamre.org/p/pt/pt26e5.htm where *hesed* is rendered as "great mercy."
99. Weiser, *Psalms*, 828.

306

"He opens his hand and can satisfy the needs of every living creature" (v. 17). The psalmist, both by the alphabet acrostic structure, and by his repeated use of the word "all" (some seventeen times, most of them as the poem builds to a conclusion in vv. 14–21) is trying to convey the notion of comprehensiveness.[100]

Lest all this sound like incipient universalism, the last main stanza (vv. 19–21) makes clear that God is close to those who: (1) call on his name; (2) in sincerity (literally with singleness of heart); (3) fear him; and (4) love him. For them, he fulfills their desires, hears their cries, saves them, guard them, but then in v. 21b we hear "but all the wicked he will destroy." The psalm ends where it began with an exhortation to self by the psalmist to always praise God, and then he exhorts "all flesh" to bless his name forever and ever. Notice, as Terrien says, that nothing dampens the optimistic mood of this whole psalm. There is no mention of the injustices of nature or history, unless the references to those who are bowed down counts.[101] What is assumed however is that all creatures ought to praise their Maker while they have breath, for as the Westminster Catechism says, it is the chief end or purpose of humankind to glorify God and enjoy him forever. Goldingay points out that it is a psalm like this that seems to have inspired Jesus's formation of the Lord's Prayer, for many of the same topics are used to praise and petition God.[102] What really undergirds the similarity (which does not amount to a direct use of the same phrases) is the shared assumption about God's character and how he relates to his people when they call upon him. The Lord's Prayer of course should really be called the disciple's prayer, as it is the one he encouraged his followers to use when praying to God.

In his excellent exposition on the intertextual allusions in Luke's presentation of the Sermon on the Plain in Luke 6:27–38, Hays points out that one of the main reasons for the differences with the Matthean form of the same material is indebtedness to the language about God found in Psalm 145 in its LXX form, particularly the exhortation, "you will be children of the Most High; for he is kind to the ungrateful and the wicked. Be merciful just as your Father is merciful." As Hays carefully demonstrates, these two adjectives used to characterize God, kind and merciful, are not found in the parallel passages. What stands in the background of such language is the LXX version of psalms such as

---

100. Brueggemann and Bellinger, *Psalms*, 605.
101. Terrien, *Psalms*, 906.
102. See his treatment of this in Goldingay, *Psalms: Volume 3*, 705.

Psalm 85:5 (LXX) and Psalm 144 (LXX) is Exodus 34:5–7 (LXX). What Hays however fails to notice is that *hesed* in the LXX version of our psalm (144 in the LXX, 145 MT and English translations) is not translated "steadfast love" or covenant loyalty or the like, it is translated "mercy," and mercy has to do with forgiveness, not something owed or a covenant obligation.[103] He is absolutely right however that, "the Lukan passage echoes the full resonance of the psalm [145:8–9], which in turn invokes the story of the revelation of God's name on Sinai."[104] What he does not note is the important difference between Psalm 145 (MT and English), which speaks of God not listening to, indeed destroying the wicked, whereas Luke 6:35–36 says explicitly that God is *kind* to the ungrateful and wicked. Luke's Jesus is not talking about God's covenant loyalty to Israel, he is talking about mercy on sinners of whatever sort; *hesed* on the lips of this Jesus means mercy, just as the LXX translators told us. It does not mean covenant love and loyalty. Yes, it is also true that we hear about God's faithfulness to his promises to his people in Exodus 34, but that is not conjured up by the word *hesed*/mercy, which has a much more universal valence for Luke and Paul and others. Indeed, I would say it usually has a much broader meaning in the Psalms as well.

There is a small echo of Psalm 145:15 in Matthew 24:45 in the phrase "to give them their allowance of food at the proper time," which is part of a parabolic saying of Jesus, but of course the psalm is talking about God distributing food in due season, whereas the parable is about how the master (perhaps God) has put one of his household servants in charge of seeing to that task. Nearer in thought to Psalm 145:15 is 1 Timothy 6:17, where there is the exhortation to the rich to set their hope on God not on riches, for it is God "who richly provides us with everything for our enjoyment." The concept of God providing whatever is needed at the appropriate time is found in both Psalm 145:16 and in Acts 14:17: "filling you with food and your hearts with joy."[105]

Psalm 145:17 says that God is "just in all his ways," which is alluded to in Revelation 15:3, "just and true are your ways, King of the nations." Indeed the whole song in Revelation 15:3–4 could be said to be a reframing of Psalm 145 in miniature, for it reads: "Great and amazing are your deeds [cf. Ps 145:4], Lord God the Almighty! Just and true are your ways [cf. 145:17], King of the nations [cf. 145:1 and 13]. Lord who

103. Hays, *Echoes of Scripture in the Gospels*, 213–15.
104. Ibid., 215.
105. Marshall, "Acts," 588 mentions in passing a possible echo of Psalm 145 in Acts 14:17.

will not fear [cf. Ps 145:19] and glorify your name? For you alone are holy, all nations will come and worship before you, for your judgments have been revealed [cf. 145:21]." Here the "song of the Lamb" owes more than a little to Psalm 145.

The concept of whom God will respond to when they pray is front and center in Psalm 145:18-20—he is near to those who sincerely call on God, to those who revere him, hearing their cries and saving them, but not so the wicked. This is the very thought process expressed in John 9:31 when the formerly blind man lectures the Jewish authorities about Jesus saying, "we know that God does not listen to sinners, but he does listen to one who worships him and obeys him." The Psalms taught Jews to think in a particular way about how, when, and why God answers prayer, and for whom.[106] Speaking of misinterpreting the NT on the basis of not recognizing the Psalms material in the background we turn to Philippians 4.

Philippians 4:4-6 has often been misinterpreted as a reference to the nearness of the second coming. This totally ignores that Paul is now recasting the language of the psalms in both these verses: "rejoice in the Lord always, again I say rejoice. Let your gentleness be known to everyone. The Lord is near. Do not be anxious about anything but in everything by prayer and supplication with thanksgiving make your requests known to God." This particular passage owes more than a little to the praise psalms, including Psalm 145. One can even suggest that since "the Lord" in v. 4 is likely to be God the Father, this is also true in v. 5, not least because the rest of these phrases refer to petitioning God the Father. The particular verse that is echoed in Philippians 4 is Psalm 145:18, "the Lord is near to all who call on him in truth." This is not a reference to the temporal nearness of Christ, it is reference to the spatial nearness of God to his sincere worshipers and those who sincerely pray to God (cf. Acts 17:27). *It is always a mistake to underestimate the influence of the Psalms on prayer and praise and song passages in the NT. Indeed, one can say that the Psalms would quite naturally come to mind when the Christian writers of the NT were composing such passages, not least because almost all of them were raised as Jews, or perhaps in the case of Luke, were God-fearers.*

---

106. See, rightly, Köstenberger, "John," 461. And it should be noted, as Köstenberger points out, that there is a major difference between Jesus and the later rabbis on whether God listens to and has mercy on the wicked or not; cf. Luke 6:35-37 to b. San. 90a; b. Ber. 58a.

The Lexicon of Faith: The Broader Use of Psalms 107–150

Psalm 109:8 is cited at Acts 1:20. The original psalm is about a slanderer of King David, or the psalmist, and so we have a series of imprecations against that person, one of which reads in the LXX, "Let his days become few, and may another seize his position." Actually only a part of this is cited in Acts 1:20, the very end phrase, and it is combined with another citation from Psalm 69:25. Peter is applying this combined citation from the Psalms to Judas, explaining why God wants him to be replaced among the Twelve after his demise. The point of the first citation is that Scripture allowed for the creation of a vacancy in the leadership circle.[107] Verse 25 of this same psalm says, "I am the object of scorn to my accusers; when they see me they wag their heads." In both Mark 15:29 and Matthew 27:39 this, along with Psalm 22:7, provide the scriptural language for the evangelist to use to describe those who taunt Jesus while on the cross. Like the sufferer in the psalm, Jesus suffers the same sort of mistreatment and ridicule when *in extremis.*[108]

In 2 Corinthians 9:9, as part of a discourse encouraging the Corinthians to give to the collection for the poor in Jerusalem, Paul cites Psalm 112:9, only possibly with a dramatic difference. In the psalm, the psalmist is talking about a righteous person as follows, "they have distributed freely, they have given to the poor. Their righteousness endures forever." The LXX has, "he scattered; he gave to the needy, his righteousness endures forever and ever." In both cases the subject of these remarks is a pious and righteous Israelite, not God. In 2 Corinthians 9:9, which is closer to the LXX rendering, the natural antecedent, having just talked about God providing generously in vv. 8 and 10, is God. The ambiguity here serves Paul's purpose because he is encouraging his audience to model or imitate the generous character of God, and they are assured that God will provide for them in a way that will allow such generosity.[109]

The description of idols in Psalm 115:4–8 is interesting:

> Their idols are silver and gold, the work of human hands. They have mouths but do not speak, eyes but do not see. Ears but do not hear, noses but do not smell. They have hands but do not feel; feet but do not walk.

107. See Marshall, "Acts," 530.
108. Blomberg, "Matthew," 98.
109. See the discussion in Peter Balla, "2 Corinthians," in Moyise, *Commentary on the New Testament Use,* 777–78.

They make no sound in their throats. Those who make them are like them; so are all who trust in them.

These sorts of vivid descriptions of pagan statues provided all kinds of ammunition for various NT writers to critique Greco-Roman religion in various forms. For example, in 1 Corinthians 12:2 Paul reminds his Corinthians that when they were pagans they were enticed and lead astray to idols "that could not speak." Or again, in Revelation 9:20 we hear about those who refused to give up their idols: "they did not repent of the works of their hands or give up worshiping demons and idols of gold and silver and bronze and stone and wood which cannot see or hear or walk." The echo of Psalm 115:4–8 is much stronger here in Revelation, and it is interesting that the only place Paul mentions demons is in his discussion of idols in 1 Corinthians 10.[110]

Psalm 116:3 says, "the snares of death encompassed me, the pangs of Sheol laid hold of me." This seems to be echoed in Acts 2:24 where Peter says that Jesus was freed from "the pains of death." The distress/near death/rescue psalms proved to be very serviceable material to provide sacred language to talk about the death and resurrection of Jesus, as we have already seen in this study.

Paul, like the rest of the writers of the NT, quite naturally resorts to the language of the Psalms when praises come to mind, including quoting or alluding to specific psalms quite directly. Psalm 117:1 reads, "Praise the Lord all you nations, extol him all you peoples." In Romans 15:11 as a verse in the middle of a catena of quotes we find, "Praise the Lord, all you gentiles/nations and let all the peoples praise him." (cf. the LXX αἰνεῖτε τὸν κύριον πάντα τὰ ἔθνη, ἐπαινέσατε αὐτόν, πάντες οἱ λαοί; exactly the same as in Romans 15:11 except for the word order in the first phrase and the addition of the word "and" in the second phrase). Notice the clear distinction made between "the people of God" (οἱ λαοί) and the non-Jewish nations (τὰ ἔθνη) in both the psalm and in Romans. Wagner is completely correct in arguing that Paul is talking about two groups here, as he does in his use of Isaiah 65:1–2 and Psalm 17.[111] Paul is enough of a linguist to follow the MT doing his own translation or the LXX, whichever best suits the occasion, but here surely he is following the LXX quite literally.

At Hebrews 13:6, Psalm 118:6 is quoted in its LXX form: "the Lord is my helper; I will not be afraid. What can anyone do to me?" (κύριος

---

110. On which see ch. 6 above.
111. See Wagner, *Heralds*, 313–15.

ἐμοὶ βοηθός, οὐ φοβηθήσομαι τί ποιήσει μοι ἄνθρωπος). The author of Hebrews is clear that his own Jewish Christian audience has every right to repray this prayer, but now "the Lord" in question is Jesus (cf. Rom 8:31). An interesting echo of Psalm 118:20 appears in John 10:9 where Jesus says, "I am the gate. Whoever enters by me will be saved and will come in and go out and find pasture." The psalm verse reads, "this is the gate of the Lord; the righteous shall enter through it." We have progressed from the Lord opening the gate, to the Lord being the gate mentioned in the psalm.

Psalm 118:22–26 deserves a fuller treatment as it is not merely quoted multiple times and ways in the NT, it becomes the crucial basis for a whole series of arguments about Christ as foundational to the new community of his followers. We will present both the MT and the LXX translations here first.

MT Psalm 118	LXX Psalm 117
22 The stone that the builders rejected has become the chief cornerstone. 23 This is the Lord's doing; it is marvelous in our eyes. 24 This is the day that the Lord has made; let us rejoice and be glad in it. 25 Save us, we beseech you, O Lord! O Lord, we beseech you, give us success! 26 Blessed is the one who comes in the name of the Lord. We bless you from the house of the Lord.	22 A stone which the builders rejected, this one became the chief cornerstone. 23 This was from the Lord, and it is marvelous in our eyes. 24 This is the day that the Lord made; let us rejoice and be glad in it. 25 Ah Lord, do save! Ah Lord, do give success! 26 Blessed is the one who comes in the name of the Lord. We bless you from the house of the Lord.

What was the meaning of this passage in its original setting? The section of the psalm of concern to us is the second part, where we have a toggling back and forth between the voice of the psalmist and the voice of the community. Notice that the one who comes in the name of the Lord (vv.10–12) is said in v. 26 to be blessed. The person in question seems to have survived a dangerous situation. The corporate prayer in vv. 22–25 is on the lips of the congregation. Notice that the psalmist or worship leader speaks, is addressed, and is spoken about.[112] The generic nature of the psalm (who is the individual, what the crisis was, are things not clearly delineated) lends itself to multiple applications after the fact.

The saying in v. 22 seems to have been a proverb about reversal of

112. See Mays, *Psalms*, 375 on all this.

expectations and unexpected outcomes for someone in particular. Who rejected the stone, and who selected it to be the chief cornerstone, or perhaps keystone? It is difficult to say, but one can imagine the psalmist thinking of David, who was not the one selected initially to be king, and even when a replacement among Jesse's sons was being considered he was not "the natural" pick at all. But he was the one that God selected to found the Davidic monarchy as instrumented through Samuel the prophet. Furthermore, there were periods of danger and even rejection for King David, even by his own son Absalom. But David escaped many close scrapes and continued to be king. Perhaps this was originally a psalm used in a celebration of some events in David's life, but we cannot be sure. The psalm is too generic to be certain. Goldingay helpfully points out:

> A stone unsuitable at one stage might be exactly what was required later. A nuance of this is the reusing of stones from demolished buildings, which had a practical rationale, but in connection with a temple would also symbolize and embody continuity between a rebuilt temple and its predecessor. A recycled stone might even end up in a key position, perhaps holding together two walls at right angles at the corner of the building, in the building's foundation or at the top of the superstructure. Jeremiah 51:26 mentions both a cornerstone and a foundation stone. These might be different stones or different descriptions of the same stone. The cornerstone seems to be part of the foundation in Job 38:6 (cf. Isa 28:16), but in Zech 4:7 the headstone seems to be the top stone.[113]

In one sense, a few verses in Psalm 118 became in miniature, in the hands of the evangelist, the description of Christ's last week of life. In all four Gospels, Psalm 118:26a is used by the crowds entering Jerusalem with Jesus to proclaim and acclaim him (Matt 21:9; Mark 11:9–10; Luke 19:38; John 12:13). This is all the more natural if the psalm was originally part of an entrance liturgy for those processing into the temple.[114] Jesus is the one who is blessed as "coming in the name of the Lord." But the portion about "the stone that the builder rejected" is taken to refer to the rejection of Jesus by the "builders of Israel," namely the Jewish authorities and then Pilate. He was cast away by them, but he was selected by God, and so quite to everyone's surprise, Jesus survives the rejection, and the words of Psalm 118:17, "I shall not die but live," come true, again in an unexpected sense, for

---

113. Goldingay, *Psalms: Volume 3*, 361–62.
114. See Brueggemann and Bellinger, *Psalms*, 506–7.

Jesus did die, but lived again by resurrection. The further word about becoming the chief "cornerstone" (v. 22b) through the efforts of God alone, came to be understood as Christ being the foundation or keystone of a whole new community, a new "temple" so to speak, around which stone believers would be built into this new entity. Now the enigmatic nature of this psalm in its original setting has to be admitted and has often been debated. This is so, not least because the Hebrew here has רֹאשׁ פִּנָּה (r'oš pinnâ), which is literally head of the corner, perhaps a stone joining two walls together at the top. The LXX renders this as κεφαλὴν γωνίας, exactly what we also find in the Gospels, which literally reads "head of the corner" as well.

This is why some scholars have suggested the translation cap or keystone, as in a stone which is above, rather than cornerstone which would be at or below ground level. The Testament of Solomon 23:4 cites Psalm 118:22 and seems to view the stone as the most important one in the building of the new temple, a "crowning stone."[115] The problem with this comes in the Christian combination of this text with Isaiah 28:16 which seems clearly enough to refer to a cornerstone (see 1 Pet 2:4–7). From a later theological point of view, with Christ viewed as in heaven and holding things together for God's people from "above" (see e.g., Ephesians), the image of the keystone made better sense. But then we are talking about metaphors, and Jewish and Christian writers were famous for mixing metaphors, so perhaps "head of the corner" and "cornerstone" are ways of talking about Jesus in two different roles, foundational in the latter case, and holding things together from above in the former.

The first citation of Psalm 118:22 in our earliest Gospel comes at Mark 12:10–11 immediately following the telling of the parable of the tenants in the vineyard. As Hays says, without the resurrection, this citation is an unimaginable ending for that parable which concludes with the killing of the son and the casting of his body out of the vineyard.[116] He is right that this sort of combination was only possible with the benefit of hindsight, after the Easter events. Matthew has the position of this citation in the very same place, just after the parable of the tenants in the vineyard, in this case in Matthew 21 (see vv. 33–42). Luke as well has the same placement of the citation after that parable, but as one can see from even a cursory look at Luke 20:17 the evangelist only cites half of the Psalm 118 saying we find in Matthew and Mark.

---

115. See the discussion in Watts, "Mark," 214.
116. Hays, *Echoes of Scripture in the Gospels*, 44.

In both Luke and possibly Matthew there is an additional stone saying which brings the section to a close, a saying we don't find in Mark, namely, "Everyone who falls on this stone will be broken to pieces; and it will crush anyone on whom it falls." Most of the best witnesses include Matthew 21:44 as part of the original text, but it is missing from D and some other important manuscripts. In favor of its being a part of Matthew's Gospel from the start is that its placement is different than in Luke, and the form of the saying varies a little from the Lukan form as well.[117]

In the endless debate about how Paul uses the term "Israel" in his letters (does it refer to non-Christian Jews, Christian Jews, the church as a whole?), one of the more debated texts is Galatians 6:16. Had more attention been paid to the overtones of the text, and its allusion to the Psalms, maybe there would have been less heat and more light on the subject. Psalm 128:6, like Psalm 125:5, has the phrase "peace be upon Israel." Galatians 6:16 has, "as for those who will follow this rule, peace be upon them, and mercy, and upon the Israel of God."

First of all, there is no doubt that the psalmist is referring to ethnic Israel. Second, in Paul's somewhat convoluted sentence he wishes peace on two groups—not one. The rule he is referring to is the recognition that now with the new creation in Christ, neither circumcision nor uncircumcision is anything. Paul suggests to his audience, and perhaps to the Judaizers as well, that if they will follow this principle peace and mercy be upon them. The final clause appears almost as an afterthought, and "also peace be upon the Israel of God." I take this to refer to the very same entity that "Israel" refers to in Romans 9–11—namely, non-Christian Jews.[118] The recognition of the allusion to the two psalm passages should have helped make this conclusion easier to come by.

In the last verse of Psalm 130 we hear of Yahweh that "it is he who will redeem Israel from all its iniquities." In the NT of course this general idea is predicated of Jesus himself, for instance, Matthew 1:21 talks about Jesus saving people from their sins, but the language of rescue and the language for sins is different from either the Hebrew or the LXX, which speaks of ransoming/redeeming Israel from all her "iniquity." Titus 2:14 says of Jesus, "he it is who gave himself for us that he might redeem us from all iniquity" (λυτρώσηται ἡμᾶς ἀπὸ πάσης ἀνομίας). The Titus use of the passage does not mention Israel, and the LXX has the word "its" modifying "iniquity," but otherwise they are

---

117. See the discussion in Metzger, *Textual Commentary*, 47.
118. On this see also Miller, *Israelite Religion*, 319–36.

very close, such that we can speak of an allusion here. Of course the concepts are different, Yahweh rescuing his people does not involve Yahweh offering a human sacrifice, much less sacrificing himself. But this is precisely what Paul is talking about.

In Psalm 132:5 we have the interesting reference to David refusing to go to bed until he has found a house for the God of Jacob or, as he puts it, "until I find a place for the Lord, a dwelling-place for the Mighty One of Jacob." In discussing David, Stephen in Acts 7:46 says that David, "found favor with God and asked that he might find a dwelling-place for the x of Jacob." Some manuscripts fill in the blank with the word "house" some with the word "God" and the text critics have concluded that the reading "house" is better supported and more difficult and so should be preferred.[119] But is it too difficult? After all, David did not ask permission to build a dwelling place for "the house of Jacob," and what would that phrase mean anyway? The Hebrew has לַאֲבִיר יַעֲקֹב (la'abîr ya'akōb), which refers to a dwelling place for the Mighty One of Jacob and the LXX simply has "God." In view of the numerous echoes of the Psalms in this speech, it seems likely that Psalm 132:5 is echoed here, and that the original reading in Acts was "God of Jacob" as in the LXX.

In discoursing about David in comparison to Jesus, Peter reminds his audience at Acts 2:30, "since he [i.e., David] was a prophet, he knew that God had sworn an oath to him that he would put one of his descendants on his throne." In as much as what comes before and after this pronouncement reflects clear indebtedness to the Psalms, it will come as no surprise that in this sentence as well the Psalms are echoed or alluded to, in this case Psalm 132:11, "the Lord swore to David a sure oath from which he will not turn back: one of the sons of your body I will set on your throne." The allusion here is closer to the MT than to the LXX.

Luke 1:69, yet again in a poetic speech (called a prophecy in v. 67), has these words, "He has raised up a horn of salvation for us, in the house of his servant David"; this is at least an echo of Psalm 132:17, for the psalmist, after speaking of salvation, adds "there I will cause a horn to sprout up for David" (the LXX and MT agree).

The sermon of James is redolent with wisdom language, including both the wisdom language of the OT and of his brother Jesus.[120] At James 1:17 we find a characterization of God which has seemed odd to some. He is called the father of lights right after James speaks of God

---

119. See Metzger, *Textual Commentary*, 308–9 for discussion.
120. On which see Witherington, *Jesus the Sage*.

as the one from whom every good and perfect gift comes down from above. James is probably alluding to Psalm 136:4-9, where the psalmist is rolling through a list of the creation gifts God has given us all, and we are told he is the one who "made the great lights, for his mercy endures forever." A careful reading of James in light of the Psalms, particularly the praise Psalms, can illuminate several of the dark corners of that sermon.

It is a good thing from time to time to remind ourselves not merely of the ways that the NT quotes, alludes to, borrows from the Psalms in many ways, but also of the ways it profoundly differs from it, indeed even disagrees with the sentiments of one psalmist or another. An excellent example of this is when we hear the psalmist in Psalm 139:19-22 say

> Oh that you would kill the wicked, O God,
> and that the bloodthirsty would depart from me—
> those who speak of you maliciously,
> and lift themselves up against you for evil.
> Do I not hate those who hate you, O Lord?
> And do I not loathe those who rise up against you?
> I hate them with a perfect hatred.
> I count them my enemies.

Contrast this with Jesus's words in Matthew 5:43-44: "you have heard it said 'you shall love your neighbor and hate your enemy.' But I say to you, love your enemies and pray for those who persecute you so that you may be children of your Father in heaven" (cf. Rom 12:14-21: overcome evil with good).

It would appear clear that Jesus, who regularly draws on the Psalms in many ways, including in his last words on earth, feels free to differ from the psalmist in this matter—indeed differ strongly. Furthermore, he tells his disciples that if they obey the teaching he gives in Matthew 5:43 they will be *like their heavenly Father in character*. Here is one more opportunity to remind ourselves that the Psalms are a revelation of what was genuinely on the heart of the psalmist—good, bad, or ugly. The Psalms speak to God, they are not always speaking for God, and should not always be seen as oracles revealing God's character and will. A critical discernment of the substance of the Psalms is necessary. Not seldom genuine human nature, desires, will, is all they reveal—not the character of God, or the will of God, which Jesus sees very differently than the psalmist who wrote Psalm 139, as does Paul, taking his cues from the teaching of Jesus.

The prayer practices of early Israel were shaped by the Psalter, not only in the use of language, but in the prayer gestures or postures followed. One good example of this is the lifting up of hands in prayer. This is referred to in various places in the Psalter (see, e.g., Ps 141:2) and we hear in 1 Timothy 2:8 the exhortation to the Christian men in Ephesus that they too should lift up holy hands in prayer, a gesture of sincerity but also of reaching out to God and pleading with God.

Psalm 143:2 involves a confession of the psalmist who admits that none are righteous before God. The LXX of this has οὐ δικαιωθήσεται ἐνώπιόν σου, which should sound familiar to students of Romans 3, which reads at v. 20: οὐ δικαιωθήσεται . . . ἐνώπιον αὐτοῦ. The psalmist asks for God not to enter into judgment with him for "none will be judged to be righteous before you." The psalmist is not talking about a legal fiction called "justification," he is talking about the actual moral quality of being righteous. I would suggest that Paul, especially in light of the references to the law and the knowledge of sin = unrighteousness, is talking about the same thing.

We have already had occasion to note how the Psalms have been drawn on to cast the narratives about Jesus on the Sea of Galilee, sleeping in the boat and stilling the storm, or walking on the water. In Matthew 14:30–31 we have a further instance of this; it echoes Psalm 144:7, which is a prayer for rescue, much like Peter's cry to Jesus when he was sinking, and it reads, "stretch out your hand from on high; set me free and rescue me from the mighty waters." This story is unique to Matthew's Gospel, and what it tells us is that not just Luke, but also Matthew had a way of drawing on the language of the Psalms to frame his gospel material.

Upon the release of Peter and John they return to their community in Jerusalem to report, and praise is given to God in Acts 4:24 in the form "almighty Lord, who made the heaven and the earth, the sea and everything in them," an extended phrase which we also find on the lips of Paul in Acts 14:15; in both cases this is an allusion to or even a partial quotation of Psalm 146:6: "God, who made heaven and earth, the sea and all that is in them." The LXX of this verse has τὸν ποιήσαντα τὸν οὐρανὸν καὶ τὴν γῆν, τὴν θάλασσαν καὶ πάντα τὰ ἐν αὐτοῖς, which should be compared to both Acts 14:15: ὃς ἐποίησεν τὸν οὐρανὸν καὶ τὴν γῆν καὶ τὴν θάλασσαν καὶ πάντα τὰ ἐν αὐτοῖς and Acts 4:24: σὺ ὁ ποιήσας τὸν οὐρανὸν καὶ τὴν γῆν καὶ τὴν θάλασσαν καὶ πάντα τὰ ἐν αὐτοῖς. I do not doubt that many early Jewish Christians framed their prayers drawing on the familiar language of the Psalms that they had sung and prayed before, but the community in Acts 4 surely must have prayed in Aramaic. It is surely Luke who has taken his Christian source material, whether from the words of Jesus or Peter or Paul, and often drawn on the language of the Psalms in the LXX to convey in Greek what they said.

Psalm 147:9 reads, "he gives to the animals their food, and to the young ravens when they cry," which seems clearly alluded to in Luke 12:24, "consider the ravens [τοὺς κόρακας]: they neither sow nor reap . . . and yet God feeds them" (cf. Matt 6:26). Here, clearly enough Luke is following the LXX which has καὶ τοῖς νεοσσοῖς τῶν κοράκων, whereas in Matthew the more generic word for birds is used, providing us with yet more evidence that Luke frames his discourses and even his narrative using the language of the LXX, in this case the Psalms.

As we have mentioned earlier in this chapter, the language of the Psalms was the ready resource for NT writers when songs, or prayers, or praise exclamations were being written about, for example, notice the echo in Mark 11:10 // Matthew 21:9 where we have the familiar phrase Ὡσαννὰ ἐν τοῖς ὑψίστοις. Whereas the Hebrew has the word "Hallelujah" at Psalm 148:1, in the LXX we have αἰνεῖτε αὐτὸν ἐν τοῖς ὑψίστοις.

Finally, as Paul begins probably his most famous poetic passage in 1 Corinthians 13, he speaks of being like a clanging cymbal if he has no love. First Corinthians scholars have scrambled to find parallels from the Greco-Roman environment of Corinth, but perhaps at the end of the day, what brought this image to mind was the very last psalm in the Psalter which at v. 5 says, "Praise him with clanging cymbals, praise him with loud crashing cymbals." The LXX of this verse has κυμβάλοις εὐήχοις and Paul has κύμβαλον ἀλαλάζον but the instrument mentioned is the same as is the adjectival concept modifying it.

Conclusions

We examined Psalms 107, 110, 119, and 145 in some detail in this chapter, and also Psalm 118 in the crucial verses so often used in the NT. We did not detect a difference in the way the Psalms from book 5 were used by the NT writers than psalms from the previous four books, except that it is noticeable that the songs of ascent and the final five psalms in the Psalter do not come up for much use at all in the NT, but then we do not have a hymnbook in the NT, nor do we have any real discussions about pilgrimages or festivals in the Epistles in the NT. In fact, what we find is evidence that the early Christians were not going to perpetuate the priests, temples, and sacrifices approach to ancient religion, if by that one means literal sacrifices in literal temples offered by literal priests. The death of Jesus is seen across the NT as the end to that whole sort of approach.

What we need to do is ferret out evidence of early Christian hymns and attitudes toward worship through mostly indirect evidence or small hints. We do know that the earliest Christians sang the psalms, and indeed are instructed to do so in Ephesians 5:19. We may assume that the Psalter continued to be a go-to resource for early Christian worship, just as it was for early Christian reflection on the Christ event, and on the early Christian life.

The notable difference in early Christian piety and emphasis can be seen, for example, in this chapter in how little is done with the great torah song, Psalm 119. Yes, some phrases and key verses are plucked from this gigantic song and recycled, but by and large is does not come up for the kind of use that some of the verses in Psalms 110, 118, and 145 do, and this should not surprise us. The earliest Christians, by and large, did not see themselves as perpetuators of the Mosaic covenant, but rather of a new covenant, and so even when they drew on the law or the Psalms' recycling of legal material, they saw it as one form of wisdom along with the teaching of Jesus and the Apostles, but not "the" source of wisdom.

The very remarkable use of Psalm 110 vv. 1 and 4 as well as the use of the stone passage in Psalm 118 shows a creative use of certain key psalm verses for christological purposes. This was not just a matter of transferring things previously said of others to Christ, it also was an attempt to make divine claims about Jesus, he is David's lord, and not only so, he is reigning at present at the right hand of God. This psalm material was seen not only as particularly suitable for talking about Jesus's present role in heaven (not merely ruling but serving as a high priest in the heavenly sanctuary interceding for believers), but also about his previous role on earth, as the stone that the builders of early Judaism rejected. Not surprisingly, it was Paul who managed to find a way to use Psalm 110:1 to talk about Christ's future role on earth when he returns and "puts all of his enemies under his feet."

As we have already seen, narrative poems, including salvation historical review poems, could serve to provide color and descriptors for narratives in the NT about Jesus and his first followers. Such a poem is

Psalm 107, the language of which could be used to describe Jesus stilling a storm on the Sea of Galilee, or to describe the future messianic banquet attendees and where they came from. Such psalms also provided patterns of how to pray when in distress, or even how to sing when in distress, like Paul and Barnabas did in jail. They also provided assurance that God answered such distress signals coming from his people.

A psalm like Psalm 145 provides a clear clue about how the teachings of Exodus about the character of God (see vv. 8–9) were still valid, a form of enduring wisdom that God was merciful and kind and compassionate. We saw reasons to doubt that the correct translation of *hesed* was covenant love and loyalty when the discussion was about God's way of relating to sinners, or even gentiles to whom he owed no loyalty and had no covenant with. The strain of universalism in some of these psalms (for example the talk of "the sons of Adam" rather than "the sons of Jacob") helped the NT writers as well to find scriptural language that suited their gospel message and attempt to bring good news to both Jew and gentile alike.

Some of the most creative uses of the material in the fifth book of the Psalter could be seen in the small turns of phrases, some of the echoes that are often overlooked in the study of citations and clear allusions. For example, the use of Psalm 143:2 to talk about the righteousness of God and about being "reckoned righteous" seemed clearly to indicate that the discussion was about God's character and the character he wanted replicated in his people, but also that God was prepared to take Abraham's trust, or Phinehas's intervention, and credit it as righteousness. This was the language of business, not the courtrooms, and it was not about some legal fiction or alien righteousness being imputed to Abraham or Phineas. Nor is that the case in Romans either.

One of the more stark contrasts between what we find in some of these psalms and what we find in the teaching and attitudes of Jesus and Paul comes clearly to light when one examines the imprecations or curses in some of these psalms. Jesus calls for love of enemies, not cursing them, and indeed he calls for his disciples not to use any kind of oaths at all, not even affirming ones. The fact that Jesus and his followers, while certainly seeing the Psalms as God's word, could nonetheless disagree with the views of some of the psalmists is striking, and we have suggested at various points that this sort of approach was possible because it was known that the Psalms were a true revelation of the human heart, not always of God's heart, and as such they could be read and used critically, carefully, and selectively. Sometimes, the wisdom of Jesus and his followers amounted to saying "go and do likewise" to some things said in the Psalms, and sometimes "go and do otherwise." *This critical approach to the Psalter is something we did not see when it came to the handling of Isaiah in the previous volume. There was no critique explicit or implicit of the oracles in Isaiah, but that is not the case when it comes to the material of the Psalms.* In our concluding chapter we will discuss various of these things in more detail and draw together some of the key insights from all the Psalms and how the earliest Christians read them.

8

"The Song Remains the Same"

When indeed the Holy Spirit saw that the human race was guided only with difficulty towards virtue, and that because of our inclination toward pleasure, we were neglectful of an upright life, what did he do? The delight of melody he mingled with the doctrines, so that by the pleasantness and softness of the sound heard we might receive without perceiving it the benefit of the words, just as the wise physicians who, when giving the fastidious rather bitter drugs to drink, frequently smear the cup with honey.
—Basil of Caesarea, Homily on Psalm 1:1

A hymn is the praise of God with song; a song is the exultation of the mind dwelling on eternal things, bursting forth in the voice.
—Thomas Aquinas, *Commentary on the Psalms*, Preface.

On[1] the surface of things, one might think or assume that the enormous amount of use of the Psalms in the NT, whether citations, allusions, echoes, or simply use of language or ideas might mean "the song remains the same . . . second verse, same as the first." But in fact, this would not be quite correct in various ways. For one thing, the psalmists are not talking about a dying and rising of the sufferer in their right-

---

1. With apologies to Mssrs. R. Plant and J. Page for the title.

PSALMS OLD AND NEW

eous sufferer psalms. They are talking about last minute rescues of someone about to die or be killed during various sorts of crises.

And yet the language could be partially reappropriated and reused to good effect in the NT to talk about Jesus and his death, and the trials and tribulations of his followers. The operating principle was *analogy*, not "this equals that," nor even necessarily "this is what that old text was truly and originally about." But then the very nature of poetry, especially wisdom poetry, which is inherently metaphorical, involves the use of *analogy*. When the poetry is often as generic and universal as the Psalms, speaking to the general human conditions (the fears, the hopes, the dreams, the foibles, the prayers of humans hoping for divine help), then the door is left wide open for later meaningful appropriation in ways that go beyond, but not against, the original meaning of the poetry.

How the Psalms could and would be used depended in part on what fit in well with the already preexisting Christ narrative (including his words and deeds), as well as the experiences of his first followers. The primary narrative was the new one, freshly told and newly written, the gospel story, the newly minted living word, and the stories of his followers in Acts.[2] The secondary source of language and material was the OT, and especially the Psalms and Isaiah. The death and resurrection of Jesus had flipped the script, and the old, old story said or sung, was no longer the primary one.

Richard Hays in his helpful reflections on the way the resurrection affected the reading of the OT, suggests that a conversion of the imagination happened to the earliest Christians that caused them to read the OT differently, not as an end in itself, but rather as something which foreshadowed or prefigured a greater reality yet to come, which they were convinced had indeed come in the person of Jesus. But just the coming of Jesus was not enough. It was his bodily resurrection, demonstrating that God's yes to life was louder than death's no—even after death had done its worst in the case of Jesus—that led to a reading of the OT with Easter eyes, so to speak. They read it with eschatological hope, read it as though all the different major sections of Scripture, the Law, the Prophets, the Psalms in one sense or another bore witness to Jesus (see Luke 24).[3]

---

2. In an oral is primary, written is secondary culture this is hardly surprising. Notice that the phrase "word of God" in the NT *never refers to a written text*. It refers in a couple of places in Johannine literature to the Son of God, but mostly the phrase in Paul and in Acts and in Hebrews refers to the oral proclamation of the gospel; cf. 1 Thess 2:13 and Ben Witheringon III, *The Living Word of God: Rethinking the Theology of the Bible* (Waco, TX: Baylor University Press, 2007).

But no one would have ever known this if Jesus had not risen from the dead, and left clues as to how the OT should now be understood in the kingdom age. The understanding of this was only possible after the resurrection, in retrospect, and with the guidance of the now indwelling Holy Spirit. The end of the story made clear that the understanding of the earlier portions of the story had been somewhat askew (mistaking the part for the whole), or inadequate, or most certainly incomplete for the story was not over yet. About this fact, that the story was far from over, both followers of Jesus, and all sorts of other early Jews could agree. God was not finished with Israel yet.

One of the factors that led to this *conversion of the imagination* was the beguiling nature of the Psalms. Athanasius, realizing this, says:

For this . . . is the curious thing about the Psalms; that in reading the other books lectors tend to proclaim the sayings of the holy authors whatever subjects they are talking about, *as concerning those about whom the books are written, and listeners will understand that they themselves are different people from those dealt with in the text. But . . . the person who takes up this book [i.e., the Psalter] will read out . . . the Psalms as if they were their own words; and the ones who hear them will be deeply moved, as if he himself were speaking, and will be affected by the words of these songs as if they were their own.*[4]

The Psalms, in short, speak not only "for us" but if we read them and embrace them they speak "as us."

The Psalms change the human heart not only from the outside in, like hearing a true prophecy or a late word from God does, but from the inside out, for they become our words in the sincere recital of them. Indeed, total immersion in the Psalms happened because they were sung, they were heard, they were responsively read, they were taught, they were memorized, they were preached to a degree unlike any other form of the OT. To our knowledge, the prophecies were not sung in the synagogues or in early Christianity, nor were the laws, nor were the historical narratives unless they were retold in the Psalms. In an oral culture such material that was so ubiquitous in worship and in instruction, and in personal piety as well, naturally funded the lexicon of faith and led to psalm material showing up in one form or another on almost every page of the NT.

In the view of the writers of the NT, God himself had planted some

---

3. Richard B. Hays, "Reading Scripture in Light of the Resurrection," in *The Art of Reading Scripture*, ed. Ellen F. Davis and Richard B. Hays (Grand Rapids: Eerdmans, 2003), 216–38.
4. Athanasius, *Ep. Marcel.*, 11, PG 27.21 (emphasis added).

seed ideas, concepts, even institutions like the monarchy and the priesthood that are rhapsodized about in the Psalms. In the view of those NT writers, God all along intended those ideas and institutions to only fully realize their promise, or come to full expression in the messiah, and in the eschatological age he ushered in. Was this more than the psalmist's realized or understood? Probably so, but then poetry is always a risky thing—it can mean more than you realize when first you create it. They might well be surprised how things turned out and came to fruition, but I doubt they would have objected to the use made of the Psalms by the NT writers because they would *not* have seen it as *at odds with or contradicting* what they said and meant in the Psalter. Plenty of stories have striking and unexpected twists and turns before they reach a climax or even a surprising or unforeseen ending, and the story of the Davidic king and his "seed" is one such story. What the Psalmists would *not* likely have said is that the story as the NT writers told it was a contradictory story to the one they originally imagined.

It is interesting that one's evaluation of how the Psalms are used in the NT depends in part on one's own theology. If, for example, one doesn't believe that Jesus ought to be considered part of the divine identity, God's unique Son, then obviously one will find the transfer of passages which in the OT are clearly referencing Yahweh to Jesus as not merely audacious but even *illegitimate*. But clearly enough, for various NT writers they are not content to just apply royal psalms to Jesus as a latter day king. They also apply passages that refer to Yahweh to the Christ, for example, passages dealing with the final judgment of all human beings. One could further pursue this line of thinking by pointing out that if one doesn't believe the eschatology of the NT, in particular that Jesus will return to judge the living and the dead, then one will also find the transfer of that role of final judge from Yahweh to Jesus also to be a misuse of a psalm that was originally about someone else.

The writers of the NT did *not* read the Psalms uncritically. A different kind of theological and ethical judgment seems to be already in play on the part of these writers in various ways. What I mean by this is that in light of the life and teachings of Jesus, there were certain things said in the Psalms about the king that did not comport with their christology. For example, if one were to take Psalm 51 as a royal confession, it would not fit Jesus. Or if one were take the example of the imprecatory psalms, such as the pronouncements about the Edomite babies, again the NT writers would bypass such material due to what they now believed about both the merciful character and will of God and of his

Christ and of the need for mercy and forgiveness even of enemies by
Jesus's followers as a result of Christ's teaching. Or again the emphasis
on lament in the Psalter did not suit the eschatological mood of the NT
writers for the most part. Or the focus on the law also did not become
a major emphasis in the new community of Christ, so it is unsurpris-
ing that the torah psalms, especially Psalm 119, come up for almost
no mention in the NT. *The psalm material would have to be read critically
because what it mainly revealed was what was on the psalmist's heart.* I would
suggest that these factors help to explain the rather clear selectivity in
the use of some particular psalm verses and not others in their appropriation of psalm material.

There were other factors in play as well that led to selectivity in the
case of the evangelists, namely the givenness of the life of Jesus. There
were some things in the psalms that could be used to tell the story of
Jesus because they corresponded to what was known of the story about
his passion, but there were also some things that could not be used, for
example, Jesus would not be rescued from the very brink of death. As I
have said, the primary story was the story of Jesus, which normed how
the stories of the righteous sufferers, whether in the Psalms or in Isaiah, could be used to illustrate, to express, to add color to the passion
narrative. Yes, in some cases fulfillment proved to be the appropriate
term for the relationship between a psalm like Psalm 22 and the suffering and abuse of Christ on the cross.

One of the things that we discussed repeatedly in the Lexicon of
Faith sections of the exegetical chapters is that the language of the
Psalms provided a very significant portion of the vocabulary of faith
for the NT writers. By the principle of analogy, and because they
believed they were dealing with the same God as the writers of the
Psalms, they found the language of the Psalter accurately described
their own experiences and were happy to use it for that purpose. As
we have stressed, this did not amount to contextual exegesis of the
OT and should not be faulted for not perfectly cohering with that sort
of interpretive approach. We have called this a "homiletical" use of
the Psalms, not an attempt to suggest "this is that" or even "this fulfills that" necessarily. Obviously, this sort of creative use of the language does assume some continuity between how the language was
used before and how it is used in the NT, or else the reuse doesn't really
work, it isn't apt. Rather, *similar experiences led to the use of familiar sacred
religious language to express one's own perspectives on such experiences.*

We saw in the examination of Psalm 41 that the language in the verse in question was suitable in both contexts (the psalm and the Gospel contexts) , but the contexts were notably different. In the psalm the person in question was ill and his "friends" stopped eating with him; not so at the Last Supper in the case of Jesus and Judas. This is only problematic if one insists that the NT writers were attempting to do contextual exegesis of the psalm, and did it poorly. They were not. They were simply using psalm diction to describe another meal in a different context.

One of the things that becomes very clear, besides the obvious fact that the earliest Jewish Christian writers were likely to remember and turn to the Psalms when they were composing their own songs, hymns, poems, benedictions, doxologies, and prayers, as we have seen again and again in this study, is that the NT writers were diligently searching the OT Scriptures, including the Psalms, to explain the novelties, the surprising aspects about the story of Jesus. No early Jew I know of was expecting a Davidic king to rule in heaven over God's people or be a heavenly high priest according to the order of Melchizedek, but somehow Psalm 110 vv. 1 and 4 helped the earliest Christians envision this as all part of God's plan from the beginning. No early Jew that I know of expected a massive, almost universal rejection of their own messiah by his fellow Jews, but Psalm 118:22–25 helped the earliest Christian writers make sense of this in terms of God's salvation plan. It was especially *the surprising and even scandalous aspects* about the story of Jesus, especially its ending, that required scriptural support, explanation, and illumination again and again. The Psalms regularly were put in service to provide a guide for the perplexed or those who were skeptical about Jesus of Nazareth and his remarkable and shocking career.

If we ask what was the catalyst for the eschatological and christological use of the Psalms in the NT, no doubt some credit must be given to the charged Jewish atmosphere that existed in and around the Holy Land during the early first century, which produced those sorts of reflections in the Qumran community, by John the Baptizer, and of course by Jesus. Jesus's own use of the Psalms in these ways surely must have provided some precedent and impetus for his earliest disciples and the writers of the NT to follow suit, and follow suit they did, especially in the use of parts of Psalms 2, 22, 110, 118, and various other texts as well.

At the same time, the NT writers realized that the use of the Psalms of the historical Jesus was one thing, and the use of the Psalms of the exalted Jesus, at the right hand of the Father, was another. Psalm 110

vv. 1 and 4, for instance, went from being a promise in Mark 12, to being an assumed reality for the many NT writers who used Psalm 110:1 of the exalted Christ, and especially the author of Hebrews who focused so prominently on Psalm 110:1 and 4. What this meant was that the application of the Psalms to Jesus was not exhausted and did not become unprofitable after the ascension, rather there were just other sorts of applications of a variety of verses that could now be offered to speak of Christ's role in heaven, or in the future at the eschaton.

From time to time we have stressed not only the poetic quality of the Psalms and how that should affect our interpretation of them, but we noted as well that they are songs, meant to reach the affective side of the human personality as well as the cognitive side. They are brimming over with emotions of all sorts. It is then not surprising that in the few places we hear about Jesus's emotions or inner spiritual life in the Synoptics or in John, the Psalms come into play. For example, Psalms 42–43 recounts the feelings of a troubled and grieving praying person, and this same language shows up in Mark 14 on the lips of Jesus to describe his inner turmoil as he is about to pray in the garden of Gethsemane. We may also think of the reference to Jesus having compassion on the crowd because "they were like sheep without a shepherd," another allusion to the Psalms. We should not neglect the emotional character of such language, nor ignore that once again it was some of the obviously emotive language of songs/psalms that was drawn on to express inner feelings and the state of one's spirit.

In our study of the remarkable and lengthy use of Psalm 95 in the homily called Hebrews we stressed the following: *the OT is being handled in a thoroughly Jewish manner, even with all the new christological insight and readings. The Christians were of course not alone in reading the OT in a contemporizing manner, nor were they alone in reading it in an eschatological and messianic manner. What we find almost never in the NT is a use of the Psalms or other portions of the OT in the manner we find it so often used by Philo, the great allegorizer of the OT. The relentlessly **historical** orientation, including a focus on future history (eschatology) of the NT handlers of the OT is apparent again and again, even in Hebrews. In our particular text under scrutiny the author of Hebrews makes the argument, on the basis of the assumption that if David (as the LXX suggested) was the author of this psalm, then obviously since David lived well after the time of Joshua and the initial entering of the promised land, then he could not have been referring to that event when he talks about entering into God's rest, rather he was looking mainly to the future,* *though through catchword connection based on the word "rest" he is able to connect Psalm 95 with the story of God's original resting in Genesis 2.* The use of the Psalms in the NT is seldom ahistorical like Philo's use of the OT, even at its most creative (e.g., when we are told that it is the voice of Christ himself speaking in a Psalm). All of the writers of the NT have a sense of history and of progressive revelation, and these presuppositions undergird and affect their use of the Psalms. The principle of analogy assumes a historical before and after, as does the use of typology.

As we said at the end of the discussion of book 4 of the Psalter: *Not all the use of the Psalms was christological, sometimes it was just logical. Not all the use of the Psalms was exegetical or alluded to larger OT contexts, sometimes it was just homiletical. Often the language of the Psalms was appropriated to address some very different subjects than the psalmist addressed. When that happened, it was not because the author took a cavalier approach to interpreting the Psalms, it is because he found the generic and multivalent character of much of the Psalms' poetic language open to all sorts of reuse and relecture. Its very openness, universalness, evocativeness, and metaphorical character fairly begged for a variety of applications and repurposing.*

The conclusion we drew at the end of chapter 5 proves suitable as a conclusion for this whole study: *The Psalms were the language of devotion, the language of hopes and dreams, the language of emotional expressions of the joys and sorrows of life, the language of aspiration and inspiration, and the writers of the NT not only knew this, they embraced it. The Psalms were the language with which the devout reached out to God and unburdened their hearts and souls. It is how they prayed and thought about God. And in the NT, it is how they thought about and expressed their faith in Jesus. Yes, the prophets provided oracles, and previews of coming attractions, but the Psalms taught people how to embrace their faith and their God, even in the midst of suffering, sin, and sorrow, even when the promises of God seem to have failed.*

Finally, if we were to compare the finding from *Isaiah Old and New* and this study it is interesting that there is some overlap, in part because the Psalms sometimes quote divine oracles (e.g., Psalm 110:1 and 4) which the earliest Christians found especially helpful as ways of explaining the unique features of the Christ event, but also because both Isaiah and the Psalms uses poetic language to make their points. What is different is that the NT writers feel free to take a more critical approach to the Psalms because they are the true expressions of what was on the psalmist's heart, not always the true expressions of what God had in mind. I do not detect this same critical approach to the oracles of God in Isaiah. In other words, the NT writers, while seeing all this material as Holy Writ, also had some hermeneutical sophistication in recognizing the differences in the genre of literature and the character of the content. It was taken for granted that what Isaiah said, God said. By contrast, it was not taken for granted that everything the psalmist said revealed the heart and mind and will and character of God. Often it did do the latter, but not always, and it had to be sifted through the filter of the Christ event and the fullest revelation of God's character in Christ and his teachings. Sometimes, the Psalms were just a truthful and insightful revelation of what was on the human heart of the person who penned the song.

Appendix A

Psalms References in the Nestlé-Aland Novum Testamentum Graece, 28th edition

This index of citations, arranged by Psalm verse, comes from the 28th edition of the *Novum Testamentum Graece* by Eberhard Nestlé and Kurt Aland (Deutsche Bibelgesellschaft, 2012), 783–88. As close scrutiny will show, various of these references are not to citations, allusions, or echoes of the Psalms in the NT, but in many cases just to general ideas or key terms or assumed background material from the Psalms that appear in the NT. This index represents the maximum one could claim when it comes to the use of the Psalms in the NT. Note that the references in italics are seen as quotations of some sort.

Psalmi

1:1	Acts 24:5	**2:9**	*Rev 2:27, 12:5, 19:15*
3	Matt 21:41	11	2 Cor 7:15
5	Matt 13:49	**4:5**	*Eph 4:26*
2:1f.	*Acts 4:25*	**5:10**	*Rom 3:13*
2	John 1:41 Acts 4:27 Rev 11:15, 17:18, 19:19	**6:3**	Matt 15:22
7	Matt 3:17 Mark 1:11 Luke 3:22 John 1:34 *Acts 13:33 Heb 1:5, 5:5*	4f.	*John 12:27*
8	*Heb 1:2 Rev 2:27*	9	*Matt 7:23 Luke 13:27*

7:10	Rev 2:23	**18**:50	*Rom 15:9*
13	Luke 13:3	**19**,2	Rom 1:20
8:3	Matt 21:16	5	*Rom 10:18*
4	Rom 1:20	8	Jas 1:25
5–7	*Heb 2:6*	10	Rev 16:7
6f.	Acts 17:28	15	Acts 7:35
7	*1 Cor 15:27 Eph 1:22*	**21**:10	Jas 5:3
9:9	Acts 17:31 Rev 19:11	**22**:2	*Matt 27:46 Mark 15:34*
14	Matt 15:22, 16:18	3	Luke 18:7
10:5.10	Matt 20:25	6	Rom 5:5 Phil 1:20
7	*Rom 3:14*	7	Mark 9:12
14, 18	Jas 1:27	8	Matt 27:29, 39 Mark 15:29
16	Rev 11:15	8f.	Luke 23:35
14:1	Titus 1:16	9	*Matt 27:43*
1–3	*Rom 3:10*	14	*1 Pet 5:8*
7	Rom 11:26	15	Matt 26:37
15:2	John 8:40 Acts 10:35 Heb 11:33	19	*Matt 27:35 Mark 15:24 Luke 23:34 John 19:24*
16:5f.	Luke 10:42	22	2 Tim 4:17
8–11	*Acts 2:25*	23	John 20:17 *Heb 2:12*
10	*Acts 13:35*	24	Rev 19:5
17:15	Rev 22:4	25	Heb 5:7
18:1,3	Luke 1:69	29	Rev 11:15
6	Acts 2:24	**23**:1	Rev 7:17
7	Jas 5:4	2f.	Rev 7:17
17	Matt 14:31	5	Luke 7:46
18	Luke 1:71	**24**,1	*1 Cor 10:26*
21, 25	Jas 4:8	2	2 Pet 3:5
30	Matt 6:13	3f.	Matt 5:8

25:5	John 16:13	**34**:3f.	Luke 1:46
8	Luke 6:35, 18:19	8	Heb 1:14
9	Matt 22:16 Mark 12:14	9	*1 Pet 2:3*
10	John 1:17	13–17	*1 Pet 3:10*
11	Luke 18:13	14	Jas 1:26
20	Rom 5:5	15	Heb 12:14
26:2	Matt 6:13	19	Matt 5:3
6	Matt 27:24	20	Acts 7:10 2 Tim 3:11
27:2	Rev 17:16	21	*John 19:36*
7	Matt 15:22	**35**:8	Rom 11:9
12	Matt 26:59 Mark 14:56	9	Luke 1:47
28:4	Rev 20:13	11	Mark 14:56
29:3	Acts 7:2 Eph 1:17	16	Acts 7:54
3f.	Rev 10:3	19	*John 15:25*
31:1f.	*Rom 4:7*	23	John 20:28
6	*Luke 23:46*	**36**:2	*Rom 3:18*
10	Matt 26:37 John 12:27	8	Matt 23:37 Luke 13:34
20	Titus 3:4	**37**:2	Luke 12:28
25	1 Cor 16:13	4	Matt 6:33
32:2	John 1:47 Rev 14:5	11	Matt 5:5
5	1 John 1:9	12	Acts 7:54
9	Jas 3:3	13	Heb 11:40
33:3	Rev 14:3	14, 32	Jas 5:6
6	John 1:3 2 Thess 2:8 Heb 11:3	25	Matt 6:33
9	Heb 11:3	**38**:1	1 Cor 11:24
10	1 Cor 1:19	12	Luke 23:49
11	Luke 7:30	14–16	Matt 26:63 Mark 14:61
19	2 Cor 1:10	**39**:4	Luke 24:32

39:6	Jas 4:14	**50:**9–13	Acts 17:25
7	Luke 12:20	12	1 Cor 10:26
9f.	Matt 26:63 Mark 14:61	14	Heb 13:15
12	Jas 4:14	15	Jas 5:13
13	Heb 11:13 1 Pet 2:11	20	Luke 2:14
40:4	Rev 14:3	23	Heb 13:15
7	Eph 5:2	**51:**6	Luke 14:18 *Rom 3:4*
7–9	*Heb 10:5*	7	John 9:34 Rom 7:14
11	John 1:17	14	Mark 14:38
41:10	Mark 14:18 *John 13:18* Acts 1:16	15	Matt 22:16 Mark 12:14 Luke 22:32 Jas 5:20
14	Luke 1:68 Rom 9:5	**53:**5	2 Cor 11:20
42:3	Acts 14:15 John 3:2 Rev 22:4	**55:**16	Rev 19:20
6–12	*Mark 14:34*	23	Luke 10:41 1 Pet 5:7
6, 12	*Matt 26:38*	**56:**14	2 Cor 1:10
43:5	Matt 26:38 Mark 14:34	**57:**2	Matt 23:37
44:4, 6	Luke 1:49	**61:**5	Matt 23:37
23	*Rom 8:36*	6	Rev 11:18
27	Matt 15:25	**62:**11	1Tim 7:17
45:7	Heb 12:26	13	*Matt 16:27 Rom 2:6 2 Tim 4:14*
7f.	*Heb 1:8*	**63:**2	John 19:28
46:4	Luke 21:25	3	Acts 7:55
5	Rev 22:1	10	Eph 4:9
7	Heb 11:34	**65:**5	1 Cor 3:17
47:9	Rev 5:7	8	Matt 8:26, 14:32 Mark 4:39 Luke 8:24, 21:25
48:3	Matt 5:35	**66:**10	1 Pet 1:7
49:8	1 Tim 2:6	18	John 9:31
8f.	Matt 16:26 Mark 8:37	**67:**3	Luke 3:6 Acts 28:28
17–21	Luke 12:21	**68:**2	Luke 1:51

68:19	*Eph 4:8*	**73**:26	Luke 10:42
30	Rev 21:24	28	1 Cor 6:17
30–32	Acts 8:27	**74**:2	Acts 20:28 Heb 12:22
35	John 9:24	17	Acts 17:26
36	2 Thess 1:10	**75**:9	Matt 26:39 Mark 14:36 Rev 14:10
69:2	Matt 14:31	**76**:6	Rom 1:21
5	*John 15:25*	**77**:19	Heb 12:26
9	Mark 3:21	20	Rom 11:33
10	*John 2:17 Rom 15:3 Heb 11:26*	**78**:2	*Matt 13:35*
15f.	Matt 14:31	4	Matt 21:15
22	Matt 27:34, 48 Mark 15:36 Luke 23:36 John 19:28	8	Acts 2:40
23f.	*Rom 11:9*	15f.	1 Cor 10:4
25	Rev 16:1	18	1 Cor 10:9
26	Luke 13:35 *Acts 1:20*	23	Rev 4:1
29	Rev 3:5	24	*John 6:31 Rev 2:17*
70:1	1 Cor 11:24	24f.	1 Cor 10:3
6	Matt 15:25	31	1 Cor 10:5
71:2, 15f., 18	Rom 3:21	35	Acts 7:35
19	Luke 1:49	36	Mark 7:6
20	Rom 10:7	37	Acts 8:21
24	Rom 3:21	41	Matt 16:1
72:2	Rev 19:11	44	Rev 16:4
10	Rev 21:26	45	Rev 16:13
10f., 15	Matt 2:11	56	Matt 16:1
17	Luke 1:48	68	Rev 20:9
18	Matt 21:15 Luke 1:68	70	Rom 1:1
73:1	Matt 5:8	70–72	Luke 2:8
13	Matt 27:24	71f.	John 21:16

79:1	Luke 21:24 1 Cor 3:17 Rev 11:2	**89**:11	Luke 1:51
3	Rev 16:6	12	1 Cor 10:26
5	Rev 6:10	18	Luke 2:14
6	1 Thess 4:5	20	Luke 9:35
9	Luke 18:13	21	Acts 13:22
10	Rev 6:10, 19:2	23	2 Thess 2:3
12	Luke 6:28	27	1 Pet 1:17
80:2	John 10:4	28	Heb 1:6 Rev 1:5, 17:18
9f.	Mark 12:1	37	John 12:34
9–17	Luke 13:6	38	Rev 1:5
9–20	John 15:1	49	Luke 2:26
81:17	Mark 1:6	51	1 Pet 4:14
82:2	Luke 20:21	51f.	Heb 11:26
6	*John 10:34*	**90**:4	2 Pet 3:8
85:11	John 1:17	5f.	Matt 6:30 Luke 12:28
86:5	Luke 6:35	**91**:4	Luke 13:34
9	Rev 3:9, *15:4*	11	*Luke 4:10*
10	Matt 21:15	11f.	*Matt 4:6, 26:53 Mark 1:13*
87:2	Rev 20:9	12	*Luke 4:11*
5	Gal 4:26	13	Luke 10:19
88:9	Luke 23:49	15	Jas 5:13
12	Rev 9:11	**92**:16	John 7:18
89:2	Luke 1:50	**93**:1	Rev 19:6
3	Rom 15:8	**94**:1	1 Thess 4:6
4f.	John 7:42 Acts 2:30	11	Rom 1:21 *1 Cor 3:20*
7	Rev 13:4	14	*Rom 11:2*
8	2 Thess 1:10	**95**:7	John 10:3 Rev 21:3
10	Matt 8:26, 14:32 Mark 4:39 Luke 8:24, 21:25	7f.	*Heb 3:15, 4:7*

95:7–11	*Heb 3:7*	**104:4**	*Heb 1:7*
10	Matt 11:16	12	Matt 13:32 Mark 4:32 Luke 13:19
11	Heb 4:3, 5	27	Matt 24:25
96:1	Rev 14:3	**105:21**	Matt 24:47 Acts 7:10
5	Rev 9:20	24	Acts 7:17
11	Rev 12:12	26	Rom 1:1
13	Acts 17:31 Rev 19:11	30	Rev 16:13
97:1	Rev 19:6	38	Rev 11:10
3	Rev 11:5	39	1 Cor 10:1
7	*Heb 1:6* Rev 7:11	**106:9**	Mark 4:39 Rev 16:12
10	Luke 1:74 Rom 12:9	10	Luke 1:71
98:1	Rev 14:3	14	Luke 23:42 1 Cor 10:6
2	Rom 1:17 Rev 15:4	16	Mark 1:24 Luke 4:34
3	Luke 1:54, 3:6 Acts 28:28	19	Acts 7:41
9	Acts 17:31 Rev 19:11	20	Rom 1:23
99:1	Rev 11:18, 19:6	23	Luke 9:35
6	1 Cor 1:2	31	Rom 4:3
100:5	Luke 1:50	37	1 Cor 10:20
101:5	Jas 4:11	48	Luke 1:68 Rev 19:4
102:12	Luke 12:28	**107:3**	Matt 8:11 Luke 13:29
26–28	*Heb 1:10*	9	Luke 1:53
28	Heb 13:8	10	Luke 1:79
103:3	Mark 2:7	10–16	Acts 12:17
7	Rom 3:2	13–16	Acts 16:26
8	Jas 5:11	14	Luke 1:79
17	Luke 1:50	20	Acts 10:36
19	Matt 5:34 Rev 4:2	25–27	Mark 4:37
104:2	Rev 12:1	25–29	Matt 8:26

107:26	Rom 10:7	118:17f.	2 Cor 6:9
28f.	Mark 4:39	19f.	Rev 22:14
30	John 6:21	20	John 10:9
109:8	*Acts 1:20*	22	Mark 8:31 *Luke 20:17* Acts 4:11 1 Pet 2:4, 7
16	Acts 2:37	22f.	*Matt 21:24 Mark 12:10*
25	Matt 27:39 Mark 15:29	24	Rev 19:7
26	Matt 15:25	25f.	*Matt 21:9 Mark 11:9 John 12:13*
110:1	*Matt 22:44, 26:64 Mark 12:36, 14:62, 16:19 Luke 20:42, 22:69 Acts 2:34* Rom 8:34 *1 Cor 15:25* Eph 1:20 Heb 1:3, *13*, 8:1, 10:12	26	*Matt 23:39 Luke 13:35, 19:38*
4	Rom 11:29 *Heb 5:6*, 6:20, 7:3, *11, 17, 21*	119:30	2 Pet 2:2
111:2	*Rev 15:3*	32	2 Cor 6:11
4	Jas 5:11	43	Jas 1:18
9	Luke 1:49	46	Rom 1:16
112:4	2 Cor 4:6	57	Luke 10:42
9	*2 Cor 9:9*	89	Luke 21:33
10	Matt 8:12	98	2 Tim 3:15
113–118	Matt 26:30	103	Rev 10:9
113:5	Heb 1:3	120	Luke 12:5
114:3, 7	Rev 20:11	137	Rev 16:5, 7
115:4–7	Rev 9:20	142, 160	John 17:17
5	1 Cor 12:2	164	Luke 17:4
13	Rev 11:18, 19:5	165	1 John 2:10
116:3	Acts 2:24	176	Matt 18:12
10	*2 Cor 4:13*	122	John 4:20
11	Rom 3:4	6	Luke 14:32
117:1	*Rom 15:11*	123:1	Matt 14:19 Mark 6:41
118:6	Rom 8:31 *Heb 13:6*	2	Luke 9:16
15f.	Luke 1:51	125:5	Gal 6:16

126,2f.	Luke 1:58	**140**:4	*Rom 3:13* Jas 3:8
5f.	Luke 6:21	**141**:2	1 Tim 2:8 Rev 5:8
128:6	Gal 6:16	9	Matt 13:41
130:8	Matt 1:21 Titus 2:14 Rev 1:5	**143**:2	Rom 3:20
132:5	Acts 7:46	**144**:7	Matt 14:31
11	Acts 2:30	9	Rev 5:9, 14:3
17	Luke 1:69	**145**:13	1 Cor 10:13
134:1	Rev 19:5	15	Matt 24:45
135:1	Rev 19:5	15f.	1 Tim 6:17
14	*Heb 10:30*	16	Acts 14:17
15–17	Rev 9:20	17	*Rev 15:3, 16:5*
20	Rev 19:5	18	Acts 17:27 Phil 4:5
136:2f.	1 Cor 8:5	19	John 9:31
3	Rev 17:14	**146**:6	*Acts 4:24, 14:15 Rev 5:13, 10:6*
7	Jas 1:17	**147**:8	Acts 14:17
26	Matt 11:25 Luke 10:21	8	Matt 6:26 Luke 12:24
137:8	Rev 18:6	15	2 Thess 3:1
9	Luke 19:44	18	Acts 10:36
138:1	1 Cor 11:10	19f.	Rom 3:2
139:14	*Rev 15:3*	**148**:1	Matt 21:9 Mark 11:10
21	Rev 2:6	**149**:1	Rev 14:3
21f.	Matt 5:45	**150**:5	1 Cor 13:1
140:2	2 Thess 3:2		

Appendix B

LXX or Old Greek, Hebrew Bible or MT?

If the study of the Bible were a business, one could say that the study of the Greek Jewish Scriptures has become something of a growth industry in the last thirty years, after many years when it was mostly a subject for specialists.[1] It is still however in its nascent stages in some regards, for example, there are still *not* critical editions of all the books in the LXX, and so even from the point of view of text criticism the full picture eludes us on many fronts as to how to evaluate a variety of issues. Let's start with the issue of the Hebrew Bible (HB) and work backwards.

I say backwards because the MT is the main basis of modern translations of the HB. It is in turn mostly based on the earliest complete manuscript of the OT, the Leningrad Codex, which only dates to 1008 CE, a full millennium after the time of Christ! It is thus surprising that even with over fifty years of studying the discoveries at Qumran under our belts, many OT scholars and even more translators are rather dogmatic about sticking with the MT as the basis for study and translation.

R. Timothy McLay finds this more than a little puzzling,[2] and I must admit I do as well. Shouldn't we make a better effort at getting back to the earliest form of the text of the HB with the help of all the evidence, including the evidence from Qumran, Naḥal Ḥever, and indeed even the oldest Greek evidence of the translation of the Hebrew text that predates the Masoretic text by a lot? It is all very well to say

---

1. See recently, e.g., Wagner, *Reading the Sealed Book*, and also the essays in *The Old Greek Psalter: Studies in Honour of Albert Pietersma*, ed. Robert J. V. Hiebert, Claude E. Cox, and Peter J. Gentry, JSOTSup 332 (Sheffield: Sheffield Academic, 2001).
2. See the first couple of chapters in McLay, *Use of the Septuagint*.

that the Qumran material *mostly* demonstrates that the producers of the MT were remarkably careful and conservative in preserving the HB text. Yes, but sometimes it doesn't demonstrate that, and it often sounds like special pleading when someone defends the MT by claiming that we likely have an "eclectic" or "sectarian" text of the HB in various manuscripts at Qumran. But perhaps the tide is turning in a less "traditionalist" direction, to judge from remarks by Robert Bergen, who says, "Serious concerns—and frequently highly negative evaluations—have arisen concerning the quality of the text transmitted to us in the MT. . . . The majority of modern researchers who have studied this issue conclude that in most cases where there is disagreement in the wording of a passage, the LXX's reading is superior to that of the MT." He is talking about the text of Samuel and how the Dead Sea readings, particularly where they cohere with the LXX against the MT are to be preferred. Of course the text of 1 and 2 Samuel is one of the most textually problematic parts of the HB, but nevertheless Bergen provides a good caution against always preferring the MT to the LXX reading of verses where the two traditions differ. Indeed, he provides a rationale for giving a very balanced appraisal of the Hebrew and Greek texts in terms of which is closer to the original form of the verse in question.[3]

Any study of the NT use of the OT has to deal with the evidence as we have it *now*, for scholarship is *always* a work in progress, it is never finished and always subject to revision, and until we get more clarity about the original form of the HB, we must go with what the majority of OT scholars base their work on, which is indeed the MT. That is why we have stuck with offering translations of the MT in this series. Similarly, it is why I have stuck with offering translations of the LXX. These are still the *best* starting points we have, especially if we are addressing not a specialist scholarly audience, but rather a broader one of rabbis, pastors, priests, seminary students, and educated laity.

As for the Old Greek texts of the Jewish Scriptures, including the LXX, a few important things need to be said, not least of which is *to repeat* that there is much scholarly work to be done before we have critical editions of all the LXX books. *Until then*, we have to go with the good translations, such as the NETS version used in this manuscript, done by good careful scholars.

I agree with McLay that by and large it appears that the NT writers

---

3. Robert D. Bergen, *1, 2 Samuel*, NAC 7 (Nashville: Broadman & Holman, 1996), 26.

drew quotations and allusions from written sources, though not always. Written sources presuppose available documents, whether in the form of whole book scrolls, or collections of key texts in written form such as catenae. Sometimes, as we have noted in these studies, the Scripture seems to be cited or paraphrased from memory, especially when no citation formula is used and the precise text in question is uncertain, or we seem to have a blending together of, for example, several psalm texts into an amalgam of some sort.

I am unpersuaded however by McLay's arguments that the canon of the OT was not basically closed in the NT era. The historical evidence suggests otherwise, not the least of which is that no book not found in the HB is ever cited as Scripture in the NT.[4] None! Furthermore, none of the *extra books* of the LXX, books not found in the HB, are cited as Scripture either, though clearly a document like Wisdom of Solomon has influenced some of the way Paul and others have framed their material.[5]

Nor am I persuaded that there was the degree of flux and chaos in regard to the fixity of the OT texts that scholars like McLay seem to think there was. Why not? I will give an analogy. Paraphrases of biblical texts have been done in all eras of biblical history, and what they *presuppose* is a more fixed text, from which they can paraphrase or improvise creatively. *It is a mistake to take evidence for paraphrases of this or that biblical text, for instance in the NT, as compelling evidence for fluidity or flux when it comes to the baseline text. This is rather like arguing that because we have John Coltrane's remarkable improvised jazz version of "My Favorite Things" that ergo there must not have been a fixed or canonical version of the song extant. This would be incorrect.* Or to use another analogy Eugene Peterson's *The Message* provides no evidence whatsoever that there aren't some quite literal translations of the NT available and widely known.

---

4. McLay, *Use of the* Septuagint, 138 tries to claim the use of 1 Enoch 1:9 in Jude 14 as evidence to the contrary, and he also suggests the Martyrdom of Isaiah shows up in Heb 11:37, and then there is the reference to Jannes and Jambres in 2 Tim 3:8. None of these examples pass muster. The strongest of these is the Jude text, but Jude does not say he is citing a scriptural text, he says he is quoting a saying of the prophet Enoch, which is a different matter. This is no different than Paul citing a Cretan poet who once said, "All Cretans are liars." A mere citation does not provide evidence for a wider corpus of Scriptures. Neither the verse in Hebrews nor 2 Tim 3:8 involve any kind of citation of an extrabiblical text at all. They simply reflect knowledge of such texts, but the information is not said to be scriptural. Something doesn't have to be in Scripture to be consider true or worth citing or using.

5. See McLay's discussions in *Use of the Septuagint*, 1–76; and cf. Ben Witherington III, *What's in the Word: Rethinking the Socio-rhetorical Character of the New Testament* (Waco, TX: Baylor University Press, 2009), for the relevant essays on canonization.

I do however agree that overall, it appears that the Greek versions of the OT provided the *main source* for the NT writers to learn the OT, and in particular the LXX was a key resource.[6] It is not mainly the HB that was the source drawn upon and used by the NT writers when they used the OT Scriptures. At this juncture some reflections on Moisés Silva's study of the Greek Psalter in Paul's letters, and McLay's analysis of the impact of the LXX on the NT are in order.

Of the some 107 clear quotations of the OT in Paul's letters, some 24 come from the Psalter. As Silva points out, for most of these citations, "there are no substantial differences among the . . . MT, the OG, and the Pauline texts."[7] It is also important to note that there are *no* instances where Paul agrees with the MT against the OG in a citation with one possible exception—2 Cor. 9:9.[8] There are only three instances where there are significant differences between Paul's text and the OG: Romans 3:10–12 (Ps 14:1–3 // Ps 53:1–3); Romans 11:9–10 (Ps 69:22–23), and Ephesians 4:8 (Ps 68:18).

Overwhelmingly, the citations from the Psalter come up in Romans, 1–2 Corinthians, and Galatians, with one from Ephesians. They are mainly found in Romans and 1 Corinthians. A remarkable six of the sixteen Psalm citations in Romans show up in one place, Romans 3:10–18. As the table in Silva's study shows, Paul ranges over all five books of the Psalter from Psalm 5 to Psalm 143. His knowledge of the Psalms is extensive.[9] There are clear examples where Paul cites the Greek OT text verbatim: Romans 3:13a = Psalm 5:10; Romans 3:13b = Psalm 139:4; Romans 4:7–8 = Psalm 31:1–2; Romans 10:18 = Psalm 18:5; Romans 15:3 = Psalm 68:10; 1 Corinthians 10:26 = Psalm 23:1; 2 Corinthians 4:13 = Psalm 115:1; 2 Corinthians 9:9 = Psalm 111:9. In another eight cases, the quotations are not quite exact, but the discrepancies are trivial, and in the three examples where there are significant differences between what Paul has and the Greek OT, these "should be attributed to Paul's own rhetorical interests," not to his knowledge of more than one Greek OT text of the Psalter.[10] In the three cases where there are significant differences between Paul's text and the Greek OT text of the Psalter, in every case Silva has provided a clear and, to me compelling argument,

---

6. McLay, *Use of the Septuagint*, 136.
7. Moisés Silva, "The Greek Psalter in Paul's Letters: A Textual Study," in *Hiebert, Old Greek Psalter*, 277.
8. On which see "The Lexicon of Faith," in ch. 7, above.
9. Silva, "Greek Psalter in Paul's Letters," 279 and Silva is only touching the tip of the iceberg, because he is only dealing with citations.
10. See Silva, "Greek Psalter in Paul's Letters," 280–81.

that it is Paul's rhetorical adaptations and modifications we are dealing with, *not evidence of multiple OG texts of the Psalms.*

Paul does reflect some knowledge of the Hebrew text, and he may on a few occasions be making his own translation into Greek, but on the whole the changes seem to reflect purposeful adaptation of the Psalm text by Paul, rather than just doing a new translation from the Hebrew.[11] Silva concludes: "the weight of the evidence speaks loudly in favor of textual stability and continuity. Out of the 24 Pauline citations from the Greek Psalter, 22 clearly reflect the critically restored text." Silva is also prepared to say that in view of how often Paul uses the Psalms, it would be more than a little surprising if a different conclusion could be drawn, for instance, from his use of Isaiah. This is a totally different viewpoint from the one you get from reading McLay.[12]

Though McLay is wrong about non-HB books being cited as Scripture in the NT, and also wrong about the degree to which the OT canon was mostly fixed by the first century AD and the degree of fluidity and flux of the texts of the Jewish Greek Scriptures in the NT era (rhetorical and stylistic changes by a NT author of an OT citation are *not* evidence of alternative translations of a text), nevertheless some of his most important conclusions are correct and needed to be emphasized here: (1) the citation of the Greek Jewish Scriptures numerous times, indeed most of the time in the NT, rather than citing the HB in a fresh translation clearly shows that the writers of the NT trusted the Greek text and treated it as a reliable form of Holy Scripture. This point I think is not debatable; (2) the use of the OG or LXX to make an important theological point that could not be made on the basis of the HB or MT text is another crucial point. Whether one considers Amos 9:11–12 in Acts 15:16–18 or Deuteronomy 32:43 in Hebrews 1:6 or, say, Isaiah 29:13 in Matthew 15:9 (and there are more examples he rightly presents), it is clear enough that the Greek OT provided some important theological grist for the mill, and support for ideas and concepts that could not have been derived from the HB or MT.[13]

In sum, the new research into the origins of the HB and the origins of the LXX is important, and we look forward to a day when we do indeed

11. Notice that this is also the conclusion of Christopher D. Stanley, *Paul and the Language of Scripture: Citation Technique in the Pauline Epistles and in Contemporary Literature*, SNTSMS 69 (Cambridge: Cambridge University Press, 1992). Creative use of a rather fixed text, rather than multiple texts of the Psalms being used, is the verdict.
12. Since Paul is chronologically our earliest witness to the state of the OT text, and he provides strong evidence for a relatively fixed OT canon and text, we may assume that the later NT writers were not dealing with OT texts in greater flux than Paul did.
13. McLay, *Use of the Septuagint*, 169–70.

have critical editions of all the LXX books. But in the enthusiasm for this new development of an already important field of study, there has been an overreaction to the idea of a relatively fixed text and canon of the OT by the time we get to the NT era. Pluraformity has been overemphasized in the heat of the enthusiasm for new vistas in OT research. On further review, Silva and others have rightly cautioned that the NT itself does *not* suggest a situation of great flux when it came to which books counted as Scripture or how stable the texts of those books were. As we pointed out, Silva demonstrated this with relative ease in his study of the Psalms in Paul's letters. I would add, that because of the vast use of the Psalms in so many different ways in the NT era, and in so many different venues, and with a clear help from what we find of the Psalter at Qumran which largely matches the MT, if the early evidence for the Psalms do not suggest great fluidity of texts in Hebrew or Greek, we should *not assume* that would be the case with the other OT books in that era, including the other OT books drawn on in the NT. What we must reckon with is the creative and rhetorical and even homiletical use of the OT, especially of Isaiah and the Psalms, by the writers of the NT in various ways.

Let us consider now some of the salient points that have come to light from the detailed study of some of these Psalms. First, Jamie A. Grant has suggested that the reason the royal Psalms continued to be retained in the Psalter, even when there was no king, is because even these psalms were *generic enough* to be reapplied to all sorts of persons, and not just to kings, and more particularly they could be readily reapplied to messianic hopes for a future king.[14] I think this is partially correct, but what also made this material multivalent or at least open to later use is the *poetic* quality of the material.

What Grant also fails to mention is that texts like 2 Samuel 7 prompted the belief among many Jews, it would appear, that God would not allow the Davidic monarchy to end altogether or to disappear from history. In other words, it was partially the form of the material, partially the more generic content of the material, and partially the belief that God would be faithful to his promises vis à vis the Davidic monarchy, that likely kept this material in the Psalter even during many centuries when there was no king in Judah or in Israel. Put another way, they clung to the belief that God would not renege on his promises or allow his word to fail. If we doubt how big a factor this

---

14. See Jamie A. Grant, "The Psalms and the King" in Johnson, *Interpreting the Psalms*, 101–18, see esp. 113–16.

sort of thinking might be for a devout Jew, consider the reasoning of Paul in Romans 9–11 where he applies precisely this sort of argument to explain that God has not forsaken his first chosen people Israel or his promises made to them. Paul's response to the rhetorical question, "So then has the Word of God failed?" is a robust "Absolutely NOT!!!" He is even prepared to argue for an eschatological fulfillment of those promises to Israel when Jesus returns so sure is he that God will be true to his word. I doubt the collectors and final compilers of the Psalter felt much differently. There has to be a reason why the Psalter begins by extoling God's word in the form of torah and why the longest single Psalm is Psalm 119.

A further important point that we have mentioned at several junctures is that the influence of these Psalms on the writers of the NT cannot even begin to be assessed if all one does is stick to citations or clear allusions to the Psalter in the NT. I put it this way toward the end of the first major exegetical chapter:

> Through prayer, and singing, through public reading out loud, teaching and memorization, the language of the Psalms gradually became the language of many early Jews, which they used to express their own thoughts and feelings. Because the Psalms are poetry, and are often more generic and universal in character, they lent themselves quite naturally to expressing common human experiences of the pious Jew of the NT era, including Jesus himself. This kind of use of the Psalms was apparently common and was not so much a kind of exposition of the OT text as an appropriation of the language of the Psalms to describe a similar thought, feeling, or experience of the Jewish speaker. Devout early Jews spoke a kind of "Biblese" and the OT, particularly texts like the Psalms or Isaiah provided the vocabulary, the lexicon for self-expression, or articulation about current events.

As this study progressed, I became progressively less enamored with pronouncements that the NT writers were using the Psalms in ways that did not in any way correspond with the original meaning of the Psalm. This it seems to me is to ignore a large number of important factors: (1) the multivalency of Hebrew poetry, especially more generic poetry that comments on the universal human condition; (2) the rhetorical hyperbole of such poetry. It is precisely the hyperbole, for example in the royal psalms, which make them so fruitful and easily reapplied to Christ, not least because what was clearly hyperbole when applied to ancient Davidic kings could be said to be fulfilled or would be fulfilled literally in David's greater son, David's lord. In other words, if you're going to be pedantic about literal fulfillment of the meaning of the Psalms, then Jesus does a better job of it than David, or Solomon, or Hezekiah, or Josiah; (3) precisely because of its hyperbolic and metaphorical character this poetry was seen to have prophetic potential, by which I mean the potential to be better fulfilled by the messiah than his forebears; (4) in order to actually argue that the NT writers were misapplying the Psalms, one would need to show that their use of it was *contradicting* the original meaning of the psalm, rather than just amplifying it or further developing it; and (5) perhaps most importantly, the NT writers are often just using the Psalms homiletically or as a source of vocabulary or imagery. *They are mostly not attempting to either exegete the psalm or to deal with its original contextual meaning.* You can object to their hermeneutics if you like, but you cannot complain about their exegesis if they are not engaged in such an enterprise. Let us take one example, the very first psalm we exegeted in this study, Psalm 2.

We said in the first exegetical chapter the following:

> James L. Mays puts it this way: Psalm 2 "is the only text in the Old Testament that speaks of God's king, messiah, and son in one place, the titles so important for the presentation of Jesus in the Gospels."[15] While in its present context in the Psalter it served as something of an introduction to the other royal psalms (Psalms 18, 20, 21, 45, 72, 89, 110, 144), in the hands of the earliest Christians it became a rich resource for talking about Jesus.

We ask now, was it somehow inappropriate when Psalm 2 spoke of messiah, son, and king that the NT writers felt this psalm was especially appropriate to apply to Jesus, for instance at his baptism and reception of the Spirit? No, the psalmist did not have Jesus specifically in his sights, but yes he was indeed talking about the Davidic king that was God's choice and no one fit the poetic portrait painted in Psalm 2 better than Jesus. Call this fulfillment without prediction if you like, but clearly the aftermath in the Gospels would not have made the sense it does without the before in Psalm 2. As Paul said about the resurrection, the seed may look rather different from the plant to the sower, but the seed and the plant are united as part of one living entity. Defending the integrity of the original contextual meaning of this or that psalm does not require objecting to what the NT writers were doing with the Psalms, or suggesting that they got the meaning wrong.

Were there limits to the creativity in which the Psalms would be

15. Mays, *Psalms*, 44.

350

handled by the NT writers? The answer to this question I think must be yes, in several respects. First of all, you will notice that there is no attempt to use even the salvation historical narrative psalms for the sake of some sort of Christian allegory. Even when Christ is sometimes said to be the speaker of this or that psalm (see, e.g., Hebrews or Romans 15) this is not because some character in the Psalms is treated as the preincarnate Christ, rather it has to do with the early Christian belief that Christ is part of the divine identity and so at least sometimes Christ may have inspired what is said in the psalm, or even speak directly in a divine oracle within a psalm. You will notice as well the specific, almost vehement denial that Christ is "the angel of the Lord," or any angel, in the book of Hebrews. This is not because the author has a "low" christology, this because he has the highest sort possible, Christ is part of the divine identity, indeed what was previously said of Wisdom could now be said of Christ (as also in 1 Corinthians 10). In addition, even the author of Hebrews recognizes the before and after of the biblical text, as they have a strong sense of the progressiveness not only of biblical history, but of biblical revelation in the OT and will only say, for example, on the basis of Psalm 110:4 that Christ is a priest after the order of Melchizedek, not that he was Melchizedek in disguise in OT times. So the psalms are not used allegorically in the NT, not even the salvation historical ones, and this differentiates what the NT writers are doing in comparison to Philo.

One of the fundamental assumptions made by the NT writers again and again is that God's character has not changed over the course of human history, nor has humanity's need for salvation and rescue changed either. This is one reason why the writers of the NT see immediate relevance and application of much of what is said in the psalms to their own situation and also to the situation that existed during the earthly life of Jesus. Furthermore, it is the very incompleteness of the story, and of the revelation in the psalms, and the very generic or universal character of the poetry in the psalms that opens the door to seeing a relationship of promise and fulfillment, or a relationship of the seed to the fruit, or a relationship of partial to whole when treating the psalms in the NT. Ironically, it is precisely because all of the hyperbolic rhetoric about the king and his kingdom was not literally fulfilled that propelled the later psalmists, and the collector of the Psalter, to look forward with hope to the promises coming true in the future. Indeed, the buoyant spirit and nature of some of these psalms, even some of the ones that likely originated in the postexilic period when there was no Davidic king, suggests that the composers of these songs believed that "the future was still as bright as the promises of God."[16]

We have had occasion to evaluate the suggestions of Hays and others that metalepsis is in play in the use of the Psalms in the NT in various places. I think that there is some evidence for this that is rather convincing, but it is not something that the NT writers assume or suggest most of the time, because much of a particular psalm would not suit an application to Christ or the early Christians, and so going back and reading the rest of a psalm in light of the Christ event would not be profitable. For example, we point to the following in the first major exegetical chapter:

> Sometimes in the use of the Psalms in the NT there is an apologetic tone and motive detectible and the use of Ps 41:9, "even my friend in whom I trusted, who ate of my bread, has lifted the heel against me." In its original context, the story the poem tells us is of a person who is sick, perhaps even deathly ill, and even his supposed friends are abandoning him as was the case with Job (see v. 3), but that is not all. This person believes he has also sinned against God and needs spiritual healing (v. 4). Obviously, the whole of this psalm could not be applied to Jesus, and in fact in this case it is not helpful to argue that this psalm is used in the NT in a way that suggests that the readers were supposed to go back and consider the whole psalm. We are not dealing with that kind of intertextuality here, we are dealing with the use of only the particular verse that is seen as apt, and as fulfilled in the life of Jesus.

---

16. This phrase has sometimes been attributed to William Carey, but it appears to have originated in something which was said by his fellow missionary Adoniram Judson, a missionary to Burma. The original form of the saying seems to have been, "the prospects are as bright as the promises of God."

Appendix C

Gospels, Acts and Psalms Chart

This chart was created by Professor Dale Brueggemann, and is used by his kind permission here. It originally appeared in his article "The Evangelists and the Psalms," in Johnson, *Interpreting the Psalms*, 264-66.

Psalm	Language	Gospels and Acts
2:1–2	"Why do the nations conspire, and the peoples plot in vain? The kings of the earth set themselves, and the rulers take counsel together, against the LORD and his anointed"	Acts 4:25–26
2:7	"You are my son, today I have begotten you."	Acts 13:33
6:3	"My soul is sorely troubled." (LXX)	John 12:27
6:8	"Depart from me, all you workers of evil"	Matt 7:23; Luke 13:27
8:2	"Out of the mouth of babes and nursing children you have perfected praise." (LXX)	Matt 21:16
16:10	"For you do not give me up to Sheol, or let your faithful one see the Pit. You show me the path of life."	Acts 2:28–31; 13:35
22:1	"My God, my God, why have you forsaken me?"	Matt 27:46; Mark 15:34
22:7–8	"All who see me mock at me; they make mouths at me, they shake their heads; 'Commit your cause to the LORD; let him deliver—let him rescue the one in whom he delights!'"	Matt 27:39, 41–43
22:15	Thirst	John 19:28

Psalm	Language	Gospels and Acts
22:18	"for my clothing they cast lots."	Matt 27:35; Mark 15:24; Luke 23:34; John 19:23–24
31:5	"Into your hand I commit my spirit"	Luke 23:46
34:20	"He keeps all their bones; not one of them will be broken."	John 19:36
35:19	"those who hate me without cause"	John 15:25
41:9	"who ate of my bread, has lifted the heel against me."	John 13:18
42:5, 11; 43:5	"soul ... cast down/deeply grieved"	Matt 26:38; Mark 14:34
62:12	"you repay to all according to their work."	Matt 16:27
69:4	"hate me without cause."	John 15:25
69:9	"It is zeal for your house that has consumed me"	John 2:17
69:21	"for my thirst they gave me vinegar to drink."	John 19:28–30
69:25	"May their camp be a desolation; let no one live in their tents."	Acts 1:20
78:2	"I will open my mouth in a parable; I will utter dark sayings from of old."	Matt 13:35
78:24	"he rained down on them manna to eat, and gave them the grain of heaven. Mortals ate of the bread of angels."	John 6:31
82:6	"You are gods"	John 10:34
89:20	"I have found my servant David"	Acts 13:22 (cf. 1 Sam 13:14)
91:11–12	"For he will command his angels concerning you.... On their hands they will bear you up, so that you will not dash your foot against a stone."	Matt 4:6; Luke 4:10
104:12	"the birds of the air have their habitation ... among the branches."	Matt 13:32; Mark 4:32; Luke 13:19
110:1	"The LORD says to my lord, 'Sit at my right hand'"	Matt 22:44; Mark 12:36; Luke 20:42–43; Acts 2:34–35; cf. Matt 26:64; Mark 14:62; Luke 22:69

Psalm	Language	Gospels and Acts
118:22–23	"The stone that the builders rejected has become the chief cornerstone. This is the LORD's doing; it is marvelous in our eyes."	Matt 21:42; Mark 12:10–11; Luke 20:17; Acts 4:11; cf. Eph 2:20–22; 1 Pet 2:4–8
118:25–26	"Hosanna" and "Blessed is the one who comes in the name of the LORD."	Matt 21:9; 23:39; Mark 11:9; Luke 19:38; John 12:13
132:11	"The LORD swore to David a sure oath from which he will not turn back: 'One of the sons of your body I will set on your throne.'"	Acts 2:30
146:6	"who made heaven and earth, the sea, and all that is in them"	Acts 4:24
148:1	"praise him in the heights!"	Matt 21:9; Mark 11:10

Appendix D

Psalm 110:1 and Related Texts: A Reflection on the Work of Richard Bauckham

Richard Bauckham has established something of a reputation for writing seminal and stimulating essays, densely packed with information, which change the state of play in the discipline. His collection *Jesus and the God of Israel* contains more than one such essay. Almost all the essays in this volume have appeared as independent discrete essays, and they remain in that state here, but they all contribute to the larger project which Bauckham is undertaking to produce a large technical study, provisionally entitled "Jesus and the Identity of God: Early Jewish Monotheism and New Testament Christology." Bauckham would have us see the essays in this volume as answering some questions along the way, and as working papers toward the larger project. As such these essays deserve a thorough discussion and review.[1]

The initial, and in some ways, most important, essay in this volume has been published in an earlier form in a 1999 book entitled *God Crucified: Monotheism and Christology in the New Testament*, which in turn was, in the main, a publication of Bauckham's Didsbury Lectures given in 1996.[2] The essence of Bauckham's thesis was, and is, that the categories of ontology and function when applied to the issue of christology have seriously skewed the analysis of the data. Opting instead for the rubric of "divine identity," which includes aspects of being and doing, Bauckham seeks to show that: (1) the earliest christology

---

1. Richard Bauckham, *Jesus and the God of Israel* (Grand Rapids: Eerdmans, 2008). This Appendix appeared in a different form as a book review in *The Asbury Seminary Journal* 64 (2009).
2. Richard Bauckham, *God Crucified: Monotheism and Christology in the New Testament*, Didsbury Lectures (Grand Rapids: Eerdmans, 1999).

was the highest one, as early Jewish thinking was already structurally open to the development we see in early Christian christology; (2) the division of NT data into doing and being in fact amounts to imposing later Greek categories on the data; whereas (3) the concept of unique or characteristic divine identity bridges this divide even to the point where Bauckham can say that the revelation of the divine identity comes not merely in the deity of Christ, but in Jesus's human life and passion as well, "in a way that is fully continuous and consistent with the Old Testament and the Jewish understanding of God."[3] This thesis is to be distinguished from the attempts to find a model for christology in the discussion in early Judaism about "two powers in heaven" or in general in the discussion of semidivine intermediary figures. If some of this sounds rather like Moltmann's theses in his seminal work entitled *The Crucified God*, this is no accident, since Bauckham has clearly been influenced by that work and has been one of the major interpreters of Moltmann in Europe.[4] Bauckham thus approaches the study from a different angle than, say, Larry Hurtado in his *Lord Jesus Christ* or *One God, One Lord*,[5] and indeed, Bauckham would disagree with those who try to find precedent for NT christology in the discussion of angelic and other divine intermediary figures (see, e.g., Alan Segal's important study *Two Powers in Heaven*).[6] There was an absolute distinction in early Judaism between the one creator and ruler, God, and all other things and beings as created, and all those intermediaries always stood on the other side of the creator-creation distinction. By contrast, says Bauckham, Jesus is included directly in the unique identity of the one God of Israel. Both in what we have anachronistically called his divine and human natures and traits, Jesus reveals the identity of the one God. What is crucial here is what counts as "identity," for Bauckham sees early Jews as strict monotheists who had a rather clear fix on what the unique and consistent traits of the divine identity were. Monolatry, that is, the exclusive worship of the one biblical God, was the appropriate and natural human response to the recognition that there *was* only one God—but what was meant by the term "one" in the Shema and elsewhere? This is a key question as well for Bauckham, and here

---

3. Bauckham, *Jesus and the God of Israel*, x.

4. Moltmann, *Crucified God*.

5. Larry W. Hurtado, *Lord Jesus Christ: Devotion to Jesus in Earliest Christianity* (Grand Rapids: Eerdmans, 2003); Hurtado, *One God, One Lord: Early Christian Devotion and Ancient Jewish Monotheism*, 3rd ed. (London: Continuum, 2015).

6. Alan F. Segal, *Two Powers in Heaven: Early Rabbinic Reports about Christianity and Gnosticism*, SJLA 25 (Leiden: Brill, 1977).

is some of his answer: "Jewish monotheism did not characterize the uniqueness of God in such a way to make the early inclusion of Jesus in the unique identity of God inconceivable. Those scholars, including many New Testament scholars, who assume that no Jewish monotheist could have accepted divine Christology, including Jesus in the divine identity, without abandoning Jewish monotheism have not understood Jewish monotheism," and its flexibility.[7] For example, to say, as the Shema does, that God is "one" refers to God's uniqueness, not to God's being numerically one person. So, Bauckham adds, "Nothing in the Second Temple Jewish understanding of divine identity contradicts the possibility of interpersonal relationship within the divine identity but, on the other hand, there is little, if anything, that anticipates it."[8] In other words, what we find in the NT is a legitimate development of what is found in the OT, but there are few precursors already in the OT to the high christology found in various places in the NT.

The problem in the way NT scholars have configured this sort of discussion in the past is caused by their thinking of the data in light of the later Greek philosophical model of things, namely, to think in terms of *what* God is, focusing on divine nature or being, rather than focusing on *who* God is, namely, the divine identity and its characteristic traits.[9] This way of putting things leads to confusion when it comes to including the human identity and actions, including death, of Jesus within the divine identity. On the later Greek way of thinking, the humanity of Jesus and his death become a theological problem for affirming the divinity of Jesus and his equality with God. Bauckham suggests that his model of analysis avoids this dichotomy and problematizing of the data.

The other seven (also previously published) essays in this volume can be seen as providing supporting data and corroboration for the thesis laid out in the first essay. The essay on biblical monotheism in chapter 2, published initially in a collection in 2004, initially reacts to the discussion of Nathan MacDonald on monotheism in Deuteronomy, based on his 2001 Durham doctoral dissertation.[10] Bauckham is convinced that MacDonald is right that what Deuteronomy is insisting on is monolatry for Israel, not monotheism in the modern Enlightenment sense. Rather, Deuteronomy argues that Israel's God is the "god

---

7. Bauckham, *Jesus and the God of Israel*, 53.
8. Ibid., 56.
9. Ibid., 58.
10. Nathan MacDonald, *Deuteronomy and the Meaning of Monotheism*, 2nd ed., FAT 2/1 (Tübingen: Mohr Siebeck, 2012).

of gods," in effect the only true god, and the only one who deserves to be called "the God." This does not imply a denial that there are other gods, but simply that they do not deserve the title *God* with a capital G. What is being asserted is the uniqueness of Yahweh, that Yahweh is God in a class by himself. Included in this notion is not merely that Yahweh is the sole God in relationship to Israel and the sole God Israel can and should recognize, but also the more universalistic notion that Yahweh has unrivalled power and sovereignty throughout the cosmos. "By contrast, the gods of the nations are impotent nonentities, who cannot protect and deliver even their own peoples."[11] In other words, Bauckham is resisting the suggestion that Yahweh is presented as the supreme tribal deity in Deuteronomy, while agreeing with Mac-Donald that the modern framing of the question of "monotheism," in purely ontological terms, is anachronistic and should not be read back into Deuteronomy. "Though called gods, the other gods do not really deserve the term, because they are not effective divinities."[12] Thus, one can say this theology is beginning to drive a wedge or ontological division through the middle of the old category "gods" with the result that Yahweh appears in a class all of his own.[13] In some ways, the reader will be reminded of Paul's argument in 1 Corinthians 8–10 that while it is true that there is only one true God, nonetheless his converts should not go to pagan temples and dine because they will be dining with demons, who certainly do not deserve the title "gods" but nonetheless are real spiritual entities.

One of the main points Bauckham makes forcefully is his caution against assuming that historical processes develop in an analogous fashion to biological evolutionary processes. I quite agree with this point, and it is a point we should have already taken into account when talking about theological and christological developments, not least because of the evidence of the bankruptcy of comparing these developments to developmental philosophical ones along the lines of the Hegelian model. History and historical developments are neither purely intellectual developments that could be reduced to a history-of-ideas approach (praxis and behavior involves and effects belief), nor are they strictly analogous to biological processes such as evolution. Bauckham then provides a useful and necessary caution when it comes to how we con-

---

11. Bauckham, *Jesus and the God of Israel*, 70.
12. Ibid.
13. Ibid., 71.

ceive of monotheism and its permutations and combinations through history.

Bauckham is equally concerned with the attempt by Robert Gnuse and others in effect to talk about Israelite monotheism and do biblical theology by means of a very tenuous and tendentious historical reconstruction of the origins of Yahwism.[14] In other words, what is assumed to be behind and generating the text steers and, indeed, straitjackets the discussion of what is in the text. In Bauckham's view, there is an inherent exclusive yet inclusive monotheism in texts like Deuteronomy that are not merely a result of late monotheistic editors doing their dirty work *ex post facto*. He is also unhappy with the attempt to separate the issue of particularity from the issue of universality when it comes to monotheism. He puts it this way: "it is fair to say that universalism and particularism are not contradictory aspects. Jewish monotheism is characterized by its way of relating YHWH's particularity as Israel's God to his universality as Creator and sovereign Lord of all."[15] Bauckham sees a "monotheizing dynamic" in many and varied OT texts, not limited to those reflecting late redactional activity. In fact, he argues that even the polytheistic texts in the OT are subject to this monotheizing dynamic such that they serve the purpose of establishing that only Yahweh is the true God, the one who deserves to be called "the God," the one who created and rules all and saves his people.

> So my proposal does not suppress the diversity of the texts, but does show how the whole of the Hebrew Bible can be read in accordance with early Jewish monotheism. It rejects a developmental reading of the texts. . . . Undoubtedly, the texts emerge out of a complex history, but they do not contain sufficient or sufficiently clear traces of their own pre-history to make tradition history a viable vehicle for biblical theology.[16]

It is thus hardly surprising that Bauckham's reading of the Shema, and similar OT texts that say that God is one, involves the conclusion that "the Shema asserts the uniqueness of God, not his lack of internal self-differentiation."[17] Thus, when Paul (1 Cor 8:4-6) modifies the Shema in a christological way, Bauckham argues that Paul is not adding a Lord to a God in the faith and worship of Christians, which would be di-theism,

---

14. R. Gnuse, *No Other Gods: Emergent Monotheism in Israel,* (Bloomsbury/T&T Clark, 1997).
15. Ibid., 84.
16. Ibid., 92.
17. Ibid., 106.

but rather is saying that the God and Lord who is called one in the OT includes, as it turns out, both the Father and the Son. Jesus is included within the divine identity, which is what "I and the Father are One" (John 10:30) is also taken to mean, not merely that the Father and the Son are closely united or in agreement or the like.

The third essay, "The 'Most High God' and the Nature of Early Jewish Monotheism," is one of the most recent of these essays (published first in 2007), and provides us with a detailed tabulation of where and how the phrase "the most high God" is in fact used in early Judaism. Some of the more interesting conclusions include: (1) the term was more frequently used in Palestinian Jewish texts than in diaspora texts; (2) nevertheless it was often used in discussion with polytheists; but (3) at Qumran the term ʾel rather than ʾelōhîm or even ʾel ʿelyôn is consistently used, apparently to make clear that the biblical God does not belong to a class of beings called gods, but rather stands alone and unique in class; (4) the term is used to indicate the sovereignty of the biblical God over all of creation and all creatures, including any extant supernatural created beings. The data confirm "the strong impulse to draw an absolute distinction of kind between YHWH and all other reality, characteristic of Second Temple Judaism."[18] The phrase pictures the biblical God's transcendent supremacy over all things, and is not being used to situate the biblical God in relationship to lesser gods, much less acknowledge that there are actually other gods worthy of the name.

Because the phrase "the most high" was in widespread use in the Greco-Roman world where a pantheon of deities was believed in, it is understandable why some Jews might use this phrase so their gentile interlocutors would have a point of contact, but then the Jewish apologist would go on to explain that they were referring to the supremacy and sovereignty of their God over all else. However, in fact, as Bauckham shows, diaspora literature tends to avoid the phrase, perhaps precisely because of its possible polytheistic overtones when gentiles were the dialogue partners. Josephus only uses the term once when quoting the emperor, and Philo only uses it when addressing gentiles, but with a specific disavowal that he is implying there is more than one real God (see *Leg.* 3.82), much less a pantheon of them. The avoidance of the phrase or its severe qualification in the diaspora reflects the exclusive monotheism in early Judaism whether in Israel or the diaspora,

---

18. Ibid., 119.

and thus the attempt to avoid suggesting that Yahweh was merely one God among many, or one God supreme over other true deities.

The chapter on the worship of Jesus in early Christianity is a substantial expansion of the older *Anchor Bible Dictionary* article Bauckham wrote many years ago, and in particular it interacts with the works of Larry Hurtado published after he had written the article, not surprisingly, since he largely agrees with Hurtado's conclusions. Worship of Jesus began in the earliest Jewish Christian communities in Jerusalem and elsewhere and was not seen as a step away from Jewish monotheism but rather as an "internal development" within it. The worship of Jesus was conceived as part of the worship of God as it had always been practiced and as such involved prayers to Jesus, hymns and doxologies about Jesus, and the like. Jesus is conceived as exalted and sitting on God's throne and as a part of the divine identity deserving unalloyed loyalty and true monotheistic worship. The extensive case is by now familiar from the lengthy studies of Hurtado and, before him, Hengel, and so we pass on to further chapters. It is important to note that the older thesis of W. Bousset and others, which suggested it was when Christianity became hellenized and gentilized that Jesus became the object of worship, will no longer pass muster in the light of the evidence from early Jewish Christianity.[19] For example, both Matthew and Revelation, two of the most thoroughly Jewish of early Christian documents, are two of the documents most clear about the worship and deity of Jesus. What this chapter adds to the discussion is that it takes the evidence up to about the time of Nicaea, demonstrating the consistency and christological character of Christian worship in the first three centuries of the Christian movement. "Jewish monotheism and the worship of Jesus were mutually conditioning factors in the development of early Christian faith."[20] The belief in the former did not curtail the practice of the latter, nor was the worship of Jesus seen as a violation of biblical monotheism.

What one believes about some being is revealed by whether or not one is prepared to worship that being. In chapter 5 of his essay collection, Bauckham discusses the early Jewish texts that have to do with the throne of God. The uniqueness of the biblical God implied and called for the exclusive worship of this God only; hence Josephus's explanation of the Shema: "the first word [i.e., commandment] teaches

---

19. W. Bousset, *Kyrios Christos: Geschichte des Christusglaubens von den Anfangen des Christentums bis Irenaeus,* (Vandenhoeck and Ruprecht, 1965).
20. Ibid., 141.

us that God is one and he only must be worshiped" (*Ant.* 3.91). This requirement of worshiping only and exclusively the one biblical God made early Judaism stand out from all the other religions in the Mediterranean crescent in that era. Worship was the real test, or better said, evidence, of who was deemed deity in that religion. Bauckham stresses that divine identity is the right category for a discussion of the biblical God, as opposed to divine nature, because the relevant texts in question almost invariably focus not on *what* God is, but rather on *who* God is.

Unlike Greco-Roman religion, where there was a gradient of obeisance and devotion and worship, a sort of ascending scale where one gave each more-than-merely-mortal being their due according to where they were assumed to be in the hierarchy of things, in Judaism there was no such gradient—only one being who deserved to be worshiped, the one who was the unique and true God who is the sole creator, ruler, and redeemer. Abraham figures large in this discussion in early Judaism precisely because he is seen as the first and paradigm of one converted from idolatry to the true worship, service, knowledge of, and faith in the true God (see e.g., Testament of Job 3–5; Josephus, *Ant.* 1.155–56).

But what about all those exalted intermediary figures that crop up from time to time in early Jewish literature, which are shown respect and even a form of reverence in the literature? Bauckham argues that the key litmus test to determine whether they are viewed as divine or not is this: Is this figure included within the unique divine identity in that literature, or not? Clearly in the case of God's Spirit, or the personification of Wisdom or his Word, the answer is yes, but these are not viewed as beings who are in some sense independent of God. Principal angels and exalted patriarchs, however, fall into a different category. They are not viewed as an inherent part of and expression of the divine identity. This is why one finds the insistence in various places by angels that they are not to be worshiped (see, e.g., Revelation 19–22). Both angels and patriarchs are creatures of God, and thus fall on the other side of the line of the creator-creature distinction that determines who should be worshiped.

Bauckham argues that the concern in early Jewish literature is to protect the unique identity of God, not for unitariness of God, which he claims is a facet of Jewish monotheism that arises after the biblical period, which is to say, after the NT era.[21] Bauckham dissents from the opinion of Segal and others that there is commonly a pattern in some

early Jewish literature of a designated single mediator or plenipotentiary of God who is second-in-command to God and helps rule the universe. Bauckham sees such an idea only in Joseph and Aseneth 14.8–9
(applied to the archangel Michael), at Qumran (1 QS 3.15–4.1, applied
to the Spirit of truth or Prince of light, i.e., Michael), and Philo's Logos
figure. Bauckham sees these as exceptions to the general pattern in
early Jewish literature, but still they are examples that should not
be lightly dismissed or ignored. Bauckham's point, then, is that such
exalted mediatorial figures are rare rather than common in the literature. Rare or not, the question becomes on which side of the creator/
creature distinction do they belong, and only the *logos* figure might fit
in the former category. But the *logos* in Philo seems clearly to be a *what*,
not a *who*.

The remainder of this particular essay focuses on the throne of God
as the ultimate symbol of divine sovereignty over all things (see, e.g.,
Ps 103:19). Normally, God alone is said to sit on this throne, and even
when the discussion is about God's final judgment on the earth when
God comes down for the Yom Yahweh, God alone is said to sit on that
throne (see, e.g., 4 Ezra 7:33; 1 Enoch 90:20; Rev 20:11). This is what
makes a text like Daniel 7 so remarkable since here and later in the
parables of Enoch a human-like figure sits on a throne along with the
Ancient of Days for this judging exercise. Bauckham points out that in
the case of images of a heavenly council, there are subordinates who
are said to sit on thrones (see, e.g., the elders in Revelation 4; cf. Testament of Job 33), but the action of the elders in worshiping the only
one in the vision depicted as God, makes clear that they are not sitting
jointly on God's throne with God. The issue then becomes, who can sit
on God's throne? Analogous to this are the images of angels sitting on
thrones in the lower heavens but worshiping only God (see, e.g., Ascension of Isaiah 7:14–33). Even when "throne" becomes a name for a rank
of angels (Testament of Levi 3:8) these angels are occupied with praising God, and are even said to stand in 2 Enoch 20:1–4. Typically, it is
only God who sits on an ongoing basis on a throne in heaven. Everyone else either stands, as servants would in a royal throne room, or is
quickly shown to be standing up and offering worship to the one God.
In short, the literature stresses the sole sovereignty of the one who
continually sits on the throne in heaven. It follows from this, according to Bauckham's logic, that when one finds texts about someone or

21. Ibid., 159.

something that continually inhabits the throne of God in heaven with God or is seen as part of the sole figure on the throne, this implies that that being is part of the divine identity.

Thus, for example, Wisdom is portrayed as God's adviser who sits with God on his throne (see 1 Enoch 84 and Wisdom of Solomon 9) and is thereby depicted as something inherent or intrinsic to the divine identity, not as a separate entity. In Ezekiel the Tragedian's work, Moses is depicted in a dream as on the throne of God, but the function of the parable is to make clear that Moses will rule on earth, or at least in Israel in a parallel way to God's rule in heaven on his throne. The story arises as a sort of exegesis of Exodus 7:1 where God tells Moses he will make him god in relationship not to the whole universe but to the situation of the Hebrews in Egypt. This story then is not an exception to the rule that only God sits on a heavenly throne ruling the universe. In Daniel 7 and in the parables of Enoch based on Daniel 7, there seems to be an exception to this rule for God himself places the son of man figure who represents God's people on his throne to judge the world. The figure does not participate in the divine judgment until the eschaton, but at that juncture he does indeed sit on God's throne and continues to do so. This is why, both in Daniel 7 and in 1 Enoch 46:6; 48:5; 62:6, 9, the son of man is said to be worshiped while sitting on the divine throne, which ergo means he receives divine worship, not mere obeisance. "What Ezekiel the Tragedian attributes only figuratively to Moses, the Parables of Enoch attribute literally to the Son of Man though only in the eschatological future. . . . Wisdom portrayed as sharing God's throne, and the Son of Man, according to the Parables of Enoch, provide the only precedents for the Christian claim that the exalted Jesus shares the heavenly throne of God."[22]

Bauckham however is not inclined to commit the etymological fallacy of assuming that these texts can explain where high christology came from in early Christianity, not least because these texts do not give a role to Psalm 110:1 in the formulating of ideas, which is so crucial to the Christian depiction of things christological. Bauckham believes that early Christian thinking about Jesus being part of the divine identity came to expression or was articulated *chiefly through creative exegesis of texts like Psalm 110:1.* The exegesis articulated a theological rationale or explanation for what was already practiced, namely the worship of Jesus as God, as included in the divine identity. He shows

22. Ibid., 171.

that in the first one hundred years of early Christianity no text was more frequently used for such purposes than Psalm 110:1 (found some twenty times quote or alluded to in the NT alone, but also in such diverse places as Polycarp, 1 Clement, the long ending of Mark, Barnabas, Ascension of Isaiah, Apocalypse of Peter, and elsewhere). It is this text that was often linked with Daniel 7:13–14 and Psalm 8:6 in the interpretation of the Christ and Christ event. This prevalence of use of Psalm 110:1 must be contrasted with the complete absence of use of this text in other sorts of early Jewish messianic formulations, and shows that early Christian thinking about Jesus was creative and sometimes novel. It was not simply a matter of transferring earlier Jewish ideas about messiah to Jesus. What was shared in common with messianic Judaism of other forms was this propensity to do creative exegesis for messianic purposes.[23]

> The concern of early Christology was not to conform Jesus to some pre-existing model of an intermediary figure subordinate to God. The concern of early Christology from its root in the exegesis of Ps. 110:1 and related texts, was to understand the identification of Jesus with God. Early Jewish monotheism provided little precedent for such a step, but it was so defined and so structured as to be open for such a development.[24]

It is thus not surprising that Bauckham does not find the study of Jewish intermediary figures as particularly helpful or connected to the study or explanation of early Christian christology.

On one point I would differ from Bauckham. It appears clear to me that Jesus himself applied texts like Daniel 7 and Psalm 110 to himself in his public discussions about who he was. Further, it appears clear to me that in some ways he presented himself as Wisdom (see, e.g., Matthew 11). This being the case, *it is not early Christian exegesis where we should look to find the origins of the novelty and creativity in the first instance, but rather to the historical Jesus himself.*[25] Bauckham however is clearly able to demonstrate that the various NT texts which portray Jesus as being given divine sovereignty over all things, or being worshiped by humans or angels (including Matthew 28), or being exalted to the heights of heaven and sitting on God's throne are all clearly indi-

---

23. Ibid., 174–75.
24. Ibid., 176.
25. See Ben Witherington III, *The Christology of Jesus* (Minneapolis: Fortress, 1990); Witherington, *Jesus the Sage*; Witherington, *Jesus the Seer*.

cating that Jesus is seen as part of the divine identity of God, which is why he may be worshiped as God the Father is worshiped.

In a lengthy chapter 6, Bauckham turns to the evidence pertinent to discussing Paul's christology of divine identity, and the evidence is hardly meager. At the outset of this chapter, Bauckham reiterates his approach to early Jewish monotheism, only here he now, helpfully, makes some distinctions between creational, cultic, and eschatological monotheism—God the creator, God the only one to whom worship is due, God the final judge of all creation. With these categories in hand, he seeks to show how Paul places Christ in all three of these categories quite readily. One of the virtues of this chapter is it shows how often Paul takes Yahweh texts in the OT and refers them to Christ.

Bauckham easily demonstrates this is not a rare phenomenon, but rather a persistent pattern in the Pauline corpus. Bauckham realizes that *kyrios* in the LXX was a regular circumlocution for the divine name YHWH, and he believes Paul is well aware of this too. *Kyrios* should not be seen or said to be a translation of YHWH. Remarkably, Paul is able to apply the divine name to either God or Christ *even when citing the same OT text in different contexts* (e.g., Isa 40:13; cf. Rom 11:34 and 1 Cor 2:16). This tells us something important about Paul's view of Christ, namely that he doesn't simply transfer Yahweh texts from the Father to Christ, but rather divides them up. Bauckham finds a clue as to why Paul does what he does with the divine name by suggesting that "a major factor in Paul's application of texts about YHWH to Jesus is his Christological reading of the eschatological monotheism of the Jewish Scriptures."[26] In other words, texts taken to refer to God as final judge and redeemer Paul tends to apply to Christ (cf., e.g., Rom 11:26–27 drawing on Isaiah 59, among other texts, and 2 Thess 1:7–12). A good example of how this works can be seen in the second half of the Christ hymn in Philippians 2:5–11, where it is Jesus who is given the name above all names and will be worshiped as Yahweh was to be worshiped, not least because he fulfills the role only God can fulfill—ruling over all. What is interesting about this is that this eschatological naming and worshiping Paul views as already happening in the present, though it will also happen in a consummate way in the future when Christ returns (see Rom 11:25–27). What such texts require is that one be able to do justice both to the differentiation of Jesus from the Father, but also to the identification of the two as part of the divine identity. "The identifying

---

26. Bauckham, *Jesus and the God of Israel*, 191.

name YHWH names Jesus as well as God his Father, and in such a way that they are certainly not two gods."[27] One of Bauckham's more interesting reflections on Philippians 2:10 is that since the name Jesus is in fact Yehoshua, which means "Yahweh is salvation," it is possible that when Paul says, "at the name of Jesus" every knee will bow, he is not merely applying Isaiah 45:23 to Jesus and calling him Yahweh in eschatological mode; rather "it could be that the name Jesus is regarded as a new kind of substitute for and even form of the divine name such that Phil. 2:10–11 means 'at the name YHWH-is-Salvation every knee should bend . . . and every tongue confess that Jesus Christ is LORD (i.e., YHWH)."[28]

The problem with this conjecture, however, is that Paul assumes his largely gentile audience will understand what he means on the basis of what he literally says in Philippians 2, not on the basis of the etymology of an Aramaic or Hebrew name of Jesus, which does not appear here, even in transliteration. Bauckham helpfully correlates Philippians 2:10–11 with Hebrews 1:3–4, where the name that is inherited cannot be the name that the person already has (in this case Jesus, in the case of Hebrews, the Son), so it seems best to say that Jesus inherits the name YHWH at his eschatological exaltation. Bauckham is one of a growing chorus (along with Hurtado, Fee, and others) that rejects James Dunn's argument that one should read Philippians 2:5–11 as an example of Adamic christology and not full-blown monotheistic christology, not least because it is hard to get around the reference to the preexistent Christ who made a decision to become a human being.[29] Adam, even in the late apocryphal Life of Adam and Eve, is not a figure said to have preexistence. Much more fruitful is the reading of Philippians 2:5–11 in light of Isaiah 45, 52, and 53. As Bauckham goes on to point out, the reason it is appropriate to worship Jesus as Yahweh in the eschatological end is because he already had "equality with God" in the beginning as Philippians 2:6 makes clear. That is, he was already part of the divine identity before he took on flesh.

One of the questions regularly and appropriately asked of Bauckham's way of dealing with Pauline material—which is to say, his way of finding complex allusions to the OT, not to mention partial quotations and echoes, and then using this intertexuality as a hermeneutical

27. Ibid., 196, a point he illustrates from Rom 10:13, where Joel 2:32 is drawn on and applied to Christ.
28. Ibid., 199n38.
29. J. D. G. Dunn, *Did the First Christians Worship Jesus? The New Testament Evidence*, (Westminister/J. Knox, 2010).

tool to provide an explanation of the meaning of this or that Pauline text—is: How in the world could Paul's mostly gentile audience be expected to catch these echoes and allusions or even recognize most of the quotations? For example, there is no more textually dense portion of the Pauline corpus than Romans 9–11, and yet this is a portion said to be specifically addressing gentiles (see Rom 11:13). Presumably the answer must be that Paul assumes there are enough Jewish converts and God-fearing converts in the audience that he is expecting them to explain the deeper and richer implications of his discourse to those who have simply converted from paganism. Being apostle to the gentiles did not mean he converted only former pagans, or even only gentiles. But there is another possible conclusion: namely that Paul sometimes, even deliberately, spoke over the heads of his audience, as a rhetorical tactic to make clear to them there is much they did not understand, in this case about the future of Israel and God's plans.

The discussion of 1 Corinthians 8:6 by Bauckham is simply a somewhat expanded edition of the earlier discussion in this work, and requires no further comment, other than that it provides further ammunition for the conclusion that Paul was deliberately including Christ within his understanding of the divine identity. But Bauckham is also concerned to show that Paul's theological bent is not a unique or eccentric one, and so he proceeds in this same chapter to provide examples from elsewhere in the NT of the use of OT YHWH texts with Jesus as the referent.[30] Some of these possible examples are more convincing than others, but he establishes his point well enough that Paul is not exegeting in the dark or in splendid isolation, but as part of a larger enterprise involving various early Jewish Christians including Jude, Peter, John of Patmos, and the author of Luke-Acts, who may have been a God-fearer. The other side of this demonstration follows, in which Bauckham deconstructs the efforts of Maurice Casey, William Horbury, and others to find some sort of precedent in early Jewish language about less than divine figures (angels, patriarchs) to explain texts like Philippians 2:10–11 or 1 Corinthians 8:6. Here it must be said Bauckham has the better of the argument, showing that Melchizedek in some of the Qumran texts, and Yahoel in other texts, refers to angelic figures given priestly roles and given the privilege to bear the divine name as God's priestly representative, but always clearly distinguished from God.

30. Ibid., 219–21.

The same can be said of texts that closely associate the function of messiah and the functions of God (e.g., 1 Enoch 46:4; 62:2; 4 Ezra 13:10–11). In other words, these texts are not talking about a being sharing in the divine identity in the way NT texts do in regard to Jesus. Scriptural texts about YHWH are not applied to such angelic figures in this literature in the way we find texts applied to Jesus, and thus do not provide a parallel or precedent for what we find in Paul and elsewhere in the NT.

Chapter 7 of this study provides us with a paper Bauckham gave at the 2006 St. Andrews Conference on Hebrews. Bauckham admits that the primary concern of NT writers was with a christology that addressed issues of eschatology and soteriology, but this in turn led quite naturally to addressing issues of protology as well, since Jesus was to be well and truly included in the divine identity from stem to stern, or to use a Johannine phrase, as Alpha and Omega. In Hebrews Bauckham sees the three main titles Son, Lord, and High Priest used in ways that require Jesus being included not only in the divine identity, but also as sharing in full human identity as well. The prologue in Hebrews 1:1–4 is seen by Bauckham as making a clear statement about the full and eternal deity of the Son as established by a long catena of Scriptures in 1:5–14.[31] Jesus is exalted above all the angels, and not merely supreme among the angelic class. But of only God is this said in early Judaism.

Here Psalm 110:1 already comes into play, which is why some commentators have seen Hebrews as something of a creative sermon on the christological implications of Psalm 110 and related texts. In Bauckham's view, the author of Hebrews does not think in terms of Jesus becoming the Son at some particular point in time, but as having always been and always being the Son. "Son" is not the name he inherits but rather the divine name, according to the prologue in Hebrews 1:1–4. Because he is eternally the Son, as the angels are not, he inherits a better name in the end than they do. Bauckham does not agree with those who think the angels feature prominently in Hebrews 1 because our author is critiquing an angelomorphic christology, or even a practice of worshiping angels. No, says Bauckham, the angels function as something of a boundary marker, for the Son is above them before all time and when he is exalted, and he is below them as a human being for a while during the incarnation.[32] The angels

31. Ibid., 237.
32. Ibid., 240–41.

serve to mark out the cosmic territory and they worship the Son. In "three key respects—creation, sovereignty, and worship—the Son is related to the angels precisely as God is."[33]

When the author wishes to speak about the Son as sovereign, what he wants to stress is that the Son is almighty to save, and indeed he attains his eschatological lordship over all by humbling himself, becoming human, dying, and serving as the high priest of all humankind who is one of that race. "So the high priestly work of atonement is the way in which he comes to exercise his sovereignty in the way he does—salvifically."[34] The twist in the tale comes when the Son is said to be a priest forever, like Melchizedek, without ancestors or descendents, or in other words, the Son is said to need to be an eternal being, divine, in order to fulfill this priestly role, which distinguishes his priesthood from all others. Thus, it was necessary that he be both human and divine to fulfill this role. Christ is this sort of priest not because of his ancestry, but because he has "the power of an indestructible life," something only God the Eternal One has. Interestingly, Hellenistic language about the eternal quality of a true God is applied to Christ in conjunction with the Jewish firm assertion of monotheism. There is only one being who is truly eternal. Interestingly, it is as high priest that the Son sits down on the heavenly throne.

> That Jesus sits on the throne, not only as king but also as high priest . . . indicates surely that his completed work of atonement is now permanently part of the divine rule over the world. In this way, this priesthood, unlike the Levitical, does belong to the unique identity of God. This high priest is the perfect mediator; he not only represents his people to God, in sacrifice and intercession, but also embodies the grace and mercy of God to which his sacrifice now gives permanent expression. Therefore, for the people of God, the heavenly throne is the throne of grace (4:16) [and not of condemnation].[35]

What comports with all this are statements like Hebrews 13:7, which indicate that the identity of the Son is the same throughout eternity, as an eternal being, or the Scripture quotation in Hebrews 1 where Christ is addressed as "God," or the places in Hebrews where Christ is said to have spoken this or that OT Scripture. The author insists on both the full humanity and full divinity of the Son.

33. Ibid., 243.
34. Ibid., 244.
35. Ibid., 251.

The final chapter in this fine study is an exegetical and theological reflection on the so-called cry of dereliction from the cross in Mark 15:39 and parallels. Not surprisingly, Bauckham wants us to see this as not an isolated citation of Scripture, but rather as a "web of allusions"[36] to Psalm 22 and other lament psalms in Mark's passion narrative (e.g., Mark 14:18 = Ps 41:10; Mark 14:34 = Pss 42:5, 11; 43:5; Mark 14:57 = Pss 27:12; 35:11; 69:4; Mark 15:24 = Ps 22:18; Mark 15:29 = Ps 22:7; Mark 15:32 = Pss 22:6; 69:9). Bauckham makes the interesting point that while we ought to interpret the cry in light of the whole of Psalm 22, nonetheless, since Jesus does not quote the Psalm in Hebrew, but rather does his own appropriation of it in Aramaic, only drawing on these specific words, we must take absolutely seriously the element of God-forsakenness in the words.

Furthermore, Bauckham stresses that this is not merely about Jesus's feelings of abandonment, for the psalms often speak about actually being left by God to suffer and die. Jesus is exegeting his actual experience out of the psalm. Bauckham argues that here Jesus not merely identifies with the original psalmist but with the plight of forsaken Israel as well who chanted these psalms. He comes to this conclusion because the allusions to this psalm are intertwined with allusions to the suffering servant of Isaiah 52–53 who suffers for God's people as their representative. Bauckham suggests that Jesus asks the question of abandonment not on his own behalf, but on behalf of God-forsaken Israel, now under occupation.[37]

I find this unconvincing as exegesis of Mark, not least because Jesus chooses a verse that speaks about "my God" (twice over), but asks about personal abandonment of the individual. Here it seems to me the well of elaborate intertextual echo runs dry. Psalm 22 is not intertwined with Isaiah 52–53. Rather Jesus is speaking out of and for his own experience. Perhaps one can say he shows trust by calling God "my God," but it is right to make something of the fact that this is the only place in this Gospel where Jesus addresses God in this way, rather than as Abba or Father. Furthermore, Jesus had hitherto been depicted as knowing he would be killed, not that he would be crucified in total public humiliation and in the nude. Mark's Gospel is stark and dark and this is the climax of the darkness for Jesus in particular. Bauckham rightly follows C. Meyer's interpretation that Mark's Gospel is punctuated by apocalyptic revelatory moments at the baptism, transfiguration, and the

36. Ibid., 255.
37. Ibid., 260.

cross and in each of these stories there is a revelation of the true identity of Jesus as Son of God.[38]

Thus, the conclusion of Bauckham is apt: "Jesus' divine identity is revealed not only in his deeds of divine authority nor merely in his coming participation in God's cosmic rule, but also in his godforsaken death."[39] But what exactly does this mean in the latter case? Bauckham suggests, "The centurion represents all the godforsaken who find the presence of God in Jesus' self-identification with them, the godforsaken. . . . God redeems and renews humanity in this way, by entering the situation of humanity at the deepest level of the human plight: the absence of God."[40] It is appropriate to hear echoes here not of Scripture but of Moltmann, who has certainly influenced this reading of Mark's account, and for the better.

In the end, Richard Bauckham provides us with a rich exegetical and intertextual feast in the various and varied essays in this volume. Some are more convincing than others, but all provide us with a fresh way of evaluating NT christology. Instead of parsing things into functional or ontological categories, Bauckham suggests a singular category that includes both—the various ways Jesus is said to be part of the divine identity, part of who God is, rather than addressing the question of what God or Jesus is by nature. It is fair to say that this insight will continue to challenge us all going forward, and we look forward to the main course on this same subject for which, amazingly enough, this is only the very large, rich, and filling appetizer.

I have left this discussion here in this appendix for the very good reason that this volume is part of a series of discussions on exegesis, intertextuality, and hermeneutics, and not specifically on their theological or christological implications. Having said that, I stand by my earlier conclusion that it was *not* elaborate detailed early Christian reflection on the OT that was the initial impetus for focusing on Psalm 110:1 as an explanation for the exalted nature of Christ. It was rather the use of the text by Jesus himself, and the implications of the way he used it, that set this fruitful train of thought moving down the track, and many NT writers followed him in this. Nevertheless, I agree with Bauckham that the concept of the divine identity is probably the most fruitful way to discuss the divine oneness and yet distinction made between the Father and the Son in the NT.

---

38. C. Meyer, *Binding the Strong Man. A Political Reading of Mark's Story of Jesus,* (Orbis: 2008).
39. Ibid., 266.
40. Ibid., 267–68.

Bibliography

The following is just a sampling of some of the works consulted and is a listing of those that I found *most helpful*. It is not intended to be anything like a comprehensive bibliography.

Psalms Commentaries

Brueggemann, Walter, and W. H. Bellinger. *Psalms*. NCBC. Cambridge: Cambridge University Press, 2014.

Charry, Ellen T. *Psalms 1-50: Sighs and Songs of Israel*. BTCB. Grand Rapids: Brazos, 2015.

Craigie, Peter C., and Marvin E. Tate. *Psalms 1-50*. 2nd ed. WBC 19. Dallas: Word, 2004.

Goldingay, John. *Psalms: Volume 1; 1-41*. BOTCWP. Grand Rapids: Baker Academic, 2006.

____. *Psalms: Volume 2; Psalms 42-89*. BOTCWP. Grand Rapids: Baker Academic, 2007.

____. *Psalms: Volume 3; Psalms 90-150*. BOTCWP. Grand Rapids: Baker Academic, 2008.

Hossfeld, Frank-Lothar, and Erich Zenger. *Psalms 2: A Commentary on Psalms 51-100*. Edited by Klaus Baltzer. Translated by Linda M. Maloney. Hermeneia. Minneapolis: Fortress, 2005.

Kidner, Derek. *Psalms 1-72: An Introduction and Commentary on Books I and II of the Psalms*. TOTC. Downers Grove, IL: InterVarsity Press, 1973.

____. *Psalms 73-150: An Introduction and Commentary on Books III-V of the Psalms*. TOTC. Downers Grove, IL: InterVarsity Press, 1975.

Kirkpatrick, A. F. *The Book of Psalms*. CBSC. Cambridge: Cambridge University Press, 1902.

Kraus, Hans-Joachim. *Psalms 1-59: A Commentary*. CC. Minneapolis: Augsburg, 1988.

____. *Psalms 60-150: A Commentary*. CC. Minneapolis: Augsburg, 1989.

Longman, Tremper, III. *Psalms: An Introduction and Commentary*. TOTC. Downers Grove, IL: InterVarsity Press, 2014.

Mays, James L. *Psalms*. Interpretation. Louisville: John Knox, 1994.

Murphy, Roland E. *The Psalms, Job*. Proclamation. Philadelphia: Fortress, 1977.

Terrien, Samuel L. *The Psalms: Strophic Structure and Theological Commentary*. Grand Rapids: Eerdmans, 2003.

Weiser, Artur. *The Psalms: A Commentary*. OTL. Philadelphia: Westminster, 1962.

Wesley, John. *Psalms: Explanatory Notes and Commentary,* Middletown DE: Hargreaves Publishing, 2016.

Non-Psalms Commentaries

Bergen, Robert D. *1, 2 Samuel*. NAC 7. Nashville: Broadman & Holman, 1996.

Craddock, Fred B. "The Letter to the Hebrews." *NIB* 12:1–173.

Witherington, Ben, III. *The Acts of the Apostles: A Socio-rhetorical Commentary*. Grand Rapids: Eerdmans, 1998.

____. *Conflict and Community in Corinth: A Socio-rhetorical Commentary on 1 and 2 Corinthians*. Grand Rapids: Eerdmans, 1995.

____. *The Gospel of Mark: A Socio-rhetorical Commentary*. Grand Rapids: Eerdmans, 2001.

____. *Grace in Galatia: A Commentary on St. Paul's Letter to the Galatians*. Grand Rapid: Eerdmans, 1998.

____. *Letters and Homilies for Jewish Christians: A Socio-rhetorical Commentary on Hebrews, James and Jude*. Downers Grove, IL: InterVarsity Press, 2007.

____. *The Letters to Philemon, the Colossians, and the Ephesians : A Socio-rhetorical Commentary on the Captivity Epistles*. Grand Rapids: Eerdmans, 2007.

____. *Matthew*. SHBC. Macon, GA: Smyth & Helwys, 2006.

____. *Paul's Letter to the Romans: A Socio-rhetorical Commentary*. Grand Rapids: Eerdmans, 2004.

Monographs

Alter, Robert. *The Book of Psalms: A Translation with Commentary*. New York: Norton, 2007.

Anderson, Bernhard W., and Steven Bishop. *Out of the Depths: The Psalms Speak for Us Today*. 3rd ed. Louisville: Westminster John Knox, 2000.

Anderson, Gary A. *Sin: A History*. New Haven: Yale University Press, 2009.

Beale, G. K., and D. A. Carson, eds. *Commentary on the New Testament Use of the Old Testament*. Grand Rapids: Baker Academic, 2007.

Bonhoeffer, Dietrich. *Psalms: The Prayer Book of the Bible*. Minneapolis: Augsburg, 1970.

Brown, Raymond E. *The Death of the Messiah: From Gethsemane to the Grave; a Commentary on the Passion Narratives in the Four Gospels*. ABRL. New York: Doubleday, 1994.

Brueggemann, Walter. *Spirituality of the Psalms*. Facets. Minneapolis: Fortress, 2002.

Cole, Robert L. *The Shape and Message of Book III (Psalms 73-89)*. JSOTSup 307. Sheffield: Sheffield Academic, 2000.

Collins, John J. *The Scepter and the Star: The Messiah of the Dead Sea Scrolls and Other Ancient Literature*. ABRL. New York: Doubleday, 1995.

Cullman, Oscar. *The Christology of the New Testament*. Rev. ed. Philadelphia: Westminster, 1964.

Damen, Ulrich. *Psalmen-und Psalter-Rezeption im Frühjudentum: Rekonstruktion, Textbestand, Struktur und Pragmatik der Psalmenrolle 11QPs^a aus Qumran*. STDJ 49. Leiden: Brill, 2003.

deSilva, David A. *Perseverance in Gratitude: A Socio-rhetorical Commentary on the Epistle "to the Hebrews."* Grand Rapids: Eerdmans, 2000.

Dodd, C. H. *According to the Scriptures: The Sub-structure of New Testament Theology*. London: Nisbet, 1952.

Eriksson, Lars O. *"Come Children, Listen to Me!" Psalm 34 in the Hebrew Bible and in Early Christian Writings*. ConBOT 32. Stockholm: Almquist & Wiksell, 1991.

Flint, Peter W. *The Dead Sea Scrolls and the Book of Psalms*. STDJ 17. Leiden: Brill, 1997.

Gunkel, Hermann. *The Psalms: A Form-Critical Introduction*. Facets 19. Philadelphia: Fortress, 1967.

Hagner, Donald A. *Encountering the Book of Hebrews: An Exposition*. EBS. Grand Rapids: Baker Academic, 2002.

Hay, David M. *Glory at the Right Hand: Psalm 110 in Early Christianity*. SBLMS 18. Nashville: Abingdon, 1973.

Hays, Richard B. *Echoes of Scripture in the Gospels*. Waco, TX: Baylor University Press, 2016.

_____. *Echoes of Scripture in the Letters of Paul*. New Haven: Yale University Press, 1989.

Heiser, Michael S. *The Unseen Realm: Recovering the Supernatural Worldview of the Bible*. Bellingham, WA: Lexham Press, 2015.

Hengel, Martin. *Studies in Early Christology*. Edinburgh: T&T Clark, 1995.

Heschel, Abraham Joshua. *The Prophets*. New York: HarperPerennial, 2001.

Horton, Fred L. *The Melchizedek Tradition: A Critical Examination of the Sources to the Fifth Century A.D. and in the Epistle to the Hebrews.* SNTSMS 30. Cambridge: Cambridge University Press, 1976.

Johnson, Philip S., and David Firth, eds. *Interpreting the Psalms: Issues and Approaches.* Downers Grove, IL: InterVarsity Press, 2005.

Lewis, C. S. *Reflections on the Psalms.* London: Bles, 1958.

Longman, Tremper, and Daniel G. Reid, *God is a Warrior.* Grand Rapids: Zondervan: 1995.

Luther, Martin, and Bruce A. Cameron. *Reading the Psalms with Luther: The Psalter for Individual and Family Devotions.* St. Louis: Concordia, 2007.

McLay, R. Timothy. *The Use of the Septuagint in New Testament Research.* Grand Rapids: Eerdmans, 2003.

Menken, Maarten J. J. *Old Testament Quotations in the Fourth Gospel: Studies in Textual Form.* CBET 15. Kampen: Kok Pharos, 1996.

Miller, Patrick D. *Israelite Religion and Biblical Theology: Collected Essays.* JSOTSup 267. Sheffield: Sheffield Academic, 2000.

———. *The Way of the Lord: Essays in Old Testament Theology.* Grand Rapids: Eerdmans, 2004.

Moltmann, Jürgen. *The Crucified God: The Cross of Christ as the Foundation and Criticism of Christian Theology.* New York: Harper & Row, 1974.

Mowinckel, Sigmund. *The Psalms in Israel's Worship.* 2 vols. Nashville: Abingdon, 1962.

Moyise, Steve, and Maarten J. J. Menken, eds. *The Psalms in the New Testament.* NTSI. London: T&T Clark, 2004. (There are a series of articles by various authors in this volume, see below.)

Skehan, Patrick W. *Studies in Israelite Poetry and Wisdom.* CBQMS 1. Washington, DC: Catholic Biblical Association of America, 1971.

Wagner, J. Ross. *Heralds of the Good News: Isaiah and Paul in Concert in the Letter to the Romans.* NovTSup 101. Leiden: Brill, 2003.

Wenham, Gordon J. *Psalms as Torah: Reading Biblical Song Ethically.* Grand Rapids: Baker Academic, 2012.

Witherington, Ben, III. *Isaiah Old and New: Exegesis, Intertextuality, and Hermeneutics.* Minneapolis: Fortress, 2017.

———. *Jesus the Sage: The Pilgrimage of Wisdom.* Minneapolis: Fortress, 2001.

———. *Jesus the Seer and the Progress of Prophecy.* Minneapolis: Fortress, 2014.

———. *John's Wisdom: A Commentary on the Fourth Gospel.* Louisville: Westminster John Knox, 1995.

Articles

Allen, Leslie C. "The Value of Rhetorical Criticism in Psalm 69." *JBL* 105 (1986): 577–98.

Attridge, Harold W. "The Psalms in Hebrews." Pages 197–212 in *The Psalms in the New Testament*. Edited by Steve Moyise and Maarten J. J. Menken. NTSI. London: T&T Clark, 2004.

Beckwith, R. T. "The Early History of the Psalter," *TynBul* 46 (1995): 1–27.

Brooke, G. J. "The Psalms in Early Jewish Literature in the Light of the Dead Sea Scrolls." Pages 5–24 in *The Psalms in the New Testament*. Edited by Steve Moyise and Maarten J. J. Menken. NTSI. London: T&T Clark, 2004.

Brucker, Ralph. "Observations on the *Wirkungsgeschichte* of the Septuagint Psalms in Ancient Judaism and Early Christianity." Pages 355–69 in *Septuagint Research: Issues and Challengers in the Study of the Greek Jewish Scriptures*. Edited by Wolfgang Kraus and R. Glenn Wooden. SCS 53. Atlanta: Society of Biblical Literature, 2006.

Campbell, A. F. "Psalm 78: A Contribution to the Theology of Tenth Century Israel." *CBQ* 41 (1979): 51–79.

Childs, Brevard. "Psalm 8 in the Context of the Christian Canon." *Int* 23 (1969): 20–31.

Condon, K. "The Biblical Doctrine of Original Sin." *ITQ* 34 (1967): 20–36.

Cross, Frank Moore, and David Noel Freedman, "A Royal Song of Thanksgiving," *JBL* 72 (1953): 15–34.

Culpepper, Robert H. "The High Priesthood and Sacrifice of Christ in the Epistle to the Hebrews," *TTE* 32 (1985): 46–62.

Daly-Denton, Margaret. "The Psalms in John's Gospel." Pages 119–37 in *The Psalms in the New Testament*. Edited by Steve Moyise and Maarten J. J. Menken. NTSI. London: T&T Clark, 2004.

Damant, Devorah. "Use and Interpretation of Mikra in the Apocrypha and Pseudepigrapha." Pages 385–91 in *Mikra: Text, Translation, Reading, and Interpretation of the Hebrew Bible in Ancient Judaism and Early Christianity*. Edited by Martin J. Mulder. CRINT 2/1. Philadelphia: Fortress, 1988.

Doble, Peter. "The Psalms in Luke-Acts." Pages 83–117 in *The Psalms in the New Testament*. Edited by Steve Moyise and Maarten J. J. Menken. NTSI. London: T&T Clark, 2004.

Enns, Peter E. "Creation and Recreation: Psalm 95 and its Interpretation in Hebrews 3:1–4:13." *WTJ* 55 (1993): 255–80.

Freed, Edwin D. "Psalm 42/43 in John's Gospel." *NTS* 29 (1983): 62–73.

Greenstein, Edward L. "Mixing Memory and Design: Reading Psalm 78." *Proof* 10 (1990): 197–218.

Howard, David M. "The Psalms in Current Study." Pages 23–40 in *Interpreting the Psalms: Issues and Approaches*. Edited by Philip S. Johnson and David Firth. Downers Grove, IL: InterVarsity Press, 2005.

Joffe, Laura. "The Elohistic Psalter: What, How, and Why?" *SJOT* 15 (2001): 142–66.

Karrer, Martin. "Epistle to the Hebrews and the Septuagint." Pages 335–53 in *Septuagint Research: Issues and Challenges in the Study of the Greek Jewish Scriptures*. Edited by Wolfgang Kraus and R. Glenn Wooden. SCS 53. Atlanta: Society of Biblical Literature, 2006.

Keesmaat, Sylvia C. "The Psalms in Romans and Galatians." Pages 139–61 in *The Psalms in the New Testament*. Edited by Steve Moyise and Maarten J. J. Menken. NTSI. London: T&T Clark, 2004.

Labahn, Michael. "The Psalms in Q." Pages 47–60 in *The Psalms in the New Testament*. Edited by Steve Moyise and Maarten J. J. Menken. NTSI. London: T&T Clark, 2004.

Mays, James L. "The Place of Torah-Psalms in the Psalter." *JBL* 106 (1987): 3–12.

McBride, S. Dean. "The Yoke of the Kingdom: An Exposition of Deuteronomy 6:4–5." *Int* 27 (1973): 273–306.

Moritz, Thorsten. "The Psalms in Ephesians and Colossians." Pages 181–95 in *The Psalms in the New Testament*. Edited by Steve Moyise and Maarten J. J. Menken. NTSI. London: T&T Clark, 2004.

Moyise, Steve. "The Psalms in the Book of Revelation." Pages 231–46 in *The Psalms in the New Testament*. Edited by Steve Moyise and Maarten J. J. Menken. NTSI. London: T&T Clark, 2004.

Neyrey, Jerome H. "'Without Beginning of Days or End of Life' (Hebrews 7.3): Topos for a True Deity," *CBQ* 53 (1991): 439–55.

O'Kennedy, D. F. "The Relationship between Justice and Forgiveness in Psalm 103." *Scriptura* 65 (1998): 109–21.

Rooke, Deborah W. "Jesus as Royal Priest: Reflections on the Interpretation of the Melchizedek Tradition in Heb 7." *Bib* 81 (2000): 81–94.

Runia, David. "Philo's Reading of the Psalms." *SPhilo* 13 (2001): 102–21.

Seow, C. L. "An Exquisitely Poetic Introduction to the Psalter." *JBL* 132 (2013): 275–93.

Sekine, Seizo. "Psalm 51." Pages 157–214 in *Transcendency and Symbols in the Old Testament: A Genealogy of the Hermeneutical Experiences*. BZAW 275. Berlin: de Gruyter, 1999.

Swanson, Dwight D. "Qumran and the Psalms." Pages 247–61 in *Interpreting the Psalms: Issues and Approaches*. Edited by Philip S. Johnson and David Firth. Downers Grove, IL: InterVarsity Press, 2005.

Thompson, Marianne Meye. "'They Bear Witness to Me': The Psalms in the Passion Narrative of the Gospel of John." Pages 267–83 in *The Word Leaps the Gap: Essays on Scripture and Theology in Honor of Richard B. Hays.* Edited by J. Ross Wagner, C. Kavin Rowe, and A. Katherine Grieb. Grand Rapids: Eerdmans, 2008.

Watts, Rikk. "The Psalms in Mark's Gospel." Pages 25–45 in *The Psalms in the New Testament.* Edited by Steve Moyise and Maarten J. J. Menken. NTSI. London: T&T Clark, 2004.

Weiss, Herold. "*Sabbatismos* in the Epistle to the Hebrews." *CBQ* 58 (1996): 674–89.

Wilk, Florian. "Letters of Paul as Witnesses to and for the Septuagint Text." Pages 253–71 in *Septuagint Research: Issues and Challengers in the Study of the Greek Jewish Scriptures.* Edited by Wolfgang Kraus and R. Glenn Wooden. SCS 53. Atlanta: Society of Biblical Literature, 2006.

Williams, H. H. Drake, III. "The Psalms in 1 and 2 Corinthians." Pages 163–80 in the *The Psalms in the New Testament.* Edited by Steve Moyise and Maarten J. J. Menken. NTSI. London: T&T Clark, 2004.

Woan, Sue. "The Psalms in 1 Peter." Pages 213–29 in *The Psalms in the New Testament.* Edited by Steve Moyise and Maarten J. J. Menken. NTSI. London: T&T Clark, 2004.

Website Resources (These provide charts on the citations of the OT in the NT)

Just, Felix. http://catholic-resources.org/Bible/Quotations-NT-OT.htm.
Kalvesmaki, Joel. http://www.kalvesmaki.com/LXX/NTChart.htm.